The publication of this book is made possible through the generosity of
The Conference on Jewish Material Claims Against Germany
Arnold and Miriam Frankel
The Jesselson Foundation

SYNAGOGUES

WITHOUT JEWS

SYNAGOGUES

WITHOUT JEWS

AND THE COMMUNITIES THAT BUILT
AND USED THEM

Rivka and Ben-Zion Dorfman

The Jewish Publication Society
Philadelphia
2000 • 5761

עטרת זקנים בני בנים
ותפארת בנים אבותם

Children's children are the crown of their elders,
And the glory of children is their parents.

Proverbs 17:6

We dedicate this book and the encompassing documentation project to the memory of our parents, Sara and Chaim Gruman, from Calarassi, Moldovia, and to Mindye and Yehiel Dorfman, from Orinin, Kamenetz Podolsk, in the Ukraine. As immigrants to America, faced with a tiring struggle for a living in the 1920s, they nonetheless provided us homes where we imbibed a love and appreciation for an enlightened Jewish tradition. Their values guided our lives and led us in our mature years to devote ourselves to synagogue art research.

The Jewish Publication Society
2100 Arch Street, 2nd Floor
Philadelphia, PA 19103

Composition by Shepherd Incorporated
Design by Deb Goedken, Shepherd Incorporated
Manufactured in China

01 02 03 04 05 06 07 08 09 10 9 8 7 6 5 4

Library of Congress Cataloging-in-Publication Data, ISBN 0-8276-0692-3

Dorfman, Rivka.
    Synagogues without Jews : and the communities that built them / Rivka and Ben-Zion Dorfman.
        p.   cm.
    Includes bibliographical references and index.
    ISBN 0-8276-0692-3
    1. Synagogues—Europe, Southern—History 2. Synagogues—Europe, Central—History.
    3. Synagogues architecture—Europe, Southern. 4. Synagogue architecture—Europe,
    Central. 5. Jews—Europe, Southern—History. 6. Jews—Europe, Central—History. 7.
    Europe, Southern—Ethnic relations. 8. Europe, Central—Ethnic relations. I. Dorfman,
Ben-Zion. II. Title.

BM653.D67 2000
296.6′5′094—dc21   00-042125

All photographs and artwork not otherwise acknowledged were done by Rivka and Ben-Zion Dorfman.
Translations from the Scriptures are from *TANAKH, the Holy Scriptures: The New JPS Translation According to the Traditional Text,* The Jewish Publication Society, 1985.

Photograph on title page spread: the synagogue in Szeged, Hungary.

CONTENTS

FOREWORD

Our Patriarch, Jacob, flees from the fury of his brother, Esau. Resting in flight, he dreams the famous dream that has become a symbol of man's existence and aspirations. This symbol of man is a ladder, "set on the ground and its top reached to the sky, and angels of God were going up and down on it" (Gen. 28:12).

Jacob felt that this dream was not only something personal, but a manifestation of the divine. He asserts: "How awesome is this place! This is none other than the abode of God, and that is the gateway to heaven" (Gen. 28:17). According to Rashi, the ascending angels were those of the Land of Israel, who had accompanied Jacob from Beersheba to this spot; the descending angels were those assigned to accompany him to the foreign land of Haran.

The deeds of the fathers mark a path for the sons. As the tribes of the Sons of Jacob wander their 40 years of tribulations in the wilderness, again there is a symbol. In the desert, and perhaps specifically in the desert, the Lord commands, "And let them make Me a sanctuary that I may dwell among them" (Exod. 25:8).

Young Daniel in his Babylonian exile arranged the windows of his house in the direction of Jerusalem, and there he prayed three times daily (Dan. 6:11 and Brakhot p.36:a). Thus, even in exile, Daniel continued the custom of Israel described by the divine poet, "Sweet was our fellowship; we walked together in God's house" (Ps. 55:15).

With the destruction of the second Temple in 70 C.E., the synagogue occupied a central position in the psyche of the Jewish nation, in its emotions and in the organization of its community life. The synagogue became a small Temple substitute, "I . . . have scattered them among the countries, and I have become to them a diminished sanctity" (Ezek. 11:16).

Our sages and prophets emphasized that the synagogue is not merely a house of assembly, but a locale for the Divine Being (Tractate *Shabbat*, 32). Isaiah prophesied that at the end of days peace and brotherhood will reign in an era of universal belief in one God: "My House shall be called a house of prayer for all peoples" (Isa. 56:7).

But who can predict the length of that road to the end of days, and who can foresee its dangers or presage its latent possibilities? Since antiquity, the house of Jacob has been dispersed to the corners of the earth. The tribes of Israel have drunk deep of the bitter elixir of banishment and exile. But even in alien lands they guarded their faith and tradition. They remained loyal to their homeland, to their Torah, and to the memory of their Temple. The synagogue could not always be resplendent in honor and respect, for not every country allowed Jews to build grand houses of prayer.

More than any other nation on the European continent, the Jews were victims of political catastrophes, of rebellions and wars. People were burned, leaving whole villages depopulated. Buildings were burned, leaving few architectural remains. Books were burned, but the sacred heritage survived. Only scholars and savants know the depths of spiritual treasure that inhabited Jewish culture to the remotest regions. Huddled in the ghetto, Jews kept ties with their nation's culture through talmudic lore, and contact with general philosophy through secular, theoretical writings.

At the end of the fifteenth century, European Jewry suffered a great catastrophe. Under the instigation of the Inquisition, Spain and Portugal banished their Jews. It was natural for these exiles to find refuge in Islamic lands of the Mediterranean basin and in the Balkan regions under Ottoman rule. Italian coastal cities, active in trade with both eastern and western ports, also absorbed many Spanish Jews. This fact explains the differences separating synagogue architectural styles in the Balkan and Mediterranean countries from those in northern Catholic and Protestant lands. But there is an expression in each region of the existential paradox of the Jews-to be equal to their neighbors while retaining their distinctiveness. Both the Renaissance and the Moorish style left their mark on synagogues.

Rivka and Ben-Zion Dorfman are to be commended for their many years of extensive research, documenting the art and architecture of eastern European synagogues in an effort to rescue this historic Jewish art from oblivion. Their project deserves special recognition because this tenacious couple concentrated their efforts on the smaller cities, remote villages, and unfamiliar towns, where every photo and each detail has become a monument in print to former Jewish communities. Infinite work, tireless devotion, and careful investigation find eloquent expression in their book. Even the occasional tear in the eye does not dim the beauty and splendor that once existed and are no more.

On the afternoon of November 10, 1938, the day after the infamous Kristallnacht in Berlin, I was among those in the dazed crowd gazing at the embers and smoke of a gutted synagogue. Standing on the sidewalk a few meters away, the only way I could express my emotions was by uttering a whispered prayer—the Eighteen Benedictions that are recited daily by pious Jews. My heart was filled with pain, but also with hope.

I write these lines more than half a century later in Jerusalem, the capital of Israel. The hope of the congregation of Israel and prayers rising from synagogues around the world have conquered despair.

Dr. Joseph Burg
Jerusalem, 1999

PREFACE

FROM THIS TOWN

Our documenting of synagogue art and architecture started innocently enough on an April vacation to Italy. The trip was inspired by a course on Renaissance art at the Hebrew University in Jerusalem and a lecture by architect David Cassuto on synagogues in Italy. The spring countryside was lush with burgeoning foliage. Flowering fruit trees on the rolling hills filled the air with a subtle fragrance. Our first stop was at the antiquities of Rome's ancient port, Ostia, where in 1962 archaeologists identified a fourth-century synagogue at a distance from the main excavated area. Its presence was so neglected, however, that museum officials could not help us find it! Pointed, eventually, in the right direction by a passerby, we walked a long way before we discerned three stone columns beckoning us from across a huge field. The isolated ruins lay hushed in the late afternoon sun as we clambered the low walls and paced the broken pavement. A fallen architrave,* engraved with ancient Jewish symbols of a menorah, shofar, *lulav,* and *etrog,*

lay on the ground near the remains of a high semicircular brick structure, thought to be the Holy Ark niche. We photographed the site as a matter of course. We did not know then that we had stumbled on a mission.

We traveled to Ravenna, resplendent with Byzantine mosaics, to Florence, flush with Renaissance sculpture and painting, and to sparkling Venice, its marble churches and palaces reflected in shimmering canal waters. Our itinerary took us also to a silent, unattended synagogue in Urbino, scant paces from the ducal palace. We saw the well-preserved synagogues of Ferrara, Verona, Parma, Soragna, and Mantua, and the tall, dust-covered, bronze candelabra of the third-floor synagogue in Sabbioneta—bereft of Jews since the century's first decade.

By the time we arrived in Piedmont and canvassed its synagogues, enclaves of art and tradition, we realized that we were on a new course. More of Renaissance Italy could wait. These synagogue treasures—the legacy of scattered Jewish communities that dotted the hills—must be documented. It was then and there that we embarked on a project that in five seasons would

*See glossary for definitions of architectural and foreign language terms.

Ruins of the ancient synagogue at Ostia, Italy, fourth century C.E.

Synagogue in Sabbioneta, Italy, eighteenth century, before restoration in 1996.

take us to 350 synagogues in eight countries—and inside almost all of them. Teachers by training and inclination, we were under compulsion to record whatever we found. Here was a story that had to be told. The work subsequently engaged us, with the help of dozens of loyal volunteer assistants, over seven additional years of research and writing, back home in Jerusalem.

The stares of townspeople on the street, in town after town, the curtains discreetly pushed aside in windows on the square, were balanced by the readiness of many older people to tell us at length of Jewish families who had been their neighbors. They recited for us which businesses the Jews had owned before the war. People living in previously Jewish-owned houses had only good things to say about the former owners. It was uncanny, incredible. In one town, when a municipal official noticed our horror at the shambles of the synagogue building, he tried to comfort us, *"Aber wir haben einen schönen Friedhof"* (But we have a beautiful cemetery).

"The capitals—Budapest, Bratislava, Prague, Vienna, Rome, Athens, Zagreb, and Belgrade—still have small, but viable Jewish communities. Their major synagogues are documented and reasonably well known, but the town and village hinterlands, a vast reservoir and graveyard of the Jewish past, are mostly unpublished. Our chosen task was to record existing synagogue buildings that are relatively unknown. These are also of lesser restoration probability, especially in peripheral locations reached by few travelers. The thought was always with us as we drove along the country roads during the long months of field activity that many of these buildings may disappear in the next few decades. When they go, nearly all trace of the former Jewish presence in these lands will vanish. Rummaging through the dusty synagogues of vanished communities was a depressing experience. As we walked the streets in these picturesque and tranquil precincts, we could not help thinking of the missing Jews who had worshipped in buildings that were now dwellings or storerooms.

There was also the excitement of new places and new people—satisfaction at the goodwill and cooperation that we encountered nearly everywhere. Municipal officials and small-town mayors received us in their offices, helped us make contacts, arranged entry into the synagogues, and then showered us with mementos as we departed. If strangers on the street could not reply to our queries, they went out of their way to find someone else who could. In the Slovak town of Svätý Jur, a neighbor of the synagogue summoned for us Genovéva Kováčová, whose historian daughter, Viola, had just written *Čas Barchesu* (The time of the Sabbath bread), her mother's engrossing memoirs of life with her Jewish neighbors in the pre-war *kehillah* (Jewish community). Through an interpreter and with many smiles, Genovéva told us of the book and gave us a Slovak typescript of it.

Our sources of information abroad ranged from local inhabitants, town historians, municipal archivists, and museum personnel to the staffs of the few extant Jewish communities. We photographed or photocopied documents as we found them and supplemented the information

from libraries in Israel. On return trips to Europe, we prepared detailed questionnaires in several local languages. The first part introduced us as researchers and asked for help in finding an interpreter and in locating the synagogue. The second part presented questions about the former Jewish community. We taped the verbal replies. Then, thanks to a devoted crew of volunteers in Israel (and even a few in Europe) for transcription and translation, the contents of document or tape were made legible to us in English or Hebrew. Information on *local* histories is hard to find. We supplemented the scant material from encyclopedias and similar sources with local publications we collected as we traveled. Compendia such as those of Hugo Gold and both general and special remembrance books from Yad Vashem, the Holocaust Martyrs' and Heroes' Remembrance Authority in Jerusalem, were especially useful. We gathered information from the database at Beth Hatefutsoth, the Nahum Goldmann Museum of the Jewish Diaspora at Tel Aviv University, and also contributed to it.

Municipal officials in European towns we visited were sometimes proud to give us copies of plans for the forthcoming restoration of the local synagogue, as in Třebíč, Moravia, Vrbové, and Liptovský Mikuláš in Slovakia. Most archivists were cooperative and eager to find historical documents to show us. There were a few, however, who insisted that we "Come back tomorrow," and on the morrow found other excuses to send us away empty handed. In one small village we showed our credentials to a housewife living in the tiny former synagogue. *"Wir haben das Haus gekauft!"* (We bought this house!) she fairly shouted in distress and slammed the door shut. But such events were not typical. The overwhelming impression is one of friendliness and a desire to help.

Several archivists and municipal officials have maintained contact with us, sending us occasional updated information. We were guests of the convivial Mayor Jaroslav Kos of Rychnov nad Kněžnou, Bohemia, in comfortable attic quarters. He arranged a private tour of the Rychnov castle-museum and obtained permission for us to photograph an illuminated eighteenth-century

Detail of illuminated *megillah* from Bohemia, *ca.* 1660, at the Kolowrat Castle Museum, Rychnov nad Kněžnou, Bohemia. (Photographed with permission at Kolowrat Castle Museum. Inv. 8722.)

Megillah (Scroll of Esther). When he brought us to the town synagogue he had never entered before, it was in use as a storeroom for a plumbing supply company. Mayor Kos was shocked and embarrassed at the desecration. He apologized for the state of affairs and promised to do what he could to change matters. Before long, he organized money and restoration activity, providing frequent photos of the work in progress until the synagogue was dedicated as a Jewish museum in 1995.

People we met casually told us of Jewish ancestors. In Boskovice, Moravia, we met a gentile woman who lives in Prague. She invited us into her grandmother's house in Boskovice where she spent weekends, to show us the evidence of her family's Jewish past: Stars of David on lamps, a prayer room in the attic, and a roof that opened up to form a *sukkah* (booth). The gentile Švagr family of Pilsen, Bohemia, took us into their hearts and home. We had met in the town of Kasejovice, where family head engineer Josef Švagr, was born, and where, holidaying on the weekend, he smoothed Czech into English

for us. Twice they hosted us during our research in Pilsen. On a return visit to Kasejovice, we handled a mid-nineteenth-century *siddur* (prayer book) from the synagogue book closet. Its identifying *ex libris:* "Josef Švagr."

People were hospitable even when we lacked a common language. We traveled almost daily, usually coming by nightfall to small towns that had neither hotel nor "pension." The *Zimmer* bed-and-breakfast tradition, forbidden under the communist regime, was slow to develop in the periphery of Hungary and Czechoslovakia after the liberation. Near Holešov we stayed with Vita Peluchoví, a high school teacher who had suffered job discrimination under the communists for his Christian piety. In Mikulov, Moravia, before the 1989 Velvet Revolution, we found shelter in the house of an old woman. She refused to accept money from us because the local Jews had been her friends, but she worried that the police might discover the violation of taking strangers into her house and repeatedly made us promise not to tell.

Imre Pogone, caretaker of the synagogue in Mád, Hungary, ran out with a broad smile, waving the big iron synagogue key in the air as soon as he spied us coming down the hill from the synagogue toward his cottage. When we returned the following year, he and his shy wife embraced us as old friends—still without verbal communication. In Győr, Hungary, Marianna Spiegel, a teacher at the music school in the former synagogue, insisted on providing hospitality in her home. There we met her parents, leaders in the pre-war *kehillah.*

Arriving in Perugia, Italy, we were dismayed to find no lodging: all rooms were reserved for delegates to a cosmeticians' convention. The head of the tiny Jewish community, Sergio Pacifici, welcomed us warmly. Honoring a custom that harks back to an almost forgotten synagogue function, he gave us hospitality *in* the synagogue, an apartment in the old Jewish quarter. The living-room area was a proper sanctuary, with *Aron Kodesh* (Holy Ark), reader's stand, and chairs. The dining room had been adequate for a community seder celebrated there a few days earlier. Two reclining chairs in another room opened into beds, a small closet contained clean linens and blankets: the comforts of home.

We made friends through the international Servas organization, named in Esperanto to mean, "I serve." Its members welcome travelers into their homes for personal contact and as a gesture of international understanding and peace. Special Servas friends are Pana and Tamás Marosváry, who hosted us in their rambling 200-year-old house, a former inn on the Danube in a northern suburb of Budapest. Complaining that we worked too hard, they entertained us with a family party to celebrate Ben-Zion's birthday. The next day Tamás took charge. Driving us to see the three synagogues of Gyöngyös, he interpreted and helped with the documentation.

The project brought us into contact with the last, or nearly last, Jews in many towns. *Shoah* (Holocaust) survivors, they eke out a living, clinging to vestiges of identity in a rapidly changing reality of diminishing Jewish significance. Our guide in Hlohovec, Slovakia, was the observant Moshe Glück, fluent in Hebrew, who

Our guide in west Slovakia, the late Moshe Glück, at a pause in Trnava, in the Status Quo Synagogue. A scholarly man and leader in the former community of Hlohovec, Moshe traveled frequently to other towns, to teach Bible, lead prayers, visit the sick, or to check on the condition of synagogue or cemetery.

lived his last year in Israel. The municipality had demolished his community's synagogue to build approaches for a bridge. Moshe never rode over that bridge. Descending from car or bus to walk the entire distance across it, he paused reverently at the side to murmur a silent *Kaddish.*

Ladislav Mareš was saved from the transports because his father was not Jewish. He

Ladislav Mareš, last Jew of Heřmanův Městec, Moravia.

Massimo del Sette of Biella, Italy, caretaker of the synagogue.

showed us the brush his mother used in Terezín to polish Gestapo boots. Recently retired, he tries to raise funds to restore the synagogue and the Jewish quarter in Heřmanův Městec, Moravia. In Biella, Italy, Massimo del Sette is a convert to Judaism and a devoted guardian of the synagogue. From a scrap he found in a synagogue bench, he enumerated for us the detailed expenses incurred by the community in celebrating the Emancipation Declaration by King Carlo Alberto, dated March 29, 1848. Jiří Mahler, last Jew of Bohemia's Světlá nad Sázavou, gave us a genealogical family tree that included the composer Gustav Mahler, a distant cousin.

Arthur Kővesí, head of the minuscule community in Szolnok, Hungary, was a septuagenarian widower when we first met him. He guided us to the former synagogue, now a glistening white art gallery. As he stood near the Ark he whispered, *"Hier habe ich geheiratet"* (This is where I was married). The following year he happily introduced us to his new wife, a fellow survivor.

Nearly all the villages we visited had been empty of Jews since the Nazi deportations. These locations attracted few foreign visitors. An exception was the rare Jewish traveler, following an ancient, binding Jewish custom: to locate the grave of a relative and there to recite the *Kaddish* prayer. Strangers in the village square, we were obviously foreigners. Our Jewish identity and the purpose of our visit soon became known to passersby, whom we approached for information about the synagogue. After a moment of acquaintance came the ubiquitous question, "Was your family from this town?"

Our family? We had spent hundreds of hours searching for synagogues and vestiges of the inscriptions in them, more hours scrambling through vines and brambles for decipherable gravestone iconography, and days poring over documents in arcane archives. Regardless of our immediate forebears, we are an intrinsic part of the endless list of anonymous Jews who populated these villages and towns. "Yes," we replied, "our family came from this town."

SYNAGOGUES WITHOUT JEWS

In history, as in journalism, there might be a tendency to report catastrophes rather than the everyday achievements of community life. Indeed, the ordinary tribulations of living pale before the onslaught of marauding armies that pillage their way recklessly through a terrorized populace. A house built with love, pain, and treasure can collapse in an hour's conflagration. Valuables accumulated over a lifetime can be swept away in a sudden flood. But despite the disasters they faced, Jews persevered. They built homes, synagogues, schools, and businesses. They married, begat children, and transmitted the living tradition of a culture infused with moral values. Less dramatic perhaps than catastrophes, these events are the real essence of their history.

Synagogues Without Jews surveys some of the synagogues we saw in the countries of central and southern Europe and the histories of the *kehillot* (the Jewish communities) who built and used them. We vacillated endlessly over which synagogues to include: What should influence our decision? Should we apply criteria of art and architectural quality, the historical importance of the *kehillah,* antiquity, or our personal preferences? The relatively well-known synagogues of the capitals did not need our coverage, but a few of the larger non-capital cities did, such as Trieste, Graz, and Pilsen. These cities are included in our book because they are mostly unfrequented by Jewish travelers and because their stories are relevant for historical balance. Ultimately we chose a representative set (barely a tenth of those we saw and documented), a set that touched on our several criteria. In retrospect we probably skimped on outright ruins despite our earlier intentions to include more of them. Along with the lights and shadows of personal and community lives, there are descriptions of events (provided by our local history sources) that illuminate the general character of the Jewish experience in Europe.

The book covers a geographical area corresponding roughly to what was once the Austro-Hungarian empire, but does so in terms of the present political divisions, as shown in the map on the back endpaper. Jewish history in Europe, that of a national and religious minority, has had a generic similarity throughout that region over the two-millennium rise and fall of Jewish settlement. Yet the factors that operated in each country to influence the relations between the Jews and the rulers, or the majority population, have varied. An indication of such similarities and differences can be found in our brief Jewish history for each country that precedes the chapters on that country's respective communities. Here you will also find some information about completed synagogue restorations; recent and ongoing or planned synagogue restorations are listed in the appendix.

We indulge our fondness for key terms in their original languages; they are an element of local color. An explanation, however, is provided immediately following each foreign expression at its first use. The glossary contains all terms used more than once in the book and usually provides a more extensive translation than appears in the text. Architectural terms are defined in the glossary only, but their meanings within the chapters are often evident from the accompanying photographs.

Four supplemental essays conclude this book. "A Gallery of Women" sketches several of the stalwart Jewish women we met in Hungary and briefly examines the historical basis for the position of women in the synagogue. Our colleagues grace the volume with other topics: Noemi Cassuto discusses the development of synagogue architecture in Italy in "The Italian Synagogue Through the Ages." Elements of Sephardic synagogue architecture and decoration that she describes in Italy apply also to Sephardic synagogues in other places, such as Greece or the former Yugoslavia. "Synagogue Interior Decoration and the Halakhah," by Shalom Sabar, compares the figurative iconography practiced in synagogues to rabbis' views on what is permissible. Rudolf Klein explores the effect of a culture's world outlook on its sacred architecture in "Spirituality and Space" and relates his findings to style in Ashkenazic synagogue architecture.

Community and Synagogue

Long after the Middle Ages, Jewish communities in Europe were still dependent on the goodwill

A detail from an eighteenth-century synagogue in Radnice, Bohemia, used as a garage before its recent restoration. This pilester is on the outside face of the interior Ark niche, and it carries a headless lion crouching with tail high.

and protection of local or sovereign rulers. Locating their settlement near a palace or castle was a commonplace practice, but Jews could be expelled from a town or a region at the whim of a monarch or of the intolerant crowd he obeyed. Between major misfortunes, Jews made out the best they could under occupational restrictions and outward behavior that was antagonistically dictated to them by a hostile Church and the popular majority it controlled. The large royal cities where the Jews made their livelihood in trade were often forbidden to Jewish settlement, so the Jews lived in myriad towns and villages within commuting distance. *Kehillah* size could be small, with the synagogue in proportion: In Radnice, Bohemia, for example, the late-eighteenth-century synagogue building, which functioned for a long time as a garage before recent restoration, accommodated exactly one vehicle. Sustained by manual arts, trade, or moneylending, Jews actively pursued a life of learning and intellectual profession, often emphasizing but not limited to narrow religious confines.

One wonders where the Jews got their tenacity—to be rebuffed again and again in the struggle for sheer survival; to have to ask for permission and to pay in coin for every breath of life; to be banished from home on short notice and then to return to the same desperate exertions on the merest invitation. They must have been nourished by a zest for life, an optimism born of faith in a tradition that held that the highest good was life itself—and the hope for a future destined to be better than the present. Mutual self-help, from family to *kehillah* to the greater community of Israel, was an intrinsic part of that tradition. The verse, *"Kol Yisrael arevin zeh bazeh"* ("All of Israel are responsible one for the other"; Shavuot 39) found and still finds its expression in communal institutions devoted to welfare and the improvement of the community and the individual.

The mainstay of communal life was the synagogue, the centrality of which as a place of congregation and prayer developed rapidly in the Diaspora as it did in *Eretz Yisrael* (the Land of Israel) after the destruction of the Second Temple by the Romans in 70 C.E. The synagogue served as a temple substitute, a hallmark of Jewish community for the next two millennia. Over the centuries, the synagogues were the places most fully charged with specific Jewish identity.

The synagogues we documented are the repository of what was artistically important to the communities that built and used them. Practicing *hiddur mitzvah* (enhancing the commandment), European Jewish communities strove to beautify their synagogues. Exteriors were plain until the mid-nineteenth-century Emancipation (whether by law or for self-protection), but the interiors were rich with color and embellished with the finest materials each *kehillah* could afford. Primary artistic emphasis went to the *Aron Kodesh* (the Holy Ark in which the Torah

scrolls were housed), which were crafted from wood, with distinctive doors, guardian pillars, and gilded highlights. Ceilings were often blue and emblazoned with random stars of gold around focal stucco forms and symbols. In some regions floral and animal motifs decorated panels of prayers inscribed on the walls. Post-Emancipation synagogues extended the symbolic and decorative elements to the exterior as well, in architectural styles suited to the times. Even in their present condition, synagogues in Europe are the most significant clue to the public aesthetics of Jewish life there.

Destruction and Decay

What is left of the once-ubiquitous Jewish presence in central and southern Europe, two generations after the *Shoah* (Holocaust)? In the cities, towns, and villages across the continent, overgrown cemeteries and synagogues that still stand may be the sole reminders of an enterprising Jewish existence that once extended to every hamlet. As we researched we were literally racing against time, against indifference, deterioration, and demolition. In tiny Pečovská Nová Ves, Slovakia, a decrepit synagogue is used as a barn today. The present owners refused us access, and we could document only the exterior and the local cemetery. In Všeruby, Bohemia, we were too late; town officials informed us that they had torn down the synagogue eleven months earlier because engineers had declared the building unsafe. That story was repeated in Podolinec, Slovakia, where officials gave us photos of the no-longer-existent synagogue facade.

Left ownerless after the Jews were deported, property was quickly seized by neighbors. Factories and workshops were reorganized under ad hoc non-Jewish management that devolved into ownership. Community buildings, such as rabbis' residences or easily convertible village synagogues, were snapped up for living quarters. Viewing the derelict synagogue buildings merely as available space, postwar authorities adapted most of them to practical use as storerooms or workshops, many for dwellings, some for churches, and a few for cultural or administrative

Joseph Sofer and his wife, from Brooklyn, visit the grave of his uncle, Rabbi Naphtali Sofer, in the east Slovak village of Pečovská Nová Ves.

purposes such as libraries, museums, or archives. In only a few instances, the buildings were given back to the fledgling post-war Jewish communities, but these communities were always too small to use more than the *beit midrash* (study room) for prayers and too indigent to maintain the buildings properly.

The Germans viciously began the deliberate destruction of synagogues on Kristallnacht, November 9 and 10, 1938, and kept it up through World War II. The destruction continued even after the war. At Humenné and at Michalovce in Slovakia, synagogues in good condition were demolished for being "too close" to newly raised Communist Party headquarters. Under communism in Hungary, an elegant 1914 synagogue in Makó by architect Lipót Baumhorn was deliberately torn down.

Ironically, the status of the synagogues that still stand may worsen as democracy strengthens its foothold in central Europe. The present dynamics of social change are accompanied by political unrest and outbursts of national patriotism, too often with an anti-Semitic bent. Towns and cities are undergoing rapid physical alterations under the vagaries of economic conditions. The old synagogues are in the midst of this turmoil because they were commonly built on choice locations on or near town centers. Previously only moderately safe under stagnant regimes, the new political dynamism subjects them to the possibility of accelerated attrition.

Preservation and Restoration

Jewish communities in the capitals have been too preoccupied with problems of daily living to be concerned about the restoration of synagogues that are miles away in towns that no longer have Jews. During our research in the early 1990s,

Facade of abandoned synagogue, built in 1797 in Tarcal, Hungary.

synagogues in various states of disuse or decay, we thought about the religious significance of such desecration. Certain talmudic passages (*Megillah,* 26a–b, 27a–b) evaluate the sanctity of the synagogue. The buildings are sacred when they contain at least one Torah scroll in an *Aron Kodesh,* but both the *Aron Kodesh* and the synagogue lose many degrees of sanctity if the Torah is missing. However, a defiled Holy Ark or an empty synagogue is still precious because the residual sanctity derives from the activities that belonged to them. When no longer in Jewish use, "the synagogue building may not be sold for any unclean purpose such as a bath, a tannery, a laundry, or even for a *mikveh* (ritual bath)."

The Holy Ark is holier than the synagogue. Remains of an Ark that has fallen into disuse must be preserved as carefully as damaged Torah scrolls. Ruins of a synagogue may be used for certain secular purposes only, because the building retains some of its sanctity. Ideally, a ruin should be left untouched, with weeds growing around it to arouse compassion in the viewer. "For the country shall be all thorn bushes and thistles" (Isa. 7:24). "I will lay your cities in ruin, and make your sanctuaries desolate" (Lev. 26:31).

Some Jews maintain that, once defiled, synagogues bereft of Jews should be razed rather than be put to mundane use. In our view, every synagogue and cemetery still standing in central Europe is the landmark of a former Jewish presence. We believe that wherever feasible, these synagogues should remain. Let them stand as monuments across the continent of Europe, each a witness to a *kehillah* that was born, flourished, and vanished.

Synagogues, especially those designed by major architects after the Emancipation, are impressive structures, well suited for general cultural use. Restoration for public enrichment where there are few or no Jews carries the weight of mixed factors—aesthetic, historical, emotional, and economic. Sensitive, authentic restoration of the structure for cultural purposes and the inclusion of a Jewish museum area can enhance rather than disturb a former synagogue's new function. The well-renovated buildings in

Jewish officials in the urban centers of Bratislava, Prague, and Budapest had little accurate information on the state of synagogue buildings located far from the capitals. Ironically, it was a report of our findings that helped community officials in Bratislava, then preparing restitution claims, to assess the extent and disposition of synagogues still standing. Our report went also to the Jewish Heritage Council of the World Monuments Fund and was instrumental a few years later when the Council conducted an extensive survey of the Jewish built heritage in the Czech Republic.

The hundreds of synagogues that still stand all across Europe—deserted or used for menial purposes—raise the question of what to do with them. As we traveled from town to town and saw

Apostag, Hungary; Holešov, Moravia; and Gorizia, Italy, are fine examples of Jewish art and architecture. Serving now as cultural centers, they also recall past community achievement and status.

Unfortunately, not all restorations were so sensitively executed in the past. The sparkling neo-Moresque exterior of the synagogue in Kecskemét, Hungary, is authentic, but no sign remains of the original magnificent interior. The Functionalist 1934 synagogue in Žilina, one of the most beautiful in Czechoslovakia, was drastically modified. It now serves as a technical school auditorium, and all indications of its Jewish origin have been abolished. Many current synagogue restoration projects show greater concern for the building's essential character. Responsible officials are careful to affix a plaque acknowledging the building as a former synagogue and commemorating the Jews who died in the *Shoah*.

Selecting candidate buildings for restoration involves architectural and artistic evaluation of a building's importance as well as the availability of funding. Since all former synagogues cannot be rehabilitated, it is important that at least the significant synagogue buildings in towns without Jews should be preserved. A national committee, including architects, historians, and representatives of the Jewish community, should determine the criteria for selecting which buildings will be restored. Even in buildings where restoration costs are high and work schedules drag on for years—as in Mikulov and Třebíč, Moravia, or St. Pölten, Austria and Novi Sad, Croatia—the final results justify all the efforts. Other synagogues for which extensive restoration is not possible should at least be minimally renovated, clearly marked as former synagogues, and used for some respectable public purpose.

In undertaking to restore a synagogue for cultural use, municipalities have often turned to Jewish sources for support. Sometimes former residents responded to the nostalgic appeal with generous contributions and were pivotal in the success of the venture—as in Slavkov, Bohemia and other places. In our view, however, the Jewish charity agenda, for all its nebulous breadth, has goals enough without adding on the respon-

Restored interior of synagogue in Rychnov nad Kněžnou, Bohemia, 1995. The work was initiated and sponsored by the municipality under the energetic leadership of Mayor Jaroslav Kos. (Courtesy of J. Kos.)

sibility of financing cultural shrines for towns that are *judenrein* (without Jews). Fundraising should be a local or national obligation. The people of Apostag, for instance, have set an example for excellent restoration achievement with minimal funds. There is hope, too, that international agencies concerned with the preservation of national monuments will succeed in aiding some localities to rescue and restore extant remnants of the Jewish built heritage.

Synagogue restoration in historic Jewish locations has shown itself to be a wise investment. The international crowds that swarm the Jewish quarter in Prague, the Dohány synagogue in Budapest, and the Ghetto Nuovo in Venice are vivid proof that tourism to Jewish sites is big business. (These lands are also destinations for Jews searching for their roots.) With the Cold War over and the tide of Western tourism swelling to central Europe, municipalities have begun to recognize the tourist potential of Jewish sites and many have organized some preservation or restoration.

Judaica

Although synagogue artifacts are not central to our theme, their inherent association with the synagogue impels us to include them in the context of the changes affecting the synagogues of Europe. Furniture and ceremonial objects for the synagogue received the same attention to artistic quality as synagogue design. Candelabra, once the primary evening light source and often enhanced with reflectors (as in Mondovì, Italy) and lamps in unlimited variety, illuminated and decorated the synagogue space. Craftsmen devised ritual objects of precious materials: silver Torah crowns, Torah shields, *rimmonim* (finials), or brocade *parokhot* (Ark curtains). People marked major personal events with gifts of such articles for the synagogue. Parents celebrated a son's first visit to the synagogue with the gift of a wimple—an embroidered linen Torah binder. Wealthy Jews may have commissioned artistic ceremonial objects such as illuminated *Megillot* (scrolls of the Book of Esther), porcelain *seder* plates, and silver *hanukkiot*

(Hanukkah candelabra) for their homes, but the ordinary folk experienced Jewish art mostly at the synagogue.

Judaica shared the fate of the synagogues in the *Shoah,* except for the distinction that the Judaica was portable. Some of it was, therefore, saved in hidden places and returned, as in Ioannina, Greece. But portability meant that anyone could take it without having to answer for it—and untold numbers of stolen Jewish artifacts from synagogues and Jewish homes still enrich houses, shops, and museums throughout Europe. An exception of sorts took place in Czechoslovakia, where the Germans plundered the artifacts systematically and shipped them to the State Jewish Museum in Prague. There they were carefully catalogued by Jewish experts under coercion and stored in any available space for the Nazis' intended museum of "decadent Jewish art." A sizable synagogue building is still used to hoard just a portion of the stolen *parokhot.*

One positive consequence of this Judaica concentration was the Torah Scroll Project, described in our chapter on Kojetín, in which Torah scrolls were rescued, repaired, and distributed to active *kehillot* worldwide. The State Jewish Museum, now the Jewish Museum, in possession of the Czech Jewish community in Prague since 1994, has considered returning individual artifacts to their places of origin wherever suitable Jewish museums are established. Returning Judaica items to small local museums in restored synagogues is historically justified, but risky because of the danger of theft.

Starting in 1952 the late Umberto Naḥon located, bought, and transferred to Israel 40 items, including furnishings and whole synagogues. Among the rescued articles is the synagogue from Vittorio Veneto, now in Jerusalem's Israel Museum, and the furnishings from the synagogue of Conegliano, now arranged as the Italian synagogue in Jerusalem. In 1972 the Italian government ruled that synagogue remains are the legacy of the Italian nation and may not be exported.

This issue is part of the broad-based, current activity concerning the disposition of Jewish material losses in the *Shoah.* It touches on real estate, factories, bank accounts, insurance policies, works of art, and former Jewish property—personal as well as communal—and compensation for unpaid forced labor. Unfortunately, the discussion and adjustment is taking place so long after the events that caused the Jewish losses that the number of surviving victims among the claimants is rapidly diminishing.

Restricting our attention here to communal Judaica artifacts, we may ask, *who* in justice is the proper heir of the vanished communities? Although the Jewish world sees Jewish artifacts as precious material remains of their lost *kehillot,* the above examples illustrate that host countries claim the art in their domain as *their* cultural heritage. One might expect countries that are finding plundered Judaica within their borders to offer it gratis to Jewish institutions for distribution and use in living Jewish congregations anywhere. At the least, there should be a readiness to negotiate with Jewish art experts and historians to produce a feasible plan for the transferral of a reasonable proportion of these Judaic treasures to Israel and Jewish communities worldwide.

ITALY

The Italian peninsula is the one European region where Jews have resided without interruption since the second century B.C.E. They settled initially in Rome and its environs; more than half of the 50,000 Jews in the region lived there during the empire's first century. Julius Caesar regarded them as a cohesive element of the empire and granted various exemptions to allow them religious autonomy. In 70 C.E., when Titus and Vespasian suppressed the Jewish revolt in Judea, the Roman legions destroyed the Temple, committed widespread massacre, and transported about 6,500 Jewish prisoner-slaves to Rome. Many of the slaves eventually attained freedom and integrated into the local Jewish population or returned to Judea. Of the thirteen synagogues known to have existed in ancient Rome, the ruins of one of them—from the first and fourth centuries C.E.—have been excavated in the city's ancient port at Ostia.

Catacomb inscriptions, and frescoes in Rome and its outskirts, indicate that some elements of the pagan Roman population took an interest in Judaism. Remnants of this funerary art trace the gradual separation of the early Christians from their Jewish origins as they adopted pagan Hellenistic elements into their beliefs, practices, and iconography. Toleration of the Jews came to an end in the late fourth century C.E., with the adoption of Christianity as the official religion of the empire. Church Fathers secured laws to restrain Jewish religious practices and to limit the Jews economically. The gradual disintegration of the Western Roman Empire, finalized by the deposition of the last Western Roman emperor Romulus Augustulus in 476 C.E., deepened the fragmentation of Italy. The disintegration persisted for more than 1,400 years, as control of the peninsula's various regions shifted among foreign powers, local nobles, and the papacy.

The Jewish population was concentrated in the southern regions during the late Middle Ages (1100 to 1300 C.E.). Some decrees affecting the Jews offered protection from assault and forced conversion, whereas others placed them in a position of perpetual serfdom and compelled them to wear a yellow badge. The powerful Inquisition, instituted in 1233, advocated mass conversion and persecuted Jews on every pretext. By 1294, half of the nearly 15,000 Jews in the south had been forced to abandon their religion, entire communities had been annihilated, and many synagogues had been converted to churches.

Near the turn of the fourteenth century, several factors opened a niche for Jewish loan banking: The Church prohibited moneylending by Christians, small merchants needed financing, and Jews possessed liquid capital realized as they were forced to move about. The fourteenth and fifteenth centuries, therefore, were periods of modest economic prosperity for the Italian Jews, and they established nearly 300 small Jewish communities up and down the peninsula. Although Jewish bankers began to adopt the customs and manners of the Italian upper classes, they adhered to their intellectual and religious heritage. These two centuries of the Renaissance were marked by unprecedented cultural activity and by many Jewish contributions to intellectual, artistic, and scientific endeavors.

Increasing anti-Jewish propaganda by Franciscan friars in the mid-fifteenth century incited the populace to riot. Jews were consequently expelled from many cities. Spain exercised its sovereignty over Sardinia and Sicily to include the Jews of these islands, 40,000 from Sicily, in its expulsion edicts of March 1492. The exiles found brief refuge in the kingdom of Naples until they were expelled from there early in the sixteenth century. Later they settled in the relatively tolerant central and northern cities of the peninsula where refugees from Spain were also received. A decree excluding Jews from the south took effect in 1541 and remained in force for more than three centuries.

Local rulers in the northern cities and towns welcomed Jews from the southern regions because of the banking skills they introduced. The new *kehillot* grew and matured, and absorbed Ashkenazic Jews fleeing from persecutions in southern Germany and France. The house of Medici in Florence, the Este dukes in Ferrara, the Gonzaga dukes in Mantua, and some

of the popes were reasonably well disposed to Jews in their jurisdictions and encouraged their talents. As the growing specter of Protestantism began to threaten the hegemony of the Church, Catholic tolerance disappeared in the decrees of the Counter-Reformation. The popes turned with particular harshness against the Jews, confining them in ghettos, restricting their economic activity to menial occupations, and burning books of the Talmud.

The prohibition against Jews living among Christians was central to the anti-Jewish program of Christian religious orders from the early fifteenth century, especially in Italy. By the sixteenth to the mid-seventeenth century, the ghetto was an established institution for nearly 30,000 Italian Jews. Up to 7,000 Jews lived in the cramped ghetto of Rome. Cosmopolitan intellectual life was limited, but Jewish exegesis and the study of Talmud and Kabbalah (mysticism) flourished. When Napoleon's army entered the land (1796 to 1798, and in 1800), there was a flurry of liberation and ghetto demolition, but the 1815 French retreat allowed restoration of the old repressive order.

With the support of local middle classes, freedom and equality for Jews came to various parts of the peninsula at different times. Appealing to workers and students as well as to Jews, the Risorgimento liberation movement (1750 to 1870)—to free the peninsula from oppressive reactionary regimes and unite Italy—aimed to eliminate anti-Jewish discrimination as well. Pope Pius IX ordered the abolition of ghettos in Rome and other Papal States during the 1848 revolution. Italy and Italian Jewry were liberated with the annexation of Rome to a united Italy in October 1870.

Emancipation and integration into Italian society wrought radical changes in the Jewish communal structure in the decades before World War I. With new careers available in the cities, migration to the larger centers emptied the smaller rural communities of Jews.

Mussolini's Fascist government did not at first interfere with Jewish social and legal rights, but as ties with Nazi Germany strengthened in 1936, Italian Fascism turned to overt anti-Semitism. The severe antiracial restrictions of 1938 were followed by Italy's entry into World War II in June 1940. Italy's surrender in September 1943 left the south in the hands of the Allies, but the Nazis controlled central and northern Italy. This spelled disaster for Italian Jews, who suddenly found themselves victims of the "Final Solution" along with thousands of Jewish refugees from France and Yugoslavia who had fled to the safety of Italy in the earlier stages of the war.

The Germans systematically hunted the Jews in the principal towns, herded them into jails or into concentration camps in the north, and sent many of them to extermination camps, mainly to Auschwitz. Some Jews escaped to Switzerland, and others joined the partisans in the mountains. Many found refuge within the Italian population, which, unlike other ethnic groups, had seldom shown intense anti-Semitism. Jewish victims in Italy numbered about 7,750 out of a pre-war population of 35,000. Most of the Italian rabbis fought with the underground and, if captured, they, too, were deported to Auschwitz.

In post-war Italy, fewer than 30,000 Jews struggled to rebuild communities diminished by deportation, conversion, and emigration. Twenty-six thousand refugees from central and eastern Europe thronged the northern Italian cities while awaiting passage to Palestine; some of them settled there. More immigrants arrived from North Africa, Egypt, Hungary, and other eastern European countries, and also integrated into these communities.

Since the local population had scant interest in destroying the synagogues and the Germans had had little time to wreak the kind of damage they did in other parts of Europe, many Italian synagogues remained intact. Most of Italy's standing synagogues are in a reasonable state of repair, including several that are in towns without Jews. A few vacant synagogues have recently been restored with funding by both municipal and Jewish interests. The majority of extant synagogues in Italy are in the Sephardic pattern, with bi-focal arrangement and facing benches, or with a central *bimah.* Some follow the Ashkenazic layout, placing Ark and *bimah* together, at the east.

Over the centuries, some Italian *kehillot* had developed a *nusaḥ Italki* (Italian rite), a distinctive tradition of prayer order and melodies. This *nusaḥ* is still practiced in Rome's Jewish community and in Jerusalem's Italian synagogue, although most other *kehillot* in Italy have accepted Sephardic, and some the Ashkenazic traditions. In Piedmont, the Afam *nusaḥ* was favored in Asti, Fossano, and Moncalvo. The name applied in the Italian and Sephardic traditions to the Holy Ark is *Heikhal* (temple). The reader's platform may be called either *bimah* (platform), or *tevah* (box). While *tevah* usually refers properly to the reader's desk, it may be applied to the entire platform, especially when the latter is a self-contained internal structure, as in the Piedmont region. In Ashkenazic usage, the respective terms are *Aron Kodesh, bimah,* and *amud.* The usual layout of older synagogues in Italy followed the bipolar floor plan, with *Heikhal* and *bimah* at opposite ends, or sides, of the synagogue.

The central organization of Italian Jewry today is the Union of Italian Jewish Communities. The Union represents Jewish interests with respect to the government and coordinates activities between the communities. Italy's 35,000 Jews are concentrated in Rome (15,000), Milan (7,000), Turin (1,200), Florence (1,000), and Livorno (700) and are present in small numbers in 23 other cities and towns. International Jewish organizations, such as WIZO and B'nai B'rith, and youth groups, such as B'nai Akiva and Hashomer Hatza'ir, have branches in some of the larger cities. Italian Jewry is in the forefront of the country's liberal forces in the struggle against the extreme right-wing separatists of the Northern League and the neo-Fascists.

A SPARK OF THE DIVINE

Ancona was a welcome sanctuary for Jews in the early sixteenth century. Persecuted in Iberia by forced conversion or recurrent expulsion, they could neither survive there as Jews, nor find any peace by conversion. As "New Christians," derisively called *marranos* after a Spanish word for swine, or—less pejoratively in modern times, *conversos*—they were ruthlessly pursued by the Inquisition. The Inquisition's *auto-da-fé* (burning at the stake) was never far away. Thousands of Jews sought refuge wherever possible. Open to them were only Muslim lands, Protestant territories, and, occasionally, the Papal states under exceptional, relatively benevolent popes. Enjoying a period of rapid expansion, Ancona was an independent city willing to augment its Jewish population in order to benefit from its skills. The refugees came and integrated into an older community, a *kehillah* with roots.

The hilly Marche region of eastern Italy descends gently to the Adriatic Sea. Ancona, its capital, dates from the fourth century B.C.E., when Sicilian traders skirting northward along the coast sighted its unusual topography. They perceived the superb quality of the natural harbor and remained to found a port. The city

sprawls along the slopes of a rocky promontory that forms an acute angle with the mainland, a geometry that inspired the Greeks to name the city *Ankon,* meaning "elbow." Ancona was a major point of departure for the Crusades, and was more often influenced by the Levant, the lands bordering the Aegean and the eastern Mediterranean seas, than it was by the West.

The port's brisk maritime commerce attracted merchants, including Jewish traders with Levantine ties. Jews were landholders in the vicinity as early as 967 C.E., cultivating olive orchards and vineyards. The community grew so rapidly that by 1300 its Jewish population was second in size in Italy only to that of Rome. The more affluent Jews dealt in trade or moneylending, especially after the 1274 Church Council decree against the practice of usury by Christians. In an attempt to cope with widespread economic distress, many towns in central Italy granted Jews *condotte,* contracts, to open loan banks. Twenty-seven such locations in the Marche region developed into Jewish communities, each with its complement of rabbis, poets, and doctors. Among the coastal *kehillot* were the communities of Fano,

View of the busy harbor of Ancona from a southern hilltop.

prosperous by 1332; Senigallia, with its frequent fairs; and Pesaro, a center for scholars. In Urbino, perched on the inland hills, Jewish bankers and savants mingled with the nobility at the court of Duke Federico. Between the fourteenth and sixteenth centuries, Ancona was one of the most flourishing cities in central Italy. In 1348, its *kehillah* absorbed an influx of Ashkenazic Jews from Central Europe, refugees fleeing persecutions kindled by the first occurrence of the Black Death plague.

The Franciscan order reacted antagonistically to the legalization of Jewish moneylending and fought back with cutthroat competition. They founded a loan bank, Monti di Pietà (Funds of Piety), in an expanding network to lend money at little or no interest. Their branches extended to Ancona in 1490 and seriously encroached on Jewish livelihood. Still, townspeople often called on Jews when the friars had exhausted their own means, or for supplementary large loans.

The renowned Jewish poet and scholar, Immanuel of Rome (1261–1328), left Rome about 1321 and traveled the towns of central Italy as an itinerant spokesman and tutor to wealthy patrons. Speaking for the Ancona *kehillah,* he appealed to Jewish officials in Rome to exempt his client from the special levy they had imposed on the communities of central Italy. His letter begged for grace, in consideration of his employer's "poverty." Although he was one of the most gifted Italian Jewish poets, his mellifluous language did not convince the *parnassim* (officials), who well knew that Ancona was one of the wealthier *kehillot* of the region. Immanuel was a prolific writer of hymns and erotic poetry full of wit, puns, and word play based on biblical expressions. Rabbis frowned on his licentious flippancy and restricted the circulation of his collected works, *Maḥbarot Immanuel* (The Compositions of Immanuel).

Assembling a crusade at Ancona in 1455 against the Turks in the Holy Land, Pope Callixtus III tried to cover the expense by levying a five percent income tax on Jews in papal lands. His successor, Pope Pius II, rapaciously demanded

The red velvet cover of the reader's desk in the *Scuola Levantina.* Heavily embroidered in a lush garland of flowers, ferns and foliage, the inscription acknowledges the donor: "In praise of the Lord and his Torah, by the honorable Moshe Polinio, may the Almighty protect him. In the year 5652 (1892)."

five percent of Jewish *capital* and urged the Italian states, against their better judgment, to collect it. Milan replied that it already taxed its Jews to the limit, while Venice shrewdly insisted on an international guarantee that the crusade would indeed embark. The scheme failed for lack of money and would-be crusaders sold their arms to Jewish pawnbrokers in Ancona to finance their homeward journeys.

Early refugees from the 1492 expulsions from Spain and Portugal landed on Italy's western coast to a bleak reception. In Genoa, ardent friars wandered among the famished arrivals at the piers. With bread in one hand and a crucifix in the other, they offered food in return for conversion. Thirty years later, Ancona, on the east, became a haven for *converso* families fleeing the Portuguese Inquisition and for Jews expelled from Spanish territories in southern Italy. The city eagerly invited Levantines and Jews to help develop its commerce when it came under the Papal State in 1532. At first, Papal authorities concurred with the wisdom of that policy and

guaranteed protection in Ancona to a hundred Portuguese *converso* families.

The attitude changed drastically when the former head of the Inquisition took over the Papacy as Paul IV (r. 1555–1559) and launched one of the most wretched periods in the history of Italy's Jews. He immediately decreed a ghetto in Ancona and excluded Jewish worship from all but a single synagogue. Buildings prohibited from use were deliberately left standing—for tax purposes. Paul IV fanatically opposed any form of apostasy; *conversos* were the special target of his vicious pursuit, particularly those of Ancona. In 1556 his emissaries precipitated a tragedy that rocked the Jewish world. They threw a hundred *conversos* into prison and the tribunal of the Inquisition condemned 50 of them to die.

The indomitable Doña Gracia Nasi (1510–1569) rose to the occasion. Born to a family of Portuguese *conversos,* she had left her homeland after the death of her husband, Francesco Mendes, and lived successively in Flanders, Venice, Ferarra, and—finally—in

Constantinople. Stateswoman, patroness, and business magnate, Doña Gracia was the outstanding Jewess of her day, known and loved for her unceasing effort to aid Jews in their struggle against the Inquisition. She enlisted the intervention of Sultan Suleiman the Magnificent on behalf of the Turkish subjects among the Ancona captives and thereby saved them. The remaining twenty-six Jews were burned at the stake. This atrocity aroused Jews throughout the Mediterranean basin to their first militant act against the popes' excessive power. Doña Gracia initiated a substantially successful boycott of Ancona's port and prevailed on the sultan to comply. Boycott-observant trade sailed north to the port of Pesaro. Two years later, commercially deprived and in fear of more papal reprisals, the Jews of Ancona reluctantly decided to terminate the boycott.

The Church adjusted its policy to extract revenue at every turn. Expelling the Jews from papal cities in 1569, it exempted a few large *kehillot,* such as Rome and Avignon. Ancona also was spared because its Jews were important in the Levant trade, but they paid ten *scudi* annually, as did those in Rome, for each of the 115 closed synagogues left behind in the emptied ghettos. Hundreds of refugees, unable to find places to settle in the overcrowded ghetto of Rome, swarmed the ports of Senigallia and Pesaro awaiting ships to Turkey or Palestine. Help came from Joseph Nasi, Duke of the Greek island of Naxos, nephew and son-in-law of Doña Gracia. He transported many refugees on his ships to a colony that he established in Tiberias where they found new homes and employment.

Amatus Lusitanus (1511–1568), a Portuguese *converso* and one of the greatest physicians of the sixteenth century, was among the many savants attracted to this cosmopolitan community. The fame of his hundred-case medical histories, *Centuria Curationum,* and his treatises on medical botany caused popes, nobility, and cities to invite him to serve their medical needs. Ostensibly a Christian, he retained his loyalty to Judaism. After his home was looted, with loss and damage to many of his books and manuscripts, Lusitanus managed to escape across the Adriatic to Dubrovnik. He settled in

Salonika, where he practiced Judaism openly and spent his last years treating Jewish patients.

Because wealth led to ostentation and extravagance by the rich merchants, importers, and textile magnates, Ancona rabbis felt it necessary in 1766 to post Hebrew broadsides in the ghetto to announce rules of constraint. Regarding wedding feasts, they limited expenditures for flowers and *ketubbah* illumination, the number of dishes that

Detail of the *Heikhal* in the Scuola Levantina. Symmetrical, fluted rose marble columns support an elaborate curved and broken architrave and cornice, topped by a group of black marble urns. Blue marble panels garnished with gilded ornaments separate the columns along the wall.

might be served, and the number of guests—although not the number of invited poor. They also restricted the number of torches that might accompany bridegrooms when they went to fetch their brides. In contrast to the moneyed elite, however, life of the city's proletarian Jews was harsh, monotonous, and dreary. Conforming to legally imposed degrading occupations, they were mostly itinerant peddlers, rag pickers, tailors, or dealers in second-hand clothing.

With Napoleon's victorious invasions came welcome change. Immediately upon their February 10, 1797 entry into the city, Jewish soldiers in the French forces rescued Ancona's Jews from rampaging mobs who blamed them for the Italian defeat. The soldiers tore the yellow badges from Jews' hats, replacing them with French tricolor cockades, then joined their fellow soldiers in breaking down the ghetto walls. Ancona's Jews rejoiced, but their felicity was muffled in the realization that more than half of the 240,000 piaster levy imposed on the city by the victors would fall upon the Jewish community.

The French occupations were brief—1797 to 1799 and 1800 to 1814—but during these periods, Jews enjoyed full civil equality. Three of Ancona's 1,400 Jews, Sanson Costantini, David Morpurgo, and Ezekiel Morpurgo, were appointed to the town council. With Napoleon's final retreat in 1814, all the former restrictive conditions were restored. The ghetto was reinstated. Hospitals expelled sick or wounded Jews. Jewish employment of Christians was strictly forbidden and patrols stalked the ghetto alleys on the Sabbath to intercept Christians who might light a fire for a Jew.

From the moment of Napoleon's fall, the Jews of Italy threw themselves wholeheartedly into the Risorgimento struggle for unification. Ancona was one of the last cities to be liberated. Its ghetto was abolished in 1830, and the 1848 uprising brought about a more liberal attitude toward the Jews. Nevertheless, during the siege of the city in 1860, the papal commander demolished the Levantine synagogue building, clearing the site for defense barricades. The sacrifice availed nothing, however, because, in the following year, the city fell to the liberating armies

Sylvia Fano, a young congregant whom we met at the Italian-rite synagogue in Ancona four years before her untimely death. The few young adults of the *kehillah* have problems meeting other young Jews. Under the auspices of the Federazione degli Giovanile Ebrei Italiani, (Federation of Young Jews of Italy), they gather periodically in various Italian cities for social activities.

of the Risorgimento. The region of the Marche joined the kingdom of Italy, and the Jews of Ancona were granted full civil rights.

Emancipated, the Jews integrated fluidly into Italian society, to the detriment of traditional customs and values. The frequency of intermarriage rose. On the other hand, some Jews of Ancona took interest in the Jewish national revival. The first Zionist society in Italy was organized in Ancona in 1896. During the persecutions of World War II, individual Ancona Jews were able to save their lives by paying large sums as ransom. Four hundred members of the Ancona *kehillah* survived the war.

Around the turn of the twentieth century, affluent *kehillot* in Turin, Florence, Milan, Rome, Vercelli, and Trieste constructed monumental temples in their cities. In contrast, the Ancona *kehillah* was satisfied with its two traditional synagogues, neither of which occupies its original site today. After the 1860 demolition of the Levantine-rite synagogue, Scuola Levantina, originally completed in 1550, the congregation built a new structure in 1879 on via Astagno, a steep, cobblestone alley not far from the harbor, and reconstructed their synagogue on the two upper floors. Today, the Scuola Levantina serves the synagogue needs of the few hundred Jews that comprise the present community.

THE LEVANTINE SYNAGOGUE

As is typical in pre-Emancipation Italy, no outward markings suggest the presence of a synagogue. An arched stone portal in the austere facade frames heavy wooden doors at the entrance. The prayer hall of the present Scuola Levantina is a stately room, higher than the original hall, with many fine Renaissance features: wide, round-headed windows, paired pilasters, and gracefully vaulted windows at the gallery level. The high east windows admit some daylight, but most of the effective lighting comes from the many lamps and chandeliers. An unusual glass lantern, serving as skylight and ventilator, pierces the vaulted ceiling of carved stucco. Intriguingly, its inscription advises, *"Da ma l'ma'ala mimkha"* ("Know what is above you"; *Avot*, 2:1).

Under the influence of modernizing trends, the *parnassim* of the Levantine synagogue introduced changes in the layout during the renovations of 1935. Significantly, they abandoned the previous bipolar plan. They raised the *Heikhal* onto a wide platform and bounded it with a decorative wrought iron balustrade. They dismantled the elevated *bimah* and moved its functions to an expanded *Heikhal* platform. High-backed benches on the long axis gave way to rows of chairs facing the *Heikhal*. In the spirit of the times, the renovation architect freed women from dark restricted positions behind north and south wall grilles and gave them a bright, open *matroneo* (women's gallery), projected over the hall on three sides.

In its opulence, the massive Ark in the Scuola Levantina shows an affinity to Baroque altars in Italian church art. A huge gilded crown under a velvet canopy hangs over the *Heikhal*. A dominant *parokhet* (Ark curtain) of red damask protects the repoussé silver Ark doors behind it.

Scuola Levantina, archival photo. In the former bifocal arrangement the *Heikhal* stands on the short east wall, facing the *bimah* on the west wall. (Courtesy of Umberto Naḥon Museum of Italian Jewish Art.)

The Levantine synagogue, Scuola Levantina, built in 1550, refurbished in Baroque style, and still in use by the Ancona Jewish community. The synagogue was installed here in 1879 after the original structure was demolished in 1860. The rich Baroque *Heikhal* under an elevated canopy dominates a high, bright room. Open balconies for the women were added in 1935.

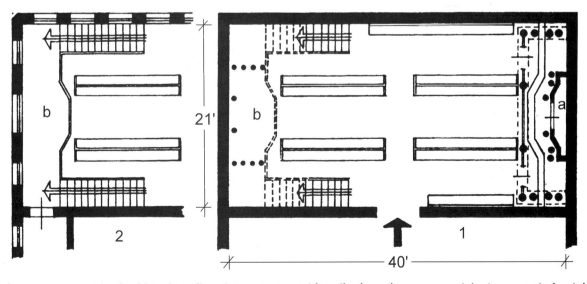

Bipolar arrangement in the historic Italian-rite synagogue (described on the next page) in Ancona: a) the Ark; b) the *bimah*. 1) main floor; 2) the high *bimah* level, 13 steps above the sanctuary. At its present lower ceiling location, the *bimah* sits at floor level. (Adapted from J. Pinkerfeld, *Synagogues in Italy;* Hebrew).

THE ITALIAN RITE SYNAGOGUE

The Italian-rite synagogue, Scuola Italiana, built in 1635, is smaller, more intimate and more lavish than the Levantine synagogue. Situated formerly at the lower corner of via Astagno, the building was torn down in 1932 to make room for a bank, now a cinema. Its furnishings found a safe haven on the ground floor of the 1879 Levantine substitute building and here the Italiana remains as a museum. The original prayer room of the Scuola Italiana had been a long rectangle, about 36 by 19 feet. Thirteen steps led up to a *bimah* platform, directly over the room entrance on the narrow west wall. The women sat behind grilles on a slightly elevated south side platform. Wooden benches for the men on the long axis faced the center aisle and afforded a view to both *bimah* and *Heikhal*.

The bipolar plan was retained when the Scuola Italiana was transferred to its present location in 1933. The smaller size of the new chamber, however, dictated structural changes and rearrangements in which portions of both *tevah* and *Heikhal* assumed new roles. The *tevah* was lowered because of the low ceiling. Placed at the west wall on a low octagonal wooden base, it now carries the six carved wooden panels that had previously adorned the high platform. The open Rococo screen from the *Heikhal*, with its three garlanded and floral-embossed wooden arches and a group of columns, were all transferred to this *tevah* as decoration.

The *Heikhal* dazzles the eye even without its resplendent entrance arch. Like a regal jewel box on the east wall of this tiny synagogue, it glistens in an effervescent wealth of Rococo detail. Helical and straight embossed and gilded pillars, broken tympanum, garlanded architrave and silver doors all vie for attention.

On the wall in the street entrance corridor, a stucco-framed inscription in Hebrew greets all comers:

Man of Israel, as you enter, may your heart
* be filled with awe.*
Lower your head facing this holy place
And note well the spark of the divine that
* rests upon it.*
Each morning rise with the sun
And pour out prayer and praise to the Lord.
Then will He bless you and sustain you
And fulfill all your wishes.

The *Heikhal* of the Italian-rite synagogue, Scuola Italiana before it was moved in 1932. Constructed in Baroque style in 1635, the synagogue underwent Rococo renovation about a century later. This archival photograph shows the three-bay Rococo screen on pedestals and its low metal balustrade that separated the raised *Heikhal* from the prayer room. (Courtesy of the Umberto Naḥon Museum of Italian Jewish Art, Jerusalem.)

Rococo screen and *tevah* of the Scuola Italiana in their present location. Formerly mounted in front of the *Heikhal* before the synagogue was moved, the ornate screen is now positioned around the *tevah*. A red velvet ḥuppah, formerly also over the *Heikhal,* now hangs above the *tevah* and graces the infrequent weddings. In contrast to the changes made in the Levantine synagogue, the bipolar arrangement of the Scuola Italiana was retained, keeping the benches parallel to the long walls.

Lower right of repoussé silver door of the *Heikhal,* Scuola Italiana. The central motif features a bold flower burst, highlighting a giant sunflower in a deeply fluted urn. The urn and the kidney-shaped container below it are sculpted in high relief in the grand manner of the Italian Rococo. Conical scrolls frame the inscribed medallion above the sunflower. Decorations of both lower doors are identical but the inscriptions differ. This one asserts:

> *In front of this door,*
> *All men who wish*
> *To worship the Lord*
> *Shall raise their voices.*
> *A precious treasure lies within*
> *—Concealed and well hidden—*
> *Beyond comparison with*
> *All honor and glory.*

WHISPERING WALLS

Whole *kehillot* were on the move when Jews were expelled from France in 1306, 1332, and 1394. Avoiding the pirates of the Ligurian Sea, they braved the hazards of the Alpine passes to reach a safe haven in the Piedmont region. In 1430, as the trickle of refugees swelled to a torrent, Amadeus VIII, Duke of Savoy, tried to check the growing Jewish settlements in his duchy by issuing a discriminatory code. He decreed occupational restrictions and forbade Jewish residence in proximity to Christians, as well as the construction of new synagogues. He burdened the Jews with extortionate taxation and forced them to wear a badge on their clothing. This system waxed and waned at varying degrees of enforcement, but did not entirely disappear until after Emancipation of the Jews in Italy. The rulers occasionally threatened expulsion, but they were ambivalent about it. They had to balance their desire to rid themselves of Jews against their need for Jewish services—and ransom payments would occasionally blunt the threats.

Settlement in the scattered Piedmont towns often developed by accretion. When a local lord contracted by *condotta* for a banker to serve his town, the resourceful Jew brought along his household—in essence, a nascent *kehillah: moreh, mohel, shoḥet* (teacher, ritual circumciser, slaughterer), and their families, and before long, a rabbi. Amid the castles, orchards, and vineyards on the limestone massif of Monferrato, the town of Casale recognized an organized community 100 years after such fifteenth-century seeding. Its members were active in commerce and loan banking. In 1560 Duke Guglielmo Gonzaga granted a privilege to the *kehillah* freely to engage in commerce, to keep a synagogue, and to worship according to its customs and ceremonies.

The building on via di Po, used as the earliest synagogue, was barely adequate for Casale's original 40 Jewish families—some 200 persons. The space was certainly far too small for the many Jews who streamed into the town in the late sixteenth century, after economic recession and expulsions sent Jews packing from Lombardy, and the 67 Casale families decided to build a larger synagogue; it was completed in 1595 and still stands at 44 vicolo Salomone Olper, in the heart of the old ghetto. By 1627 the

The synagogue in Casale Monferrato, 1595. Located on a narrow alley in the former ghetto, the unadorned exterior has a simple entrance and a row of high windows.

Monferrato district counted 575 Jews, and the capital, Casale, listed 385 in 77 families. After much discussion, the *kehillah* expanded the synagogue in 1663, adding 60 seats.

The Gonzaga dukes of Mantua held sway in Monferrato from 1536 to 1703. Whereas at home they related to familiar Jews with a casual benignity, they treated the anonymous Jews of distant Monferrato with the customary discrimination of the time, including frequent harassment. On a Sabbath in the fall of 1575, the town inspector burst into the Casale synagogue to verify whether the worshippers were wearing the badge in the prescribed form, "a strip of yellow silk on the right sleeve, long till the third of the arm." Transgressors paid ten crowns to the treasury and five to the delighted informer. On the following Monday, the inspector sequestered the Jewish loan bankers' books for scrutiny.

An early-seventeenth-century charter opened new trades for Piedmont Jews, permitting them legally to engage in commerce and the crafts, particularly in the textile industry. By the eigh-

teenth century, they owned silk and cotton mills in Casale and elsewhere. Jewish dominance implanted a professional jargon in cloth manufacture, based in part on Hebrew words. A dotted garment, for example, *na vesta a kinim,* took its name, according to one source, from the lice—*kinim*—of the third plague with which Moses afflicted the ancient Egyptians. Occupations diversified. The population grew and prospered, for a while.

The annexation of Monferrato in 1703 by the house of Savoy brought in its wake a deterioration in the Jewish circumstances. Ghettos, decreed in 1724, mandated a painful compulsory translocation of people from smaller communities to urban centers large enough to encompass ghettos. Thus the overcrowded Casale ghetto perforce had to absorb the Jews from San Salvatore.

Casale fell to the French in 1799. Jews received the occupying troops with rejoicing and

Seating plan of Casale synagogue in 1663. Plan shows the original orientation, with the *Heikhal* on the east, an entrance from the west, a central *tevah* (in canopied Piedmont style), and seats along the four walls. The seats are labeled in an alphabetical sequence, starting at the left of the Ark. The added benches are designated, "benches for the public." (Courtesy of Adriana Ottolenghi.)

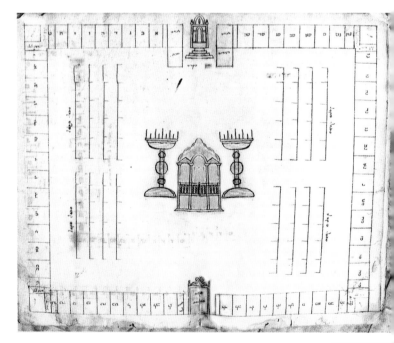

THE SYNAGOGUE IN CASALE MONFERRATO

The typical, unadorned row-house facade and entrance of the synagogue in Casale stemmed from official architectural restrictions and the need for the safety of anonymity. An ordinary door leads to the courtyard of the complex and to an open loggia lined with stone benches along the synagogue's west wall. Entry to the prayer room, one flight up, is from the north. Originally, the entrance was from the west, in the middle of the loggia.

The sparkling interior is a magnificent example of Piedmontese late Baroque and Rococo, as successively improved by an affluent community in the spirit of Jewish tradition. It is a spacious, pleasantly proportioned room, 30 by 60 feet, with a ceiling 30 feet above the floor. Light permeates the space from twelve high narrow windows on east and west walls. The earlier central plan—*Heikhal* on the east, benches facing a central *bimah*, and entrance from the west—has been altered to a post-Emancipation layout.

The current arrangement dates from the expansion of 1853 to 1866, when the architect Archinti enlarged the prayer room to the south. He placed the *Heikhal* on that wall, and moved the entrance from the west to the short north wall. He eliminated the central *tevah*, replacing it with a low *bimah* bordered by a wrought-iron grille before the Ark. The benches lined up frontally, facing the Ark in the new style of the times.

The *matroneo*, stretching along north, west, and south walls, hides behind a series of wooden grilles, exquisitely carved and gilded. Although the intention in decorating was "to inspire concentration and contemplation," the resulting opulence of gilded ornaments and the profusion of inscriptions dazzle the visitor.

Heikhal, upper portion. The *Heikhal*, built in 1761, anticipates the neo-Classical style, with a row of Corinthian columns supporting an ornate tympanum, gilded with flowering oak motifs in the large central panel. The multiple wooden pillars were originally painted to resemble white marble, but were repainted brown in 1852 as a sign of mourning over the death of King Carlo Alberto. A narrow inscription above the doors advises: *"Da lifnei mi atah omed"* ("Know before whom you stand;" *Avot* 3:1).

Synagogue interior to the *Heikhal*. The splendor of the interior contrasts sharply with the austere facade. The entire hall and its ceiling vaults are decorated in lavish Rococo style with a multitude of inscriptions in ornate cartouches. In an unusual orientation, the spacious *Heikhal* and *bimah* occupy the south wall as a result of major changes introduced in the 1866 renovations. In the style of contemporary church design, the architect introduced a pulpit, accessed initially by a spiral stair, but now, only by a portable ladder.

joined them in tearing down the ghetto gates. A legend tells of French Jewish soldiers singing psalms around the campfire in Hebrew to the tune of the "Marseillaise." After a brief withdrawal, Napoleon conquered Piedmont again in 1800 and granted Jews full civil rights. In 1807, with the intention of "a renewal of the ancient *Sanhedrin,*" he convened in Paris an assembly of 71 rabbis and scholars from France and the Italian peninsula. Italian *kehillot* dispatched 29 participants, including Emilio Viotta of Casale as one of the secretaries. The assembly drafted regulations to align Jewish behavior with the spirit of freedom initiated by the French Revolution: Jews must engage in useful professions; as citizens, every Jew must regard the home country as his fatherland.

The Casale *kehillah* prospered and flourished culturally in the Napoleonic era. Vittorio Emanuele I repulsed the French in 1814 and restored discrimination and ghetto walls. The prosperity collapsed and the flurry of culture as well, but the temporary breath of liberty had changed the Jewish outlook: freedom and equality were now of primary importance. Jews associated these goals with the Risorgimento aspirations for a united Italy, an Italy liberated from the reactionary regime of Austria and the petty tyrants who ruled many of the cities. With the encouragement of rabbis and support of bankers, Jews played a significant role in the revolt. Jewish intelligentsia formed close bonds with members of the revolutionary movements, sharing in the secret work of the *Carbonari*

Decorated ceiling. Embracing the upper space, a series of ornamented, symmetrically arranged trusses carry the vaulted basket-handle ceiling as they sweep down to the window line. Three major panels in the central ceiling area appropriately proclaim: *"Zeh sha'ar ha'shamayim"* ("This is the gateway to heaven"; Gen.28:17).

gilded inscriptions in Hebrew and Italian commemorate the *Statuto Albertino* that he issued:

On the twenty-fourth day of Adar II in the year 5608, March 29, 1848, King Carlo Alberto, and on the eighteenth day of Sivan, June 9, the National Parliament, issued decrees removing all earlier interdictions, granting freedom to all the Jews in the sub-Alpine kingdom, that they should forget the injustices and pain of former edicts and become free men in their homeland. In their love for her shall they ever prosper. For everlasting memory, by the holy Kehillah *of Casale.*

That day was the 332nd anniversary of the establishment of the world's first ghetto in Venice. The king opened the ghetto gates that day for the last time and lifted all legal discrimination.

Euphoria spread through the Piedmont *kehillot.* They rejoiced and jubilated amid effu-

Heikhal interior, lined with red damask. The inner side of the doors is painted cobalt blue with gilded Decalogue, menorah, and shofar carved in bas relief.

(charcoal burners), members of a secret, politically radical Christian society, and its successor, Giovani Italia (Italian Youth), which, along with the struggle for freedom, also opposed anti-Semitism. Much of the activity took place in Piedmont, especially in Turin.

Jewish participation in Italian unification brought the issue of Jewish rights to the attention of statesmen, writers, and jurists. Liberals appreciated the undeniable confluence of their national aspirations with the Jewish struggle for emancipation. Under recurrent pressure of protagonists for the Jewish cause, the king of Sardinia extended civil rights to Jews and other non-Catholics. Flanking the synagogue *Heikhal,* two

sive declarations of Jewish loyalty to the monarch. This provided the occasion for consulting with major architects to plan new grandiose synagogues; thus, to establish in stone the newly acquired Jewish respectability. Grand synagogues were built in Turin, Alessandria, and Vercelli, while extensive renovations were made in some of the older synagogues, as in Asti, Cuneo, and Casale. As residents in the first region of Italy to gain emancipation, Piedmont Jews secured a leading position. Its many small communities displayed religious zeal and intellectual energy far beyond expectation and Casale became the intellectual center of the north.

The Jewish communities paid a hidden, but heavy price for freedom. Assimilation made devastating inroads within a generation of the Emancipation. Following the post-Emancipation pattern of migration to the large cities, the *kehillah* in Casale declined from a high of 869 in 1839 to a pre-World War II count of 160. In contrast to the 108 synagogues that served 65 *kehillot* in 1830 Italy, only 35 were still in use a century later, half of them functioning irregularly.

When the Fascist party rose in 1919 as a militant patriotic organization, many Piedmont Jews were among its earliest supporters. The new Jewish bourgeoisie identified with the party's anti-socialist stance and felt comfortable with its extreme nationalism. The tragic implications of Fascist doctrine became evident only much later. By World War II, Italian Fascism was more openly anti-Semitic and the die was cast for the attempted destruction of Italian Jewry. The racial laws, transports, battles all took their toll. Fewer than half of the pre-war 4,000 Jews of Piedmont survived the upheaval. Despite former good relations between Jews and their Christian neighbors, the Fascists succeeded in deporting 30 Jews from Casale. The synagogue was ransacked and many ceremonial silver objects were stolen, never to be recovered.

After the war, the small group of survivors tried to reestablish the *kehillah,* combining in part with the small group in nearby Vercelli. For some years all prayed together in Vercelli on Rosh Hashanah, and in Casale on Yom Kippur. When the Vercelli synagogue fell into ruin, the few remaining individuals could assemble only at Casale.

Regional authorities chose the Casale synagogue for restoration as a museum because of its singular beauty. Under the direction of Piero Vignola and Giulio Bourbon, the work was completed in 1969. Giulio Bourbon remained as museum director. Of the 23 *kehillah* members in 1994, only seven adults and three children lived

Adriana Ottolenghi, one of the leaders of the small, but devoted *kehillah.* Forebears of her husband, Salvatore Giorgio Ottolenghi, who presides over the community, arrived in Casale in 970 as civil servants of Emperor Otto I of Germany. "In the last decades before the war most of the Jews were merchants, and on the high holidays the majority of the stores on the main street were closed. Now we open the synagogue for prayer to serve our few members and tourists only once a year, on Yom Kippur."

in Casale. The oldest member was eighty-five and the youngest, four.

By far, the most remarkable feature of the synagogue is the abundance of inscriptions that line the walls, each within its circular or rectangular cartouche. Together, they cover nearly every available surface. The lower rows quote biblical verses, a custom common in many sixteenth- and seventeenth-century synagogues in central Europe. Important prayers were often lettered on the walls, especially in the women's gallery. The upper row of inscriptions here fulfills another function. Like heady phrases in a stirring novel, they whisper highlights of the multifaceted story of the generations that sat on the benches below:

- *This tablet is witness that this house of God was prepared in the year 5355 (1595) for the glory of the Lord of Israel.*

- *The Spanish Purim: "In memory of divine protection during the siege by Spanish troops, 21 Adar II 5389 (1629), and 10 Tishri 5391 (1631)."*

- *Purim of the bombs: "A day of paean and praise, for God was our protector and refuge from the grenades of the besieging enemy, 7 Iyar 5416 (1656)."*

- *"This tablet in the wall testifies that the holy Ark in elegant splendor was built of precious wood and the capitals coated with pure gold in the year 5547 (1787)."*

- *"A day of radiance and joy, in memory of the salvation granted us by the Lord from the afflictions of the Austrian troops besieging the city, 2 Nisan 5609 (1849)."*

- *On major renovation: "With the leaders' advice, the congregation's wish and contributions by the people, this temple renewed its youth like a phoenix. It expanded in length toward the Holy Ark, and was dedicated in great jubilation and song in the year Yasisu v'yismeḥu, 'Be glad and rejoice [in You]' 5626 (1866; Ps. 70:5)."*

Interest in the synagogue history was continuous. Noting that the inscriptions were fading, the congregants carefully copied them all into a notebook in 1842 for secure preservation. During the extensive renovations of 1866, artisans refinished the walls and reapplied the inscriptions, condensing some and omitting others. One of those left out was in appreciation of Shmuel Yitzkhak, who gave "green decorations in honor of God." The reference is to two beautifully executed stucco reliefs, painted green to imitate old copper, representing the holy cities of Jerusalem and Hebron, on the east wall and west wall respectively, both close to the *bimah.*

Jews of northern Italy and those formerly of Casale; rabbis from Milan, Genoa, Turin, and Trieste; local clergy and town officials—all were among the nearly 500 guests at the celebration of the Casale synagogue's 400th anniversary, on Sukkot 5755 (1995). The *ḥazzan* chanted, "From east to west the name of the Lord is praised" (Ps. 113:3), and worshippers waved their *lulavim.* The weeklong festivities

Cartouche inscription on north wall. Rows of gilded cartouches cover the walls, the lower row with biblical quotations, the upper level marking memorable events in *kehillah* history. The inscription reads: "Who may ascend the mountain of the Lord? Who may stand in His holy place? He who has clean hands and a pure heart, who has not taken a false oath by His life or sworn deceitfully." (Ps. 24:3-4).

included a regal dinner, conferences, and a concert of Sephardic Jewish music from the ancient pre-expulsion tradition.

The wide corridors of the synagogue *matroneo* were reopened as a Judaica museum containing valuable historical documents and texts, precious silver and fabric ritual ornaments. The items on exhibit were collected from the *kehillot* of Vercelli, Turin, Alessandria, Asti, and Genoa, as well as contributions from Jewish families in Piedmont and purchases on the antique market. Among the unusual objects on display are a bronze Hanukkah lamp from the fifteenth century, a silver *brit milah* set and a ceremonial chair for the *sandek* at the circumcision ceremony from the nineteenth century. The extensive historical archives of the community, reorganized in 1989, contain a total of 817 publications arranged in chronological order, allowing researchers to trace the life of the community over the centuries.

One notebook entry not preserved in wall inscription concerns a synagogue event in 5521 (1761). The congregants blended Yom Kippur solemnity with exuberant celebration as they dedicated a new *Heikhal:* "They carried the Torah scrolls around the synagogue from the old Ark to the new one on the night of Yom Kippur . . . with great song and the sound of a bell, *calusa* . . . by candlelight and torchlight . . . chanting: 'As the doors of the *Heikhal* are opened wide, so may the gates of our prayers' acceptance be opened at the end of the fast.' "

OVER THE BRIDGE TO SALCANO

On the morning of October 6, 1788, between Rosh Hashana and Yom Kippur, Jacob Moises Gentile, actuary of the Gorizia *kehillah,* came to the executive committee to report. After years of diligent work, he had finally put the community's archive into order—from the earliest documents of the neighboring cities of Gorizia and Gradisca, dated 1509, to the then current year. He trusted the leaders' wisdom to provide a recompense, although he reminded them that "like the ants of Solomon's Proverbs, he had to prepare in summer the supplies for winter." Three days later, Moisè Morpurgo, Jacob Senigaglia, Hermann Levi, Iseppo Bolaffio, Nadàn Luzzatto, and the other *parnassim* voted him 20 florins for his work. While most of the early documents have since been lost, the *kehillah* archive still contains many records from the eighteenth and nineteenth centuries, as well as references to earlier annals that are missing. Giuseppe Bolaffio, a descendant of one of those leaders, reviewed the papers in fascinating detail in 1957 in the journal of Italian-Jewish history, *Rassegna Mensile di Israel* (RMI). These accounts present a mosaic of Jewish life in that community.

Gorizia, in Italy's northeast corner of shifting borders, remained culturally Italian but politically Austrian for more than 400 years. It returned to Italy, in 1919, after ferocious battles during World War I. In later World War II settlements, Italy ceded eastern areas, including part of Gorizia, to Yugoslavia. The Gorizia *kehillah,* only about 35 miles north of the larger Jewish center in Trieste, maintained close ties with that community and shared in its history.

Ashkenazic Jews reached this fertile region as they fled from persecutions in Germany in the mid-fourteenth century, appearing in Gorizia records as early as 1349. Sephardim, expelled in 1569 by Pius V from the south, joined the earlier nucleus, although each group retained its own tradition. The earliest settlement was located on the castle slopes in an open area surrounded by trees and shrubbery that provided some isolation during the frequent epidemics.

The process of herding Jews into ghettos, begun in sixteenth-century Italy, effectively excluded them from the countryside and from towns and villages where forming a ghetto was impractical. To this exclusion and existing occupational restrictions, the Church added literature censorship, clothing badges, and obligatory attendance at Catholic sermons. The Jews of Gorizia were afforded some protection by the local nobility who appreciated their role in the economy. When the ghetto was instituted in 1697, a policy unique to the Hapsburg-controlled northern region of Italy allowed the heads of 14 prominent Jewish families to buy 16 designated houses on the present via Ascoli near the San Giovanni Church. By the close of the seventeenth century, the community numbered 270 people in 53 families. Crowding caused considerable internal friction, especially a century later, when it numbered 300, four percent of the Gorizia population. The congestion was so severe that it swayed the *kehillah* in 1779 to refuse 15 Jewish families admission to Gorizia after they were banished from the neighboring town of San Danielle.

Life inside the ghetto was not easy. Jewish leaders often turned to the Royal Council of Gorizia and Gradisca for help. An official circular issued September 23, 1775, informed the *kehillah* that "the Council has learned that the members do not live in harmony; that such lack of harmony has a bad influence on their public and private businesses; and it is ordered that all members of the community appear at all *kehillah* meetings, under threat of punishment." Members not only missed meetings, they were often remiss in payment of *kehillah* and city taxes and contributions. In June 1794, ghetto leaders turned to the city magistrate with a request that he assign the military to persuade recalcitrant members to pay their debts.

The *kehillah,* along with most Italian Jews from pre-Renaissance times and well into the nineteenth century, had troubles of a more serious nature—the concern for Jewish continuity. Both forced conversion and apostasy posed serious problems. It was impossible to persuade the Church to relinquish a newly baptized person, regardless of baptismal circumstances. Zealous lower clergy often ignored the explicit disapproval of higher ecclesiastic authorities toward baptizing abducted Jewish children and denying them a chance to return to their families. In 1739

Row of wooden benches on the *tevah.* The running inscription above the benches commemorates the ghetto fire of 1761, when "blazing flames licked up to the synagogue and suddenly stopped on the threshold." The *kehillah* celebrated that date and its miracle for many years as a "minor Purim."

the nuncio of Vienna forbade this practice, but it continued nonetheless. Reacting episodically to recurrent tragic events of forced conversions, the monarchs sought to control the problem each time with an expedient change to limit what the Church was permitted to do. As evaluated by Bolaffio from Gorizia's archive, each refinement and every expansion of the imperial "ban" on forced conversion emerged only after persistent Jewish complaints of repeated painful and widespread violations. Rescripts by Maria Theresa in 1768; Joseph II in 1782, 1787, 1789, and 1790; and by Leopold II in 1791, defined and successively reduced the circumstances under which Jewish children might legally be baptized. The rules eventually restricted conversion to persons exercising mature, informed, and overt volition—but enforcement was weak or nonexistent.

The best-known event of forced conversion in Italy was that of seven-year-old Edgardo Mortara (1851–1940), whom papal police abducted from Bologna to Rome in 1858. They acted on the strength of a claim by a domestic that she had secretly baptized him five years earlier, when "he was about to die." Deathbed baptism was a Church-approved practice, considered valid even against parental will. A universal outcry over Mortara's abduction, as well as efforts by Napoleon III and Sir Moses Montefiore, were futile against an adamant Pope Pius IX. Mortara was nominally released 12 years later when the Church lost its secular power with the success of the Risorgimento, but by then he was an enthusiastic Augustinian novice. Titled an "apostolic missionary" by Pope Leo XIII, he became an ardent conversionist and had a long career as a canon and professor of theology.

Gorizia's *parnassim,* however, had apostasy problems of an opposite nature. In 1782 a Gorizia Jew came to the town council with a complaint. He had decided to become a Roman Catholic and his sister Rebecca, 26, was inclined to do likewise, though concern for their beloved father gave her pause. Her brother planned to take her to Venice where she might freely decide, but he could not find her, an event that he attributed to "that most iniquitous plot of those heads of the ghetto." A week later, without any evidence of her whereabouts, the council ordered the ghetto leaders to "free" Rebecca within 24 hours, on threat of personal arrest. Rebecca's fate was not recorded.

Lower lobby of the synagogue. With vaulted ceiling supported by a central row of rusticated pillars, this spacious room once served as the prayer room of the community's Polish Jews.

In an echo of *The Merchant of Venice,* a Gorizia girl of 17 developed an intimacy with an officer from Tuscany in 1801. Reacting to her father's harsh reproach, she ran away to nuns in the local Ursuline convent. Her father's desperate appeals to Church authorities to allow him a private encounter with his daughter yielded no more than a single brief meeting under the domineering presence of political and Church commissaries. He even petitioned the emperor, "The ecclesiastics torment me, legitimate defender of my daughter's morality." The Church neither married the girl to her lover, nor returned her to her family.

In 1764, the *parnassim* summarized Jewish property and occupations for municipal officials. Most ghetto Jews owned their houses and many also had rural holdings. A census of 1788 cites 25 houses in the ghetto, housing 52 families, with 79 bachelors and widowers, and 137 women. The majority managed shops, selling assorted merchandise: silk thread, cloth and remnants, iron goods and tools, foodstuffs—particularly oil—and hides. Early in the eighteenth century, Jews introduced the silk industry into the counties of Gorizia and Gradisca, and encouraged the peasants to cultivate silkworms. Wealthier families ran factories that wove silk cloth. Only one Jew ran a mortgage bank, testifying to the strength in Gorizia of the Franciscan-managed Monti di Pietà. Jewish merchants were active also in the importing and warehousing of grain. Using their connections with Alexandrian Jews in a time of scarcity, they succeeded in importing *catamboseia,* an Egyptian grain previously unknown in Italy. A large shipment of it greatly benefited the needy.

The archive tells of an 1819 appeal by Jewish elders to the Austrian government to prevent an infiltration of German Jewish propagandists for religious reform. Within a decade, however, the *kehillah* grew more receptive to new ideas. Promoting liberalism in Judaism and an early pioneer of the *Haskalah* in northern Italy, Gorizia's Rabbi Isaac Samuel Reggio (1784–1855) was influential in establishing a rabbinical seminary in Italy, the Collegio Rabbinico. The Collegio functioned in Padua from 1829 to 1871, with a curriculum that included far-ranging secular studies, at Rabbi Reggio's insistence. The compelling leader in the Padua Collegio was Rabbi Reggio's close associate, Samuel David Luzzatto, a Trieste-born philosopher, scholar, and poet. The Collegio reopened in Rome in 1887, educating rabbis in a modern spirit. For a hundred years, the majority of rabbis in Italy earned ordination at this institution. By incorporating modern scholarship, Italian Jewry avoided a clash between religion and science. As a result, it remained immune to the controversies over religious reform that plagued northern and central European Jewry. Rabbi Reggio translated the Pentateuch into Italian and wrote critical commentaries that provoked fierce antagonism from the Orthodox rabbinate in Germany.

The Gorizia community reached a maximum membership of 314 in the mid-nineteenth century, but the count fell to 256 by 1890. Between the world wars, an outstanding teacher, Angelo da Fano, taught refugee children from central Europe. He introduced Zionist youth activities, often over parental objection. He was a dynamic leader in the Hatikvah and Menorah organizations, many of whose members realized their dream of *aliyah* to *Eretz Yisrael* and helped found religious settlements there.

After absorbing the *kehillot* of Udine and San Daniele in 1930, the pre-World War II Gorizia community numbered 288. Many fled with the outbreak of hostilities, leaving only about 80 by the time of Italy's capitulation in November 1943. The Nazi roundup of Jewish residents in that month ensnared 45 persons, aged 1 to 89 years, whom they deported to the camps. The small post-war *kehillah,* that functioned until Trieste annexed it in 1970, dedicated a deportees' memorial plaque in the synagogue courtyard.

Today there are no Jewish residents in Gorizia. In the center of the former ghetto, an old gate on via Ascoli leads to the gardens of a large house that once belonged to Graziadio Isaia Ascoli (1829–1907). The most famous scholar of the Gorizia *kehillah,* Ascoli became a philologist and held the chair of linguistics at Milan University for over 40 years. He made important contributions to comparative linguistics and devoted himself to Jewish historical research,

publishing papers on the medieval Jewish tombstones of southern Italy, inscribed in Hebrew, Latin, and Greek. A large portrait of Graziadio Ascoli, acclaimed by his native city as scholar and senator, hangs in the city hall. His house is now a protected historical site, open to the public.

Not far from the Ascoli house stands the synagogue, one of the early buildings on the street, erected in 1699. It was modified and enlarged in 1756, and again in 1894, serving the community until the deportations on November 23, 1943, when vandalism replaced care. Synagogue treasures, secretly walled up during the war in an attempt to save them, were discovered and confiscated when the Nazis turned the synagogue over to Church custody.

Forty years later, under the inspired guidance of a former mayor of Gorizia, Antonio Scarano, civic-minded residents formed the Associazione degli Amici d'Israele (the Friends of Israel Association). They appreciated the Jewish contribution to the development of their town and devoted themselves to the preservation of the Jewish-built heritage in Gorizia, to authentic restoration of the synagogue, to preservation of ghetto houses, to a study of the history and traditions of the lost *kehillah,* and to exposure of their young people to this knowledge. At a cost of half

Members of Associazione degli Amici d'Israele (Friends of Israel) in Gorizia with former resident, Bertie Eckert, fourth from the right, with his daughter, Tamar Milo, and granddaughter, Dana. Bertie returned to his birthplace in May 1997 for the first time since his emigration to Palestine in 1939. (Photo: Bernardo Bressen, Gorizia.)

THE SYNAGOGUE IN GORIZIA

Two tall wooden doors set in a high wall afford access to the courtyard where the building is surrounded by a garden. The courtyard wall has simple, classic lines with Moorish decorative elements. Recently repainted in a pale beige, the wall features a small eight-pointed rosette and Tablets of the Law at the summit. Simple and harmonious, the facade gives the appearance of a country villa, blending well with other buildings on the street. The internal entrance leads to a spacious hall, with a vaulted ceiling supported on a row of four broad columns. At the far end of the room, a door opens to the small lobby and to the grand marble double staircase that leads to the synagogue on the floor above.

The large prayer room has an air of restrained elegance. Sunlight entering through the 12 tall windows and reflected on the polished marble floor fills every corner. Although the founding community followed the Ashkenazic rite, Italian tradition influenced the synagogue layout. It prescribed the bipolar arrangement: *Heikhal* on the short east wall, opposite the *tevah* on the west entry side and the benches in long rows facing north and south. The *Heikhal,* with its black marble helical pillars and ornate Baroque pediment, provides an element of contrast in the otherwise subdued neo-Classical interior. Here, on the dark marble steps of the *tevah,* on the eve of Tisha b'Av, the white-clad elders gathered in the darkness with lighted candles and bemoaned the destruction of the Temple.

Crowned by an elliptical *matroneo,* the synagogue is reminiscent of the demolished Scuola Grande in Trieste or the extant Ashkenazic Tedesca Synagogue in Venice. The Venetian community expressed elegance with rich fabrics and gilded ornamentation. The Gorizia *kehillah* fulfilled the desire for enhancement, *hiddur mitzvah,* by

lavish use of marble: in the *Heikhal* structure, in the neo-Classical window frames, in the bold black-and-white geometric floor design, and in the four tall inlaid-marble candelabras.

The synagogue in Gorizia on via Ascoli. Built in 1699, it served the community until World War II. When the diminished Gorizia *kehillah* was dissolved in 1978, its Trieste guardians donated the building to the municipality of Gorizia for cultural use. Restored by municipal and private funding, the synagogue was reopened as a museum on September 2, 1984. We were the only witnesses when Pesach Ostishinsky of Netanya, Israel, and Rabbi Eliyahu Richetti of Trieste affixed a *mezuzzah* on the synagogue door post on July 22, 1988.

Elevated *tevah* on the west wall near the entrance. It is located in the middle of the short west wall and approached by a double set of five slightly curving steps. Slender helical pillars, supporting the modest cupola, echo the style of the *Heikhal* pillars.

Synagogue interior to the *Heikhal.* In bipolar fashion, marble *Heikhal* and decorative bronze grate dominate the east wall, opposite the *tevah* on the west. Above, an oval Venetian-style *matroneo* has a finely carved balustrade and moveable latticed shutters.

a million lire and years of painstaking effort, the newly restored building made its debut as a Jewish museum in 1984.

The municipality paved a narrow path through the synagogue garden down to a peaceful brook that served the *kehillah* for *Tashlikh* some 200 years ago, but not in this century. Gorizia native Bertie Eckert, of Kvutzat Yavne, remembers walking to a distant river for the *minhag,* and he marvels at the scholarship of the Amici in trac-

ing the older venue. On his 1997 visit to the house where he grew up, the present owners showed him 200-year-old relics of Jewish ownership of the house, found in recent renovations. Chiseled grooves that had been plastered over in four stone door posts yielded *mezuzzot* with parchment intact. Large stone basins in the basement were a former *mikveh,* and a small hammered copper plaque on a heavy door depicted the sacrifice of Isaac.

Gorizia's Jews, as well as the neighboring *kehillot,* once buried their dead in the Jewish cemetery located in a part of town ceded to Yugoslavia. Called Nova Gorica, that section is now in Slovenia. A high fence behind the northern railroad station designates the border, and the old burial ground lies on the other side. This is possibly the earliest Jewish cemetery in Slovenia, with nearly 700 graves; the oldest stone dates from 1371. Most of the stones have disappeared and weeds cover the scarcely legible remainder. After the post-World War II border change split the town, Gorizia Jews escorted their burials to nearby Gradisca.

Even pastimes and enjoyments of bygone days come down to us in dated legal documents. Bolaffio reports a City Council warning to the ghetto *parnassim:*

On June 11, 1764, several carriages of Jews of both sexes left the ghetto over the Isonzo River bridge for the village of Salcano, where they spent the whole day in the trattoria of Bartolomeo Cargnei, eating and dancing until late at night. You have to refrain from making such entertainment outside the ghetto. Otherwise you will have to pay 100 hungars and sustain corporal punishments.

On that and other occasions, the *parnassim* asserted themselves in terms of basic civil rights. "Life in the ghetto is not attractive for young people. They want to have normal escapades and to spend some hours of freedom in a more lively and cheerful environment." Availing themselves of testimony by the innkeeper that it had been a simple recreation, "without any indecency, scandal, or publicity," the leaders explained that malevolent people had artfully distorted the facts. "No law forbade Jews to go, on foot or by carriage, to the surrounding villas," and what had happened at Salcano was strictly private, not a "crime or something illicit, deserving penal prohibition."

They ended by pleading that Jews be granted the freedom to go to any of the surrounding villages, "to enjoy the greenery together with honest people as was commonly done in Vienna and even in Rome under the eyes of the Pope, who tolerated only honest behavior."

Like the cemetery, the village of Salcano now lies across the border in Slovenia, and is part of Nova Gorica. Border guards usually permit free passage between the two sections of the divided city. Do the young people from Gorizia still cross the river to eat and dance in the *trattoria* of Salcano?

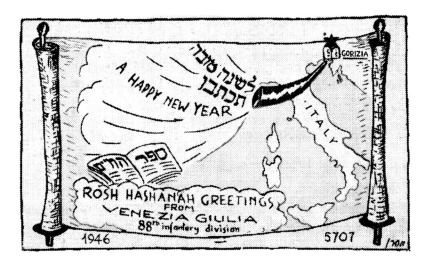

New Year's greeting card, 5707 (1946), sent home by soldiers of the American 88th Infantry Division. The card depicts a huge shofar emanating from tiny Gorizia in Italy's northeast. Stationed there at war's end, Captain Rabbi Nathan A. Barack had the synagogue cleaned and reopened for services on Rosh Hashanah. (From C. Bulfoni, *La sinagoga di Gorizia.*)

GHETTO WITHOUT A GATE

*T*he inspiration to delve into this topic [the Jewish plight] *stems from memories of my 15-day train trip through Austria, Germany, and Poland on the way to the Russian front in August 1942, as a soldier in the Alpine Division of Mussolini's army. Along the tracks of every station on the way, there were lines of barefoot Jews in ragged clothing, engaged in menial jobs under the constant watch of German guards. All bore yellow* Jude *patches. The women, some of whom still had traces of faded beauty, were bent over from hunger and weariness. Silent and frightened, they dragged themselves through the trains, carrying pail and broom, as their eyes begged for bread. The suffering of this tortured humanity penetrated deep into my soul, and I searched for the reason for this continued inhuman persecution.*

Thus Roberto Arnaldi, Italian scholar and historian of the Monregale region in Piedmont, introduces his booklet, "Remembrances of the Jewish Past in Monregale." He was alerted by a newspaper article in 1981 describing a project of the previous summer by Jewish youths from Turin who surveyed unused synagogues in the

Piedmont hills and chose to refurbish the one in Mondovì. The project was launched by Israeli architect David Cassuto during a convention of Italian Jewish youth held in Florence the previous year. With other volunteer help and the guidance of experts, they cleaned up the synagogue furniture, *Heikhal,* and *tevah.* They carefully identified and catalogued the ritual objects, books, and documents, many of which had been stored in the benches. This was the first step in the long process of preserving this jewel of a synagogue.

Mondovì's origin in 1198 directly relates to a despotic bishop in Asti. Fleeing his harsh dominion, free-minded villagers of Vicoforte, Carrasone, and Vasco in Monregale moved to a clearing on top of the Regale Mountain where they founded the village of Mondovì Piazza. At the foot of the mountain, now linked to the summit by a funicular railway, lay the newer district, Mondovì Breo. The town was a fief of various rulers, passing unpredictably by force or politics between the House of Savoy and the French until the region became part of the Italian kingdom in the twentieth century.

Jewish presence in Mondovì dates from 1580, when Jews banished from Spain and southern France found refuge on the slopes of Monregale. These wooded hills once sheltered numerous minuscule Jewish settlements that have barely left a trace. In the tiny village of Vicoforte, in the valley below Mondovì, the street called Ghetto leads to a group of houses dating from the fifteenth century. Through high gateways, the massive posts of which suggest that they once bore heavy gates, one arrives at a series of joined, enclosed courtyards that, as local legend has it, once housed Spanish Jewish families.

Bishop Gerolamo Scarampi of Monregale chronicles that the 1582 Council of Trent confirmed the need for avoidance of "excessive closeness to Jews," expressed in the 1555 papal decree confining Jews to ghettos. Nevertheless, the Savoy dukes delayed compliance with that decision, finding the Jewish moneylenders vital to their economy. The hilly terrain, with Mondovì divided into an upper and lower town, was also problematic. Finally, in 1720, a ghetto was established in the upper town on via Vico behind the church. Since that street was an important artery, it could never be closed and therefore had no gate. Christians continued to live in many of the houses near the Jews, and the clerical prohibition

against Jewish dwellings in proximity to a church was quietly disregarded. The *kehillah* in Mondovì remained small, leaving a visible imprint only in the ghetto: a synagogue and a few Jewish buildings located between via Vico and Piazza d'Armi. The uncrowded ghetto afforded relatively comfortable living conditions.

Deeply indebted to Jewish moneylenders, Carlo Emanuele I granted Mondovì's clerical Monti di Pietà (loan banks) less monetary support than it enjoyed in other Italian cities. He permitted an influential Jewish banker, Aron de Sacerdoti, to live in Mondovì in 1588, with a

The ghetto street and synagogue on via Vico in Mondovì, Baroque, ca. 1700. No mark distinguishes the synagogue building, center left, from other attached houses in Mondovì Piazza, the upper section of the city.

View of the countryside from the synagogue porch, looking down on the village of Vicoforte Fiamenga.

privilegio to deal in money. It was a limited permit, subject to periodic renewal and dependent on extravagant payments. Sacerdoti, however, gained notoriety because of alleged criminal activity. He was sentenced for insulting the duke and for suborning a witness. After he escaped over the border, smuggling money and valuables, officials convicted him *in absentia* and confiscated his property.

A census by Carlo Emanuele III in 1761 listed 19 ghettos in the province of Piedmont—with a Jewish population of 4,186 in 808 families, including 12 Mondovì families that numbered 64 individuals. An 1839 census in Mondovì counted 79 Jewish males and 68 females, including those in the valley villages who participated in the *kehillah.* The population rose to 200 within 30 years.

Relations between Mondovì Jews and Christians were unusually cordial and harmonious. When the Piazza ghetto became too crowded, several Jewish families found temporary hospitality with Christians. The population was content to do business with the Levi, Momigliano, and Lattes families, to deposit money in their banks, and to pay reasonable interest on loans. During an economic crisis that caused the collapse of all the regional banks, Mondovì citizens with deposits in the Lattes family bank stoically accepted its bankruptcy. *"Il latte é andato sul fuoco,"* they consoled each other, "The milk ran over into the fire." Branches of the Ottolenghi, Iona, and Foa families, prominent throughout northern Italy, settled in Mondovì also. Favorite personal names of women, gleaned from town documents, included Giuditta, Graziosa, Clelia, Diamanta, Sara, Vittoria, Rachele, Ester, and Bona.

Donato Levi founded the Mondovì Bank of Exchange and Discount in 1820, and his family conducted it in continuity. Even the clergy patronized the Levi bank when the Monti's interest rates went up. Ettore Levi managed the bank from 1917. His son, Dr. Marco Levi, followed him, joining the corporation in 1928. Dr. Levi reopened the bank after World War II with his uncle, Gabriele Segre, and managed it until they merged with other Italian banks in 1972.

Many Mondovì Jews were tradesmen, dealing mainly in the products of the spinning and weaving industry from the surrounding countryside where Jews specialized in raising silkworms and in producing fine silk cloth. Although Jews were well-accepted in the town, an incident of 1776 points up their marginality. A maidservant accused "two Jews" of kidnapping a Christian child, saying she "saw someone in a red cloak committing the deed." Two Jews owning red cloaks were duly arrested, but the maid could not identify them in a lineup among Christians, all in red cloaks. For lack of evidence, the accused, who had languished 44 days in prison, were exonerated and released. The child, having run away as a prank, later returned home unharmed.

The Mondovì *kehillah* contributed regularly to Jewish charities and was generous to all of the city's poor. In the heady celebration on April 2, 1848 of the Edict of Emancipation by Carlo Alberto, the *kehillah* organized a series of events. The highlight was a festive banquet for the town's residents, including the clergy. A few days later, after communal prayers by Jews and Christians, Fortuna Estella Levi led the Jewish women and their Catholic

Mobile *sukkah* lamp of hammered copper in the open-canopied *tevah.* Mirror strips on the conical base enhance candlelight by reflection. Copper flowers on curving stems raise metal disc faces inscribed with biblical phrases relating to Sukkot.

neighbors in a campaign to collect clothing and other necessities for families of Piedmontese soldiers fighting for Italian independence.

Jewish horizons expanded in the wake of the Emancipation. As new legislation opened up areas of residence, higher education, and the professions to Jews, many migrated to the populous cities: Turin, Genoa, and Milan. They developed careers in public service, in business and cultural spheres, in the army, and in banking and industry. The Levi family bank was influential in starting a large ceramic industry that, during the 50 years until 1982, employed 120 workers. After moving to an industrial zone that allowed expansion and modernization, it reopened under new management. The Jewish engineer Giorgio Bassani, and his partner, Manfredi, established a foundry that produced special cast iron for the Italian Air Force during World War I. They continued production for civilian use until World War II.

Mondovì's Felice Momigliano (1886–1924) was an author and man of politics. From his high-school study of philosophy, he acquired a socialist outlook for which he was persecuted at quite an early age. He wrote, "Education molds the soul towards an awareness of beauty, truth and goodness." A dedicated pacifist but still a devoted patriot, he was proud that his father had been among the first to be drafted in the 1848 revolt. The first Mondovì Jew to achieve competence in philosophy and literature, he was driven by an insatiable thirst for knowledge to leave Piedmont for study in Rome. His brothers also pursued university studies. In 1959 a memorial tablet in his honor was affixed to the synagogue building, noting his role in promoting both the ideals of the prophets and the theories of one of Italy's unifiers, Giuseppe Mazzini. Momigliano bequeathed his extensive collection of books to Mondovì's municipal library.

In conformity with 1931 legislation relating to Jewish communities, Turin annexed the small Mondovì *kehillah,* along with the other *kehillot* in Piedmont. The few Jews there took the seemingly sensible step of transferring the archives, the precious Judaica, and 13 of their 14 Torah scrolls for safekeeping to the synagogue in Turin. But even the best laid plans often go astray. The Turin synagogue suffered a direct hit from an Allied fire bomb in World War II and most of these treasures were destroyed. The remaining Mondovì Torah and other artifacts had better luck. Just one day before the Germans entered town, Dr. Marco Levi concealed the items behind a concrete wall in his home. This cache survived.

Mondovì citizens respected their Jewish neighbors and honored the bond of human solidarity during World War II. The six remaining Mondovì Jews, along with other Jews who fled from Turin to the hills, found shelter with local residents and clergy who endangered their own lives to save them. Marco Levi's family hid in the Istituto Sacra Famiglia in nearby Dogliani, where the nuns of the Dominican Order

The last Jew of Mondovì, Dr. Marco Levi—descendant of a founding family of the Mondovì *kehillah.* A bachelor, Levi cares for the tiny synagogue and maintains ties with the family of his sister Lidia in Turin.

THE SYNAGOGUE IN MONDOVÌ

Upon entering the small, irregular prayer room, the visitor immediately encounters the octagonal *tevah,* positioned centrally opposite the entrance. Carved of dark painted wood, it nearly obscures the *Heikhal* on the far wall. Two steps off the floor, it has six low carved and decorated panels and two open sides for entry. A graceful, airy, wood baldachin is carried on eight short, marble-painted pillars with gilded Corinthian capitals. This style is unique to Piedmont synagogues, and survives today only in specimens from Chieri, Carmangnola, Cherasco, and Mondovì. On a side table sits a wooden charity box, divided into sections labeled "for the school," "for the poor," and "for *Eretz Yisrael.*" An older, well-worn *tzedakah* (charity) board, covered with knotted strings, lies nearby, leaning against the wall.

Limited to a small prayer room with few windows, and unable to afford marble for *Heikhal* and *tevah,* Mondovì's Jews were lavish with painted decorations and biblical quotations. On three sides of the room, 14 trompe l'oeil images of broad, purple-draped windows cover the walls. Among the biblical verses on the panels above the painted windows is the message from Isaiah 56:7, *"Ki beiti bet t'fila yikarei l'khol ha'amim"* ("For My House shall be called a house of prayer for all peoples"). Another passage expressed the philosophical outlook of the Mondovì *kehillah, "Ki tov yom b'ḥatzeirekha me'elef"* ("Better one day in Your courts than a thousand [anywhere else]"; Ps. 84:11).

Among the treasures found in the benches of the prayer room during the restoration of 1980 were a *ketubbah* (marriage contract) from 1750 and loose pages of micrography, the writing visible only with the aid of a magnifying lens. Embossed Torah crowns with rich relief decorations, including one with the name Mondovì in Hebrew letters, are in seventeenth-century Baroque style. The elegance of these ritual objects contrasts sharply with the modest furniture and decorations in the room, suggesting how this community of limited means stretched its budget to follow *hiddur mitzvah* and commissioned extravagant ornaments for their holiest and most precious possessions, the Torah scrolls.

The exceptional walk-in *Heikhal,* now empty, stands on the east wall opposite the entrance. Of carved and gilded wood, its main decorative elements include a pair of helical columns ornamented with a climbing grapevine and a seven-branched menorah with red flames painted on the upper doors. The Ark structure stands between two towering Corinthian pillars frescoed on

continued

Tzedakah board, with membership list on the right and varying money amounts enumerated along the top. On the Sabbath, each congregant could indicate his intended contribution by pulling the knotted string to the column of his choice without doing the "work" of writing.

the wall. The low approach platform is bordered by two wrought-iron grates that carry iron candle-cups. Oil lamps hang in front of the Ark, including a permanently lit *ner tamid,* and eight others that were lit on special occasions. A heavy bronze Hanukkah lamp stands near the Ark, and five large hanging chandeliers sparkle with soft candle light from a myriad crystal faces.

In a corner of the entrance landing outside the synagogue door there is a stone basin served by a stone funnel that collects rainwater for ritual hand washing. A short narrow corridor leads to the intimate *matroneo,* on the left, that does not hide the women behind latticed shutters. The women, on three rows of plain wooden benches, could follow prayer-room proceedings through wide open windows. The corridor ends in a broad enclosed porch that accommodates the depth of the walk-in *Heikhal.* The porch also housed the diminutive *ḥeder,* evidenced by an old school desk with an indecipherable name carved into the top. Day-dreaming *ḥeder* boys could feast their eyes on the green hills spread before them through the tall east windows.

Synagogue chandeliers and frescoed walls. There are 14 elegantly curtained windows painted around the room, each with a biblical verse written in its architrave. Water damage has left bright stains on the walls.

respected their Judaism. He tells of another Jew hidden there, who, garbed in the flowing robes of a pious monk, hoed the garden daily while softly mumbling the words of the "Ḥad Gadya" to himself. A total of 407 Jews were deported from Piedmont by the Fascists; 31 returned. Of the thousand Jews who fought with the Italian partisans, seven received gold medals for bravery.

The small synagogue, dating from the early eighteenth century, is on the third floor at 65 via Vico, above apartments once inhabited by Jewish families. It had been closed for nearly two decades in the 1920s and 1930s and so it escaped attention and desecration. A Christian family on a lower floor keeps the key and opens the synagogue for infrequent visitors.

Mondovì Jews used the corner of a seventeenth-century cemetery below the Mondovì fortress where the thousands of people who died of the plague in 1630 were buried. When the city opened a new cemetery in the lower part of the city, Mondovì Breo, in 1865, it allotted a portion for Jewish use to which the old gravestones and human remains were moved. A monument the municipality erected in 1954 at the side of the cemetery road names the Piedmont victims of the Nazis and lists those from Mondovì: Anna Segre Levi, Beniamina Levi, Pia Levi, Aldo Levi, and Professor Delfina Ortona.

Interior of the walk-in Ark. The synagogue once owned 14 Torah scrolls bound with silk ties and decorated with damask *me'ilim* and silver ornaments. The Ark, one of the last of its kind in Piedmont, projects into the rear porch.

Matteo Neppi Modona, grandnephew of Marco Levi, holds the curtain of the early eighteenth-century wooden Ark. In keeping with the diminutive proportions of the synagogue, the Ark platform is only about four inches above the floor.

In the late 1980s, the octogenarian Dr. Marco Levi was the last Jew still living in Mondovì. "We still use candles in the synagogue," he admitted. "The synagogue fell out of use before we could install electricity. Our last rabbi, Ferrucio Servio, left in 1905 when we were no more than 10 families. The rabbi from Cuneo came to open the synagogue in 1923 for my Bar Mitzvah. The last wedding in the synagogue took place in 1924, when my aunt Pia Levi married Marco Levi of Saluzzo. He died about 10 years later. Pia and her family were deported to Auschwitz." In 1935, when his sister, Lidia, married Dr. Bruno Neppi Modona, of Turin, Dr. Levi hosted the wedding in his home.

In the synagogue, Dr. Levi drew our attention to a fading Jewish National Fund certificate hanging on the *matroneo* wall, with its message, "A forest grove in the area of Yatir in Israel is dedicated to the memory of the

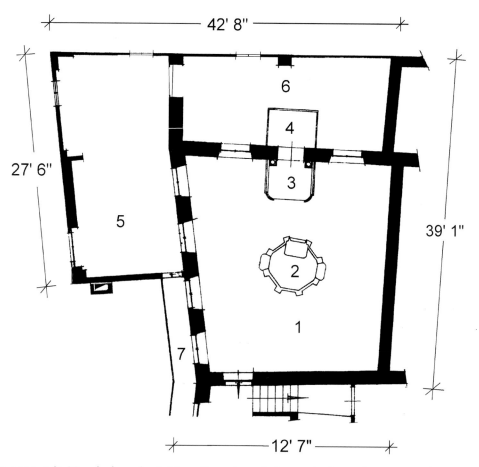

Plan of the synagogue in Mondovì, early eighteenth century. Entrance is through a narrow door at the head of the stairs, with a narrow porch on the left leading to the *matroneo*. 1. prayer room, 2. *tevah*, 3. Ark platform, 4. walk-in Ark, 5. *matroneo*, 6. *ḥeder*, 7. passageway. (Courtesy of Marco Levi.)

kehillah in Mondovì, Piedmont, *'Ir v'em b'Yis-rael'* ('a mother-city in Israel'; II Sam 20:19) August 5, 1986. When the young people arrived from Turin to clean up the synagogue, he greeted them and asked, "It is good that you are refurbishing the synagogue, but how do we make it into a cultural and religious center for a community that no longer exists?"

"CITY OF JOY"

The Renaissance was a remarkable period for the Jews of Italy. It was an era of Diaspora history to rival that of the Golden Age in Spain for its singular synthesis of Judaism and the local culture. True Renaissance personages successfully blended multiple interests: the physician was often a rabbi-scientist, the playwright a historian, the loan banker an astronomer-mathematician, and the Torah scribe a dancer-impresario. Jewish scholarship and ingenuity played a significant role in the revival of the arts and classical learning.

Of all Italian cities, *gloriosa* Mantua in the heart of Lombardy led her sister cities in creating a milieu of luxurious living touched by hedonism and embellished by artistic achievement on every side. This occurred under the noble house of Gonzaga, which governed Mantua from the turbulent fourteenth to the eighteenth centuries, with rank of marquis from 1433, and later as dukes. Avid patrons of the creative arts, the Gonzagas and the Jewish bankers whom they sponsored provided the necessary support for a Golden Age in a Mantua that Jews knew as *Kiryah Alizah,* "Joyous City." The glory lasted until Church intolerance, foreign conquest, and plague decimated and despoiled the Jewish community and the city itself. Nothing that happened after the seventeenth-century assault on Jewish Mantua's muse could rekindle its genius.

When the ghetto walls rose up in 1620 around the Jews of Mantua, the last of the large Italian communities to be enclosed in a ghetto, cultural contact between Jews and Christians was curtailed. The Jews now concerned themselves with the sciences and the arts, and confined themselves nearly entirely within the limits of halakhah and mysticism. But echoes of the Renaissance resounded in the late seventeenth and eighteenth centuries, when rumblings of the emancipation spirit of the French Revolution reverberating through Italy roused the Jews to participate again in the cultural and political effervescence of their times.

The beginnings of Jewish life in the city were much more modest. By legend, Mantuan soldiers of Titus' army brought Jews home as menials after the 70 C.E. fall of Jerusalem. The small low-status *kehillah* there in the Middle Ages was one of the few in northern Italy. Abraham ibn Ezra (1089–1164), wandering poet and scholar, resided briefly as a guest or tutor in a wealthy Mantua household, and

Daniel Norsa, his Family and the Madonna della Vittoria. St. Jerome carries a Model of the Church

The Norsa banking family in disgrace. Although he had paid for permission to remove a Madonna painting from his newly purchased house, public outcry and the duke's edict forced Daniel Norsa to replace the house with a church. In a fifteenth-century altar painting by an artist of the Mantegna school, now in a side chapel in Mantua's Basilica of St. Andrea, St. Gerome holds a model of the small church, the Madonna sits enthroned, and the Jews are at her feet. (Illustration after S. Simonsohn, *History of the Jews in the Duchy of Mantua*.)

there he wrote a Hebrew grammar, *Sefer haZakut* (The Book of Purity).

In the thirteenth and fourteenth centuries, economic pressures—including a sequence of war, plague, and famine that generated a public need for loans—motivated Jewish moneylenders from Italy's southern regions to migrate northward to Lombardy. By the early fifteenth century, eleven Jewish families operated seven loan-banks in Mantua. Expulsions from Spain, Sicily, and southern Italy, and religious persecutions in France and Germany drove Jews to northern Italy, shifting the demographic center of gravity of Italian Jewry from south to north. Mantua drew many of the emigres. The earliest

mention of a cemetery and synagogue in the city, and hence an established *kehillah,* is 1420.

Inaugurating an age of intellectual and artistic achievement, the Gonzaga rulers enthusiastically patronized artists and scholars, many of them Jews. Jewish bankers shared the supportive role and accumulated manuscript libraries. The city began palpably to flourish in 1480, after Marquis Giovanni Francesco II married Isabella d'Este, daughter of the Duke of Ferrara. She was a superbly cultured woman and one of the foremost Renaissance persons of her day. She set the stage for an era of feminine emancipation that liberated Jewish women no less than their Christian peers. Jewish women became physicians, involved themselves in education, especially in humanist subjects, and some took up the pen as scribes. Unfortunately, few names of these Jewish women appear in Mantua sources.

A singular exception is Estellina Conat, the wife of Abraham Conat: physician, talmudist, and the first Hebrew printer in Mantua, active mostly from 1475 to 1477. The beautiful typeface he used is a paradigm for fonts in modern luxury editions. Estellina helped her husband print the book, *Beḥinat Olam* (Examining the World), by Jedaiah Hapnini, and set the type for printing the astronomical tables called *Netiv Ḥokhmah* (Path of Wisdom), by Mordecai Angelo Finzi. Finzi (d. 1476) was a loan banker, physician, and scientist. He was known for original mathematical and astronomical works, such as lunar calendars and day-length tables, and for translations of such scientific material into Hebrew.

Mantua became the center of a new humanistic spirit in Jewish scholarship. Physician, scholar, and rabbi Judah Messer Leon published a textbook of logic, *Nofet Tzufim* (Sweetness of Honey), in Mantua before 1480. The first book by a living writer that was printed in the Hebrew language, it examined the Bible from a purely literary viewpoint and extolled the oratory of the Hebrew prophets above that of the Greek and Roman philosophers. Leon's other works were treatises on grammar, medicine, and science, as well as commentaries on Aristotle.

The greatest Jewish historian of the Italian Renaissance was Azariah ben Moses de' Rossi (1510–1578), an outspoken humanist scholar and relative of the composer, Salomone de' Rossi. In *Me'or Einayim* (Enlightenment for the Eyes), Azariah de' Rossi described the disastrous 10-day Ferrara earthquake of 1571 and its effect on the population. He noted that whereas Jews tended to see Divine intervention in the event, other scholars often searched for natural causes. Delving into Jewish antiquity, de' Rossi was an expert in Jewish sources. He also cited more than a hundred non-Jewish authors to trace the development of the Bible, Jewish history, chronology, poetry, and culture. Invoking a remarkable spirit of free inquiry, he regarded talmudic legends as legends per se, not to be taken literally.

Me'or Einayim aroused opposition even among enlightened Jewish scholars in Italy. Many rabbis forbade reading it or possessing a copy without special license—proving, incidentally, that the Church had no monopoly on banning books. When Rabbi Joseph Caro avowed that the book was dangerous and should be burned, Mantuan rabbis offered a compromise, permitting the book only to persons over 25. Used and quoted over the years by Christian scholars, *Me'or Einayim* was not republished by Jews until the founders of the Reform movement in nineteenth-century Germany recognized it as a source of fundamental ideas for their interpretation of Judaism. Leopold Zunz, leader of the movement, *Wissenschaft des Judentums* (Science of Judaism), edited the new edition.

Jewish physicians in Italy were esteemed for their medical ability. A galaxy of Jewish doctors attended nobles, princes, and popes. Laymen assumed that the Jews' knowledge of literature gave them access to Arabic medical treatises and secret doctrines unknown to Christians. The most famous family of physicians in Italy was the Portaleone dynasty that loyally treated Italian nobility in Mantua and Padua for 300 years. Abraham ben David Portaleone (1542–1612), one of the most illustrious members of the clan, attended Duke Guglielmo Gonzaga and his successor, Vincenzo I. A writer of great reputation, he composed two important medical works in Latin and a compendium on the construction of the Temple, *Shiltei Hagibborim* (Shields of the Mighty; Mantua, 1612), in Hebrew. It was a massive discourse dedicated to his sons, compiled while he was partially paralyzed, shortly before his death. The book opens with details of the Jerusalem Temple, its instruments, and service, and includes a discussion of Temple music and general instrumental music. It goes on to discuss all the branches of science known in his day and uses the 10 languages in which Portaleone was fluent.

Dramatizations of Purim's Scroll of Esther provided the earliest Jewish theater experience; they were so popular that Christian neighbors

Detail of the *Heikhal*. Typical Baroque vegetative motif decorates the doors, and a grape vine entwines the pillars.

keenly followed the performances, in violation of Church interdiction. As Jewish amateur theatrical groups expanded their repertoire, they were invited to perform secular productions at the Gonzaga court and other palaces. Judah Leone de' Sommi (1525–1590; also known as Sommo), a scion of the Mantuan Portaleone family, unexpectedly chose the field of theater arts. He had been a calligrapher, Torah scribe, and private tutor in his youth, but he became a prolific playwright and the first theatrical producer in history. Vincenzo's ascension to the Dukedom of Mantua in the summer of 1587 brought the full spirit of Renaissance splendor to the city. Vincenzo encouraged every form of art, with special emphasis on plays and pageantry, and engaged the talented Leone de' Sommi to write plays and arrange their production.

The pageants of the house of Gonzaga vied with the carnivals of Venice. Mantua emerged as

Bimah apse with damask-covered *tevah* and a pair of tall bronze candlesticks.

a leader in the new theater arts of Italy, while the *kehillah* provided dramatists, impresarios, performers, musicians, and often the dancers for many of the spectacles. Normally, the *kehillah* carried the expenses for the performances and the responsibility for mobilizing its members to participate. The cast abided by religious scruples, informing the duke, if need be, "We must begin the comedy early enough today to finish before the Sabbath commences."

In 16 manuscript volumes, de' Sommi wrote pastoral comedies in Italian and some in Hebrew, all with instructions for lavish scenic backdrops. His comprehensive *Dialogues on the Representative Art* presented a detailed guide to the multiple aspects of stagecraft, a theater history first. De' Sommi's pastoral drama for a Purim performance, *Zakut B'diḥutah d'Kiddushin* (The Comedy of Wedlock), rediscovered and published in the 1940s, is the first original drama written in Hebrew. The presence a century later of two copies in a Mantuan Jewish library suggests that it was a viable repertoire element over an extended period.

Longer performances included an intermezzo with music and dance, which sometimes almost outdid the play. Mantua, where music and dance were integral to Jewish education, resonated with Jewish musical activity. Outstanding instrumentalists were Abramo dell' Arpa and Isacchino Massarano. A talented composer, choreographer, singer, and harp player, Massarano was independently wealthy. Mixing freely with Mantuan nobility, he often entertained Duke Guglielmo and company in his spacious home. Preparing the wedding celebration in 1583 of his son and heir, Vincenzo—who was Massarano's close friend—Guglielmo commissioned Massarano to choreograph dances for a gala performance by the Jewish theater.

The greatest Jewish musician of the period was Salomone de' Rossi. Partly influenced by Palestrina and an occasional collaborator of Monteverdi, he published compositions from 1589 to 1623, introducing the musical spirit of the Renaissance. De' Rossi aimed to improve aesthetic standards in synagogue cantillation.

His works were composed of passages from the liturgy, including psalms, hymns, and prayers for Sabbath and holidays. These pieces of remarkable virtuosity lack traditional elements of either Arabic or eastern European influences and are pure Italian Renaissance. Although his music was sung and performed in Mantua and in neighboring communities, the forces of musical conservatism were too strong. His music was not republished after 1623 and was seldom heard again before the twentieth century. His cantata *Hashirim Asher l'Shlomo* (The Songs of Solomon), a collection of 33 songs he wrote for the synagogue, was recently republished in a modern edition in New York. Members of de' Rossi's family were musical in their own right. His sister, nicknamed "Madame Europa" after one of her successful theatrical roles, often included her musician sons in performances at the ducal court.

Both genius and charlatan, Abraham Colorni (1544–1599) was the only notable engineer among Mantuan Jewry. His talents in applied mathematics, engineering, and weapons invention endeared him to the dukes of Mantua, Ferrara, and Savoy. Many of his ingenious military devices—designed, but never executed—were remarkably ahead of his time: bridges that could be thrown over rivers within minutes, folding ladders for assaulting bastions, and musical instruments that could quickly be converted into weapons.

Mantuan Jews flourished in the particular social ambiance of Renaissance Mantua. Those who could afford it fell in line with the surrounding hedonism. Copying habits of extravagant dress, they often engaged in gambling and card playing, activities discouraged in Jewish tradition. The fraternization existed against a broader background of popular and Church intolerance, and amid the intensifying spread and militancy of the Counter-Reformation. Mantua duly observed the 1553 papal anti-Talmud campaign, for example, with the local difference that Cardinal Ercole, of the house of Gonzaga, forewarned the Jews a few days before taking action to confiscate or burn books. Other repressive anti-Jewish measures—ghettos, property-ownership bans, yellow hats, and maximal occupational restrictions—that were strictly enforced in Rome and most Italian cities, restrained Mantua's 3,000

Interior of the synagogue dome. Its eight segments decorated with a low frieze of palmettes, the dome also contains low windows on east and west sides above the *Heikhal* and *Bimah*.

Jews of the seventeenth century with a relatively benign laxity. They had their share in the prescribed occupations, as peddlers and ragpickers, but many of the non-elite were artisans, shopkeepers, and moneylenders. Ultimately, external forces nudged Mantua closer to the national norm of intolerance: the clothing badge became obligatory and a ghetto was set aside for the 480 families in 1612.

When German mercenaries hired by Austrian Emperor Ferdinand II set siege to Mantua in 1629, Jews helped to build defensive fortifications. Work continued even on the Sabbath, with rabbinical dispensation in view of the national danger. A devastating plague spread through both camps, but, despite heavy losses, the invaders were able to exploit the Mantuans' weakness and to capture the city. Mantua fell on the perennial disaster day, the 9th of Av, in 5390 (1630), initiating the lamented "Sack of Mantua." The jubilant soldiers started their looting in the ghetto, first emptying Jewish banks of 4.8 million lire, then killing their way into houses. Limited by their commander to three hours in the ghetto, they hurried to the town and to the ducal palaces for plunder, stripping them of the art treasures amassed by the Gonzagas, and all else of value.

A few days later, the Austrian commander expelled the Jews on three days' notice, limiting removable possessions to three ducats per person on pain of death. On the 22nd of Av the Jews huddled in the nine synagogues of the ghetto for a final prayer before their mournful departure the next morning. During the following four months, wagon convoys rolled out of Mantua, carrying booty from ghetto, palaces, and town. Later that year, with the emperor's permission, only about a thousand of the 1600 survivors chose to return to their looted homes in Mantua. The saga of the long siege, the plague, and the ferocious battles, the exile, and the return is eloquently described in *Hagalut V'hapedut* (The Exile and the Redemption; Venice, 1634) by eye-witness Abraham Massarano, son of choreographer Isacchino Massarano.

The reorganized *kehillah* was a shadow of its former self. Its later annals are no more than an anemic semblance of broad historical events.

Following numerous wars of succession, the duchy of Mantua passed to Austrian rule soon after the turn of the eighteenth century and enlightenment crept in, lagging slowly after intolerance. On a background of still virulent popular anti-Semitism, regal action abolished the yellow badge and the limitations on property ownership. By the century's end, Jews nominally had complete equality. When Napoleon's troops, in 1797, knocked down the walls of the ghetto, its principal square—derogatorily called Piazzetta dell' Aglio, "Garlic Square" —was patriotically renamed Piazza della Concordia, "Peace Square."

The city's Jews were active in the Risorgimento movement for the unification of Italy, claiming two heroes: Giuseppe Finzi and the writer Tullo Massarani. Ever shrinking, the *kehillah* numbered 669 in 1931. When the Nazis occupied Mantua, they seized 40 Jews and dispatched them to the death camps.

In the 1980s the 160 Jews who still lived in Mantua maintained a solitary extant synagogue, the last of the six they had used in the nineteenth century, when they numbered more than 2,000. The building has been declared a national architectural monument.

West facade of the rebuilt Norsa synagogue in Mantua. Baroque style, 1751. This was the first public synagogue in Mantua, originally built in 1513 in the home of the banker Moses ben Nathaniel Norsa. The complex at number 11 via Govi, now housing a synagogue and community office, contains a large wing where Jews were incarcerated before deportation during World War II. The low apsidal protrusion on the unadorned facade contains the *bimah*.

THE NORSA TORRAZZO SYNAGOGUE IN MANTUA

The Italian-rite Norsa Torrazzo synagogue occupies the former Jewish rest home in the building complex of 1825, at No. 11 via Govi. The furnishings scrupulously installed there in 1899–1902 were from the 1751 restoration of the original sixteenth-century synagogue. The latter was demolished early in the twentieth century. Mahogany doors under an arch in the inner courtyard open to a vestibule, with a stairway to the *matroneo* in the north end of the synagogue. Centered on the long east and west walls in a bipolar arrangement, apses contain *Heikhal* and *bimah* respectively, both adorned with richly embroidered vestments. Although of modest dimensions, the *bimah* apse is elaborately decorated in a style that matches the *Heikhal* apse on the opposite wall and provides a pleasing architectural balance. Rabbi and *ḥazzan* sat on carved and gilded wooden benches under four bay windows that are framed by helical pillars identical to those decorating the *Heikhal*.

Elaborate stucco inscriptions decorate the walls, quoting biblical passages or extolling the virtues of the respected Mantuan Norsa family of bankers, printers, and scholars. Old wooden benches and prayer desks, dating from an eighteenth-century renovation, run parallel to the short walls to face the central space. Bronze lamps and an old, now-electrified chandelier hang from the ceiling. High, arched, and latticed openings conceal the *matroneo* above the entrance on the north wall.

Community Secretary Jare Dante, at the *Heikhal*. Three curved marble steps lead up to the gilded wooden Baroque *Heikhal,* resplendent with deeply carved doors and six helical pillars.

The synagogue contained a precious archive. Early in the twentieth century, Rabbi Bonaiuto Isac Levi compiled *kehillah* documents of the years 1522 to 1810, into a 10-volume historical encyclopedia. Today, the community houses only a portion of this rich library. Most of the Hebrew volumes printed in the sixteenth, seventeenth, and eighteenth centuries are stored in the municipal library in via Ardigo, along with 162 Hebrew manuscripts. Other manuscript fragments are stored at the Diocesan Historical Archives.

One of the real treasures of the *kehillah* is far away in the Vatican Library (Codex Rossi 555). Commissioned by a Mantuan Jewish banker in

Synagogue interior to the north. *Heikhal* and *bimah* nestle in small apses in the centers of the long east and west walls.

1436, this sumptuously illuminated manuscript of Jacob Ben Asher's ritual code, *Arba'ah Turim (Four Sections),* contains a remarkable rendition of a fifteenth-century synagogue interior in Mantua. Perhaps the most vivid depiction of the spirit of life in fifteenth-century Jewish circles of Lombardy and Veneto is a drawing of dancers in a page from the Rothschild Miscellany, ms 24, now in the Israel Museum, Jerusalem. Thus Jews danced in Venice, in Ferrara, in Padua, and in Mantua when it was *Kiryah Alizah,* the "City of Joy."

Three couples in festive garb dance to the tune of a lute, a miniature, on a page in the Rothschild Miscellany. This is one of the most delicately executed Hebrew illuminated manuscripts from the north Italian school, and it displays the influence of artists from Ferrara and Venice. (ca. 1470, Ms. 24, folio 246v; courtesy of the Israel Museum, Jerusalem.)

GATEWAY TO ZION

Close to a shifting border like its inland neighbor Gorizia, the bustling port city of Trieste was culturally Italian but politically Austrian for much of its history. During the long centuries of Hapsburg rule it became the hub of cosmopolitan culture in Italy. Since it was central Europe's major harbor on the Adriatic Sea, the sovereign sought to develop its potential maximally. Jews were perceived as useful for that purpose and were accorded some relief from the customary repression. Trieste Jews who came to Vienna could stay in good hotels rather than in the two run-down and unsanitary inns that were obligatory for Jews from other places. Ghettoization was relatively late, lax, and early abolished. At the turn of the twentieth century, the port was one of the major European embarkation points of mass emigration to the Americas. Three decades later Trieste was the port of emergency exit for perceptive Jews who anticipated the worst and whose important destination was *Eretz Yisrael.*

Stretching across the rolling hills above its half-moon bay, Trieste is only 72 miles northeast of Venice, its glamorous ancient and powerful competitor. Jews settled sporadically in the Adriatic's northern ports, including Trieste, from the eleventh century. Under Austrian dukes, an influx of Ashkenazic Jews in the fourteenth century helped to consolidate a growing Jewish mercantile nucleus. A small community without recognition, it held services in a private house for lack of a synagogue, but it set up a cemetery in via del Monte in 1446.

The Counter-Reformation, begun with the expansion of papal rule in 1555, spread northward quite slowly. Rejoicing in the Christian defeat of the Turks, Vienna decreed a ghetto for Trieste Jews on December 2, 1693. The official order arrived four months later, a delay that afforded the strong-willed and spirited group of 60, in a city of 3,000, an opening for protest and unprecedented delaying actions, lasting until 1696. The clerical commission chose Corte di Trauner (Trauner's court), for a ghetto location in a decision much opposed by the Jews. The Trieste council ignored their protest and ordered them to appear in that court to select their houses. As carefully recorded in its archive, the Trieste Jewish community

Canal Grande in Trieste, lined with small fishing boats and pleasure craft. City streets sprawl from the crowded harbor area up over the hills.

Jerusalem scholar, lawyer, and historian, Dr. Paolo Colbi researched the story of his maternal ancestors, the illustrious Levi family of Trieste. (Photo: Mark Feffer, Jerusalem.)

argued that most of the family heads were absent: "Samuele Levi is in Senigallia for his son's wedding, Aron Morpurgo is in Pirano, David Parente in Gorizia, Salomon Parente in Venice, and poor Giustina Gentilli is ill." Unheeding, the council ruled that "town experts would forthwith assign houses to the various families, *in absentia.*"

The Jews refused invitations to repair the assigned houses, claiming, "Family heads are still missing, the weather is bad, and properly speaking, it is the owners who should make the repairs, not the tenants." This argument angered the council members. They dispatched the vice chief of police to deliver the house keys. None of the family members present would accept the keys, so he simply left them on a bench. By now the Jews realized that further protest would be futile, if not also dangerous. They gave up the struggle and reluctantly moved their belongings to the assigned ghetto.

The Jews had a friend in the amiable ghetto gatekeeper, Cristoforo della Spada, who was as lax as his inmates were disobedient. Sometimes he had to wait up for the young people until two or three in the morning. Despite his loyalty to them, the Jews were careless and even ungracious, owing him the sum of 41 lira, 5 soldi within a year. The Jews later moved to the more spacious Riborgo quarter and accepted the 13 houses allotted there. Three of the four pre-Emancipation synagogues of Trieste stood in the ghetto square.

The prominent Levi family of Trieste was descended from venerable Ashkenazic forebears.

A scion of that Levi family, Dr. Paolo Colbi—now an octogenarian Jerusalem resident—left Trieste for Palestine in 1939. Lawyer, historian, and scholar (he was Israel's Ministry of Religious Affairs' Advisor on Christianity for many years), Colbi traced the Levi family forward from *kehillah* head, Rabbi Leone Levi, in the second half of the seventeenth century. In a 1949 essay in *Rassegna Mensile di Israel,* he portrayed episodes in the family's social, cultural, and vocational history. *Ketubbot* testify to wealth by the generous dowries and to status by naming bridegrooms from distinguished families in distant towns. Funerary inscriptions give evidence of erudition by the excellence of their Hebrew.

In 1684 Giacomo, son of Samuele Levi, earned a doctorate in philosophy and medicine from the University of Padua. The parchment Imperial Diploma is profusely illuminated with floral and symbolic motifs. On the 14th of Adar, 5459, in the spring of 1699 Giacomo married his cousin Esmeralda, daughter of Rabbi Leone Levi. Their ornate *ketubbah* and his diploma are both preserved in the Umberto Naḥon Museum of Italian Art in Jerusalem. Leone Levi and Caliman Parente won *privilegio* (contract) renewal in 1696 from Emperor Leopold I (King of Bohemia, 1656 to 1705) for their loyalty to the crown and for providing "a great amount of wheat without requesting any price, when plague and famine struck Gorizia." A tragedy followed in 1733, when two members of the family died of the plague. The double tombstone bears an inscription in flowery Hebrew, mourning the death of young Leone, the son of Dr. Giacomo and Esmeralda, and Ezechia, son of the elder Rabbi Leone.

Diploma of Dr. Giacomo Levi, granted in 1684 by the University of Padua. The illuminated parchment, in Latin, bears a profusion of symbols: a miniature medallion portraying the doctor within a laurel wreath, floral motifs, peacocks (and bees gathering nectar—an allusion to imbibing wisdom). Another sheaf features clusters of fruit and the Levi family shield. (Photo: Dorfman, by courtesy of I. Timnat, Haifa and the Umberto Naḥon Museum of Italian Jewish Art, Jerusalem.)

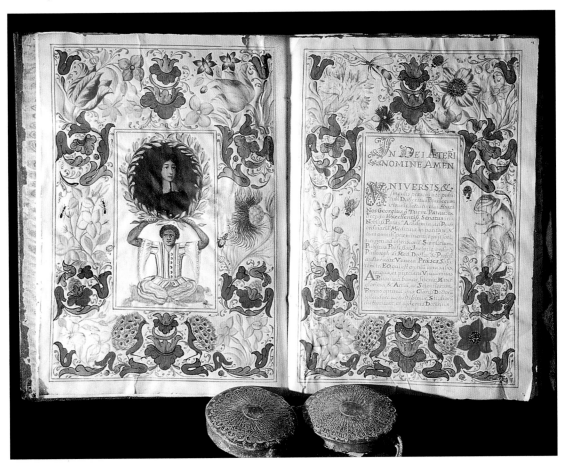

Esmeralda's younger son, Giacomo Raffaele Vita, married Allegra Luzzatto of Gorizia as late as 1754, and he lived until 1802. His only son, Leone Zaccaria, married Tranquilla Sinigaglia of Gorizia in 1799. Colbi notes that whereas Zaccaria celebrated his nuptials with a "mediocre sonnet in pompous Italian," Raffaele's earlier song had been written in good biblical Hebrew. The dynasty continued with Giacomo Samuele Levi who had three sons—all learned men of liberal ideas. Only the youngest, Giuseppe, had a son, Giacomo, who, like his forebear, studied medicine. This Dr. Giacomo Levi died of influenza at the age of 32 in the epidemic of 1918 and thus ended the male line of the Levi family. There remain 45 great-grandchildren, 41 of whom live in Israel, the others in Turin and Rome.

In 1717, Emperor Charles VI (r. 1711–1740) declared Trieste "a free port." In the mid-eighteenth century, Empress Maria Theresa (1740–1780) expanded the policy of developing the Adriatic city and kept it open to all. She drained the seaside salt marshes that choked the city and built a new 'Theresian Quarter.' The town of 7,000 inhabitants was becoming a center for Mediterranean trade.

The *kehillah* organized itself officially in 1746. The Sephardic rite, introduced by immigrants over the previous century, struck root and continued side by side with the Ashkenazic. Trieste found it economically advantageous to ease some of the oppressive restrictions on its Jews and the 1782 Toleranzpatent (edict of tolerance) by Joseph II canceled others. Wealthier Jews spilled out of the ghetto before it was abolished by decree in 1784, but some felt secure in the ghetto and reluctant to live in proximity to Christians. This was so despite the offensive brothels that nudged the ghetto and increased in number with the city's growth as an international port. Situating brothels around the ghetto was a conscious urban choice by a populace that held prostitutes and Jews at the same level of contempt and branded them both with the same yellow scarf. After the ghetto walls came down in 1785, the Jewish population spread throughout the city and grew rapidly from 670 in 1788, to 2,000 in 1811.

One of Trieste's most illustrious Jewish sons, Professor Samuel David Luzzatto (1800–1865; known by his acronym, *ShaDaL*), was a philosopher, poet, Bible scholar, and translator. He was appointed in 1829 to direct the newly established seminary, Collegio Rabbinico in Padua, and spent the rest of his prolific, scholarly life there. His doctrines bridged traditional enlightened Jewish scholarship and the Jewish intellectual revival emanating from northern Europe. He corresponded widely with scholars, edited medieval Jewish poetry, collected ancient manuscripts, translated the Bible into Italian, and created a new basis for the science of Hebrew philology and grammar. In *Avnei Zikaron* (Remembrance Stones, 1841), about Hebrew tombstone inscriptions in Toledo, he was the first to treat gravestone epitaphs as a primary source for Jewish historical research. Luzzatto's literary circle included other poets, among them his cousin, Rachel Morpurgo of Trieste (1790–1871). Luzzatto taught her Hebrew and guided her in Bible and Talmud. Her poetry, sonnets, elegies, and wedding poems, in the style of the Spanish Hebrew religious poets and the Italian Renaissance, related mostly to family and biographical incidents.

The hope of religious freedom and political emancipation brought the Jews in Austrian-controlled parts of Italy to support the revolution of 1848. Although most Trieste Jews were not of Italian origin, they identified culturally and politically with their Italian compatriots and they rallied to the Risorgimento (Unification of Italy) until its final success. Backed by the *kehillah,* Jewish intellectuals were in the forefront, struggling for the union of Trieste with Italy.

More than 1,000 Italian Jews received decorations for valor at the end of World War I. The peace settlement brought Trieste into the kingdom of Italy in 1919, but the port declined.

Immigration from central Europe and the Balkans swelled Jewish numbers to 6,000, and Trieste became the third largest Italian Jewish center after Rome and Milan. With mercantile involvement in many Italian cities, and not overly Zionist in outlook, Trieste Jews felt themselves to be Italian rather than Austrian or

Torah scrolls dressed in damask and velvet mantles. Crowned with silver Torah crowns and finials, and bedecked with silver Torah shields, the scrolls are taken out on the major holidays. Community dignitaries carry them around the synagogue on the red plush carpet. Weekly Sabbath services are conducted in the smaller *beit midrash*.

Jewish and acted accordingly in political matters. They held a pivotal position in the city's economy: in trade, banking, and insurance. The Assicurazioni Generale Company, founded by the Morpurgo family, still has branches in many countries. The Morpurgo name associates the family to Marburg, Slovenia, a haven for expellees from Graz at the end of the fifteenth century. The impact of the Emancipation on community life was profound, violating barriers that had remained firm across centuries of oppression. Assimilation spread unchecked, especially through the middle and upper classes. Intermarriage in Trieste in the early twentieth century grew to alarming proportions: more than one of three.

In 1910 the affluent Trieste *kehillah* approved an unlimited budget for the construction of a grand synagogue to replace four smaller

buildings. Three were ghetto synagogues dating from the eighteenth century. The most sumptuous of them was the fourth one, Scuola Grande, built in 1805 outside the ghetto. All of them followed the Venetian synagogue model: bifocal rectangular rooms, with Ark and *bimah* on the opposite short walls.

The new grand synagogue is one of the most prominent buildings in the city, even by comparison with the imposing houses of worship permitted by the Austrian monarchy to the Serbian Orthodox, Greek Orthodox, and Lutheran minorities. A relic now of a bygone era, it is more of a massive tribute to the prosperity of the community that built it than to the piety and devotion of its congregants. A local humorist described it soon after the well-attended dedication in 1912 as "a mixture of an Assyrian temple and an Egyptian tomb."

Emigration across the Atlantic increased substantially in the nineteenth century. Between 1820 and 1918, about 41 million persons—four million of them Jews—landed on North American shores, having left Europe chiefly from Hamburg, Bremen, and Trieste. As the Americas reduced permissible immigration afterward, Trieste continued as an embarkation point from central and eastern Europe to Palestine. After 1933, families fleeing Nazi Germany flooded Trieste, the main European exit to *Eretz Yisrael*, and blessed the city with the name, *Sha'ar Tzion*, "Gateway to Zion."

The *kehillah* reacted quickly to the school and job discrimination enacted in 1938. It opened a private secondary school, Scuola media ebreica, in the Talmud Tora building in via del Monte 3. The excellent high school and university personnel ousted from previous positions by the racial laws served as teaching staff, and the

THE GRANDE SYNAGOGA TRIESTE

Designed by architect brothers, Ruggero and Arduino Berlam, the synagogue stretches from via Donizetti, along via S. Francesco to via Zanetti. It is a monumental structure, reminiscent indeed of ancient Near Eastern architecture—with columns, mullioned windows, and designs engraved into the facade of limestone from the nearby Istrian peninsula.

High above the main portal and under a huge rectangular tower, an inscription reads: *"Pithu li sha'arei tzedek, avo bam odeh Yah"* ("Open for me the gates of righteousness, that I may enter them and praise the Lord"; Ps. 118:19). The upper band of the cartouche contains two fruited palm trees flanking splayed sheaves of grain, all symbols of the Trieste *kehillah*.

The cavernous main hall is articulated into a nave and two aisles, ending in a large apse that contains the towering *Heikhal*. In the spirit of the Emancipation, the architects elevated and enlarged the *bimah*, merging it visually with the massive Ark. This was the ultimate step in the creation of a unified focal center for the ritual as influenced by contemporary church architecture. Dark green marble covers the walls of the apse under a gilded cupola. A spacious *matroneo* gallery on three sides is witness to the large number of women at the congregation who used to throng these aisles.

The great synagogue in Trieste. Eclectic style with Romanesque and classical elements, Ruggero Berlam and Arduino Berlam, architects, 1912. Situated in a bustling section of the city, it has a protruding apse and a long wide-arched arcade. Oversize rose windows add architectural variety.

Synagogue side portal on via Zanetti. Inscription in the heavy rectangular cartouche reads: "*Ze hasha'ar l'Adonai, tzadikim yavo'u bo,*" ("This is the gateway to the Lord; the righteous shall enter through it"; Ps. 118:20). A series of stepped round-headed arches, separated by slender Moorish columns, forms a dramatic, rhythmic architectural pattern, relieving the massiveness of the limestone walls.

Synagogue interior. The expansive hall is dominated by the striking apse and its multilevel Ark. Since the *matroneo* is no longer in use, the women sit at the rear behind a perforated wooden *meḥitzah.*

school gave the children a supportive social and educational framework despite the wartime limitations. The school operated from October 1938 until October 1943, when the Germans took direct control of the city. On August 18, 1942, Italian Fascists broke into the large synagogue and desecrated it. The smaller synagogues were later destroyed completely.

The Nazi threat prompted half of the city's Jews to flee by 1940. In the winter of 1944, 837 Trieste Jews were arrested and brought to the Risiera de San Sabba. The Risiera became a prison, a deportation and genocide center for Jews, Slovene partisans, Italian and Croat anti-Fascists—the only such compound with a crematorium in Italy. The Nazis blew up the crematorium when they retreated, but the site has since become a memorial museum.

When the Allies liberated Rome on June 5, 1944, the Jewish Brigade from Palestine saw much action under the British flag. As they followed northward on the heels of the German retreat, these Jewish soldiers were among the first of the Allied forces to liberate Jewish communities and to reopen synagogues and other Jewish institutions in Italy. Trieste Jews among the partisans took an active part in Italy's liberation. In all, about 1,500 Trieste Jews remained in the city after the liberation. The survivors reorganized community life and restored the grand synagogue. From one of the older, smaller ones that were destroyed, Umberto Naḥon rescued a *Heikhal* and shipped it to Israel. It is now in use at the Smuts Street synagogue in Tel Aviv.

Dr. Colbi recalls the feverish atmosphere in the Jewish community during the uncertain days of summer and fall, 1939. Many searched for a way to escape as long as exit permits were available—for those with means. Others of the many assimilated Trieste Jews chose to pursue safety by conversion. Israel Zoller, rabbi in Trieste and later in Rome, took shelter in the Vatican. He unabashedly abandoned his community and fled to the welcoming arms of the Church.

The Adriatica Steamship Company operated two ships on the Trieste–Haifa route, the *Galilea* and the *Gerusalemme,* whose Jewish captain, Umberto Steindler, boasted over a hundred trips to Palestine between the world wars. Veteran Trieste residents remember how the ships' decks resounded with the voices of ḥaluzim singing nostalgic songs in farewell to Old Europe, while the port workers answered with the strains of "Hatikvah," in Triestine dialect. The *Gerusalemme* left Trieste on September 1, 1939, on its last sailing but was turned back to its home port from Rhodes because of the outbreak of war. The captain weighed anchor again on September 4 and arrived safely in Haifa harbor on September 9. Among the 600 *olim* on board was Paolo Colbi.

Rabbi Elia Richetti, rabbi of Trieste from 1980 to 1993, at the *bimah.* A giant cast menorah and a pair of oversized bronze candelabra on marble pedestals tower above the *bimah.* "When services close with *Neilah,* on Yom Kippur," Rabbi Richetti explained, "we have about 500 people. This includes Jews from other nearby towns . . ." he paused, "and the non-Jewish spouses and family members. In the *kehillah* there is one old man who is the last Jew in his family. He comes alone to pray every Shabbat, but on Yom Kippur his whole non-Jewish family comes to join him."

CROATIA AND SERBIA

The Balkan peninsula, especially the former Yugoslavia, is a crossroads between East and West in southern Europe, where diverse and intense identities—ethnic, national, and religious—vie for control. Yugoslavia was home to several South Slavic peoples: Slovenes, Croats, Serbs, Bosnians, Montenegrans, and Macedonians; and among them, various national minorities: Albanians, Hungarians, Turks, Roma, Jews, and others. By religious affiliation, they included Roman Catholics, Greek Orthodox, Protestants, Moslems, and Jews. Within this complex human presence the Jews played a minor, yet significant role. Not numerous in any single community, they contributed their varied skills to the development of trade, commerce, and culture. Periods of prosperity and persecution in Jewish community histories reflect the fortunes of the host countries. An important factor, especially in the twentieth century, is the close contact between the Balkan Sephardic *kehillot* and their east European Ashkenazic counterparts.

Croatia

Borders of the independent states within Yugoslavia, determined initially by geographic factors, were often modified by concessions made to the victors after bloody battles. Croatia's present borders encompass a large portion of the Danubian Plain in the north, a section of inland mountains to the west, and then a narrowing sector southward that includes the major part of the Dalmatian coastline. Although Jews arrived in these regions during the Roman era as merchants and traders, the major waves of immigration came after their fifteenth-century expulsion from Spain and Portugal. Ottoman Sultan Bayazid II welcomed the Sephardim, whose skills, craftsmanship, and trade connections enhanced his multi-ethnic empire, and he encouraged many of them to settle in the Balkans. Communities developed in Split and Dubrovnik, where the Jews enjoyed autonomy in internal community matters.

The Sephardic newcomers kept themselves largely aloof from the native Romaniot Jews and the Ashkenazic settlers from central and eastern Europe, but together they developed a flourishing Jewish cultural and economic life until the decline of the Ottoman Empire in the nineteenth century. Ashkenazim who had settled in the northern and western sections of the Balkans in earlier centuries, and had suffered periods of banishment, returned in greater numbers in the eighteenth century. They soon established thriving settlements in the northern regions under Hungarian rule, in Zagreb and Osijek, Croatia; and in Novi Sad and Subotica, Serbia.

By the mid-nineteenth century, the problem of religious reform became acute and divided many Ashkenazic communities between the Neolog reform majority and the Orthodox minority. A more marked division was found between the Ashkenazic communities in the northern industrialized cities—comprising about two-thirds of the Jewish population—and the Sephardic communities that lived in the less prosperous southern and eastern areas. In the mid-nineteenth century, Jews were granted full equality by the Croatian *Sabor* (parliament), and by the end of the century there were 21 established Jewish communities. Osijek and Zagreb numbered 3,000 persons each. At the turn of the twentieth century, the Zionist ideology gained popularity—an issue of conflict with the more numerous proponents of assimilation. At the outbreak of World War II, 23,000 Jews lived in Croatia.

Serbia

The largest of the five republics, Serbia, has no outlet to the sea. It stretches from the fertile Danube plains of Vojvodina in the north, southward to Albania, to the war-ravaged mountains of Kosovo, and FYR (Former Yugoslav Republic of) Macedonia. The largest number of national minorities in the former Yugoslavia lives in Serbia. Its history is still haunted by the humiliating defeat dealt by the Turks in 1389, in the Battle of Kosovo, when the country lost its independence for nearly 500 years. The Turks were tolerant of the Jews, but that favor was to Jewish disadvantage during the brief period of Austrian rule

(1718–1739). A sultan's charter in 1830 granted Serbia internal independence and conferred on the Jews equality with other citizens. Full rights for Jews were achieved with the Constitution of 1888.

Jews arrived in the northern Serbian autonomous province of Vojvodina in the sixteenth and seventeenth centuries, but the development of economic enterprise waited for the 1782 Tolerance Edict of Joseph II. Newly built towns such as Subotica encouraged Jewish influx to help develop the town's fledgling industries. By the end of the nineteenth century there were nearly 40 Jewish communities in Vojvodina, many of them Orthodox.

Serbian-Jewish relations reached a high degree of cooperation during World War I, when Jews and Serbs fought side by side against the Central Powers. With the war's end and the Hapsburg defeat, the victors created the Yugoslav kingdom from portions of its fragmented empire, a state beset from birth with enormous economic problems. Nevertheless, those post-war years heralded a period of relative harmony among the multi-ethnic and multi-religious populations. It was a Golden Age for the Jews, who enjoyed full equality in the Yugoslav kingdom until the 1938 German annexation of Austria spread anti-Semitic propaganda and anti-Jewish laws. Except for the Holocaust period, the Balkan harmony lasted for 72 years until the dissolution of the Federal Republic, with the outbreak of the Balkan War in 1991.

Holocaust and Post-War Period

Aside from the minority Ustaša Nazi collaborators, the general Yugoslav population had no deep identification with the Fascists. Hostile actions against the Jews were infrequent. The partisans of Tito's Liberation Army welcomed as comrades-in-arms the 5,000 Jews who fought valiantly at their side and lost 1,318 in battle; many Jews were decorated for valor. Of about 76,000 Jews in Yugoslavia in 1939, only some 16,000 survived. Post-war Croatia counted fewer than 5,000 Jews; Serbia about 4,000; Vojvodina, about 4,000; and some 3,000 in Bosnia. Without interference by Yugoslav authorities, more than half of the Jewish survivors emigrated to Israel, leaving behind a total of 6,000 to 7,000 Jews in 36 shrunken *kehillot*—down from a pre-war number of 121 communities.

About 2,500 Jews, many of them aged, live in Croatia now, at the turn of the twenty-first century, most of them in Zagreb, the capital. Smaller communities exist in Osijek, Split, Rijeka, and Dubrovnik. The *kehillot* of Zagreb and Osijek conduct services in prayer halls; those in Rijeka, Split, and Dubrovnik still maintain their synagogues. Serbia's Jews also number about 2,500, most of them in Belgrade, with smaller communities in Novi Sad, Sombor, Subotica, and Niš. The majority of their members are senior citizens. The only functioning synagogue in Serbia today is in Belgrade. Jews in Novi Sad and in Subotica use prayer halls.

An important factor in community reorganization after World War II had been the cooperation between the different kinds of division: Neolog and Orthodox, Zionist and assimilationist, Sephardic and Ashkenazic. Despite diminished numbers, intermarriage, and assimilation, as well as rising local nationalism and ethnic tensions, the Jewish community continued to function by virtue of the overall bonding provided by the Federation of Jewish Communities. The disintegration of Yugoslavia in the 1990s abolished the unifying power of the Federation. The central organization remains functional now only within Serbia.

In a more significant transition than ever before and in an atmosphere of intensified, narrow national fever, Jews can no longer be simply undifferentiated "Yugoslavs." The majority populations test them for local identity and are quick to raise accusations of disloyalty. Travel between the successor states is viewed with suspicion; therefore, minimal infrequent meetings in Hungary take the place of overall Federation activity. Isolated from each other within each of the successor states, the communities practice the Federation model with only a modicum of success. What hampers them most is their small and diminishing numbers. The present dangers pose an identity challenge that has caused many previously unaffiliated individuals to take a new interest in their Jewish background, though not necessarily in religion per se. Local governments cooperate to some extent with the Jews on the restitution of former Jewish property. Along with international Jewish organizations, some municipalities, such as Subotica, have provided funds for local investment and for synagogue repair. Private donations helped repair the ancient synagogues of Split and Dubrovnik in 1998.

The 1999 Kosovo hostilities put a temporary stop to public funding and restoration activity. The ethnic cleansing atrocities against the Albanian population in Kosovo by Serbian soldiers were countered by NATO's controversial bombing of Serbian cities and villages. Serbian Jews protested the NATO bombings. The Belgrade *kehillah* evacuated many of its women, children, and elderly to Budapest for safety. Many of them emigrated permanently, leaving even smaller *kehillot* behind. Israel provided temporary refuge to 200 Moslem Kosovo Albanians. The end of hostilities did not end the hate and the mutual retaliatory killings between Serbs and Albanians. With enemies at hand on all sides, anti-Semitism is superfluous and dormant. Nevertheless, the Jewish future in the former Yugoslavia does not look promising.

WHEN OUR SHIPS BROUGHT PROFIT

Split and Dubrovnik, the two oldest Jewish communities on the Adriatic coast of Croatia, trace their continuous existence back to the early fourteenth century. "Pearl of the Adriatic," Dubrovnik, also called Rhacusa and Ragusa, sits astride a fine natural harbor on the southern Dalmatian coast. In the Middle Ages, the city enclosed itself with high walls, mounted protective towers on them, and flour-ished as a trading port. As a small city-republic, Ragusa enjoyed its greatest prosperity and growth between the thirteenth and sixteenth centuries. Most of its trade was with cities on the eastern coast of Italy and in the Aegean basin, all of them locations of thriving Jewish communities. Jews were tolerated as itinerant traders in Dubrovnik from 1352, although the city initially denied them

The fine natural harbor of Dubrovnik on the Dalmatian coast.

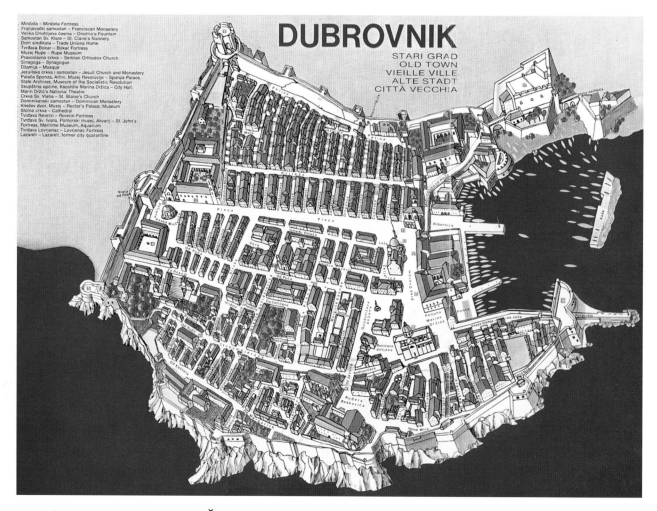

Map of the old town of Dubrovnik. Žudioská, the synagogue street is the last alley on the right off the main avenue, the Placa. (Adapted from a publicity pamphlet for Dubrovnik.)

residence. The small *kehillah* played a significant role in the commercial and maritime development of the city despite harassment and persecution.

Exiles from Spain and Portugal in the early sixteenth century augmented the small community and brought with them useful professions and skills. To curry favor with the Spanish king after the Spanish expulsions, while indulging their jealousy of Jewish maritime success, Dubrovnik competitors fabricated a blood libel (accusation of ritual murder) in 1502. Seven accused Jews, among them an eminent doctor, Mose Maralija, were speedily tried and publicly executed, and Jews were subsequently excluded from trading in the port. Balkan Jews protested both the executions and the arbitrary denial of their right to trade. Asking for reinstatement, they offered to route mercantile activities with western Europe through the port of Dubrovnik. City authorities relented in 1530, allowing Jews who had at least 1,000 gold ducats both the right to commerce and to settle in the city—as *foresteri,* "foreigners," not as *cives,* "citizens."

The community of not more than 40 persons organized itself in 1538 as *Universitas Haebreorum,* a Jewish community, under the leadership of a *Consul Haebreorum,* a Jewish consul. The city set up a ghetto in 1546 within the walls to provide dwellings for "the Jews who come daily into Dubrovnik," and yet to keep them apart, so that "they will not pass through the city streets at night." The ghetto contained five or six houses and six merchandise warehouses.

The sixteenth century witnessed the peak of economic and cultural expansion of the Republic of Dubrovnik, with intensive activity by Jewish merchants. They controlled most of the trade with Turkey and Italy through their contacts with Jews in Constantinople, Salonika, Venice, and Ancona. Much of the trade moved through Dubrovnik until Venice took the lead away at the end of the seventeenth century.

Counter-Reformation forces that gained power in the seventeenth century promulgated edicts that restricted Jewish-Christian contact to strictly business matters. Making the most of the implication that Jews used Christian blood in baking matzah, Christians were explicitly forbidden to accept matzah from Jews. To exacerbate the poisoned atmosphere, in 1622, a blood libel was launched against Yitzchak Yeshurun. His imprisonment and torture spread fear through the Jewish community. Seventeen of the 50 Jewish families emigrated, some to Venice and some to Turkey. Rabbi Aaron ben David ha-Kohen, succeeding his grandfather as rabbi while he continued to manage Dubrovnik's most successful export–import business, did what he could to allay the exiles' fears. The panic abated under his leadership and the city fathers encouraged the Jews to return.

A disastrous earthquake struck in 1667. Jews asked for and gained permission to enlarge their tiny cemetery and bury the 39 Jewish victims. Jews and all "foreign" merchants paid extra duties to cover the cost of reconstruction. As the townspeople rebuilt the city after the quake, they took care to restore the ghetto gates. By then, however, some of the wealthier Jews had established residence in another part of the city, without interference.

The Church, militantly obsessed with Jewish "heresy," regarded the Talmud and rabbinical literature as containing ideas "contrary to the laws of God and nature." An edict of January 1, 1724, ordered Jews to deliver to the clergy all books of the Talmud—whether in the synagogue or in personal possession. In March, the senate decreed that the confiscated books be burned in the town square. The senate's maximum magnanimity was to decree that former Talmud owners would go unpunished, but a fine of 500 gold pieces threatened future owners of Talmud volumes. To encourage denunciations, 10 percent of the fine was promised to potential informers.

The 78 persons in 20 families occupied 19 ghetto houses in 1756. Always overcrowded and in need of repair, ghetto houses accommodated temporary as well as permanent residents. In an effort to diminish friction with non-Jews, the community set its own restrictions in 1792: "Jews may pass from house to house in the ghetto but they may not appear on the main street from 5 P.M. of Holy Thursday until the third day after Easter. During the two nights when we have our Purim carnival, Jews may go out on the main street only to attend the synagogue, and they must always carry a light."

Small as it was, the community was capable of internal discord. In the summer of 1750, the allotment of the four seats of honor near the Ark caused such a vehement dispute within the *kehillah* that city authorities had to intervene to make peace. A municipal committee transferred the ownership of the seats to the city and ruled that members of the community could buy the seats for 20 gold pieces each, the income to be used as revenue for repairing the cathedral square. The buyers could enjoy the seats during their lifetimes, but afterward the city would sell them again on the same terms.

Though not exceptional in this regard, Dubrovnik taxed Jews excessively. A sailors' tax, *tassa degli capitani,* burdened all residents, but Jews paid an additional one, *l'annua tassa degli Ebrei,* the annual Jewish tax. The *kehillah* complained in 1786:

When our ships brought profit, we could pay the tax, but now we often have the expense of ships that bring only heavy debt. This levy of 1,500 gold pieces falls on the shoulders of a small number of families. Landlords mercilessly keep raising the rents of Jews outside the ghetto. For the Turkish merchants from Bosnia who stay in our warehouses near the port, we must furnish beds, kitchen supplies and all their needs. They have tended recently to steal the furniture and equipment—that we must replace at great expense.

The authorities heeded this complaint and reduced the tax by an unrecorded amount.

In 1808, during the brief French rule, General Marmont, governor of the occupying forces, abolished all laws of racial discrimination. Jews then enjoyed full civil equality for six years. The French administration, however, was an economic disaster for Dubrovnik and its Adriatic coast. The French sea blockade ruined the merchant fleet, and the loss of maritime import–export severely limited overland trade. Exchanging currency and lending money to the French army only partly alleviated Jewish losses. After the French defeat in 1814, Dubrovnik came under Austrian rule that lasted a hundred years. Without independence, the city lost its prominence as a seaport.

Jewish activity shifted in the 1830s from commerce to viticulture with substantial success. By 1861, of 646 Dubrovnik merchants only three were Jews. When disease beset the vineyards in 1880, Dubrovnik Jews received aid from the Jewish communities in Split and Trieste with whom they had good ties.

Civil equality, promised by Austria in 1814, came closer to reality only after 1848, but rights to own real estate and assurances of full religious freedom lagged until the 1890s. Even then, the government retained the power to determine the scope of religious activities. In the post–World War I Yugoslav kingdom, the community reorganized itself with help from the Belgrade union of Jewish communities.

As Nazism spread from Germany and Austria to Rumania in the late 1930s, refugees swamped the impoverished Dubrovnik community. Italian military forces took over the city in the autumn of 1941. Despite heavy pressure, the Italians resisted transferring Jews from their jurisdiction to the Germans. In June 1943 the Italians shipped Jews from various internment camps to a concentration camp on the north Dalmatian island of Rab. When Italy fell in November, many of the island internees joined the partisans in the struggle against the Nazis. They were immediately sent to the battle front, where 200 of the recently liberated Jews were killed. The Croatian government appropriated the Dubrovnik synagogue and rented it to the Croatian Workers' Union for the announced pur-

pose of opening a free kitchen for Moslem refugees, a plan that did not materialize. After the liberation, 23 Jewish survivors returned to the city.

In 1991 fighting broke out between Serbia and Croatia, and the historic city of Dubrovnik suffered artillery and nautical shelling. During the bombardment, the few remaining Jews watched over the synagogue. Although some of their homes and many historic buildings were harmed, there was no significant damage to the synagogue, and community members escaped serious injury.

Žudioská ulica (Jewish Street), the narrow alley of the ghetto shades the steep rise from the Placa. Paved in broad steps, the passageway hardly provides enough room for people or donkeys to pass each other because of the stone entry steps that jut out in front of every portal along the way. The synagogue occupies an undistinguished stone building in the row at Number 3, near the bottom of the alley.

Mirjam Ferera, guiding spirit of the small Jewish community, photographed in the synagogue office. In recent correspondence she writes that many changes have taken place in the community since the civil war of the early 1990s. From 23 members, six years ago, they have grown to 47 members who conduct a *minyan* and celebrate all the festivals in the renewed facilities. Restoration work proceeds under conservation experts. ". . . our synagogue can not be called [a] silent museum. . . . maybe other Jews will decide to come and stay here, and help us in our struggle to keep our community alive."

The sunless cleft of the narrow ghetto alley rises steeply from the Dubrovnik Placa, the main avenue near the market and port area. In ghetto times, the alley was closed at the top. At the lower end, near the sign Žudioská ulica (Jews' street), ghetto traffic was controlled by a gate— now gone. The synagogue was established in 1408 near the bottom of the alley, in a narrow three-storied stone building dating from the fourteenth century. High windows, ogee-arched at the second level, cut the undistinguished and essentially unchanged stone facade.

A narrow flight of stairs leads directly to the small office, where entrance tickets sell for a token fee. The walls are colorfully decorated with old photos and documents, including a list of the earthquake victims of 1667, a picture of the Western Wall in Jerusalem, and a letter from

Sir Moses Montefiore thanking the *kehillah* for its good wishes on the occasion of his 100th birthday. More steps lead up to the sanctuary. The present *kehillah* and its predecessors have lavished much care and love on the diminutive prayer room.

Access to the women's gallery behind the high wooden grilles is through the adjacent house, home of Emilio Tolentino. After Rabbi

A Torah crown and a pair of *rimmonim* at the *bimah* corner. The iron frame is there to hold the Torah scroll and ornaments during the service. The crown, of repoussé silver, has floral inserts in large ovals and a border of tiny florets. The silver finials are four sided, topped by a pyramid, crowned with a tiny flower or bird, and rimmed with miniature bells on chains. They suggest the shape of a medieval tower, after a Venetian prototype that became popular in Italy, north Africa, and parts of the Ottoman empire in the eighteenth century. These items were among the ceremonial silver loaned in 1992 to Yeshiva University Museum in New York.

THE KAHAL ADAT YISRAEL, DUBROVNIK

A dominant bearing partition, pierced by three wide arches, divides the room and the oversize *bimah* into front and back areas. Between 1652 and 1670, the synagogue was redecorated in Baroque style. To replace the women's seating, formerly in a row at the rear, a raised gallery was added at the south wall by incorporating a room from the third floor of the adjacent building. A decorative latticework separates it from the prayer room below. Men sat on high-backed benches along the north and south walls. The synagogue was probably adequate in size for Dubrovnik's Jewish community, whose numbers between the fifteenth and the twentieth centuries never exceeded the 260 affiliated persons in 1830.

A tasteful white satin *parokhet* (curtain) covers the inlaid doors of the exquisite Baroque *Aron Kodesh*. The Ark holds several Torah scrolls, one of which may have originated in Spain before the 1492 expulsions. In Sephardic fashion, bronze Florentine memorial lamps containing glass oil cups hang from chains in front of the Ark. In style, they resemble lamps of contemporary Balkan churches or mosques. Heavy maroon velvet drapes form a dramatic baldachin above the Ark and deck the windows. The community's most important work of art is a thirteenth-century Moorish carpet presumably brought from Spain during the expulsion. With floral design glowing in brilliant colors against the dark silk background, it is a superb achievement. Legend claims that it was a gift from Queen Isabella to her Jewish doctor when he was forced to leave Spain. Often hung before the *Aron Kodesh* as a *parokhet* on the High Holidays, it is presently in safekeeping until it can be displayed in the Jewish Museum planned for Dubrovnik.

The eighteenth-century *Aron Kodesh* in rich Baroque style. Three pairs of carved helical pillars, ornamented with narrow gilded bands and minute Corinthian capitals flank the Ark. The short pillars rest on raised pedestals, joined to form a gently curved base. Inlaid wood panels feature stylized floral motifs.

The oversized *bimah,* split by the arched bearing partition. The prayer hall dates from 1408. It received its present form in 1652 and was renovated several times, notably in the Baroque era. Fresh paint in a light beige color covers the walls. The polished parquet floor glistens with light from the two tall narrow windows. Not all electrified, the many hanging lamps recall a time when they were the only source of evening light.

Salamon Baruch was taken to the Italian concentration camp on the island of Rab in May of 1943 and later executed, Tolentino took over the leadership of the congregation. During the night following the German entry into the city, the Tolentino family rescued much of the ceremonial silver. They climbed past the grilles down into the synagogue, gathered the silver and the Torah scrolls and distributed them among Croatian friends. After the war, the few Jews who returned regained the synagogue treasures.

To commemorate the 500th anniversary of the expulsion of Jews from Spain and Portugal, Yeshiva University Museum in New York asked to exhibit Dobrovnik's Sephardic Judaica in 1992. The *kehillah* airlifted 54 pieces, including Torah scrolls, textiles, and ceremonial silver. After the exhibit closed, the property became the subject of extended litigation with ideological overtones. The museum refused to return the Judaica despite repeated requests by the Dubrovnik *kehillah*. Museum officials and some New York Sephardim feared the possible fate of these treasures in a shrunken Jewish community under a Catholic dictatorship like Croatia. Michael Papo, former head of the Dubrovnik community, who had arranged the loan and now lives in New York, sided with the museum. But what of the community's claim on its property? The New York State Supreme Court decided, in September 1998, in favor of Dubrovnik's Jews. Four months later the 54 precious items arrived safely in Dubrovnik. The *kehillah* is collecting money for restoration of the building, and for its museum.

Tourists are beginning again to crowd the Placa. Dubrovnik captures the heart of visitors with its natural beauty and ancient charisma. Yeshayah Cohen, sixteenth-century philosopher, poet, and Latin scholar (known by his pseudonyms Yakov Flavius and Didacus Pyrrhus) crowned his beloved city "Queen of the Illyrian Sea" and glorified her with paeans of poetry:

Si tranquilla meae sedes optanda senectae,
Ante alias urbes sola Rhacusa placet.

If I had to find a peaceful place to rest in my old age,
Above any other city I would fancy only Rhacusa.

The Placa, main thoroughfare of Dubrovnik's old city. For residents and tourists alike, the wide Placa is the favored promenade near the harbor. Lined with small shops and sidewalk cafes, it runs from the bell tower of the Franciscan Monastery, along neat rows of red-roofed houses, to the large square in front of the Sponza palace at the seaside.

ALBUMS AND IDENTITY

Zdenko Kohn is an industrial psychologist. He was in his early fifties, a vigorous leader of the community in Osijek, Croatia, when we met him at the former synagogue in May 1991. "I was born in Osijek during the Second World War," he told us simply in English. "My father fought as a partisan and he survived, but his entire family perished in Auschwitz. Now, we Jews are fewer than 50 families, with only about 20 children. We gather for holidays and have some programs for the children. They meet other Yugoslav Jewish children once or twice a year, but is that enough to give them a Jewish identity? We expect war soon between Croatia and Serbia. Yugoslavia will break up and Jews will again have to decide where to place their allegiance."

Although Kohn had a position with a large factory that manufactured agricultural machinery, a possible layoff gave him cause for worry. An exuberant guide, he took us through the "upper town," the city center, to visit the large Jewish community building on Županijská ulica. The great synagogue, not far from the main square, was torched in 1941. Zdenko remembers passing the charred shell in his youth for many years until the ruins were finally demolished during Tito's regime. A department store now occupies the site.

The *kehillah* keeps two rooms for its own use in its pre-war community building but

Zdenko Kohn, our host in Osijek.

Upper city synagogue in Osijek, Romantic style, Theodore Stern, architect, 1867 to 1869. Built on the main square, opposite the cathedral, it was part of a long row of civic and commercial buildings. A mob of Nazi collaborators burned it on April 13, 1941. (Courtesy of the Jewish community in Osijek.)

rents out the remainder. The office is drab, badly in need of painting. Portraits of past rabbis and synagogue officials share the walls with pictures of pre-war school classes and a fine drawing of the great synagogue in its prime. In the corner, a small glass cabinet displays some of the community's Judaica. A larger room, serving the community for assembly and for holiday prayers, contains a small wooden Ark and benches that can seat perhaps 40 people.

Zdenko invited us to his home, stopping on the way to buy a fresh carp in the market. His wife, Božica, a pediatric nurse, prepared a favorite Yugoslav dish, *riblja čorba,* of carp, onions, and paprika, served with noodles. As we lunched in their small dining room, we admired their comfortable furnishings, the large library, and the fine pieces of crystal. In inadequate English, Božica indicated how insecure she, too, felt about the future.

Close to the Hungarian border, the Croatian city of Osijek (Hungarian: Eszek; German: Esseg) straddles both sides of the Drava River.

This fertile region of the Danube basin has yielded interesting archeological remains, proving that Jewish settlement in the southern Slav lands is of great antiquity. Soon after the fall of Jerusalem in 70 C.E., the Romans brought Jews to these regions as slaves and as workers in the crafts. Rare findings from the third and fourth centuries C.E. point to a number of early Jewish settlements, scattered from Macedonia north to Croatia. Menorah-engraved oil lamps were found in the ruins of a second- to third-century synagogue at Salona (Split), one of the most important mercantile ports of the Romans on the north Adriatic. The archeological park at Stobi, north of the border with Greece, includes impressive remains of a fourth-century synagogue with mosaics and Greek inscriptions.

At Mursa, an ancient Roman site near Osijek, a fragment of a third-century slab bears an inscription describing the rebuilding of the *proseucha*—a Latin parallel to the Greek *synagoga*, applied to Jewish prayer rooms in the Hellenized Eastern Empire—on the occasion of an imperial visit of Septimius Severus to Mursa. This indicates the probable existence of a Jewish community there. There is no other indication of a Jewish presence in or near Osijek until the seventeenth century, when the city was part of Hungary.

To this location, a junction on the bustling trading route between the Balkans and central Europe, came Jewish peddlers driving their wagons south from Hungarian border towns. In a move to protect local merchants, the town allowed Jews to stay no more than three days, on payment of a "tolerance fee" of one to two forints a day, a steep tax for those days.

Stalwart pioneers early in 1746 were Josef Pfeiffer and the two Heschel brothers, the first Jews on record to receive permits of temporary residence in the lower city. A group of 11 courageous Jewish families from the Baranya area, north of the Drava River, followed them, and more Jews trickled in from Slovakia and Galicia. Among those listed in the *matrikel* (population register) at the end of 1746 were: Yehudah and Hirschel Benedix; Shabbat Froddle and her son, age four; Raizel and her son, age six; Yakov Benedec; and Filia Rachel Hirsh, age one, and her brothers, Natzel, 17, and Stetzel, 15. Conditions improved when Emperor Joseph II applied the Toleranzpatent to Croatia in 1783. Freedom of movement, settlement, and religion, as well as equality in educational opportunities began to be the norm, although occupational restrictions still applied. Jews gained official right of residence only in 1792.

These were observant Jews who were delighted when Jakov Lang received a special permit in 1811 to open a "Jewish kitchen in the upper city," their first public kosher eating place. Among the 40 founders of the *kehillah* in 1847 were Marcus Spiller, Yakov Shechtitz, and Dr. Mauritz Reind. The membership increased rapidly thereafter. Their first prayer room was at 393 Školska Street. They opened a Jewish school in 1856 and built a grand synagogue on the main square of the upper city in 1869. Community head Leopold Heller mobilized building donations from 22 of the most prosperous members. The Osijek *kehillah,* the largest in the province until 1890, flourished after the emancipation and expanded downriver to the "lower town." In 1900, when they numbered 1,600 people, the lower town congregation built a separate synagogue in Moorish style, completed in 1903.

Some Osijek Jews received appointments to municipal positions under the Hapsburgs. Others became doctors, lawyers, and owners of shops and factories. Many of them marketed agricultural products or engaged in banking. A few Jewish industrialists, among them Schulhof, Shmuel Gutman, Josef Kraus, and the Oberson brothers, played a decisive role in the development of the local and the regional economy. Activists in the workers' movement at the turn of the century included the Kraus brothers, Kolman Maas, Emanuel Zelig, Adolf Roth, and Nathan Schwartz, who served as secretary of the *kehillah* and teacher in the Jewish school from the end of the nineteenth century until the *Shoah.*

Father and son of the Spitzer family were leaders of the *kehillah* for almost 80 years. Rabbi Dr. Shmuel Spitzer arrived as a young man of 26. He served as chief rabbi from 1857 to 1895, and wrote 19 books on Jewish history, culture, and religion. His son, Dr. Hugo Spitzer

(1858–1934), was founder and first president of the Federation of Jewish Communities in Yugoslavia. A successful lawyer, he served on the town council and was president of the community and of the Zionist Federation of Yugoslavia until his death.

The religious conflict between Orthodox and Neolog (the Hungarian Reform movement) that plagued Hungarian Jewry flared up here also toward the end of the nineteenth century. Whereas the Orthodox were strong in northeastern Hungary, they attracted only about 20 percent in southern Hungary and Croatia. Assimilation was common, expressing itself in intermarriage, conversion, and the "red assimilation" of individuals who immersed themselves in the leftist parties or the Communist underground.

The Ashkenazic majority in Osijek was loyal to the Hapsburg monarchy and its language and culture, but retained a Jewish national identification in secular Zionism. The Zionists led the community and exerted the greatest influence upon it. The Theodore Herzl Group was the first to organize, in 1904, immediately after Herzl's death. They were followed by the Bar Giora youth, WIZO, Kaveret, "Beehive" adult Zionists, and the Miriam group, an organization of young women. In the post–World War I period, young people joined the Zionist scouts, Hashomer

A 1928 class of children with their teacher and principal in Osijek's Jewish school.

3. i 4 RAZRED ŽIDOVSKE ŠKOLE U OSIJEKU 1928. godine: Direktor Sonnenschein, Pišta Kraus, Ripp, Turi Ferber, Lippert, Fischer, Kornel Neumann, Hugo Zuckerberg, Paul Moret, Tirca Rotbart (učiteljica); sredina: Milan Kolar, Boriška Szege, Hela Mismer, Mausi Spitzer, Zlata Stein, Mira Mahler, ? , Boskovic, Feri Kohn; sprijeda: Suzi Šalgo, Edita Szilard, Lulu Kramer, Stern(-ovica, uč.), Lederer, Lang, Krakauer

Hatzair, and Akiva, a cultural organization. Community organizations included a Recreation Club that provided vacations for poor and sick children, and Židovsko opskrbilište, an organization devoted to the housing and education of orphans and underprivileged youth. Maccabee, whose sports activities included women's boating and handball, was exceptionally popular. Music lovers enjoyed opera performances conducted by Fritz Lev Mirsky.

The polarization of political and religious ideas became more noticeable when the community reorganized itself in the aftermath of the First World War. Two parties contested the community council elections, in which the voting was by party list rather than by individual candidate. The highly popular list was presented by the Židovska (Jewish) party, with traditional and Zionist identification, under the leadership of Dr. Hugo Spitzer. The other party was Izraeliticka, "Sons of the Mosaic Faith," an anti-Zionist group that perceived its Judaism in strictly religio-ritualistic terms. It was philosophically assimilationist, with pro-Croatian leanings that weakened Jewish identification. This polarity was a manifestation of the widespread perplexity among Croatian Jews after the fall of the Austro-Hungarian Empire.

The permissive and accommodating atmosphere in the early years of the Yugoslav kingdom allowed the Zionist idea to spread; its ranks expanded and its ideology dominated the community. Because of its geographic location, Osijek became a major center for country-wide Zionist activities, a location of congresses and conferences. The first Yugoslav Zionist weekly, Židovska smotra (Jewish Review), appeared here in 1909. In 1920 and 1925, Jewish youth gathered from all corners of the newly founded Yugoslav state for seminars and sports. The B'nai B'rith Society, with its small lodge in Osijek, exerted considerable impact on the kehillah because its members were influential lawyers, doctors, bankers, and industrialists. The society's objectives included mutual assistance and common action in the cultural, educational, and political life of the kehillah, as well as financial contributions for welfare and for land purchase in Palestine.

By the late 1930s the Jewish community in Osijek numbered over 3,000. Nearly all the major factories were financed and run by Jews. The main industry of the city was the manufacture of heavy agricultural machinery for export throughout Europe and beyond. Many Jews worked in the factories along with Croatian and German neighbors, meeting with no outward signs of anti-Semitism. When German troops entered the city on April 10, 1941, however, the Ustaša (paramilitary Croatian–Nazi collaborators) and the Volksdeutsche (local Germans) hailed them as heroes. Three days later mobs desecrated the Jewish cemetery and torched the great synagogue on the central square.

With the assistance of the Ustaša, the Germans initiated searches in the houses, pillaging and making mass arrests. Despite the sudden impoverishment of the kehillah, due to extreme restrictions on all Jewish economic activity, the Germans imposed a fine of 20 million dinars. In June 1942, the Jews were coerced to build a settlement near Tenje, not far outside the city, where it was promised they would be safe. Three thousand Jews from the city and the region were confined there. By August all of them were sent

Die Heilige Schriften der Israeliten (the Holy Scriptures of the Jews), illustrated by the popular Gustav Doré, a gift of the Osijek *kehillah* to the Pentecostal community.

either to Auschwitz or to the camp at Jasenovac, Croatia, where a million Jews, Roma, and Serbs were murdered by Croatian–Nazi collaborators. Only Jews in hiding and a few who had married gentiles remained in the city. Ten people returned from the camps. The resuscitated community after the war numbered 610 in 1947, including those in the surrounding region, but most of the survivors soon left for Israel.

The 1903 lower town synagogue of Osijek still stands, although it sustained severe damage from wartime arson. It lay abandoned for many years, until the Pentecostal Church of Yugoslavia bought the building complex from the community for use as a church and seminary for theology students. To symbolize the mutual ties at the time of the transfer, the Jewish community bestowed a gift on the Pentecostals. They presented them with a rare copy of the Bible, *Die Heilige Schriften der Israeliten* (the Holy Scriptures of the Jews) illustrated in 1866 with etchings by the French illustrator Gustav Doré. That Bible serves the congregation weekly and rests on the pulpit stand. The Osijek center is the largest Pentecostal seminary in the country and

Section of the lower city synagogue in Osijek. Note the design of the gallery benches and the graceful curve of the proscenium arch, echoing the line of the barrel-vaulted ceiling. (Courtesy of the Jewish community in Sarajevo.)

The lower city synagogue in Osijek, neo-Moresque style, 1903. The synagogue and school behind it were sold to the Pentecostal Church on amicable terms. The school now houses seminary students.

draws students from other countries as well. Students and faculty evince positive attitudes toward Judaism and Israel. Their deep commitment to Jesus and his message seems to be an identification with early Christian values and philosophy, a humanism not sharply different from Jewish humanism as expressed in *Ethics of the Fathers,* a tractate of the Mishnah. A young, idealistic student, Ružica Maraš, whom we met at the seminary, has been teaching herself Hebrew and identifies with Zionist goals for Israel. She became an eager volunteer to gather source material on the history of Jewish communities for our research.

Eight months after our meeting in Osijek, a telephone call from Zdenko Kohn surprised us. In elementary but understandable Hebrew, Kohn explained, "Božica and I are in Jerusalem for a day to deal with formalities relating to our work. We live in Carmiel now." That evening the four

THE LOWER CITY SYNAGOGUE IN OSIJEK
A new coat of red and white paint emphasizes the neo-Moresque features of the synagogue: the roofline dentils and the paired onion cupolas. The onion cupola is a common architectural feature of churches in the region, so the building has slipped easily into its new adaptation. In converting the synagogue to a church, the Pentecostals were careful to preserve design and decorations, except for primary symbols. They removed Stars of David from the cupolas and added a small cross above the Tablets of the Law at the apex of the portal pediment. Under a barrel-vaulted ceiling, the synagogue interior sparkles with new lighting fixtures, polished wooden pews and gallery fronts, white walls, and a restored Ark. The only change from the previous interior décor was the addition of a crucifix and an inscription above the Ark.

The synagogue interior, repainted white, but otherwise restored with minimal change. Contrary to the custom in other churches adapted from former synagogues in central Europe, the damaged Ark here was restored and returned to its niche. The only Christian symbols in the room are a gilded wooden crucifix and a Croatian inscription, "Glory to the Lord forever."

Bronze statue of a mother and child, donated in 1965 to Osijek by native son and Jewish sculptor Oscar Nemon, who moved to London after World War II. The sculpture stands at the entrance to the city park opposite the Jewish community building, a memorial to the Osijek victims of fascism.

of us met, and we learned what had happened. When hostilities broke out in May, as expected, between the Serbs and the Croats, Zdenko sent his son and daughter, college students, to Israel before the heavy fighting reached Osijek. It became dangerous to stay, but it was also dangerous to try to leave since both sides were trigger happy and regarded departure as treachery. To avoid suspicion, the Kohns prepared by loading light baggage, mostly the photo albums, into the car late at night. Early the following morning, on September 20, 1991, the Kohns and Zdenko's parents just walked out the door to the car and drove away, knowing that all their possessions would immediately be plundered. They drove all day without stopping and arrived in Budapest at midnight. The Jewish Agency arranged for a flight to Israel two weeks later.

All of them had been studying Hebrew at the *ulpan* (immigrants' classes) since their arrival. Zdenko's new name is Aharon and Božica's name is Elah. The language barrier between us, especially with Elah, had now disappeared. Communication in Hebrew was open with both of them. Aharon smiled: *"Higanu habayta,"* (We have come home!)

AN AUDIENCE WITH HER MAJESTY

Salamon Hajduška, a young observant Jew of Topola, Serbia, set out for Vienna on a bright day in 1779 to seek an audience with Empress Maria Theresa. An enterprising merchant, Hajduška had applied earlier that year to the city council of Subotica (known then as Maria Theresiopol) for a permit to open a shop. The council refused as a matter of course: Jews had been expelled from the region along with the hated Turks in 1687 when the Hapsburgs took control. Although regional fairs attracted Hungarian, Slovak, and German settlers, the city curbed immigration of Greek-Orthodox, Armenians, Roma, and Jews. Undaunted, Hajduška was determined to bring his plea to the highest possible level.

The precarious Jewish circumstances in Hapsburg-ruled Europe were always at the mercy of the rulers' intrinsic anti-Semitism. As autocratic Catholic sovereign of the Austrian domains from 1740 to 1780, Maria Theresa (1717–1780) was intolerant of Calvinists and Jews. She had no compunctions over expelling *kehillot:* from Prague, 1744; from Buda, 1746; and from Hodonín in 1774. Of the Jews, she wrote that there was "no worse plague for the state than this nation, because of its deceitfulness, its usury," which "bring the state more harm than good." She was reluctant, however, to relinquish mercantile benefits; therefore, among her other grudging, benevolent acts, she allowed Jews to establish factories—and employ gentiles. In 1749, she unified the haphazard geographic "toleration taxes" on individual Jews. The new tax to the crown promptly earned the sobriquet *malke gelt* "queen's money," among Jews of the empire. It painfully drained Jewish resources, but Maria Theresa's dependence on the income from it occasionally mitigated her anti-Jewish decisions.

As a symbol of her disdain for Jews, Maria Theresa conducted audiences with them from behind a curtain. Such was the autocratic monarch who had reigned for 39 years, to whom Hajduška appealed. His daring petition for a personal hearing caught her fancy. She heard his case and granted his request, ordering city authorities to issue a permit for him to open a business. Although the official notification did not arrive until 15 years later, Hajduška promptly set up a proper shop with a large display window under the dissenting eyes of guild members who had opposed the approval.

In another instance, Jakab Herschel from Paks, Hungary, after receiving the right of city tenancy in 1775, was allowed to trade in skins and wool. He also wangled the privilege of providing kosher food and wine to Jews who attended the fairs, at a price of three groschen per head.

Maria Theresa's oldest son and close advisor, Joseph II (1741–1790), was more in tune with the spirit of the Enlightenment than his mother. Soon after he succeeded to the throne in 1780, he instituted well-intentioned changes. Abolishing the yellow badge requirement and the payment of *malke gelt* in the Toleranzpatent (Edict of Tolerance) of 1782—and later, according to locality—he opened up university education, allowed large-scale business opportunities, and granted Jews other civil rights. Ironically, the outcome of his liberalizing action was at least partly negative for Judaism. In the monarch's aim to integrate the Jews rather than isolate them, he applied drastic conditions and succeeded much too well. The Toleranzpatent prohibited the use of Yiddish or Hebrew in commercial or community documents, confining these languages by fiat exclusively to religious ritual. This ban reduced the unifying and cohesive function of Hebrew and Yiddish in communication among Jews and thereby contributed to the gradual deterioration of Jewish education. As another thrust in the direction of assimilation, Joseph compelled Jews to adopt German family names and personal names from a restricted list. When the Toleranzpatent became applicable in Subotica in 1790, Jakab Herschel legally became Jakab Hirsch and Mordecai Marton Kis, Mark Klein.

In an attempt to protect their own limited privileges in 1786, the year the *kehillah* gained official recognition, 12 propertyless and quasi-legal Jewish families in Subotica persuaded the city council to deny new petitioners for Jewish residence. Two years later, the council reversed the former ruling, proclaiming, "The entrance of additional decent Jews would improve business for the resident Jews, and would prevent cheating of the Christian population." As the number of Jews increased with migration from Lower Austria, Moravia, and Galicia, the need for a synagogue arose. In 1802, the *kehillah* commissioned a building of 186 by 90 feet, with small annexes on eastern and northern sides. It was in rustic Baroque style with two towers and a porch added in the renovation of 1850. The building was demolished in 1913, not long after the construction of the new synagogue. In a careful census in 1807 the municipality recorded 234 Jews in 28 extended families with full residence rights, and eight temporary-resident families. Four other families without residence permits were expelled.

Exterior detail, synagogue in Subotica. Raw brick accents and brick-colored stucco ornaments on the towers, along with unexpected open arches, add visual interest and excitement.

Jakab Loebel opened a tailoring shop in 1805, nominally limited at first to Jewish clientele. There were other restrictions on Jewish activities. The community's first rabbi, Rabbi Shlomo Pulitzer, paid several fines for conducting weddings in "a foreign tongue"—Hebrew. *Melamdim* (Hebrew teachers) were harassed for "illegal teaching." On the other hand, Jews could now move about the empire with internal passports as freely as non-Jews. In 1816, they gained the right to buy real estate. As the Subotica population doubled from 21,537 to 41,707 between 1805 and 1846, the Jewish population increased ninefold, from 67 to 623. Twenty-five Subotica Jews fought in the unsuccessful 1848 Hungarian uprising against Austria. With the rebels' defeat, the victors exacted a "disloyalty fine" from the Jewish population. Subotica's share was 25,000 pairs of laced boots for the Austrian army, an amount the *kehillah* could not possibly muster. On appeal, the governor reduced the amount by 12 percent and accepted payment over a three-year period.

Nearby Novi Sad and other towns suffered extensive destruction in the 1848 fighting. Relatively undamaged Subotica emerged as the regional commercial center, to the prosperity of some of its Jews. The widening of socio-economic differences and the increasing social friction within the *kehillah* demanded attention and help for the poorer Jews. Under the energetic leadership of Babette Schiffer, a number of housewives joined together as the Women's Organization to provide mutual help and support of the needy. This organization was active until World War II, and in its last few years collected the heady sum of 12,000 forints for philanthropic purposes.

Austria extended a limited autonomy to Hungary in 1867, recognizing Budapest as the capital and confirming the new status with the name, Austria–Hungary. Subotica passed to Hungarian jurisdiction as "Szabadka." As the *kehillah* grew in numbers, Jewish professionals and academics played an increasing role in the civic life of the city. When the final barriers to full civil rights for Jews fell away, the general prosperity improved their situation and they took their place among the economic leaders of the town. Subotica Jews were owners of a steel mill and several factories that produced spirits, food products, chocolate, metal works, brick works, and cardboard.

In 1868 Hungarian Jewry divided into an Orthodox faction and a Neolog (Hungarian Reform) majority that aspired to changes in ritual and to deeper involvement in the general community and the country. A majority in Subotica opted for Neolog affiliation, but it remained loyal to a beloved Orthodox rabbi, Dr. Kutna, who served from 1861 to 1902. Rabbi Kutna never learned the difficult Hungarian language. He spoke to his congregants in either Yiddish, German, or Hebrew. Jews who moved in from neighboring villages late in his tenure swelled the Orthodox minority to 10 percent of the community.

In 1896, as part of the framework of nationwide festivities to celebrate a thousand years of the Austrian monarchy, the Women's Organization opened a public kitchen, the *népkonyha*.

Plan of the synagogue in Subotica. (Courtesy of Rudolf Klein.)

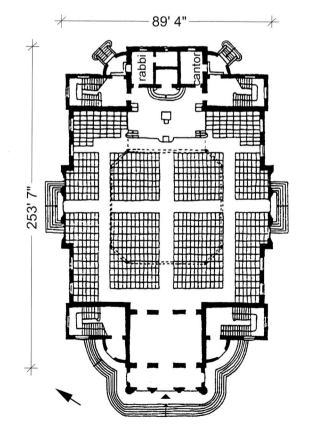

THE SYNAGOGUE IN SUBOTICA

Standing alone on the barren lot, the synagogue is an incongruous but delightful flight of fancy. The architects added Jewish symbols and concepts to the Magyar folk motifs and Oriental elements of the Secessionist (Hungarian Art-Nouveau) vernacular to present a refreshingly new interpretation of space and mass.

The most striking external feature is the Oriental three-tiered central dome, covered with shiny, green-glazed tiles, and visually balanced by smaller two-tiered cupolas on low turrets at the four corners. An elaborate arch of stucco inserts surrounds each of the four large rose windows. Stars of David in the gables and over the domes, and modest Tablets of the Law at the apexes of the gables identify the building as a synagogue. The corner towers enclose stairways leading up to the gallery.

The interior's central eight-sided area suggests the shape of the *Ohel Mo'ed*, the Israelite desert Tabernacle. The interior focuses on a massive Ark between colossal winged pillars surrounded with organ pipes above and at the sides. In the subtle asymmetry of the Secession, the stucco pediment sweeps up in free curves, bearing palm branches and a soft, central Star of David to the lofty, understated Tablets of the Law. The sanctuary contains 1,300 seats. Graceful arches and steel pillars support the galleries and the domed ceiling.

The frescoed walls bloom with stylized local wild flowers interspersed among tiny hearts and Stars of David. Architect Jakab wrote about the decoration in 1925, "The flowers in colorful harmony spread a feeling of happiness. Variations from rose to blue symbolize the rising sun, with golden rays shining on humanity from a dark blue sky. Sukkot's palm branches and angel wings endow the Ark with the temper of the desert Tabernacle and its cherubs. Floral motifs in the stained glass strive toward the dome, to connect earthly existence with Paradise." The community's acceptance of such a profusion of Hungarian folklore elements amounted to a profound social statement, highlighting the *kehillah*'s identification with the surrounding culture.

Subotica synagogue facade, Secessionist style (Hungarian Art Nouveau). Dezsö Jakab and Marcell Komor, architects, 1903. The Secessionist movement blended Hungarian folk motifs and selected Oriental elements. Punctuated by a trio of Stars of David in oriental style, each facade is dominated by a central cusped gable, with a decorated border to emphasize its undulating shape.

Interior of synagogue, east to the *Aron Kodesh*. Fresco cartouches low on the proscenium arch evoke musical acclaim from Psalm 150: *"Halleluhu b'minim v'ugav"* ("praise Him with lute and pipe"; v. 4) on the left, and *"Halleluhu b'nevel v'khinor"* ("praise Him with harp and lyre"; v. 3) on the right.

Since the number of indigent Jews was small, the kitchen volunteers provided supplementary nutrition to all schoolchildren and monetary help and food to any of the city's poor. Their work was particularly beneficial later among the numerous orphans and refugees of World War I.

Because the turn-of-the-century *kehillah* numbered 3,024 persons, the need for a new synagogue became urgent. The Subotica *parnassim* closely watched the synagogue-design contest held at nearby Szeged and eagerly snapped up the unexecuted second-prize plan. It was a joint project by Budapest architects Marcell Komor and Dezső Jakab, who had worked with Odon Lechner, the father of modern Hungarian architecture. Jews and gentiles enthusiastically subscribed to the bond-issue that covered the construction cost of 150,000 forints, barely a seventh of what the Szeged *kehillah* spent to

build its own first-prize selection. The synagogue, a prestigious Subotica landmark since 1903, is located near the city's main square, in the middle of a landscaped complex that originally included a Jewish school, community center, and ritual slaughterhouse. All but the synagogue were demolished in the 1970s.

With a grand new synagogue, the community entered the twentieth century under the devoted leadership of Rabbi Dr. Bernat Singer (r. 1902–1916), and dynamic president, Dr. Adolf Klein (r. 1903–1930). It was an era of intensive cultural, educational, and communal activities. Dr. Klein, later chief physician in the Subotica Jewish hospital, introduced a democratic regime and modernized religious services, raising the community's prestige and self-image. Subotica became one of the earliest pre–World War I communities in Hungary to embrace Zionism. It

The dome interior. High above a square central area, an octagonal tambour supports the enormous central dome, the matching diameter and height of which are 82.5 feet. The decorations are rhythmic, as on an embroidered peasant blouse: blazing rays radiate from the central corona, rows of floral clusters and vegetative designs run along the architectural lines and embrace the multiple windows. A lone Hebrew inscription above the arch, with the letters incorrectly spaced, reads: *"V'ahavta l're'akha kamokha"* ("Love your fellow as yourself"; Lev. 19:18).

of Jewish property, demobilized Jewish soldiers organized for community self-defense. Later, even as the Yugoslav kingdom stabilized, Jews had to pay "war profits" taxes and had limited access to government jobs or contracts. Distressed by the suffering multitude of the war-wounded, prosperous Lajos Pollack set up a fund to encourage and support Jewish medical students. Still not satisfied, he initiated a project to create a Jewish hospital, traveling through the country to solicit contributions. The exertion ruined his health, and he died before the hospital (named for Rabbi Singer) was dedicated in 1923—a prime achievement of the Subotica *kehillah* and the only institution of its kind in Yugoslavia.

By the early 1930s Jewish industrialists helped revitalize the city's economy with their diversified businesses. Kalman Steiner's service station for railroad cars employed 600 people; Armin Roth's hat factory, 250; Adolf Glied and Sandor Kohns' leather factory, 300; Imre Rothman's furniture factory, 150; the Goldner brothers' ice-box factory, 100; and hundreds of workers raised and processed poultry for Rafael Hartman's slaughter houses.

Numbering 6,000, six percent of the city, the *kehillah* was the fourth largest in Yugoslavia. Jewish cultural life blossomed. The synagogue choir developed into a large musical society named Kinor (Violin). The Re'ut (Friendship) society generated cultural activities. A major Zionist sport society, Koach (Strength), conducted programs and pageants on Jewish national themes. It sponsored clubs in soccer, boxing, fencing, Ping-Pong, and athletics, achieving a Balkan championship win in gymnastics. Hashomer Hatzair, Blau-Weis, and Betar flourished among the youth, as did, quietly, Communism. Zionism had the harmonious support of both Orthodox and Neolog groups. Twelve Subotica *ḥalutzim* left for Palestine before World War II. Branches of the Freemasons and B'nai B'rith were active.

Yugoslavia capitulated to the *Wehrmacht* on April 17, 1941, after ten forlorn days of fighting. The Germans dismembered the country, annexing parts to the Reich, to Italy, Hungary, and to

generated the custom of handsome contributions for building *Eretz Yisrael,* especially at family celebrations.

In the chaotic, lawless aftermath of the First World War and the wave of widespread pillage

Detail of ceiling decoration. Stylized gold-tinted plant motifs, framed in deep blue, contrast sharply against a deep orange field. Warm colors predominate throughout.

Ark detail. The long-winged cherubs who protected the desert tabernacle in the book of Exodus inspired wings for the capitals of the Ark pillars.

an independent Croatia. Hungarian troops over-ran their assigned region, including Subotica, with vicious brutality and organized the murder of communists—mostly Jews. The only resist-ance the Nazis met as they entered the city was a barrage of homemade bombs by Jewish youths, most of whom were caught and executed. Orga-nized genocide went into operation at impro-vised death camps within Yugoslavia long before the Wannsee Conference of January 20, 1942, where the Nazi Final Solution was secretly

adopted. Nearly a quarter of the Jewish youths mobilized in Yugoslav forced labor came from Subotica and most of them did not survive the ordeals of starvation and unremitting toil. In April 1944 the Nazis and local supporters herded the remaining Jews of Subotica and the Bacska county into a Jewish quarter centered in the still-functioning Jewish hospital. Deportation of these 3,200 people took place on June 16, 1944.

The partisans liberated the city on October 10, 1944. Of the pre-war Jewish population, 75 percent had perished. Some survivors returned to their pillaged homes, while many migrated to the West. Despite difficulties in readjustment, the city's Jews renewed their activities under the aegis of a protective socialist regime that promised equal rights and religious freedom. The new administration, under Tito, granted civil rights but also nationalized most of the Jewish business property. The future did not seem bright for young people. In 1947 many survivors joined the Jewish underground in smuggling refugees to Palestine. Eight hundred of the 1,200 Subotica Jews opted for *aliyah* when Israel was established in 1948.

The small postwar *kehillah* could not take care of the synagogue. It donated the building to the municipality in 1979, with the stipulation that it serve municipal cultural purposes and remain available to the *kehillah* for occasional assembly. The roof and the central dome, long in danger of collapse, were repaired, but there was no money for extensive restoration. Nearly a decade of use as a theater caused additional deterioration of the interior. Real-estate developers of the 1980s proposed to erect luxury apartments on the site. Although the scattered community buildings in the synagogue complex were torn down quickly, new construction at the site might have damaged the synagogue. Bowing to public opposition, the developers abandoned the project. In its 1996 worldwide survey, the World Monuments Fund listed the synagogue in Subotica among the 100 most endangered precious cultural sites, some of which will receive grants for restoration. The synagogue waits, silent and empty of people.

GREECE

Jewish roots in Greece reach back to the time of Alexander the Great, mid-fourth century B.C.E. and the dawn of the Hellenistic world, with its fusion of peoples, religions, and cultures. Here, on the shrub-covered mountain slopes of northern Greece, small Jewish communities first encountered the attractive, seductive elements of Greek culture and ideals. The meeting of these cultures nourished the roots of nascent Christianity and the many-faceted Western civilization.

Penetrating throughout the Near East, Greek language and culture attracted much of the upper class in Judea, the Hellenizers, putting them into conflict with the Zealots, defenders of Jewish religion and the use of Hebrew and Aramaic. The conflict was a source of tension in the *kehillot* of Greece also and in other parts of the Diaspora. In 168 B.C.E., Judea, under Hasmonean leadership, revolted against the Hellenizers and the declining Seleucid king, Antiochus Epiphanes IV. Many of the Jews sold into slavery during the war augmented the Greek *kehillot*. The victorious Hasmoneans purified and rededicated the Temple in 164 B.C.E., established an autonomous Jewish state, and set up a royal and priestly dynasty that lasted until 37 B.C.E.

The conquest of the Hellenistic world by the expanding Roman empire brought no particular upheaval to the Jewish communities. Tolerantly treated, they adopted the Greek language and engaged in Jewish proselytizing alongside their early Christian neighbors. As the Western Roman Empire began to crumble early in the fourth century C.E., Constantine established a new capital, Constantinople, on the ancient site of Byzantium and granted Christianity equal status with pagan cults. In 380 C.E., Theodosius I formally adopted Christianity to be the state religion and thereby rendered the Jewish position equivocal. Jews were a living embodiment of God's promise to his believers, but they rejected the Christian Messiah, now symbolized by the emperor. Nonetheless, the Jews of Byzantium rarely suffered persecution. By 644, after the conquest of the Persian Empire by the Arabs, most of the *kehillot* in the Diaspora found themselves under Arab–Moslem rule.

It was the Moslem caliph al-Mutawakkil who first required non-Moslems in 850 to wear outwardly distinctive signs, initially a yellow turban for all infidels. The manner of external identification went through a number of agonizing sartorial variations thereafter, but the Mamluks decreed in 1301 that Jews must wear yellow turbans, Christians blue, and Samaritans red. This ruling was the probable origin of the yellow identifying color applied uniquely to Jews in later Christian times and places.

Despite repeated foreign invasions into the kingdom, Byzantine (Romaniot) Jews continued to inhabit several large cities in the northern mainland, especially Salonika. They identified with Greek culture and had little contact with Jews from either Europe or the Near East. Brief, but fascinating descriptions of several Jewish communities in Greece appear in the notes of Benjamin of Tudela, a Jewish gem merchant from Spain who traveled to the Holy Land in 1167.

The Fourth Crusade in 1204 was harsh to the Jews in Greece. The Crusaders moved south from Salonika, distributing the land they took as fiefdoms. Several *kehillot* vanished as the Jews fled before the invaders. The Turks regrouped, and by the mid-fifteenth century nearly all the Byzantine territories in Greece came under the control of the rising Ottoman dynasty. Many Jews from mainland Greece were drafted to help repopulate and rebuild the devastated capital of Constantinople. Jews from Hungary and Provence came into the partly depopulated Greek lands, and the mass expulsion of Spanish and Portuguese Jewry (1492–1497) brought further waves of immigrants to the Ottoman Empire. The mixture of languages, rituals, and customs generated friction with resident Romaniot Jews until the more numerous Sephardic element eventually predominated. Salonika absorbed most of the Sephardic Jews, becoming the largest Jewish community in Greece until after World War II.

The long years of struggle, from the sixteenth through the eighteenth centuries, between the Ottoman Empire and the Venetian commanders over the Greek territories, were a difficult period, when many *kehillot* were destroyed. The appearance of the false Messiah, Shabbetai Tzvi, in 1665 shook the entire Jewish world and threw several Greek *kehillot,* where he had many followers, into turmoil. After Shabbetai Tzvi embraced Islam many of his disciples also converted to that faith.

During the Greek War of Independence (1821–1823) local Jews suffered harassment and even murder because of their loyalty to the Ottomans. Subsequent blood libels and angry riots encouraged many Jews to flee to Italy, Turkey, and Egypt. The loyalty of Greek Jewry to Greece during the war against Turkey in 1897 did not prevent anti-Jewish riots. Jews fled to Salonika for refuge. The first waves of Ashkenazic immigrants from Northern Europe arrived in the nineteenth century, and settled mainly in Athens. Among them was the German banking family of Baron de Rothschild, which was influential in the growth of the Athens Jewish community. Further annexations after the Balkan war (1912–1913) increased the number of Jews in Greece to 100,000.

The Lausanne Treaty of 1923 between Turkey and Greece provided for a population exchange that brought 100,000 Greeks from Anatolia to Salonika. The increased competition for jobs in this port city caused a brief deterioration in Jewish livelihood, but it did not affect Jews in other towns. The legal autonomy of the *kehillot* was offset by state policy aimed at Hellenization and assimilation of ethnic minorities. But the *kehillot* prospered, especially in Salonika. Its 75,000 Jews, comprising half the city's population in 1904, maintained 30 synagogues and religiously closed down the port on the Sabbath and on Jewish holidays. Although masses of Jews had emigrated, Greek Jewry still numbered nearly 80,000 in 1939—including 56,000 in Salonika and 3,000 in Athens—in some 40 active communities. Many *kehillot* supported extensive networks of institutions and organizations, most of them Zionist. Greek Jews enjoyed a varied cultural life, publishing religious and secular literature, and maintaining a flourishing Jewish press in Ladino, French, and Greek.

Soon after the outbreak of the Second World War and the occupation of Greece, the Nazis pressured their Bulgarian and Italian allies to implement the Final Solution on Greek communities under their jurisdiction, but the response varied among the occupied zones. By August 1943, 70,000 Jews had been deported to the extermination camps, including 48,533 from Salonika. In October 1943, Archbishop Damaskinos ordered monasteries and convents in Athens and the provincial towns to shelter Jews. His letter in defense of the Jews to the Nazi general Stroop brought threats of execution to the brave archbishop. Many Jews were saved by heroic actions of Greek clergy, police, and the resistance. Some Athenian Jews hid with Christian neighbors, escaping later by boat to Turkey. Thirteen-hundred Jews fought with the Greek partisans.

Eighty-seven percent of Greek Jewry perished in the Holocaust, leaving 10,000 survivors, most of them destitute. Only those who renounced their Greek citizenship were allowed to apply for emigration to Palestine. Rebuilding Jewish life in a post-war Greece that was torn by civil war and economic crises raised insuperable problems. Bureaucracy and tangled court procedures delayed restitution of Jewish property. The community recovered slowly, aided by its resilience and by support from the American Joint Distribution Committee and the Jewish Agency.

The Central Board of Jewish Communities in Greece (KIS) coordinates educational and philanthropic organizations and activities, and concerns itself with Jewish interests in the country, including restoration of abandoned synagogues. International support for the restorations of two synagogues, in Veroia and Hania, has come from the World Monuments Fund and from the Roth-schild Foundation, the Ronald S. Lauder Foundation, and other family foundations. Despite their economic integration, the small number of Jews in Greece, where the synagogues and all the rabbis are Sephardic and Orthodox, are reserved about their Judaism. They are respected by their Greek-Orthodox neighbors, but they tend to socialize mainly with other Jews.

Jews in Greece today number about 5,000, of whom 3,000 live in Athens. Fewer than 1,000 maintain the once-renowned Salonika community, and 350 comprise the vibrant community of Larissa. Small communities exist also in Corfu, Halkis, Ioannina, Rhodes, Trikkala, and Volos, some of them still following ancient, but disappearing Romaniot rites. The Greek government and the Greek national tourism organization view the Jewish heritage in Greece as part of their national heritage, and concern themselves with the upkeep of abandoned sites and the publication of booklets for tourists. There is much to interest the Jewish traveler to Greece and its islands.

The recently refurbished Jewish Museum of Greece in Athens houses a fine collection of artifacts covering more than 2,000 years of Jewish history in the country. Perhaps the oldest synagogue site in Greece is a ruin from the fifth century B.C.E., in Athens' ancient marketplace, the agora at the foot of the Acropolis. Other synagogue remains exist on the islands of Aegina, Kos, and Zakyntos. In Hania, on the island of Crete, the seventeenth century Etz Ḥayyim (Tree of Life) synagogue was restored and reopened in the Fall of 1999 as a research center on the history of the Jews of Crete. On the island of Delos, the intrepid traveler can still find the remains of a synagogue from the first century B.C.E., with its partially preserved marble "Throne of Moses" used, presumably, by the rabbis.

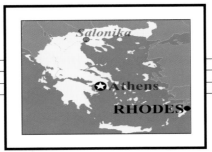

"LIGHT UP THE SABBATH LAMP, LADIES"

As the beautiful island of Rhodes rose from the waters of the Aegean Sea, the Greek sun god Helios chose it for his sacred domain. It became enchanted, always under his tender protection. Helios fell in love with the comely nymph Rhode, daughter of the sea gods Poseidon and Amphitrite, and named the island in her honor: thus, the Greek origin of the name. Jews trace the name in the lineage from Noah's son Japhet, father of Javan, progenitor of Greece, to Javan's son, Dodanim (Gen. 10:4, but rendered as Rodanim in the Septuagint and 1 Chron. 1:7), who was the progenitor of Rhodes. "From these, the maritime nations branched out" (Gen. 10:5).

Designed and built around 407 B.C.E. by Hippodamus of Miletus, the foremost architect of his time, Rhodes became the most aesthetic city in the Mediterranean basin. It was a major banking center with many public buildings, temples, markets, and wide streets leading to a harbor that sheltered by its quays ships from the Mediterranean and Africa's west coast. Rhodian merchants founded colonies on the coast of Asia Minor. The city became a center for culture and the arts and a concourse for philosophers, athletes, and sculptors.

A bronze statue of Helios, cast by the sculptor Chares in 302 B.C.E., and known as the Colossus of Rhodes, stood at the entrance to the harbor. At about 120 feet high, it was one

Rhodes town plan. 1. Jewish Martyr's Square. 2. Synagogue Kahal Shalom. (Adapted from N. Stavroulakis, *Jewish Sites and Synagogues of Greece.*)

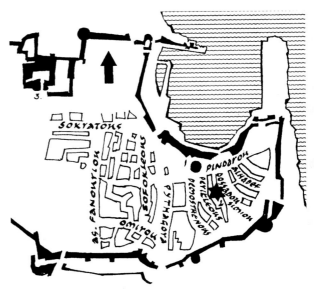

of the seven wonders of the ancient world, looming over ships in full sail as they entered the harbor between its legs. The statue collapsed in the tremors of an earthquake that destroyed the city in 227 B.C.E. and lay there shattered for nine hundred years. In 653, the Arab conqueror Mu'awiya ordered the destruction of its remains. An enterprising Jew from ancient Edessa in faraway northwest Mesopotamia is reputed to have purchased the scrap. Back on terra firma, he led a caravan of 90 camels through the desert, loaded with the valuable salvaged bronze.

In the polyglot cosmopolitan circumstances of the ancient world, Judea, also a maritime nation, was well represented in foreign ports. By the beginning of the Common Era virtually no major Mediterranean city was without an established Jewish colony. Jewish traders settled in Rhodes perhaps as early as the second century B.C.E. Hellenized Jews, estranged by the Maccabean victory in 165 B.C.E., added to their number. Contacts between Jewish traders from Rhodes and merchants from Rome, Egypt, and Asia Minor date from before the Common Era. Rome easily tolerated the Jews scattered over the empire until Christianity spread in earnest in the third and fourth centuries.

Rhodes was refuge for the Hospitalers—Knights of St. John of Jerusalem—in 1291, when the Mamelukes drove them from Jerusalem and, in a last battle, from Acre. Thirteen years later the knights controlled the island. Ruling the island for over two centuries, the crusaders amassed huge estates and much wealth. They transformed Rhodes into a center for international trade, military activity, and piracy. Renovations of the city's huge fortifications and numerous inns and castles date from this period. Jews were in great demand as outstanding smelters and metalworkers, producing prized swords and daggers. Although they lived peacefully under the crusaders' rule, they were often confined to their own section of the city, *vicus Judeorum,* under the city walls near the port, where they built their Kahal Gadol (Large Synagogue) in the fifteenth century.

In the account of his travels to Eretz Yisrael, the Italian Jewish traveler, Meshoullam ben

Menaḥem da Volterra described the Rhodians' struggles in 1480. Jewish men and women participated in battles to repel a Turkish attack by Sultan Mehmet II. Although Rhodes boasted protective towers, gates, moats, and drawbridges, the city and the Jewish quarter underwent massive destruction during the 38-day siege. Jews patriotically dragged the rubble of their ruined houses to reinforce the city walls. Their loyalty gained a reward of 100 ducats from Grand Master Pierre D'Aubusson from city revenues toward rebuilding their synagogue, but it was not rebuilt until 1522. Jews and Christians alike believed that a miracle had delivered the city from the Turks, but Rhodes did not fully recover from that attack and from the earthquakes of 1481–2. Many Jews left the island.

Only 22 Jewish families remained in 1493, living in poverty, mainly on the women's earnings in silk production. They consumed neither meat nor wine, reported Chief Rabbi Ovadiah de Bertinoro of Palestine after a visit, since they had no *sheḥitah* (ritual slaughter) nor could they produce kosher wine. Yet he found the Jews "gentle, well mannered and intelligent. They could have been princes." Other travelers commented on the beauty of the Jewish women and their outstanding skill in embroidery. The *kehillah* followed the Romaniot Greek-language tradition, the liturgy of which differs from both Sephardic and Ashkenazic traditions.

In appreciation of Master D'Aubusson's victory over the Turks, the pope elevated him to cardinal. Obsessed by pious gratitude at his sudden elevation to prelacy, D'Aubusson determined to "purify" the city. Accusing the Jews of "corrupting the Christians" and causing the severe plague of 1498 to 1499, he obtained an order from the Council of the Knights to expel whoever failed to accept Catholicism within 40 days. Children and many adult Jews were forcibly converted, while others were tortured to death. D'Aubusson died suddenly and although his demise canceled the expulsion, persecutions continued.

During the following decades, Christian pirates seized ships from which they captured more than 2000 Jews and enslaved them to work on fortifications. With no hope for succor by loyalty to the Knights, Jews put their hopes on a change of regime. When the Turks, under Suleiman the Magnificent (1520–1566), besieged the island for six months in 1522, the Jews sided with the invader. Individuals spied for the Turks. An enforced convert to Christianity, Dr. Libertus Cominto conveyed a map of the city to the Turks, an act for which Rhodian authorities had him hacked to pieces. Two to three thousand Jews, many of them former captives, helped the invaders by filling the moat with sandbags. Turkish forces entered the city in triumph as the Jews hailed the victory.

The *kehillah* prospered under tolerant Ottoman rule for nearly 400 years until 1912. Those who had forcibly been converted returned openly to Judaism. Sultan Suleiman encouraged exiles from Spain to settle in Rhodes. He awarded them a firman—an edict granting privileges such as autonomy and religious freedom, as well as free housing, a 100-year tax exemption, and guaranteed availability of kosher meat at reasonable prices. Many Sephardim emigrated from other cities in the Ottoman empire. Jews outnumbered the Turks, and created in Rhodes a major Sephardic center. The numerically reinforced Sephardim soon outnumbered the Romaniots and badgered them for changes in the liturgy. Tension between the two communities did not ease until the Romaniots completely assimilated into the Sephardic tradition. Rabbi Moshe de Vushal succeeded in forcing the union in 1668, in view of the messianism that threatened even after the apostasy of Shabbetai Tzvi and his followers. The Romaniots adopted Sephardic customs, the Sephardic *maḥzor* (festival prayer book), and the Judeo-Spanish language, Ladino. The rabbi saved the community, but lost his son Shlomo, who followed the false prophet and converted to Islam.

Community life centered around the synagogues: the large Romaniot synagogue, Kahal Gadol, dating from the Hospitalers' period in 1480, and the Sephardic Kahal Shalom, built in 1577, renovated in 1593 which is the only one still standing. Of the two other smaller synagogues, one was built by the Komondo family in

Lucia Sulam, caretaker, in the portal of the Kahal Shalom synagogue. "There were 4,000 Jews in Rhodes before the war. Now we number about 35. We have a *Pesaḥ* seder together and meet for the High Holidays. There is no rabbi, no weddings or Bar Mitzvahs. But," she gestured with a smile, "there is no intermarriage with the Greeks."

the nineteenth century. The other, formally Tikkun Hazzot, was colloquially called *Kahal de los Ricos* (Synagogue of the Rich). There were also several *batei midrash* (houses of study).

The narrow ghetto alleys echoed the sounds of daily activities and residents' greetings. Before sundown on Fridays one heard, *"Asinder, mujeres"* ("Light up the Sabbath lamp, ladies"), and before Rosh Hashanah, during the month of Elul, the cry was, *"A seliḥot, hermanos"* ("To the forgiveness prayers, brothers"). The synagogue street and the surrounding flower-decked *Juderia* (Jewish quarter) hummed with Jewish life that poured over into the nearby square. There the stalls were astir on market days, with merchants, peddlers, and customers doing business in Turkish, Greek, Italian, Judeo-Spanish, and sometimes French or English. Sounds of the tradesmen and fragrances from the open food stalls mingled in colorful confusion. The crowded taverns offered the ever-popular *raki,* a sweet Turkish liqueur.

The *kehillah* organized well: a religious council (*bet din*) and the *parnassim* governed all aspects of religious, social, and economic life.

The chief rabbi (*hahambaşi*) had the power to veto decisions of the council and to pronounce an excommunicating *ḥerem*. These governing bodies drew up agreements (*haskamot*) safeguarding all members and binding all to observance. The community received revenues from the tax assessment (*arikha*) after every Passover, and from taxes on the products Jews produced: meat, wine, cheese, and brandy. Another source of income was the auctioning of mitzvot, or ritual synagogue procedures. The proceeds supported *bikkur ḥolim* for the poor and the sick; *ḥevra de los kabarim* provided funeral services; *ozer dalim* helped the indigent to diminish beg-

THE SHALOM SYNAGOGUE IN RHODES

The building of Kahal Shalom is hardly distinguished among the other houses on the synagogue street. Just below the high rectangular windows, two stone arches bridge the narrow street to join the opposite buildings for mutual support. An unmarked stone portal affords entrance to an open pebbled corridor, with the synagogue on the left, and stairs to the *meḥitzah* at the end of the corridor. Up a few steps on its right is a small, restful courtyard planted with fruit trees and a grapevine that trails over the trellis shading the corridor. The only synagogue still standing in Rhodes, Kahal Shalom has the benefit of careful renovations sponsored by Rhodian Jews living abroad, and it functions occasionally when a minyan is available.

A choice example of Balkan synagogue architecture, the interior is sparkling in sharp contrast to an austere facade. Carved multicolored geometric capitals are painted predominantly in dark blue to harmonize with the paler blue walls. The crystal chandeliers, customary in Greek churches and synagogues, sparkle between the arches. The rectangular polished wood *tevah* is centrally located among rows of chairs facing in on three sides. The wide *meḥitzah* runs across the western wall. A row of high windows surrounds the prayer room, providing adequate, pleasant illumination. Lively frescoes cover the walls, depicting many symbols—harp, shofar, *lulav,* and menorah—all amid a profusion of flowers. Painted in the nineteenth century, the frescoes have been recently restored.

The synagogue interior, to the east from the *meḥitzah*. The graceful central arch frames the *Heikhal* area on the eastern wall where the two marble-framed Arks flank the doors leading out to the courtyard and *sukkah.* Scattered Persian rugs cover portions of the patterned stone floor.

The Shalom Synagogue (1577) interior to the west. Uneven transverse arches on stone pillars and pilasters divide the synagogue into a wide central area and narrow aisles on the sides.

ging; Sociedad de las Damas assisted pregnant women who were needy; Gioventù Ebràica di Rodi (Rhodes Jewish Youth) encouraged education, recreation, and sport.

The community reveled in the epithet, "Little Jerusalem." Native rabbis officiated along with noteworthy scholars invited from Sephardic centers in Alexandria, Constantinople, Salonika, Jerusalem, and Safed. The rabbis taught in the yeshivot and directed the conduct of the community in more than religion. With the oft-repeated claim that violations of religious law brought on calamities, they scrutinized everything, including the modes of everyday behavior: movement on Shabbat, women's dress—even at home—and how mothers should sing to children in the cradle. The rabbis' erudite *responsa* covered solemn religious issues. But some were less serious: the *kashrut* of swordfish that has scales only when it is young, or of grape leaves to which minute insects may have adhered; the use of a Turkish bath, *ḥamam,* as a mikveh; and the ritual permis-

Wall decorations. Elaborate nineteenth-century paintings decorate the walls with floral embellishments, symbols, and inscriptions. Here, a symmetrical garland embraces two elongated Tablets of the Law on which are inscribed the first two of the Ten Commandments: "I am the Lord Thy God" and "You shall have no other gods beside me." (Exod. 20:2,3). Three pairs of horns hang among the vines and flowers: cornucopias represent the classical heritage, a pair of *shofarot* and two trumpets, perhaps suggest the Levite musicians in the Temple. A *ner tamid* hangs above a ribbon banner: "Hear O Israel, the Lord our God, the Lord is one." (Deut.6: 4). The inscription above the crown on the right reads *Keter Torarr* (an error in restoration), instead of the intended *Keter Torah,* Torah crown.

Martyron Evreon (Jewish Martyrs' Square). Only a short distance from the synagogue, the square was called Calle Ancha (Seahorse Square) until it was renamed after World War II in tribute to the nearly 1,500 Jews of Rhodes who perished in the *Shoah.*

Wall plaque memorial to Jewish families of Rhodes, victims of the Holocaust.

sibility of a Shabbat promenade on ships in the harbor.

The upper echelons of Rhodian Jews managed well. Families such as Alhadeff, Notrica, Menasche, Amato, and Sourmani opened department stores and other enterprises in Rhodes and other cities of Greece and Anatolia. Sons of the prosperous families became bankers, diplomats, doctors, engineers, and international traders. The majority of the Jews on the island, however, remained poor and spent their days as peddlers, dealers in junk and rags, tailors, blacksmiths, and fishermen.

Traditional teaching methods dominated elementary education until a progressive Talmud Torah was founded in 1899. Two years later it affiliated with the Alliance Israelite Universelle and introduced modern methods and a broad curriculum. Some 30 to 40 boys continued to attend Turkish primary and secondary schools. In the absence of organized education for girls, the Catholic School of the Sisters attracted some Jewish girls and inevitably exerted its influence on them. When one adolescent girl converted to Catholicism in 1902, the *parnassim* hastily ordered the opening of a school for girls.

After the Balkan wars in 1912, Rhodes and its 4,500 Jews came under Italian rule. With the cooperation of Italian governor Mario Lago, the *kehillah* founded a Collegio Rabbinico in 1927. It was an enlightened rabbinical seminary with classes in the humanities and the sciences, and its graduates served Italian Jewry and other communities of the region.

The last great chief rabbi was Rabbi Reuven Eliyahu Israel. Descended from a line of Rhodian rabbis, he returned in 1922 from a post in Rumania and served until he died in 1932. He aimed to confer Jewish values on the younger generation and to foster a broad outlook by reforming education to include classics and other concepts of the non-Jewish world. Rabbi Israel spent many years translating rabbinical works, Psalms, and Proverbs into Judeo-Spanish. On Jewish holidays he would read aloud from his translations to an attentive and appreciative congregation. He was politically active and received many honors, including elevation to knighthood by Italy's King Victor Emmanuel.

As twentieth-century ideas and contact with Italian, French, and Greek residents influenced young Jews of the community, many of them went abroad to study and often to settle in foreign lands. Children of the poor also migrated, mostly to Argentina, Brazil, Chile, and the United States. Successful emigrants sent for their families to join them. Between 1918 and 1923, the dwindling Rhodes community experienced a temporary revitalization as over 500 Jews fled from Antalya, Smyrna, Tyre, Greece, and Bulgaria during the war for Turkish independence from Allied occupation.

In 1936 the new Fascist governor, Mario de Vecchi, introduced anti-Semitic laws. One of his first actions was to close the rabbinical seminary. On Friday night, September 1, 1938, the Fascists reactivated stringent racial laws. They expelled Jewish children from public schools and banned *sheḥitah.* The old cemetery was dug up for a park and the bodies had to be exhumed. Those Jews who could afford to escape fled to Palestine, Tangier, or Rhodesia. Germans took control of the island when the Italians capitulated to the Allies on September 8, 1943. British bombs killed eight Jews in the port area, and 26 others during another British bombing as they were leaving the synagogue on Passover. On July 19, 1944, the Gestapo entered the city and began mass deportations without any intervention by British forces. Of the 1,641 Jews deported, only 179 survived. Few returned to the island after the

Suzanna Cohen, on her first return visit to Rhodes in 1991. In 1935, when she was 17, she and her family left the island for Palestine. Accompanied by two of her three daughters from Israel, where she has seventeen grandchildren, Suzanna was overcome with emotion as she walked the alleys of the *Juderia.* Over coffee in a little cafe in the square, she recalled some happy memories of her childhood. "What wonderful weddings we had here. The whole community celebrated. Everybody, especially the children, accompanied the bride and her family on their way to *banio de novia,* the bridal mikveh, before the wedding day, and watched them carrying her dowry on copper trays for all to examine. And the foods! I still prepare for my family some of those wonderful Sephardic delicacies that my mother brought from Salonika: *travados* (honey and almond turnovers), *mustachudos* (spiced nut balls), *kayadif* (shredded pastry mixed with almonds, honey, and cinnamon), *baklava* (a sweet layered filo pastry), and *masapan* (marzipan)."

war, but they have maintained contact with other Rhodian Jews abroad.

As the Nazis rounded up Jews for deportation, compassionate Moslem neighbors helped to hide Judaica and liturgical articles. These trusted people returned the materials to the community after the war, and the items of Judaica are now on display at the Jewish museum in Athens. The restored cemetery contains some old stones from the eighteenth and nineteenth centuries that carry symbols for the vocation of the deceased. One well-marked stone from 1885 has scissors and thimble carved at the bottom to venerate a woman who embroidered silk.

Torah ornaments. On one of the four pillars in the Shalom Synagogue, a silver Torah crown and a pair of brass finials rest on a metal frame cast to include Stars of David as a shelf.

DOUBLE JEOPARDY: THE APOSTLE PAUL AND THE PROPHET NATHAN

Only a day's journey west of Salonika (Thessaloniki) for most of its two-thousand-year existence, Veroia's *kehillah* was bound to the mother metropolis by tradition, by constant interaction, and by family ties. Earliest Jewish settlers came to the town from Salonika in the first century C.E., lured by fertile vineyards and orchards, and by the trade opportunities along the Aliakmon River that drains the low foothills of Macedonia. In times of pillage or terror from foreign armies, Veroia Jews escaped to Salonika for safety. For their part, urban Jews retreated to Veroia in summer for its clear brisk air, or when pestilence swept through the crowded city streets. In the prosperous years before World War I, many rabbis chose the breezy hills of Veroia as a favored summer vacation spot.

In retrospect, it was a tumultuous existence punctuated at times by relatively large population movements, either voluntary or under duress. Twice in its history the *kehillah* was tempted by the prophets of religious apostasy and both times many members succumbed to the missionary exhortations. Nevertheless, it remained a Jewish community that was never entirely eclipsed, even in the *Shoah*.

The Apostle Paul began his career as a fanatical persecutor of Christians. He was on a priestly mission to Damascus to arrest Christians when, on the strength of a vision of Jesus, he himself converted to Christianity. Equally fanatic in his new guise, he was determined to convert the Jews as well as the pagans to Christianity and set out on missions to Cyprus, Asia Minor, Antioch, and Greece. His preaching in the synagogue of Salonika so displeased the pious elders that they "set the city in an uproar" against him and drove him out of town. Taking refuge in Veroia, he had more success there. ". . . these were more noble minded than those

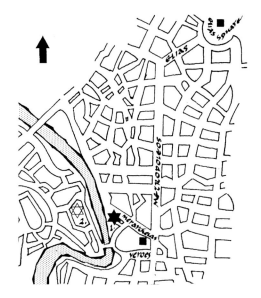

Town map of Veroia. 1. synagogue site. 2. Site of Jewish cemetery. (Adapted from N. Stavroulakis, *Jewish Sites and Synagogues of Greece.*)

in Thessalonica, for they received the word with great eagerness. . . . Many of them . . . believed." But when the watchful Salonika Jews heard of his doings, they came rushing up to Veroia, "agitating and stirring up the crowds." (Acts 17: 5–13). Veroia Jews believed that these New Testament passages influenced local Christians favorably toward them. Local people to this day will point out to the visitor the large flat stone on which Paul allegedly rose to preach in the main square.

Salonika and environs stagnated under Byzantine rule until the expanding Ottoman empire took over after the conquest of Constantinople by Sultan Mehmet II (1451–1481). To rebuild the devastated capital, Mehmet called on all previous residents, Jews in particular, to return to Constantinople, promising them "the best of the land." They came from many towns in Turkey and achieved significant improvement in their economic and religious situations. To increase their numbers, the Sultan conscripted Jews from the Greek mainland, including a large proportion of Veroia Jews. Settling in the Balat quarter of Constantinople in relatively comfortable conditions, the conscripts built their own synagogue, maintained the Romaniot *minhag* (custom), and kept close ties with the home city.

The few who remained in Veroia were traumatized by the sudden disruption of the *kehillah.*

A decade later, Sephardic exiles moved from overcrowded Salonika and augmented the Veroia *kehillah.* Castilian Spanish replaced Greek, and the Romaniot *minhag* gave way to the Sephardic ritual. The immigrants brought new techniques for processing wool and exploited the excellent quality of Veroia's waters for the rinsing. Part of the textile industry moved in from Salonika and became the mainstay of Jewish livelihood in sixteenth-century Veroia. From fleece to saleable garment—spinning, weaving, felling, and dyeing the fabric, and cutting and sewing the coats— was a labor-intensive process lasting a year. Uniforms for Ottoman troops were the primary product.

At the end of the sixteenth century, the industry suffered a sudden decline as its former markets in Europe generated competitive local producers with cheaper goods. The enterprising Veroia community reacted by developing an alternate sheep-associated industry: the production of cheese. Selling the cheese and other goods at the fairs was fraught with the risk of violence from competitors or brigands. As a ruse, Jews dressed like Turks, hid their gold in money belts, and left a provisional divorce at home to allow for their wives to remarry if they should fail to return.

Poverty, plague, and banditry were the norm in Veroia and, indeed, in much of the seventeenth-century Diaspora. In their troubles, Jews looked to religion and to mysticism for relief. Their readiness to latch on to anything that might promise change gave rise to the greatest trauma to strike the Veroia community, as it struck other Jewish communities across Europe, North Africa, and the Levant. It was a trauma enflamed by a Jew, Nathan of Gaza (1643– 1680), prophet of the false Messiah, Shabbetai Zevi (1626–1676).

Jerusalem born and educated, Nathan moved to Gaza in 1663 as the young, intellectual son-in-law of a wealthy Gazan merchant. The messianic movement had already spread and engaged the lives of many Jews. Coming from all classes of the population, they practiced fasts, mortifica-

Inscription under the eaves of a house in the ghetto. In the eighteenth century most of the houses in the Jewish quarter were destroyed by fire, but they were soon rebuilt in traditional Macedonian style, linked internally by connecting doors on the ground floor. Inscriptions and floral decorations were often painted high on the external walls. One of the houses still bears a verse under the eaves, *"Im eshkaḥeikh Yerushalayim tishkaḥ yemini,"* ("If I forget you, O Jerusalem, let my right hand wither"; Ps. 137:5), and the Hebrew date 5619 (1859).

claimed himself the Messiah. Opposed in Jerusalem, he and his 12 apostles proceeded toward Constantinople. From Gaza, Nathan proclaimed the need for mass repentance in anticipation of the Redemption. There were waves of rumor and legend ascribing miracles to the "Messiah," but neither he nor his prophet needed to perform miracles nor offer proof. Their mission demanded no more than simple faith.

In September of 1665, Nathan announced that the redemption was at hand. From his home in Smyrna, Shabbetai declared that he would unseat the sultan and proceed to the legendary Sambatyon River to return with the ten lost tribes. Since Nathan's prophetic powers were perceived as genuine, his endorsement of Shabbetai Zevi's messianism gave a critical impetus to the mass movement that swept the Jewish world. Commerce stopped in some cities as businessmen prepared themselves for the redemption. Many sold property to raise money for the journey to the Holy Land. Support for the movement came also from millenarian circles in England, Holland, and Germany, who awaited the second coming of Christ in 1666.

As they headed for Constantinople, Shabbetai Zevi and his entourage were arrested on February 6, 1666, in Gallipoli and imprisoned. The vizier treated him with unusual leniency and allowed him to hold court in the prison compound. Called to face the divan that June—in the secret presence of the sultan—Shabbetai Zevi was forced to choose between conversion to Islam or execution. Preferring life, he chose Islam. Many of his immediate disciples followed him. Surprisingly, that did not spell an end to the messianic movement. Despite the apostasy of their Messiah, many of his followers could not bear to relinquish the hope of immediate redemption. Primary among them was the prophet Nathan.

Nathan comforted the distressed masses by kabbalistic reasoning and mystical divination. He induced a faith that the apostasy would resolve itself in due time as a mission: Shabbetai would reveal himself later in all his glory as the true Messiah. Nathan spent the next decade in the region of Macedonia, Bulgaria, and Salonika,

tion, and excessive ritual baths in frenzied dedication. Nathan delved into Kabbalah, experiencing visions of the divine world. In his ecstasy, he heard a voice proclaim in God's name that Shabbetai Zevi was the Messiah, and he, Nathan, was prophet to the "son of David."

Nathan had met Shabbetai only briefly, but the mutual attraction was strong. When Shabbetai came to Gaza, it was Nathan who convinced him of his messianic mission. On May 31, 1665, Shabbetai Zevi saw visions, believed, and proin close touch with the Sephardic communities where there was a strong Shabbatean following. He visited Veroia several times, rallying an enthusiastic crowd of believers and setting up a messianic school there. When, finally, Nathan emulated Shabbetai's conversion to Islam, many Veroia Jews—like followers elsewhere—also converted. Immediately, the rabbis made provisions to divorce from apostate husbands those wives who chose not to convert. Most of the Shabbateans clung to their beliefs for a long time, long after the deaths of the "Messiah" and his "prophet." A century elapsed before the movement died out completely. In Veroia, the *kehillah* suffered ideological conflict for more than forty years.

As the Ottoman Empire shrank in influence and power during the eighteenth and nineteenth centuries, control of Mediterranean and Aegean trade shifted to the French. The economic position of the Jewish towns in the region declined. Small communities without a strong economic basis, such as Veroia, suffered more than others. The Jews of northern Greece continued their industry of spinning and weaving silk and wool, concentrating on wholesale trade, and retaining good connections with western Europe and the Orient. The busiest city was Salonika, where nearly all port activities were in the hands of Jewish stevedores, who closed the port down on the Sabbath and on Jewish festivals.

With the start of the Greek revolt in 1812, Greek-Jewish relations suffered a setback because Jews had generally been loyal to the Ottomans. In defeat, the Greeks accused the Jews of treachery, but in victory, too, they often charged them with aiding the enemy. Even Jews who fought alongside the Greeks were not always safe. The monarchy established in 1832 included only the Peloponnesus, the Attic peninsula, and the island of Euboea. During the hundred years of battles and skirmishes, many Greek Jews fled to Italy, Turkey, or Egypt. Fighting between the Greeks and the Turks was especially fierce in Thessaly, where, after a major Greek defeat in 1898, anti-Jewish riots broke out in Larissa and Trikkala. Many of their Jews fled north to Salonika and Veroia, cities still under the Turks.

The old Jewish neighborhood (*mahallasi*) of Veroia, sloping gently down toward the Tripotamos River tributary and the narrow bridge that joins the quarter to the new city. Less than 50 attached houses line the sides of the narrow unpaved street.

Construction of railway lines between Veroia and Salonika in 1894 helped the general prosperity. It is therefore not surprising to find references to the relatively large *kehillah* size in Veroia during those years: in 1905, there were 500 Jews; and in 1910, out of a general population of 10,000, their number approached 600. In 1940, there were 824 Jews in the town.

Ottoman rule in Greece ended with the Balkan Wars of 1912 to 1913, creating approximately the present borders. Veroia Jews became free Greek citizens and the *kehillah* received an accepted legal status. The 100,000 Greeks from Anatolia who arrived in Salonika under the population exchange stipulated in the 1923 Treaty of Lausanne sharpened the competition in commerce and the crafts, again driving some Salonika Jews to Veroia. In the late 1930s many engaged in farming; others ran sheet metal shops or worked in many of the crafts.

Destruction of the community during World War II was swift and merciless. About 150 Jews fled to the hills in 1943, but the Nazis deported 680 Jews to Poland. One hundred thirty-two Jews returned to Veroia after the war and found that squatters had taken over the old Jewish quarter. Among the survivors was Rabbi Obadia Shabbetai, who settled in Salonika after the war and served as religious representative of the community to the Greek authorities. The community dwindled rapidly as some moved to Salonika and most sailed for Israel. One Jewish family still lives in Veroia.

The Jewish quarter with its sagging houses dates from the early eighteenth century. Not far from the courthouse square, a covered passage within a row of connected houses leads to the quarter, called Barbouta. Even today it has the appearance of a ghetto: a small central court surrounded by houses. The external walls have small windows protected by iron bars, and inside corridors connect one house with another. The ghetto gates of heavy wood reinforced with iron bands were closed each night at sundown. The modest ghetto houses were built of stone layers interlaced with strips of lumber. They lined the court and sloped down a narrow alley to a bridge over the river. Richer Jews left the ghetto early in the

David Koen in front of his Veroia glass shop, speaking in Hebrew remembered from ḥeder days. "I was born in Salonika in 1919 and lived there until the war. Salonika, that was a city with Jews! More than 60,000 before the war. After I was liberated from the camps I came to Veroia where I met Sarah and married her. In 1970 we no longer had a *minyan,* so we couldn't pray together any more. My daughter moved to Castoria, in the mountains. My son works with me in the store. And this is my youngest grandson," he added with a wistful smile. "For his Bar Mitzvah, we will have to go to Salonika."

twentieth century and built more spacious houses nearby. Under Greek rule, the now-missing gates were no longer barred since Jews were allowed unlimited exit and fear of intrusion by drunken Turks abated. Jewish women discarded the Moslem veil outside the ghetto, worn until then to avoid harassment from Turkish ruffians.

The synagogue, built early in the mid-nineteenth century in the style of the smaller Salonika prayer houses, sits on a rise at the northern end of the ghetto. Jews once milled about this court and crowded the synagogue on Sabbaths and holidays with songs and prayers. Its *Heikhal* contained 11 Torah scrolls until 1970, when, still in Jewish ownership, it ceased to function for lack of a *minyan* (prayer quorum of 10 men).

Kehillah customs have survived in the memories of an older generation:

- The *kehillah* kept a *Genizah* where it stored scraps of discarded sacred Hebrew print or parchment. During the Hanukkah holiday, a

The synagogue in Veroia, mid-nineteenth century. The wood frame building shows construction from different periods, the earliest a mixture of brick and stone, without plaster. The main facade is exposed masonry with wooden ties. Unused for many years, the synagogue entrance is now overgrown with weeds and shrubs.

solemn procession took the contents of the *Genizah* to the cemetery across the river. The rabbi and the *parnassim* led the way, followed by the two sextons carrying sacks with the holy pages for burial, and members of the *kehillah* singing selections from the liturgy.

- A children's Purim custom was to paint a large log with a Haman face and place it in the mourners' section of the synagogue. Armed with sticks and hammers, the children would gather around the log. Each time the *ḥazzan* chanted the name of Haman during the *Megillah* (Scroll of Esther) reading, the children beat the log vigorously. When the reading was over, the children dragged the log outside to set it afire and danced around it, shouting and singing.

- Weddings took place, often in the synagogue square, with large celebrations on Mondays

and Thursdays, except in the month of Ḥeshvan, in November.

Veroia family names included Azariah, Mordechai, Pinto, Tzarfati, Istromsa, Daniel, Shlomo, and Shabbetai-Chananiah. For the most part, Jews maintained good relations with their neighbors—Greeks, Bulgars, and Turks—who had a nickname for them: *Andalusos,* after Spain's Andalusia.

During World War II, dozens of synagogues were destroyed in Salonika. In other parts of Greece, synagogues left behind by emigrating survivors in post-war years were also demolished. The nineteenth-century synagogue of Veroia and its nearly intact *mahallasi* (neighborhood) remain as an important representative of a Jewish milieu that flourished in the Greek hills for centuries. The Greek Ministry of Culture has registered the Veroia synagogue as a national

THE SYNAGOGUE IN VEROIA

The synagogue prayer room is spacious but nearly bare of furniture in a layout typical of Sephardic rite synagogues in Greece: the seating lines the walls, the *Heikhal* is on the east, and the *bimah* gains prominence in a central space bounded by columns that carry a baldachin. Within the four columns, the area is tiled in a fine geometric pattern, in sharp contrast to the rough wooden planks of the rest of the floor. A sloping reader's desk covered with a frayed damask stands in the middle of the *bimah* square. Six steps up from the floor, the wooden *Heikhal* is recessed into the eastern wall and set off from the room by its own modest wooden baldachin. Chairs and benches line the walls in a disarray that reveals a long period of disuse. This building was once home to a community of devout Jews who took pride in the synagogue and tried, within their means, to beautify it. Unable to afford marble, they marbleized with paint the northern and eastern walls, the column capitals, and the bal-dachin frame. But now, when it rains, the water drips from the ceiling and puddles on the floor.

Originally the room was square; it was first enlarged in the nineteenth century by incorporating an adjacent house on the north side for a women's *meḥitzah*. Windows cut into the wall at that time were covered with lattice strips to allow the women a view of the hall. As the *kehillah* grew in the late nineteenth century, it needed to enlarge the synagogue again. They abolished the external *meḥitzah* and sealed and plastered its windows. The synagogue was extended to the south, and a small elevated platform was put up for the women inside the prayer room, on the south wall. Women then approached by narrow indoor steps near the entrance. A tiny *ḥeder* (schoolroom) is tucked away thriftily under the sagging boards of this *meḥitzah*. The one row of dusty little chairs and attached desks tells a tale of children who learned Hebrew and fidgeted there, long ago. There is only one Jewish child in Veroria today.

The schoolroom, with a few desks tucked away under the narrow *meḥitzah* on the south wall.

Synagogue interior, view toward the *Heikhal*. The floor plan follows the Sephardic custom, with the *Heikhal* on the east wall and four widely separated columns in the center, supporting a narrow wooden marbleized baldachin above the modest *tevah,* here a wooden frame covered with a frayed and faded damask.

historic monument. Working for the municipality in 1996, Israeli architect and project manager for conservation of the synagogue in Veroia, Elias Messinas secured two grants from the Getty Foundation. These were for documentation of the structure and for preparation of a conservation plan. The study was completed, and partial restoration was done on the synagogue exterior, but he has informed us that implementation funds for the interior were not granted. The design includes a basement exhibition hall where vignettes from the kaleidoscopic history of the Jews of Veroia will be displayed.

INFIDELS IN THE OLD CITY

A piquant oral tradition among the Jews of Ioannina claims that the earliest Jews to settle in the area arrived in 70 C.E., after the destruction of the Second Temple. The Roman commander Titus, with his victorious legionnaires and hundreds of Jewish prisoners, was seaborne to Rome when violent storms drove their galley to the Albanian coast. Grateful for his delivery from the waves, Titus let the Jews go free. They made their way southward through hostile mountains and settled along the shores of Lake Ioannina. The city itself, however, was built by Byzantine Emperor Justinian in the seventh century C.E.; Jews may have settled at the town's inception, but hardly those from Titus's galley.

Ioannina's wall encircles the great fortress and the *kastro,* the old city, on a broad peninsula out into the lake. The former Jewish quarter in the *kastro* and the old synagogue, Kahal Kodesh Yashan, have been preserved. They lie in the shadow of the wall. An older synagogue—dated by a chronogram to the ninth century—stood nearby until 1810, but continuity of Jewish settlement over the whole period

Map of the Ioannina *kastro* (old city). The Jewish quarter occupied the northeast area within the walls. The synagogues are marked by Stars of David. 1. *K'K' Yashan,* 2. *K'K' Hadash,* 3. Aslan Pasha Mosque, 4. Fetiye Mosque. (From N. Stavroulakis, *Jewish Sites and Synagogues in Greece.*)

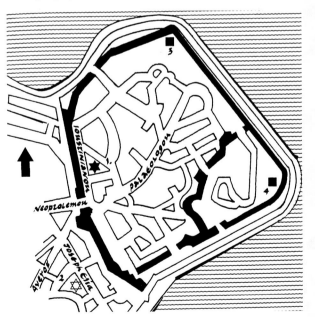

is doubtful. The province of Epirus and its capital, Ioannina, were the scene of invasions by Slavs and Bulgars, Normans who desolated the city, Uzes, Petchenegs, and Albanians. Turbulence and intrigue were the norm under Byzantium. In 1430, the city surrendered to Sultan Murad II (1421–1451) after a siege, and the province remained under Ottoman sovereignty until 1913.

People conquered by the Moslems who consented to remain under Moslem rule as second-class citizens were called *dhimmi* (protected). They were free to move, to worship, and to organize their ethnic or religious communities, *millets,* with considerable autonomy. The Jews, the city's third ethnic group after the Turks and the Greeks, resented the subordinate status accorded them but cherished their freedom to live an observant Jewish life. They were permitted to renovate existing synagogues, and the ban prohibiting new ones was commonly honored in the breach. The *hahambaşi,* chief rabbi, and his Christian parallel, the Greek patriarch, were members of the Imperial Council. In economic matters, the Ottomans discriminated in favor of

Muslims. *Dhimmi* had to pay a head tax to qualify for property ownership. At the borders, Muslim merchants paid only half the customs duties charged to the *dhimmi.*

Because of their adherence to monotheistic faiths, Jews and Christians, called *Ahl al-kitáb* (people of the book), earned respect above other *dhimmi.* Keeping military and administrative positions to themselves, the Muslims depended on the *Ahl al-kitáb* for skills they lacked and did not care to acquire. Diplomacy was one of these skills, curiously regarded by strict Muslims as "tainted and dangerous to the soul." With the Jews' widespread contacts in other Ottoman cities, bankers among them developed naturally. Ioannina Jews were also active in trade, and in crafts as tinsmiths, silversmiths, goldsmiths, dyers, and shoemakers. Special crafts included production of silk braid called *yaitan,* scarfs, veils, and silver belts for export to the Balkans, and the manufacture of garments embroidered with gold thread, popular in Albania.

With the aim of attracting the wealth and skills of Jews expelled from Spain and Sicily, in 1492, Sultan Bayezid (1481–1512) invited Jews

Market place in the *kastro.*

to settle throughout the Ottoman lands. About 100,000 Sephardim arrived: doctors, businessmen and textile manufacturers, scholars, linguists, and bankers, attaining privileged positions all over the empire. The relatively few Sephardic families who settled in Ioannina saw themselves as culturally superior to the native Romaniots and kept aloof, adhering to their own customs. Although the communities formally agreed in 1577 to remain separate, Sephardic preeminence in the Talmud and the dearth of Romaniot prayer books influenced the Romaniots to adopt some Sephardic basics. The Romaniots retained their *piyyutim,* sacred poetry, special melodies, and customs. Given an approximate unity of ritual despite the language barrier, acculturation between the two groups came about gradually and overcame the mutual reluctance to intermarry. The Sephardim eventually learned Greek and assimilated fully into the Romaniot community. This *kehillah* was one of only four in Greece that kept its Romaniot character until modern times. The others were in Khalkis, Arta, and Patra.

Among the many rabbinical *responsa* dealing with Ioannina, there is one by Rabbi Shmuel ben Moshe de Medina (1506–1589), the most famous sixteenth-century halakhic scholar of Salonika. Jewish merchants had persuaded the city authorities to forbid nonresident Jews from trading in the city. The Ioannina rabbi, shamed and upset by the restrictive action and convinced of its immorality, questioned its legality. De Medina responded in the spirit of the prophets. Recalling that the Ottomans did not prevent Christian merchants from trading in any part of the empire, he judged the regulation to be "both illegal and unfair." At issue was a matter of tax liability, not to speak of competition. In fairness, de Medina ruled that nonresidents must share in the local tax payments, in proportion to their profits.

As the empire declined and contracted after the death of Suleiman the Great in 1566, the attitudes of successor sultans to non-Muslim subjects deteriorated radically. They threatened expulsions even for minor infractions, such as prohibited costume. By decree, Jews were to behave without ostentation. Women were forbidden to appear bejeweled or to be expensively dressed in the streets. The rabbis reinforced this particular injunction with still tighter restrictions.

The Turkish traveler, Evliya Çelebi (1610–1679), observed a *kehillah* of over 800 persons in 1670, when silk manufacture occupied 160 families. He despised all non-Muslims but was especially critical of the Jews, reproaching Ioannina Jews for their "exclusiveness and fanaticism, unsociable and ill-tempered behavior in refusing to accept even a drink from a non-Jew." Visiting rabbis, who traveled the dangerous routes between Jerusalem, Hebron, Tiberias, Safed, and cities outside Palestine to generate money for their communities, fared differently with the Ioannina *kehillah.* They were warmly welcomed as fellow Jews and learned guests, whose stay often extended to months or

An unusual *shiviti* (votive tablet) of painted paper near the *bimah.* Such tablets usually contain the verse, *Shiviti Adonai l'negdi tamid* ("I have set the Lord always before me"; Ps. 16:8). With decorations appearing in many shapes and colors, shiviti often serve as amulets containing micrography and symbols, such as a *hamsa* (hand), a Star of David, a menorah or mystical verses.

years. Rabbi Moshe Halevi Nazir of Hebron, for example, sojourned in Ioannina from 1668 to 1671 while he completed his book, *Yedei Moshe* (The Hands of Moses).

Ioannina's economy expanded during the reign of the notorious Ali Pasha (1788–1822). Born in Albania, the cunning Ali became pasha of Ioannina after a series of intrigues. By 1803, he ruled Epirus, Albania, Thessaly, and Macedonia. He strengthened Ioannina fortifications and enforced the laws with a cruel hand. His personal estimate was that he had killed 30,000 people in his 33-year rule. Nonetheless, his incumbency was a period of prosperity for the *kehillah.* Ioannina became the major commercial center for Epirus and one of the most attractive cities in the Ottoman Empire. It developed into a literary capital, equipped with printing presses, new schools, libraries, and universities. Untainted by religious or ethnic prejudices, Ali allowed Jews and Christians full religious freedom and appointed outstanding individuals to his councils.

By the mid-nineteenth century, the *kehillah* of more than 250 families outgrew the *kastro* quarters and its old synagogue. In 1841, they built the Kahal Kodesh Ḥadash synagogue outside the wall, in the heart of the neighborhood occupied by the more affluent Jews. It went up on the foundations of a synagogue built in 1540 when the community had numbered 5,000. The building was rectangular, with a bipolar layout of *Heikhal* and *bimah.* The new synagogue had a very large courtyard suitable for community gatherings. A broad stone *ḥuppah* (wedding canopy) built over the synagogue entrance was a favorite location for weddings.

Christian-Jewish friction was endemic, even though most Jews lived apart within the old city walls. In the volatile Easter season, Christians shouted verbal insults and routinely threw objects such as earthen pots at the doors of Jewish houses. The Jews ordinarily countered by heckling and disturbing Christian religious processions. The skirmishes kept the Turkish authorities on special guard during the holidays of each community, but in 1829 anti-Jewish demonstrators gutted the ancient Kahal Kodesh Yashan by fire. The *kehillah* rebuilt it that year in its present form.

Relations between the Jews and the neighboring Greeks, rebelling for independence,

Courtyard of the Kahal Kodesh Yashan synagogue in Ioannina, built in 1829 on the remains of what was probably a synagogue of Byzantine times. Low concrete benches around the perimeter and under the permanent *sukkah* pergola provide some outdoor seating. A stone *lavabo* facilitates ritual hand washing.

worsened over most of the nineteenth century. By mid century, as the Greeks of Ioannina and Epirus identified with the newly established Greek state to the south, the Jews kept their loyalty to the Ottoman rulers, in the hope of protection. Such hopes often proved false. In a rash step, ostensibly toward modernizing the city, Ioannina governor Rashim Pasha set fire to the main marketplace in 1869. The loss of 160 Jewish houses and all the Jewish shops left 840 Jews homeless. Former Ioannina Jews living in Alexandria were quick to extend help. Emigration increased and many more families prepared to emigrate after a major Greek anti-Jewish riot on the eve of Easter Sunday, 1872. A Turkish military cordon surrounded the *kastro* for four days to protect the Jews. As the Greek-Turkish conflict dragged on, gangs of vicious bandits roamed the highways. The worst incident occurred when 12 Ioannina Jewish merchants, traveling together "for safety," were robbed of their goods and murdered. A few days after they left home, their ears were found floating in the *lavabo* of the synagogue courtyard.

Four thousand Jews lived in Ioannina at the turn of the century. The turbulent political situation became a main factor in the disruption of community stability. By 1905, 500 Jews had migrated to Constantinople, Alexandria, Palestine, and New York. The following year another 1,000, particularly those of the affluent strata, packed their bags for resettlement in the United States. Most of the Jews who remained were so poor that they were derisively nicknamed *spangoraménous* (tied with strings) by the Greeks because they used strings for shoelaces.

At the end of the Balkan Wars in 1913, Turkey ceded the province of Epirus to Greece. Ioannina celebrated with Crown Prince Constantine. The *kehillah* received him royally, laying down a red carpet from the marketplace to the Kahal Kodesh Ḥadash, where Rabbi Yesoula Levy, in a long white caftan, blessed the monarch in Greek. The Jews realized that their future lay with the new government and began to adjust their lives to the changed political reality, involving themselves patriotically in politics and in the army.

When he became king, Constantine, who was a brother-in-law of the German kaiser, tried to keep his country neutral during World War I, although political leadership and public sentiment favored intervention on the side of the Allies. In July 1917, the Allies expelled him for his alleged pro-German orientation, and Greece entered the war against the Central Powers. In the population exchange between Greece and Turkey after the war, more than 1,200,000 Greeks moved from Turkey, Bulgaria, and Russia to Greece. The impoverished Ioannina *kehillah* absorbed many Jewish refugees, exacerbating its economic difficulties. A disconcerting new law required stores to open on Shabbat and close on Sunday. General economic depression

Moise Eliusaf, head of the small Ioannina community, with the oversized iron key at the Yashan synagogue. "This was a mercantile community," he told us in the Alliance School Hebrew of his youth, "where the boys went into business with the fathers. I managed a clothing store, but my son, also Moise Eliusaf, is a doctor in the local hospital. The Alliance School enrolled 500 children before the war, including some Greek and Turkish children. . . We have few Jewish children today. . . ."

in the following decade, coupled with a weakening of Romaniot traditions and the lure of secular and economic opportunities in the big city, impelled many young Ioannina Jews to move to Athens or emigrate from Greece.

Nearly 2,000 Jews still lived in Ioannina at the outbreak of World War II. Some fled to the mountains to fight with the resistance forces. The occupying Italians took no severe measures and permitted flight. In June 1943, the Germans seized Epirus and made their headquarters in Ioannina a month later. The unfolding tragedy of the *kehillah* deepened when the Gestapo beguiled the influential vice president, Sabethai Cabilli, a prosperous merchant who led synagogue services, to mislead the *kehillah*. He urged the Jews to buy safety with money and goods, dispatching 250 young men to collect valuables for the Germans. Cabilli ordered parents to recall their sons from the resistance forces. Eleven of the twenty youths in the mountains responded and became entrapped in the transports. In March 1944, 1,870 Jews, including Cabilli and his family, were taken to the deportation point in Larissa and shipped to Auschwitz.

The 164 survivors who returned after the war found their homes and shops occupied by Greeks. Sluggish legal procedures delayed property restitution. The returnees received generous aid from the American Joint Distribution Society and from KIS, the Central Board of Jewish Communities in Greece. In the 1990s, the community had fewer than 60 members, mostly old people who live in Ta Evraika (Jewish Quarter), a modern apartment house on Joseph Eliya Street. The location is that of the Kahal Kodesh Hadash synagogue and school, demolished by the Germans. Most of the Jews are shopkeepers, active or retired—observant people who maintain the *kastro* synagogue, the Kahal Kodesh Yashan.

The synagogue escaped destruction because Ioannina mayor Demetrios Vlachides convinced the Germans that the city needed the building as a library. He transferred the Jewish religious articles, hidden in a secret synagogue crypt, to the local museum and made sure to return them to the survivors. Today he is honored in a synagogue wall plaque.

In 1935 the city renamed the former Max Nordau Street in memory of the outstanding

Interior of the Yashan synagogue, view northeast to the *Heikhal*. The arrangement is bipolar, in Romaniot tradition: *Heikhal* on the east and *bimah* on the west, with back-to-back benches in rows between them on the same axis.

THE KAHAL KODESH YASHAN SYNAGOGUE IN IOANNINA

The synagogue is located in the former Jewish quarter at 16 Justiananós, a narrow cobblestone street in the *kastro* just inside the ancient city wall. A high stone wall, with an arched and gabled stone portal, was erected at the end of the nineteenth century to surround and protect the synagogue compound. An inscription above the gate dates this building to 1829. The *kehillah* rebuilt it, after a fire, on the site of a seventeenth-century synagogue that stood on foundations that may have been laid in Byzantine times. Renovations of 1881 and 1987, the latter accomplished with donations from Ioannina Jews in the United States, introduced no structural changes.

The austere, one-story synagogue facade is broken on the west by a single interesting architectural element, a high apsidal projection for the *bimah,* containing a pair of tall, narrow round-arched windows. A sheltered entranceway for the men on the southwest corner opens directly into the prayer room. In contrast to the facade, the interior is rich in detail and individuality. *Bimah* and *Heikhal* face each other across an open area lined with facing benches. In a square layout common to synagogues in Thessaly, Epirus, and northern Greece, four central columns are linked by arches that support a dome. Traverse arches connect the central columns to four additional columns and to the north and south walls. The four columns under the dome define and emphasize the square, where the ample space between the benches allows for easy changing of direction during prayer and free movement of the Torah procession.

Recessed into the high west wall niche, the *bimah* is approached by a symmetrical pair of steps and is bounded by a curved balustrade. Two wide velvet banners, the upper one red, the lower, blue, each adorned simply with a pair of silver-ribboned Stars of David, hang below the balustrade.

On the opposite wall stands the marble *Heikhal,* set on a low marble plinth. A semicircular marble balustrade adds to the height of the Ark, echoing the balustrade above the *bimah,* both serving as unifying decorative elements. The mini-balcony here forms an unusual pediment, supported by a series of narrow, gray marble pillars flanking the heavily carved doors of the Ark.

The *meḥitzah* (women's gallery) is supported over six arched bays by squat square piers along the north wall. Women entered by an external stairway and sat behind a fine gold painted metal grille. The few women who now attend the synagogue sit below, on benches opposite the men. In former times the space under the gallery was assigned to students.

The *bimah,* central pillars, and decorated dome. The *bimah* enjoys special attention in Romaniot synagogues. Here it is striking in height, in decoration, and in the special apselike niche in which it is accommodated. The rabbis and cantors sat on the *bimah* on Sabbaths and holidays. For weekday prayers the reader stood at a small *tevah* (readers' stand) in the central aisle under the crystal chandelier hanging from the dome.

אל שדי

דע לפני מי אתה עומד לפני מלך מלכי המלך הקדשה

זה שער השמים

Central detail of the *Heikhal,* a semi-circular marble structure, set two steps above a marble base. Two sets of narrow pillars separate the structure into three bays. A velvet brocade *parokhet* in the wide central bay covers carved wooden doors of the Ark. *"Da lifnei mi ata omed, lifnei melekh malkhei ha'mlakhim, hakadosh barukh hu"* ("Know before whom you are standing: before the King of Kings, the holy One, blessed be He"; *Avot* 4:24) and *"Ze sha'ar hashamayim"* ("This is the gateway to heaven"; Gen. 28:17) are inscribed in the cornice above the Ark.

Ioannina-born poet and philosopher, Joseph Eliya (1901–1931), who died of typhoid. A brilliant rebel, he managed in his short life to create a rich body of original poetry and translations from Hebrew into demotic Greek. Among his earliest poems was one written at age 16 in praise of the Balfour declaration; it was deemed too Zionistic an utterance for the assimilated director of the Alliance School. "Militarism," a poem he wrote after his first taste of the Greek army, aroused his officers' anger. Eliya's voracious study of Talmud, Kabbalah, Hebrew poets, French romantic writers, and neo-Hellenic writers influenced his poetry and published works. One of his greatest achievements was an unfinished translation of the Old Testament into modern Greek, with its sublime treatment of the Song of Songs. A small municipal "Poet's Park," dedicated to the memory of Joseph Eliya contains a marble bust of the poet.

On Friday evenings and Shabbat mornings, the men of the *kehillah* climb the stone steps through the moss-covered arch in the old city wall, turning directly left for a few paces to the stone gate of the synagogue courtyard. Greeting each other warmly with a handshake, they gather for prayers in the Kahal Kodesh Yashan. With the *Heikhal* open, they may notice without concern, that two Torah scrolls are missing. To commemorate their survival and that of the synagogue, the post-war *kehillah* sent the scrolls as a thanksgiving offering to Ioannina emigre *kehillot* abroad. One went to the Kehila Kedosha Janina on Manhattan's Lower East Side and another, in its silver case, to the Beth Avraham and Ohel Sara Synagogue in Jerusalem.

AUSTRIA

Jews first came into central Europe as itinerant traders. Jewish villages, probably merchandise depots, appeared in the Austrian Alps from the close of the eleventh century. A hundred years later there was a Jewish market settlement in Vienna. In the Jewish communities of Vienna, Krems, and Wiener Neustadt, the principal Jewish occupation was moneylending, under letters of privilege by Count Friedrich II. The count guaranteed religious freedom and the protection of synagogues and cemeteries. Nevertheless, "Jewish usury" was a constant theme of hate sermons by the clergy and the cause of physical attacks. Occasional accusations of "profanation of the Host" spurred events of torture and burning at the stake. The nobility pressured Maximilian I until he consented to the mass expulsion of Jews in 1496 from the provinces of Styria and Carinthia in southern Austria. The banished Jews were allowed to settle in the east, in what is now Burgenland and western Hungary. The obligatory yellow clothing badge was introduced in 1551.

By the seventeenth century, the Vienna Jewish community had become prosperous and influential, with many of its leaders members of the court. Among the most famous were Samuel Oppenheimer and Samson Wertheimer, scholars and observant Jews who gained fame as court agents. They managed the affairs of emperors, lending them large sums of money, securing provisions for the armies and at the same time protecting the interests of the Jews. The 40-year reign (1740–1780) of Maria Theresa, who hated the Jews passionately, was a period of severe oppression. Foundations for an official Jewish community were, nevertheless, established in mid-eighteenth century, with permission for a *ḥevrah kadishah*. Communal prayers were permitted only in private prayer rooms.

The ascent of Joseph II to the throne and his 1781 Tolerance Edict eased the Jewish condition in the Austrian Empire to some degree, although its purpose was to promote Jewish assimilation into Christian society.

Viennese Jewish families established banks and factories, and cared for the needs of the Jewish community. Patronizing the arts and sciences, they sponsored musicians and founded hospitals and orphanages that benefited both Jewish and Christian needy. The first major synagogue in Vienna, on Seitenstettengasse, opened in 1826. A moderate reform prayer service, the Viennese *minhag* (custom) helped bring assimilated Viennese Jewry back to their religion, while the strictly Orthodox, mainly Polish Jews, preferred to pray in *shtiblekh* (small prayer rooms).

The revolution of 1848 gave the Jews hope for equal rights and full participation in society, a dream that they realized in 1867. Although anti-Semitism increased during the mid-nineteenth century, expanded job opportunities encouraged Jewish immigration from neighboring lands, especially from Bohemia and the provinces of the Austro-Hungarian Empire. The well-established Vienna Jews received the impoverished newcomers with some disdain. Local Jews had already played an important role in the development of Austrian commerce, science, and the arts, especially in Vienna, and they were ardent patriots.

After the First World War, the Zionists founded a Jewish National Council to fight against assimilation and the losing battle against anti-Semitism. Politically active, Jews were among the leadership of the Social Democratic Party in the inter-war period, the only party that had no anti-Semitic planks in its party platform. As Jewish numbers in Vienna before the Second World War rose to 165,946, with 15,832 more in the rest of Austria, the capital became a hotbed of anti-Semitic activity. In response, Zionist influence in Jewish public life increased sharply.

Most Austrian gentiles welcomed the *Anschluss* (annexation by Germany) of March 13, 1938, which was followed by the exclusion of Jews from Austrian society. The mass burning and destruction of synagogues in the riots of Kristallnacht on November 9–10 of that year abruptly brought an awareness of imminent dis-aster to a stunned and unbelieving Jewish population. Some 100 synagogues in Austria were destroyed, then or during World War II. About 120,000 Jews escaped over the borders before transports to the east began in 1941, but many of them were caught later. Nearly 70,000 of them lost their lives in concentration camps or by suicide.

With the war's end, nearly 30,000 "displaced persons" returned or arrived from camps or hiding. Most of them were Jews from other countries who eventually emigrated to Israel or the West, or returned to their former countries. The Austrian Jews re-established the Vienna community as well as smaller ones in Baden, Bad Gastein, Graz, Linz, Salzburg, and Innsbruck. In addition to the functioning synagogue in Eisenstadt, two synagogues have been restored for cultural purposes in cities with few or no Jews. One is the Institute for the History of the Jews in Austria, housed in the former synagogue of St. Pölten, and the other functions as the Austrian Institute for Peace Research and Education in the former synagogue of Stadt Schleining.

The steady decline in the Jewish population was reversed in the early 1990s as waves of Soviet and Iranian Jews passed through the renascent Austrian Jewish community. While most of those from Iran went on to the United States, more than 1,000 Soviet Jews settled and swelled the Jewish ranks in Vienna, but nearly as many continued on to Israel. Municipal funds for the refugees supplemented support from the Joint Distribution Committee to establish schools, community centers, and vocational programs. The large ultra-Orthodox community in Vienna maintains its own schools and *shtiblekh*. The Bundesverband der Israelitischen Kultusgemeinden (Federal Union of Israelite Congregations) is the primary communal organization of Austrian Jewry. One of its main tasks is combating frequent outbursts of anti-Semitism on the local and national fronts. The growing strength of the extreme right, and the brazen provocation of the neo-Fascists remain cause for concern.

THE HOUSE OF WOLF

The Eisenstadt *Judenrichter,* administrative head of the *kehillah,* was a lofty personage. It was customary in public for a clerk to precede him to carry the wooden mace of office, carved with a crown on top. This *kehillah* kept its political autonomy until 1938, longer than any other in Europe. It was the remnant of the tightly knit Jewry of Burgenland, a *Landjudentum* (an agrarian Jewish community), whose way of life combined rural living with traditional learning. Burgenland's *Sheva Hakehillot* (the Seven Communities)— Eisenstadt the capital, and Mattersdorf, Lackenbach, Deutschkreutz, Frauenkirchen, Kobersdorf, and Kittsee—arose and prospered under the protection of the Hungarian house of Esterházy.

Eisenstadt, the city of iron, appears in Jewish documents as Ir Barzel, or by its initials *alef shin,* Ei'Sh, which spell the word for "fire" in Hebrew. At critical junctures, the early *kehillah* had the benefit of the sagacious and philanthropic leadership of the court financial wizard, *"Judenkaiser"* (king of the Jews) Samson Wertheimer. In a later period,

Stamp of the Jewish town council. *Kof,* (letter at the right) = *kehillah; alef* (center) and *shin* (left) = Ei'Sh, for Eisenstadt, decorate a Star of David. (From Hugo Gold, *Burgenland.*)

the Wolf family developed the wine industry and used its wealth to benefit the community.

The district was part of Rome's Pannonia, a lush region of forests, meadows, and vineyards between the Hungarian plains and the Alpine foothills. The lands attracted Illyrians, Celts, Romans, Germans, Slavs, Huns, Avars, and Magyars as well as Jews. By the fourteenth century, Jews played a significant role in the economic life of the region as itinerant traders. In 1378, the bishop of Eisenstadt allowed some

Jews to settle and trade in the town. The Hapsburgs annexed Burgenland after the battle of
Mohács in 1526, when the Turks occupied eastern Hungary and Ferdinand I claimed the title on
Hungary's west.

Eisenstadt (Kismárton in Hungarian) was a
city that usually tolerated its Jews and often
served as a refuge for those expelled from other
towns. Useful Jews might even be traced: after
Wiener-Neustadt expelled its Jews, its 1550
town chronicle advised patients that their popular woman physician—whose name, sadly, is
unrecorded— was practicing in Eisenstadt.
Toward the end of the sixteenth century, expulsions from Eisenstadt proved to be temporary. In
1622, large estates in upper Hungary came under
the control of Count Nicholas Esterházy
(1582–1645). His patronage combined business
acumen with a humane approach. He enabled
Jews to return to Eisenstadt in 1626 as protected
Schutzjuden, living in ghettos within the palace
boundaries. The *kehillah* built a prayer house,
a mikveh, and a cemetery. When Emperor
Leopold I (1656–1705) dissolved the first
in-town ghetto in another abortive expulsion
of 1671, Nicholas's son, Paul Esterházy

Gateway at the entrance to the former ghetto of Eisenstadt. The inscription reads: "Entrance to the Jewish
ghetto of Eisenstadt, [formally] terminated on July 17,
1958."

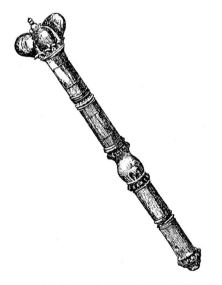

Mace of the *Judenrichter,* head of the *kehillah* of Eisenstadt, from a sketch by Alexius Wolf. The 20-inch
scepter of finely carved wood was made hollow to
house the document that listed the founders of the
kehillah. Each year the clerk added the name of the out-
going *Judenrichter* as he completed his term of office.
(Adapted from Hugo Gold, *Burgenland.*)

(1635–1713), helped the Jews to resettle in
another section of the city. He established a new
ghetto on his estate in 1675, later known as
Unterberg Eisenstadt. It was a center of intensive
Jewish life and learning, affectionately called
"Little Jerusalem." Paul Esterházy so distinguished himself in battle with the Turks, that in
1686 Leopold I conferred on him the title of
Prince, in perpetuity.

By 1688, the ghetto comprised 14 houses and
10 shops. A charter of 1690 granted Jews autonomy in return for annual taxes and occasional
gifts. Among the rights granted were: permission
to build, to practice their religion, to graze their
cattle on the meadow, to buy firewood, and—
upon payment of protection money—to trade.
For the right to bury their dead, they had to provide 30 pounds of pepper annually. Jews traded
in agricultural produce, textiles, wine, salt, and
cattle.

The two ghetto streets, which still meet at a
right angle, are called Lower and Upper. The
Upper Street ends at a wall with a gate leading to
the cemetery, where the oldest stone dates to
1671. Eighteenth-century monuments are more
numerous, but most of the stones show much

Museum model of the ghetto area in Eisenstadt. The large Wertheimer house in the middle completely encircles a sizable court. The synagogue is close by in the left wing.

erosion. Enclosed by a simple fence, a well-preserved and frequented grave is that of Rabbi Meir Eisenstadt, MaHaRam Ash (r. 1717–1744), a beloved rabbi of Eisenstadt, yeshivah head, and judge. This was a prosperous period for the *kehillah,* partly because some of the wealthy Jewish families without residence rights in Vienna paid heavily for a fictitious right of domicile in Eisenstadt.

Deportees from Vienna and Moravia sought haven and the easy-going Esterházy protection in Eisenstadt, since it was only 32 miles from Vienna. Three prominent Viennese families, Kama, Goldschmidt, and Austerlitz, having found temporary shelter in Mikulov, accepted the count's invitation to settle in Eisenstadt. (Actor-dancer Fred Astaire traced his ancestry to this Austerlitz family.)

Eisenstadt did not entirely escape pogroms. From 1704 to 1707, the Hungarian Kuruc mer-cenaries repeatedly perpetrated riot and mayhem in the ghetto, plundering and burning homes. Jews fled to Vienna, where many of them remained. Unterberg was revived, however, by the effort and generosity of Samson Wertheimer (1658–1724).

The many-faceted Wertheimer was a scholar, philanthropist, and *shtadlan*—a lobbyist for Jewish communities. At the Viennese court he was *Hofoberfaktor,* chief administrator, of the financial affairs of emperors Leopold I, Joseph I, and Charles VI from 1694 to 1709. He was equally useful to the Esterházy dynasty. The wealthiest Jew of his day, Wertheimer lent large sums to the government for its participation in the Spanish War of Succession and the war against Turkey. For his personal aid in reestablishing *kehillot* ravaged by riot and war, Hungarian Jewry awarded him the office and title of *Landesrabbiner,* (chief rabbi). For the rebuilding of Eisenstadt's ghetto,

Wertheimer provided a community synagogue, mikveh (ritual bath), school, and provision for school teachers. Prince Paul Esterházy presented him with a mansion in 1696, tax-exempt to him and his heirs, in recognition of 20 years of devoted services to the family's financial affairs. Wertheimer refurbished the mansion and installed a private synagogue, known as the Wertheimer Schul, where a house rabbi officiated until 1840.

The community synagogue was constructed about 1690, opposite the later Wertheimer mansion. It was a low building, depressed three steps below ground level in the custom of the period. Dimly lit by a few small windows, it had a domical ceiling and lacked a separate women's gallery. The building no longer stands.

The large ghetto houses, built around spacious courts, had countless additions and partitions separating as many as six families to a house while safeguarding the privacy of each. This contrasted with the important concept of *eruv,* the symbolic unification of the entire ghetto into a single homestead. Emphasizing their unity, it was customary for all the housewives to participate in baking a huge Passover

The Wertheimer house at the entrance to the ghetto. Since 1982 the house has contained a Jewish museum and a center for the study of Jewish history in Austria.

cake, appropriately called *eruv.* The Jewish population of Burgenland grew from 3,000 in 1725 to nearly 8,000 a century later.

In 1795, a severe conflagration destroyed the Eisenstadt ghetto. Some people saw the tragedy as a punishment for presumed *kehillah* sins. *"Eish,"* they mourned, "was retribution to the *kehillah* of Ei'Sh." Synagogue reconstruction waited until 1832, when the community numbered 908 persons. Karl Moreau, the prince's architect, drew the plans, and the *kehillah* funded the building cost by subscription. Great festivity accompanied the cornerstone laying on August 6, 1832. Flowers hung from the trees, and 24 frolicking children in holiday dress added color and pageantry. A descendent, another Prince Paul Esterházy, and honored guests gathered under a large pavilion on the building site. The ceremonies culminated with a 36-cannon salute. At the inauguration, two years later, members contributed ceremonial silver, a painted glass beaker for the *ḥevrah kadishah,* Torah scrolls, an elaborate *parokhet,* and a parchment megillah executed by the talented scribe Elie Gabriel.

The *kehillah* was a conservative group, carefully observant of traditions. A silver container at

The main ghetto street of Eisenstadt, shown as a wall poster in the Austrian Jewish Museum in Eisenstadt. A chain excluded vehicular traffic from the ghetto on Shabbat.

דער דא זיכט הרים ותנבעות והארברגרת אגט און דים ברכה

בָּאַ"יָ אָמ"הָ עוֹשֶׂה מַעֲשֶׂה בְרֵאשִׁית

דער דא זיבט סין מהר לדר אין גיזוערג זאגט מן ריח ברכה

בָּרוּךְ אַתָּה יְיָ אֱמָ"הָ מְשַׁנֶּה הַבְּרִיּוֹת

ILA10 Birkat Ha-mazon, Kopenhagen, Königliche Bibliothek, Cod. hebr. XXXII, fol. 10v. Obere Bild: Segen beim Anblick von Bergen, Hügeln und Wüsten. Unsere Bild: Segen beim Anblick von sonderbar gestalteten Menschen.

ILA10 Birkat Ha-mazon, Copenhagen, Royal Library, Cod. hebr. XXXII, fol. 10v.

Upper illustration: Blessing at the sight of vegetation, hills and deserts.

Lower illustration: Blessing at sight of strangely shaped human beings.

Page from an illuminated eighteenth-century Ashkenazic *Seder Birkat haMazon* (After Meal Blessings) on display in the Austrian Jewish Museum in Eisenstadt. This page illustrates two of the many blessings of thanks to the Creator for his many acts of grace. "Blessed be Thou, our Lord, King of the universe, who executed the acts of creation," and "Blessed be Thou . . . who makest different kinds of creatures." (By permission of the Royal Library, Copenhagen; Cod. Hebr. xxxii.)

the synagogue entrance offered *tzitzit* cord. Men could twist and knot the cord whenever they needed fringe replacements. It was a generous community, but it could be punitive: a mostly symbolic iron shackle and collar stood by in the synagogue vicinity, ready to restrain wrongdoers and shame them before their peers. On weekdays, the *shammash* called the men to prayer twice a day by a triple tap of his wooden mallet on the tin patch nailed to each door. Two taps signaled one worshipper fewer, a death in the community. On the Sabbath and on holidays an

official closed the gate at the upper end and latched the iron chain at the lower entrance to the ghetto. This was part of the *eruv.* It prevented the entrance of vehicles into the street, but did not limit the Jews from walking into the Christian section of the town. Weddings were always conducted under the open sky. The *kehillah* actively involved children in customs and ritual. Some of the customs mimicked, or mixed, Jewish and Christian models:

- In season, a small rabbi's gift awaited the first child to find a worm in a cherry. Then the *shammash* would loudly proclaim a ban on eating cherries without examination.
- As the children came out of the synagogue after *hakafot* on Simḥat Torah, into air heavy with the fragrance of fermenting wine, the women would pelt them with nuts and apples.
- A children's sacred billy goat was at liberty to graze in the cemetery. On the last day of Passover, children clothed and hatted it, then decorated the scapegoat with flowers and ran with it through the streets.
- At Passover's end, children paraded with a figure of a *baḥur ḥametz* (leavened bread boy). In parallel with central Europe's "straw man," burned to mark winter's end, Eisenstadt children tossed their effigy into a bonfire.

Rabbi Dr. Azriel Hildesheimer of Halberstadt, Germany, was rabbi in Eisenstadt from 1851 to 1869. He collected large sums to establish *battei meḥase,* (hostels for the poor), in the Old City of Jerusalem. Learned in Semitic studies, history, and science, Rabbi Hildesheimer embodied the rare combination of an Orthodox scholar with a modern educational philosophy and outlook. Teachers at his yeshivah taught secular as well as religious subjects and attracted students who supported the credo that Orthodoxy was compatible with the scientific study of Jewish sources. Rabbi Hildesheimer and his equable Orthodox supporters might have preserved unity at the congress of Hungarian Jewry in 1868, but polarized extremists defeated moderation.

Bronze framed glass box for memorial candle. *"Ner n'shamah shel hab'tulah Elky, aleha hashalom, bat Hindel Wolff, 5506."* ("A memorial candle for the maiden, Elky, peace upon her, daughter of Hindel Wolf, 1746.")

Eisenstadt lay in fertile wine country. Wine became its most important product, but it was necessary first to create a marketing industry. A grandson of *kehillah*-founder Benjamin Wolf Austerlitz, named Chaim Joachim Wolf ben Meir Kittsee, pioneered the sale of Eisenstadt's kosher wine to non-wine-producing areas. After a seven-year travel fling, started at age 16 on a small inheritance, he settled down to business in 1784. He took Wolf as his surname and became paterfamilias of a large and distinguished clan that brought fame and fortune to his family and town for generations. The Wolf wine business became the most important one of its kind in the Austrian empire.

Chaim Wolf's second wife, Frumet, who bore him two sons and seven daughters, was a capable businesswoman, philanthropist, advisor, and benefactor of the poor. In 1793, concerned and dismayed at the insensitive domination of community affairs by a small wealthy oligarchy, she wrote and anonymously circulated a satirical pamphlet, *Pasquil Zettelech* (Naughty Notes), lampooning the men in control and their policies. When the scandal broke, rebellious Frumet forthrightly owned up to authorship of the offending diatribe. She had to pay a fine for her audacity and suffered temporary exclusion from the synagogue. The action stirred up the community and evoked a lot of discussion, but the issue was not resolved before 1804, and it is uncertain if any lasting benefit was achieved. After Chaim Wolf died, Frumet conducted the wine business capably for 20 years, with the help of her son Leopold.

Leopold widened operations, exporting to Galicia, importing supplies from Italy and Dalmatia, and converting houses near the ghetto to wine presses and wine cellars. His sons Adolf and Ignaz continued the expansion. In 1875, they bought the Wertheimer mansion, converted the lower floors to house the central offices of the wholesale wine business, and hung a sign on the front, WEINGROSSHANDLUNG LEOPOLD WOLF'S SÖHNE (LEOPOLD WOLF'S SONS, WHOLESALE WINES). The extended family lived in the spacious rooms on the upper floor.

The family branched out to other parts of Europe and to South America, but leadership and the dynamic center remained in Eisenstadt, firmly rooted in the *kehillah* and passionately protective of it. Sandor Wolf, who succeeded his father Ignaz at the helm, had much more than business acumen to his credit. He was a scholar versed in Jewish lore, who wrote and lectured on the history and culture of the community and the city. He was an ardent collector of art and Judaica. In 40 years, he amassed a 26,000-item collection, displayed in the family home, as the Wolf Museum.

With the breakup of the empire, the unassimilated Jewish minority responded to the challenge of narrow nationalism, some with exaggerated patriotism, others by adherence to radical leftism. A minority, including bachelor Sandor Wolf, saw the merit of Zionism for the Jewish future. With three of his nephews, Sandor went to Palestine in 1923 to see for himself.

Deeply impressed with the work of the pioneering *ḥalutzim,* he embraced the Zionist cause without thought of *aliyah:* his task lay with family and community. He did all he could to keep the *kehillah* going—but it was a battle against the tide, culminating with the Nazi *Anschluss* in March, 1938.

The Nazis immediately decreed the expulsion of Jews from Burgenland, ending the 250-year autonomy of the Eisenstadt *kehillah.* Those who could not manage to emigrate fled to Vienna. By October, there were no Jews left in Eisenstadt. On November 9, 1938, an unrestrained mob devastated the community synagogue, smashed the furnishings, destroyed holy articles and books and set the building afire. In their haste to destroy, they overlooked the little Wertheimer Schul, hidden above the offices of the Wolf wine company, one of the few synagogues in Austria and Germany that totally escaped damage at that time. After the Nazis plundered his estate, Sandor Wolf moved to Trieste, and then to Palestine in 1939. He died in Haifa, in 1945, while preparing to return to

THE WERTHEIMER SYNAGOGUE IN EISENSTADT

The Austrian Jewish Museum in Eisenstadt houses the restored Wertheimer Schul, still a sanctified synagogue available to serve visiting worshippers. Early nineteenth-century neo-Gothic and Oriental ornaments decorate the walls. The *Aron Kodesh* is in Empire style, its four marble pillars topped by a semi-circular pediment. It contains four Torah scrolls and their ornaments, rescued from destroyed Jewish communities in Burgenland. A low blue-and-gold Empire-style *bimah* stands in the center, with painted wooden candlesticks at each of its corners for illumination. The oldest piece of Judaica is the heavy brass Danzig Hanukkah menorah, dating from 1680. A women's gallery, behind a wooden lattice, is three steps higher than the main chamber.

The Wertheimer synagogue in the Austrian Jewish Museum in Eisenstadt. Empire style, early eighteenth century. The synagogue is located on the mansion's second story, off a narrow balcony above the courtyard. Men entered the main chamber through the broad arch opposite. An adjacent door opens to the small women's gallery three steps up, behind a wooden lattice.

Silver repoussé Torah breastplate from the Wertheimer Synagogue in Eisenstadt. Note the lively, rampant lions atop the pillars flanking the Decalogue. The unusual inscription on the Torah cover reads: *"Mazkeret ahavat olam mibanim l'avotam."* ("A remembrance of everlasting love from sons to their fathers.")

Eisenstadt to reclaim what he could of his museum treasures.

Of the 441 Eisenstadt Jews, 245 survived the war. Three families returned to the city, but by the 1970s none remained. Some of the houses on the Upper Street were torn down to enlarge the local hospital, and the Austrian Workers' Union built its offices where the older synagogue had stood. Until 1977 the Wertheimer mansion served as headquarters of the Red Cross Organization of Burgenland. Dr. Kurt Schubert and a few others in Vienna who shared his initiative eventually recovered much of Wolf's Judaica. In 1982 the old Wertheimer-Wolf mansion was rededicated as the Austrian Jewish Museum. Its opening exhibit was devoted to 1,000 years of Jewish history in Austria.

In its catalogue, the Austrian Jewish Museum declares its mission to fight against the ignorance that breeds prejudice. A long historical survey stresses the importance of tradition in providing Jewry with new strength. Using phrases attributed to Ḥananiah ben Teradyon, martyred in the Bar Kokhbah uprising of 135 C.E. (Talmud, Avoda Zara, 18A), it concludes, "Only the parchments burn, the letters fly away."

A GUARDIAN
OF LOYALTY

The Jewish experience in Graz in the late Middle Ages typified the tensions that existed between the aristocracy, the Jews, and the gentile populace over a long period. Nobles protected Jews for their own benefit and manipulated every circumstance to extract revenue or loans from them. The Jews, jealously guarding their tradition in an openly hostile world, tried to find a livelihood within the restricted occupational niches permitted them by Church and law. Either in debt to Jews or striving to compete against them, the gentiles willingly accepted the anti-Jewish incitement of the Church as its credo and perennially demanded that the Jews be banished. While not unique to Graz, the Jewish sojourn that ended in their fifteenth-century expulsion played out these conflicting relationships. Allowed to resettle in Graz in 1861 after a hiatus of 350 years, the community they created lasted fewer than 80 years and was doomed to even greater calamity.

Jewish villages, *Judendörfer,* sprouted ubiquitously on the slopes of the eastern Alps in the eleventh and twelfth centuries. A century later, Jewish quarters rose in Vienna, Krems, and Wiener Neustadt, functioning as trading posts—the kernels of mercantile activity that evolved into the cities of the Middle Ages. In 1160 Duke Ottakar III invited moneylenders from a local *Judendorf* begun in 1147, to settle in the 30-year-old Graz: trading hub and capital of Styria in southeast Austria. A *Judenvier-*

Judendorf and Strassengel near Graz. Watercolor by Rudolf von Alt, 1844. (Courtesy of Yad Vashem Art Museum, gift of Ronald Lauder.)

tel (Jewish quarter) of 150 to 200 persons developed in the Griesviertel section of Graz near the Mur River, complete with synagogue and mikveh. It was headed by a *Judenmeister* (Jewish mayor), but a gentile, Duke-appointed *iudex Judaeorum* adjudicated legal issues between Jews and non-Jews.

Church dogma pervaded Christian-Jewish relations. The punishment for violating the prohibition on non-business contact—the Christian to be banned, the Jew to be burned—was honored in the breach, as was the Jewish obligation to wear distinctive clothing: women, a yellow veil; men, a yellow hat. Relaxed interpretation of laws against usury by Christians undermined the livelihood of Jews, effectively excluded from most other pursuits. Popular opposition to the Jews ranged from resentment of competition by the nascent middle class to the rancor of peasants in debt. The peasants' self-proclaimed vigilante group, *Judenhauer* (Jew-beaters), so viciously assaulted Jews in 1397 that a thousand of them from Styria and Corinthia fled for their lives. The *Judenhauer* were curbed eventually by a determined city council, defying their threat to burn down Graz if the Jews weren't handed over to "justice." Some Jewish houses were indeed burned by the *Judenhauer;* but their fury was spent, and Jews began to filter slowly back into the city.

An early "benign" expulsion was decreed in 1438 by the regent, Herzog Friedrich, who allowed Jews to take their moveable belongings, but confiscated their houses for the royal treasury as "compensation for the loss of future tax payments." Some of the banished Jews wandered north to Lower Austria despite the massive pogroms in that region 20 years earlier. Kaiser Friedrich III, preferring the epithet of *Judenkönig* (King of the Jews) to the loss of Jewish tax money, called them back in 1447. As an incentive he granted them a four-year tax abatement, but he appeased the burghers by restricting the number of Jews allowed to return and by not rebuilding the Jewish quarter. Only the synagogue was returned to the community.

In the midst of the unrest, the community established a school for Talmud, which over the years produced teachers and rabbis for other communities in central and southern Europe. Education was the norm, and although German was the spoken language, Jews knew Hebrew well—a language that served them for cultural and religious expression, more than Latin did for the Christians in the Middle Ages.

The career of Maximilian I (1459–1519), Holy Roman Emperor (1493–1519), encapsulates the multifaceted relations between the crown, the nobles, and the populace. Always in need of money, Maximilian regarded the Jews as an unending source of funds and treated them accordingly. He gave protection on the one hand and levied taxes to the hilt on the other. The burghers of Graz, wanting to be rid of their creditors and competitors, kept up a running barrage of demands to expel the Jews from the city. Maximilian had inherited from his father's reign a trumped-up pro-expulsion show trial against a Jew named Jonas. He insisted that Jonas get a fair trial, thereby frustrating the burghers' objective. Jonas was released after several years in custody.

Changing tactics, the burghers applied their knowledge of the sovereign's reliance on Jewish money and baldly offered cash in return for expulsion. Craftily, Maximilian sensed that he could both collect the bribe and keep his Jews—in alternate lands under his (tax) control. After delaying for several years, he agreed to the scheme—whereupon the city of Graz bargained with him over the price, arguing that the city would go bankrupt and could pay no more tax if "the expulsion of the Jews, which we ask of God, would not be carried out." Anticipating royal confiscation of Jewish property along with the expulsion, the burghers remembered to ask for priority in the right to buy it from the crown. Finally, in 1496, Maximilian compromised, accepting a mere 38,000 gulden, and wrote a letter of expulsion: ". . . the Jews killed eight young Christian children and took the blood . . . To prevent repetition we have released all Jews from Styria forever."

Resettlement of the taxpaying Jews in Hapsburg domains was exceptionally difficult, however, because prior expulsions from other

Austrian areas kept much of the country out of bounds. Place for some was ultimately found near Eisenstadt, Marchegg, and Zistersdorf, while others moved to the upper Adriatic, Hungary, and northern Italy. The wandering Jews were permitted to sell their houses in Graz—in a buyers' market—to cart off their chattels, and attempt to collect debts until 1502. This major expulsion closed large regions of Austria to Jewish settlement for a few centuries. For *kehillot* in Slovenia and Italy, however, it was a stimulating stream of Ashkenazic Jews to communities that were mainly Sephardic.

Graz Jews were allowed to settle in the western part of Hungary when it came under Hapsburg rule in 1526. They kept their German mother tongue and made frequent, forbidden forays into Styria for business. This went on for almost 300 years and led up to the second settlement period. In 1783 the Graz municipality permitted Jews to participate in the city's annual fairs. A small group of businessmen settled unofficially in the city. Leaving their families outside the country's borders, they were ostensibly in transit.

A Graz scholar and humanist, J. Kindermann, raised a lone voice in 1780 against the long mistreatment of the Jews: "Most European historians tell of the terrible deeds committed by the Jews, but they do not have the courage to admit that we, the non-Jews, were stupid and cruel. Maleficent greed and false denunciations are the inventors of those fabrications."

Until 1848, Jews were allowed to settle in Graz only after baptism, but they trickled in, in disregard of the ban. Since Graz sponsored two annual fairs of three to four weeks each, a traders' inn was indispensable. Two Jewish delegations met regent Count Stassoldo in 1860, requesting permission to establish residence. They described how vital Jews were in the business life of the city, especially as importers of Hungarian grain, suppliers to the Kaiser's army, and financiers of the steel industry and the Styrian-Hungarian railway. One leader of the second delegation was a well-known Hungarian philanthropist, Baron Philip Schey, born in Kőszeg, Hungary. The Count received them courteously, but refused their request.

In September 1861 the Styrian parliament opened the region to Jewish settlement, and in December of that year Ludwig Kaddisch obtained permission to open a kosher eating establishment. The Graz Israelitische Korporation, founded in 1863, was the forerunner of the Israelitische Kultusgemeinde (IKG, "the Jewish Society"), inaugurated in 1868, when the municipal requirement for a settlement permit was rescinded.

Settling openly in Graz, Jews made a new start, again on the south bank of the Mur River,

The city of Graz from across the Mur River, toward the general location of the demolished synagogue.

Board of Directors of the Jewish community of Graz, 1991.

THE SYNAGOGUE IN GRAZ

A square brick synagogue in the then-popular Romantic style was built to a design by Viennese architect Maximilian Katscher and completed in 1892. Its center dome rose 52 feet above the temple floor. Counting the external wooden cupola, lantern, and Star of David, the synagogue's height above the street came to 91 feet. With a large hexagonal dome, corner turrets, and two narrow towers crowned by smaller cupolas, the synagogue became a familiar landmark on Grieskai quay along the river. To its south stood the community building and school, also in Romantic style—the two buildings forming an harmonious complex surrounded by an artistic 12-foot iron fence.

Interior of the Graz synagogue before it was destroyed. (Courtesy of the Jewish community in Graz.)

in Griesviertel, where later they built their great synagogue. A wing of the coliseum building on Zimmerplatzgasse served as the first prayer hall for the 240-strong community. In the words of the *Grazer Tagespost,* September 12, 1865, it was dedicated, "Under a blue roof with golden stars, behind a balustrade of gilded bronze" where "there rose a stone altar in Byzantine style . . . all making a very fine impression!"

Of the community's many social and philanthropic organizations, the Jewish student societies deserve particular attention. Their activities engaged them in a series of cat-and-mouse skirmishes with authoritarian scholastic and municipal administrations that insisted on close formal supervision to control organizing or publishing material. The first society was Humanitas, essentially concerned with lending money to support needy students. The administration disbanded it after 20 years of unexceptional existence because the tenth issue of its satirical newspaper had offered a few off-color jokes in a New Year's issue.

Two months later, a society for the same purpose obtained approval under the name Charitas. In 1898, two law students organized a Zionist society, Ivria, that was sadly undersubscribed. The group was faced with open anti-Semitism by the student body and a university management that was worried about how the gentile students would react. Ivria dissolved in 1903. Administrative resistance to Jewish organizations diminished eventually, but the anti-Semitic student sniping continued. The seven or eight Charitas members had to defend their honor in numerous saber and pistol duels. In 1909, an offshoot of Charitas—the Jewish Finches, later renamed Emuna (Faith)—created a social house stocked with books and newspapers on Jewish affairs and open to all on Sundays.

The coliseum hall was inadequate as a prayer hall by the turn of the century, for the fast-growing *kehillah* that numbered nearly 2,000. School classes and community business had to be conducted in members' homes. Larger meetings were held in restaurants or rented quarters. Rabbi Muehsam, hired in 1877 to be the first Graz rabbi in three and a half centuries, adopted the building of a new synagogue as his top priority. The project became protracted and expensive, well beyond the congregation's financial capacity. After receiving permission from Kaiser Franz Joseph to raise funds by a lottery, Rabbi Muehsam traveled over half of Europe to collect donations. Money came mainly from Vienna, Berlin, Budapest, Prague, and Trieste, for a grand total of 40,000 gulden—about half the cost of construction.

In dedicating the synagogue on September 14, 1892, chief rabbi of Austria Oberrabbiner Dr. Guedemann declared, "There is no conflict for us between our Judaism and our Germanism. May the new House of God be a guardian of loyalty to the Fatherland, of love for the mother tongue, and for the culture of the Fatherland."

The grandiose synagogue symbolized the successful integration of the *kehillah* into the city, but that integration had a price. Austrian Jewry was on a track toward increasing assimilation. In 1900 two-thirds of Jewish marriages in Graz were mixed, although almost half of the Christian partners, mostly women, converted to Judaism. A large influx of refugees from eastern Europe arrived in the wake of World War I. Hasidim among them increased the Orthodox element in the community. The local Zionist movement was also considerably strengthened, although not many left for Palestine.

Slovak-born Rabbi David Herzog (1869–1946) of Graz taught Semitic languages at the University of Graz. A specialist in medieval Judeo-Arabic literature and the history of the Jews in Austria, he used archival material and tombstone inscriptions as historical sources in his research. In the late 1930s, when Graz became a center of Austrian National Socialism and the party's local functionaries were eager to make Graz the first city to be *judenrein* ("clean of Jews"), Rabbi Herzog was among those whose homes were raided by the Nazis. They threw him into the Mur River, but he was rescued and escaped to England, where he continued his work at Oxford University.

Immediately after the *Anschluss* on March 12, 1938, Nazi troops desecrated the cemetery. On infamous Kristallnacht, November 10, 1938, uniformed hooligans dynamited the synagogue

A class of children in the Jewish school in the 1930s.

Modern prayer room of the Graz Jewish community. The room serves the *kehillah* for prayers on Sabbaths and holidays, and for community gatherings. Wooden furniture gives the room an air of quiet dignity.

and set fire to the Ceremonial Hall of the cemetery, destroying everything. The congregational office building and its records were torched. Graz Jews were driven from their homes, and most of them perished in concentration camps.

After the war, 110 Jews resettled in the city and reestablished the community. Although their numbers rose briefly to over 400, they dropped to about 120 in the 1990s. Activities are mainly cultural, social, and philanthropic, with services conducted on the major Jewish holidays. The city inaugurated a reconciliation with the Jewish

Synagogue Square in Graz, where the synagogue stood and where the replacement synagogue will rise. The Jewish community still maintains offices and a prayer room in the building shown, although most of the building has been modified to headquarters for the fire fighting force.

Memorial monument of black granite on the site of the synagogue. Symbols on the four sides include Tablets of the Law, Star of David, a seven-branched menorah, and a Torah.

community. The mayor invited 25 former citizens now living in Israel to return to Graz as guests of the city for a week. City engineers helped plan the municipally financed reconstruction of the Ceremonial Hall at the cemetery, completed in 1991.

Postwar Austria seems to have a predilection for converting former Jewish buildings and synagogues into fire stations, such as in Rechnitz, Hohenems, and Lackenbach. Graz followed suit, and adapted the Jewish community building to be the headquarters of the city fire department. Crenelated roofline decorations have been removed, and arched windows have been changed to rectangular form. The *kehillah* maintains offices and a large prayer room on the building's second floor. The prayer room is austere and functional, with bare white walls, a large wooden Ark, wooden armchairs, and polished parquet floor. There is no visual relief in color or texture.

Synagogenplatz, once the synagogue site, was converted to a small park. A black granite monument stood at its center, a memorial to the decimated Jewish community of Graz and its synagogue. Jewish symbols were engraved on each of the four sides of the stone: the Star of David, Tablets of the Law, a seven-branched

menorah, and an open Torah scroll. The inscription below the menorah reads:

> *Under Kaiser Franz Josef I in 1892*
> *On this spot our great synagogue was erected.*
> *Under the National Socialistic violent regime*
> *On the 10th of November 1938 was our synagogue*
> *Plundered, torched, and destroyed.*

Under the community's dedication to its 2,200 Jews who were killed by the Nazis, the city of Graz wrote:

> *To preserve the memory of our Jewish citizens*
> *And their house of worship*
> *We set up this monument in November 1988*
> *As an admonition against any violent regime,*
> *Race hatred, and inhumanity.*

Not content with engraved expressions of sympathy and regret, the Graz municipality sought later to make stronger amends. With city funds, and by engaging support from Graz citizens and a national grant, the city undertook to construct a new synagogue for the *kehillah*. With symbolic reference to the Kristallnacht destruction of the former synagogue, work was begun on November 9, 1998, and the dedication is scheduled for November 9, 2000. The new building, which will serve the small *kehillah* for assembly and religious services, as well as the entire city for cultural events, will not be a copy of the one it replaces. Designed by architects Ingrid and Jorg Mayr, the modern design will emphasize the intersection of the fundamental geometric forms, the sphere and the cube. It will, however, contain a few of the original elements, such as the portal columns at the entrance and the central dome. The municipality of Graz, "increasingly conscious of its former role as a forerunner of anti-Semitism in Austria," regards the project as a memorial to Graz Jews who died in the *Shoah*.

The synagogue and community building in Graz, Romantic Style, Maximillian Katscher, architect, built in 1892 and destroyed on Kristallnacht, November 9–10, 1938. With the help of the city of Graz, a new synagogue, shown in the drawing, lower right, is under construction on the same site. Begun on November 9, 1998, the synagogue will be dedicated on November 9, 2000. (Courtesy of Mayr and Mayr.)

Blick auf die 1938
zerstörte Synagoge
vom östlichen Murufer

HOW FAIR ARE YOUR TENTS, O JACOB

Historically, Austrians have had a low tolerance for Jews. The driving force in excluding them, other than basic religious bigotry, lay with commercial interests eager to eradicate Jewish competition. Citizens cajoled rulers and magistrates to expel the Jews and to enforce exclusionary statutes—a familiar saga, meticulously recorded in official chronicles. In St. Pölten, as in Graz, the burghers scored a singular success, preventing a settled Jewish population from emerging in the city until after the Emancipation. The community that developed was small at first, but patriotic and loyal. As the *kehillah* grew and gained affluence, however, a suitable synagogue became ever more necessary. Achieving that goal took a quarter of a century—as long a time as the *kehillah* was to enjoy the use of the synagogue it built.

Jewish traders plied the roads of eastern and lower Austria as early as the tenth century, but the first mention of Jews in St. Pölten is from the fourteenth century, when St. Pölten Jews loaned money to Vienna citizens Nikolaus Holinus and Johann Hierz. In 1306 friction between St. Pölten Jewish moneylenders and their neighbors escalated into accusations of "blasphemy and desecration of the Host," and frenzied riots. Crowds poured through the Jewish quarter, killing Jews and plundering property. Anxious to maintain peace among his subjects, Duke Albrecht I quelled the riots by force. He was so enraged that he made plans to destroy the town and build a successor eight miles away, but the town's owner, Count Bernard of Passau, managed to dissuade him. Rescuing his town cost Bernard a penalty of 3,500 pounds. The local monastery sold three of its fine vineyards for 129 pounds, paid over to the Duke's coffer, as its penalty for not curbing the rioters. Such concern for Jewish residents was rare in the history of Austrian nobility.

Expulsions and threats of expulsion were the rule, not the exception. The frequent complaints and threats of banishment were directed against Calvinists as well as Jews, although both these groups were responsible for minting the local coins. City officials, aware of their joint role in the city's economy, wanted to avoid expelling them "too early." An "assurance" in

1624 that Jews could remain in the city one more year was then extended for another twelve months. During this period the authorities required the two groups "to change the local coinage, and bring good new coins into town." Despite an edict of 1628 delaying expulsion to allow Jews and Calvinists at the foundry to finish their work, only the Jews were ultimately expelled.

Bans on Jewish trade continued until the eighteenth century. A 1745 decree in the same vein by Maria Theresa forbade Jews to live in the city. Two generations later the Toleranzpatent of Josef II opened St. Pölten to Jewish tradesmen but not to Jewish residence. Attendance at the fairs was also problematic. A Jewish judge, Aron Singer of Piesling, Moravia, asked to attend the annual St. Pölten market. The council replied:

Jews from the outlying districts who were allowed to visit the annual market and trade in flax in the towns infringe on these permits to the disadvantage of the Christian trader. They remain in St. Pölten for the whole year, cheat the population by false and misleading merchandise, these Pinkeljuden, *money-Jews. Therefore the council refuses the permit. . . [and] would be happy to be rid of this scourge.*

Neighbors of innkeeper Anton Riss brought charges against him in 1798 for lodging three Jews at his inn over extended periods. The plaintiffs (Franz Unger, weaver; Johann Forster, tailor; Johann Buch, bauble maker; Johann Prilinger and Johann Mayer, coppersmiths; Georg Jung, a caster of pewter; and two unnamed hat makers) complained further that the Jews bought and sold sheep's wool, a forbidden occupation. The magistrate summoned all the parties to a hearing. Riss defended himself, saying he was willing to abide by the law and to deny lodging to the Jews, if he must, but—he noted—they were worthy of consideration because in many other locations they were not allowed to trade. Diplomatically, he stressed that he had hosted only three persons, only from time to time, mainly on Sabbath days and when they were in transit to other towns. He asked the hon-

orable court to keep in mind that business in his remote inn would be thin indeed if the Jews did not buy his beer, eggs, and butter.

The Jews pleaded in his defense. They paid higher taxes than Christians in the Austrian state. To raise these sums and to maintain their families they had to have means at their disposal. Since the law permitted trade in the outlying towns and it was troublesome to travel home for each small item, it was necessary for them to have a place to store goods. Guests Schneller and Betchowitzer had been trading in the area for many years, and were well known for their honesty; moreover, Jacob Schneller reminded the court that he had helped to apprehend thieves several times.

The complainants airily dismissed the defense arguments, maintaining that the law excluded Jews from the city except during the annual markets . . . and so be it. The hearing protocol went to the district council, whose immediate decision is unknown. Three years later a circular reemphasized the lower Austrian ruling that it was a punishable offense for Christians to give lodging to Jews. Its instructions specifically required innkeeper Riss to receive this information.

In the mid-nineteenth century, 39 families and 14 bachelors were living in St. Pölten, a total of 252 Jews. A scattering of others lived in the villages and in nearby market towns. Designation of a Jewish house of assembly awaited approval of the regional council, not granted before 1851. The first prayer room was located in the Gasser cotton factory. Within a few years they hired a teacher of religion, established a cemetery, and by 1857 achieved approval and formally organized a *kehillah* of 300 to 400 members, including those who lived on the periphery.

The community had come of age. It patently needed its own permanent and appropriate house of prayer and assembly, and it could generate the capital to cover the cost. In 1885 the growing community moved to larger temporary quarters in a renovated building on Schul Promenade. By 1888 the *parnassim* embarked on the process that would lead to construction of a satisfactory building. Particulars of that process are recorded

Synagogue in St. Pölten, *Jugendstil*, 1913, main facade. The inscription under the Tablets of the Law reads, *"Pithu li sha'arei tzedek, avo bam odeh Yah"* ("Open the gates of righteousness for me, that I may enter them and praise the Lord."; Ps. 118:19).

and they exemplify the winding path that many congregations took toward building a synagogue.

The *parnassim* first tried to acquire a site near the Linz gate but the city denied approval. A new suggestion, in 1904, was to build right next to the existing small temple on Schul Promenade. Again the city voiced objections: parts of the temple infringed on the street setback line. Protracted negotiations with the city and complicated trade-offs led to an agreement in 1911, siting the new synagogue at the corner of Schul Promenade (later renamed Dr. Karl Renner Promenade) and Lederergasse. For site acquisition, ten affluent congregants advanced almost 8,000 crowns, against future assessments. With 70,000 crowns in the building fund, the *parnassim* decided in favor of immediate action. President Albert Leicht canvassed communities of the monarchy, asking to see their respective statutes and descriptions of how and when they had built their new synagogues. Replies came from Bohemia, Austrian Silesia, and Vienna-Hietzing.

Against the advice of Vienna City Master Builder Stiegler, the community decided on a limited competition. They called for a plan with 220 seats for men and 150 for women at a pro-

posed cost of 95,000 crowns. *Kehillot* in Austria were prosperous at the time and synagogue architects were busy, but several of them, including J. Gartner, Ludwig Schone, and Theodor Schreier, tendered proposals. Schreier's plan, as adopted, adhered to the space requirements and provided for an elegant front garden as well as a covered main entrance and driveway—not on the windy, west side. Schreier announced that he would have the help of Viennese architect Viktor Postelberg.

Rabbi Adolf Schächter stipulated that no construction work was to be done on the Sabbath or the Jewish holidays unless such delay would cause severe financial loss. The extra cost of this limitation was reckoned at 4,000 to 5,000 crowns, but the rabbi had the executive committee's support. In September 1912 the builder requested permission to work on Sukkot because the crew had begun to pour concrete. Several days' interruption might cause damage. The rabbi adamantly refused, and the building committee again supported his position.

The committee strove for the best possible workmanship within their budget. The St. Pölten cabinetmaker Robert Hahnl produced the benches, the Viennese firm of Carl Geyling Erben was responsible for glazing the leaded windows, and the Vienna firm Erdman-Kleeman cast the art metal work and the striking brass grille for the *bimah*. The total construction cost came to 141,240 crowns, about a third higher than the estimate, but the sum included construction of the adjacent building containing apartments for the rabbi and *shammash* on the ground floor and classrooms on the upper floor.

After twenty-four years in the preparation—funding, site selection and bureaucratic approval, site purchase, architectural contest, and final plan—the structure went up in 14 months. The dedication was fixed for August 17, 1913, eve of the emperor's birthday. Patriots all, St. Pölten Jews wished to express their appreciation of Emperor Franz Joseph. They considered naming the synagogue in his honor and placing a bust of him on display. Since it was unthinkable to put a statue into the sanctuary and insulting to the monarch to mount the bust in an anteroom,

THE SYNAGOGUE IN ST. PÖLTEN

The synagogue complex occupies a prominent location on the fashionable, tree-lined boulevard. The architects harmoniously combined elements of the then-popular *Jugendstil* with a noteworthy Baroque octagonal dome. Despite the usage of traditional and ornamental elements, the building has a contemporary, sculpture-like appearance, notable in its modernity and individuality. Three tall rectangular windows that once held leaded glass now mirror the shifting clouds and blue skies on their clear panes. Auxiliary sections of the complex cluster in differing geometric shapes around the core octagonal structure.

The interior space fulfills the intentions of architect Schreier, proposed in 1912, "To create as open an aspect as possible; to maximize the space of the sanctuary, engendering a feeling of devotion, and, in the modest space available, to create impeccable acoustics; to use diversified painted artistry which is cheaper and makes sculpted decoration unnecessary. . . ." The high vaulted ceiling and dome provide excellent acoustics. The textile-like pattern that covers the walls and provides the main decorative element is intended to suggest the draperies that surrounded and covered the Tabernacle in the desert.

Rectangular lines offset by wide arches delineate the sanctuary. Decorated with finely detailed blue, white, and gold squares, a soaring proscenium arch rises gradually above the white stucco structure that once contained the Ark. A draped curtain conceals the empty Ark niche, forming a neutral backdrop for the grand piano on the *bimah*. Long galleries along north and south walls draw the eye to the shorter gallery on the west wall, and white framing on the wooden balustrades forms a dramatic contrast to the narrow floral bands accentuating the ceiling vaults.

The St. Pölten synagogue, *Jugendstil* (Art Nouveau). Theodor Schreier and Viktor Postelberg, architects, 1913. The stately synagogue was once the pride of its prosperous community of about 650 persons.

the committee dropped the idea. Instead, they affixed a plaque in his honor. Pleading a prior engagement, the emperor could not attend the opening, but prominent dignitaries were there, and the event had extensive press coverage.

St. Pölten Jews assembled peacefully and prayed in their synagogue for 24 years—as many years as it had taken to create it. Then came the terror of Kristallnacht. About 400 people, some in Nazi uniform, descended on the synagogue. They battered down the doors, burst into the sanctuary, smashed the windows, broke the great candelabra, and chopped the furniture. They threw religious books and ritual objects into a bonfire and bellowed Nazi political songs while the books burned.

With some partial repairs, the building served in 1942 as a reception camp for Russians in forced labor. After the war there was further deterioration of the roof, the main cornices, and the plaster on walls and ceilings. The municipality boarded up the windows, but only long after pigeons had infested and defiled the interior.

Once again in possession of the synagogue after the war, the few Jews who returned could neither restore the building nor use it as it was. They ceded it to the municipality. In 1979 the Federal Memorials Institute declared the building to be "the most significant Jewish religious structure in Lower Austria," and initiated efforts to save it. Restoration began in 1980. The com-

Synagogue interior to the east. The synagogue interior was badly damaged on Kristallnacht, November 10, 1938. It was faithfully restored in 1984. A curtain covers the space of the former *Aron Kodesh* under the restored Ark pediment and frame.

View to the west—galleries and ceiling. In perfect symmetry, the newly frescoed arches stretch to the domical vaulted ceiling.

plex was opened in 1984 for new educational and cultural functions as the Institut für Geschichte der Juden in Österreich (Institute for the History of Austrian Jewry) with support from the Ministry of Science and from the municipality. The institute's main goal is to research the history of the Jews in Austria from the twelfth to the twentieth centuries, to emphasize their contribution to Austrian philosophy and culture, and to use this knowledge in the struggle against anti-Semitism.

The restorers of the synagogue belong to a postwar generation, of which many choose to face up to the atrocities of the *Shoah* and, within their means, to make amends. Restoration of the synagogue as a memorial institute expressed the participants' feelings that "the fate of our Jewish fellow citizens is an inseparable part of Austrian history." Using almost the same phrases, Herman Fuchs, the young mayor of Kobersdorf, maintains that the Jewish story is intrinsic to Austrian history and should be taught in school. He showed us the synagogue in Kobersdorf—emptied of storeroom use and swept, but still disheveled—emphasizing the importance of restoring it as a monument to the town's former Jews. The same spirit is evident in the Austrian Jewish Museum in Eisenstadt.

Work of the institute in the early 1990s included several projects, such as researching the history of the oldest period, the twelfth to the fifteenth centuries, up to the time the Jews were expelled from Styria and Tyrol. This study involved the comparison of non-Jewish sources with rabbinical *responsa,* particularly those of Rabbi Israel ben Pethaḥiah Isserlein (1390–1460) in Hebrew and Aramaic. Cooperating with Budapest art historian David Ferenc, who had restored the fourteenth-century synagogue in Sopron, Hungary, the institute is searching with some success, notably in Bruck/Leitha, for traces of synagogues in Austria from the Middle Ages.

Dr. Klaus Lohrmann, director, and Dr. Martha Keil, senior researcher at the Institute for the History of Austrian Jewry, discussing the work of the Institute with the author. Martha Keil, explained: "We must educate the young children here in Lower Austria. They see few Jews in their life. They hear about the Jews only from grandparents and have no concept of Jewish customs or a Jewish house of prayer. The older children are less interested in Jewish matters. Perhaps we did not educate them properly."

An organized school visit to the synagogue. A staff member explains the story of the synagogue, its function, and Jewish significance. The children join in singing a familiar folk song to demonstrate the building's remarkable acoustics.

Previous assembly of a Jewish biographical lexicon of Austria and the monarchy had already yielded 15,000 names; moreover, in a related activity, the institute was collecting eye-witness reports from Jewish survivors on what had happened to them in the Holocaust. A series of international summer seminars featured Israeli experts and others on topics such as "Jewish Law on Marriage and Inheritance," in 1991, led by Zeev Falk of the Hebrew University and "The Synagogue as the Focus of Jewish Life," with the participation of Mordechai Breuer and Michael Silber of the Hebrew University in 1994.

Martha Keil of the Institute sent us an unexpected little treasure, found by her acquaintance, Dr. Morgenstern, while he rummaged through the bins in a Vienna *antiquariat* (secondhand book shop) in 1995. It is an invitation to the synagogue consecration, addressed to the Right Honorable Sir Bernhard Österreicher. The detailed three-page program sets the following imagined scene on that bright Sunday afternoon:

The gallery ladies in elegant lace and chiffon look down on a sea of men's cylinder hats below

First page of the personal invitation and program of the synagogue dedication, sent to the Right Honorable Sir Bernhard Österreicher. (Courtesy of Martha Keil.)

as the assembly rises for the solemn procession and entrance of the Torah scrolls. All chant "Ma Tovu," "How fair are your tents, O Jacob, your

dwellings, O Israel!" (Num. 24:5.) The hymn, printed in Hebrew and German, is probably sung in German. Architect Theodor Schreier then delivers the keys of the Ark to the congregation president, Albert Leicht. The Torah scrolls are reverently lifted into the Aron Kodesh *while the choir sings Psalm 24:7-10, "O gates, lift up your heads! Up high, you everlasting doors, so the King of glory may come in!" The rabbi of the Jewish community of Vienna kindles the eternal light for the first time and locks the Ark while the choir chants, "Etz chaim hi" ("For the Torah is a tree of life"; Prov. 3:18).*

Rabbi Schächter dedicates the edifice. His Excellency, the governor of Lower Austria, the mayor of St. Pölten, and the President of the Jewish community of Vienna give their blessings. The choir chants Psalm 21:2, "O Lord, the King rejoices in Your strength; how greatly He exults in Your victory!" The ceremony ends as the congregation and all their distinguished guests rise for the Austrian imperial anthem.

How reassuring it must have been for those loyal Austrian Jews in St. Pölten to have faith in their country and their kaiser on that great festive day. Of about 650 Jews living in St. Pölten prior to the Second World War, 214 were murdered by the Nazis. A memorial erected in front of the synagogue in 1992 carries their names, engraved in stone.

THE CZECH REPUBLIC

From its inception in the aftermath of World War I, modern Czechoslovakia was land-locked in the heart of central Europe. Bordered and intersected by forests and mountains, the country was composed of three historically defined regions: Bohemia in the west, with Prague as its capital; Moravia, with its capital at Brno; and Slovakia in the east, with its capital at Bratislava. Slovakia seceded from the federation in 1993 to become an independent state, leaving Bohemia and Moravia as the Czech Republic.

Jewish presence in the Czech lands dates from the early Middle Ages. Most Jews arrived as traders or crafts workers permitted to dwell near the markets or trade routes and to set up autonomous communities. Coming from Germany, Hungary, and the Byzantine Empire, they settled in Prague beginning in the tenth century. The main Jewish community developed in the late twelfth century, near Prague's old town on the right bank of the Vltava River.

Troubles and anti-Jewish persecutions alternated with measures of tolerance. The Cru-saders massacred Jews in Czech lands as they did in other parts of Europe. Legal, occupational, and residency restrictions governed what Jews did and where they lived. When ghettos became fashionable, segregation became the rule in Bohemia and Moravia as well. On the other hand, the nobility developed a symbiotic relation with the Jews, granting permission to settle on their lands and providing protection from abuse in return for high taxes and gener-ous loans. The fifteenth-century Reformation weakened the monopolistic power of the Catholic Church and the monarchy. The politi-cal balance shifted to favor the landed aristoc-racy and the new urban burgher class that was gradually invading the typical Jewish spheres of banking and trade. Although expulsion of Jews from numerous cities, including Prague, became a common occurrence, reprieves often followed a few years later.

In the mid-sixteenth century a period of relative stability followed the Hapsburg ascen-dancy over Bohemia and Moravia. Between alternating bouts of persecution and tolerance in the sixteenth and early seventeenth centuries, the Jews experienced an interval of economic and cultural prosperity. Cultural life flourished, especially in Prague. This was the era of *kehillah* expansion and the construction of the famed Prague synagogues—the Pinkus (1535), the High (1568), and the Meisel (1592)—as well as the Jewish Town Hall (ca. 1560). Under the tolerant art patron and emperor Rudolf II (r. 1576–1616), Prague became the cultural, scientific, and artistic center of the empire and a zenith in Jewish community life. The Jewish population increased in many Czech towns as Jews fled the Chmielnicki massacres (1648–1649) in Poland or were expelled from Vienna (1670). With 11,500 persons at the end of the seventeenth century, the Jewish community in Prague was the third largest *kehillah* in the world.

Enacted under Charles VI in 1726 and 1727, the Familiants Law permitted only one son of each Jewish family to marry. It limited the number of Jewish families in Bohemia to 8,451 and in Moravia to 5,106 and restricted Jewish residency to non-royal towns and villages settled by Jews before 1726. As long as it was enforced, the law caused friction in the Jewish community and large-scale emigration, mostly to Poland or to Slovakia. Some of those who were unwilling to emigrate married secretly in *bodenchassines* (attic weddings) and raised unrecognized families in evasion of the law. The Translocation Rescript of the same period ordered Jews to move into ghettos, located at a prescribed minimal or greater distance from churches and town squares. Maria Theresa exacerbated Jewish troubles with periodic expulsions and with punitive taxation whenever Jews were allowed to return.

Influenced by the philosophies of the Enlightenment that were spreading over Europe, Joseph II (r. 1780–1790) issued the Toleranz-patent (Edict of Toleration) in 1782, granting Jews and other non-Catholic minorities official recognition while expressly confirming the Familiants Law. Intending to encourage assimilation and to make the Jews useful to society and the state, he granted religious freedom and abolished economic and residence restrictions. Although he granted some of the blessings of emancipation and freedom, he also revoked Jewish judicial autonomy and commanded the adoption of the German language for family names and business use. Secular secondary and university education were opened to Jews, but so, henceforth, was military conscription.

The first Austrian constitution, in 1848, formally granted Jews equal rights with other citizens of the Czech lands. The Familiants Law was ineffective thereafter and was rescinded in 1859. With the restriction to ghettos lifted, Jews streamed to the large cities. This was a period of rapid population growth, peaking in 1890 with 94,599 Jews in Bohemia and 45,324 in Moravia. The number of Czech Jews dwindled after the turn of the twentieth century as assimilation, a low birth rate, and migration took their toll. As German substituted for Hebrew in Jewish use, Jewish writers such as Franz Kafka, Max Brod, Franz Werfel, and others became prominent in the literary flowering of Czech-German culture.

The Republic of Czechoslovakia was established on October 28, 1918. A mere twenty years later, on September 30, 1938, the Munich Pact ceded the Sudetenland to Germany. The pact brought to an end the short-lived hope for a humanistic democracy where Jews could play a constructive role. Six months later, Nazi troops occupied Bohemia and Moravia and began the systematic destruction of Czech Jewry. Of the prewar community, which swelled to 122,000 as refugees came in from Germany and Austria, 89,000 Jews were deported. Of these, 78,000 perished. In 1945 about 10,000 deportees returned to the Czech lands. In the clash with the repressive Communist regime, the survivors' attempt to rebuild Jewish life faded into a general deterioration of Jewish community ethos. Many Jews emigrated to the West and to Israel.

The Velvet Revolution that bloodlessly abolished Communist rule in Czechoslovakia in 1989 aroused Jewish consciousness and led to a renewed interest in Jewish heritage on the part of individuals and—incidentally—civic and national authorities. The Federation of Jewish Communities in Prague is the leading communal organization and is concerned with, among other matters, the restitution of Jewish property. Most of the negotiations have been successful, with either return of property or compensation paid. Struggling for survival, the community uses the money to promote welfare and economic activity. At the millennium the Jewish population hovers around 6,000—with about 1,000 Jews living in Prague, most of them aged. However, the number varies as one evaluates the definition of "Jewish." Jews are "coming out of the closet," and there is a growing interest in Jewish affairs among the young people from assimilated families. Books on a wide spectrum of Jewish topics, often written by non-Jews, draw a wide audience.

Despite the destruction of synagogues during the war and further demolition during the Communist period, more than 200 synagogues have survived in Bohemia and Moravia. Czech authorities have appreciated the historical and cultural importance of these remaining Jewish sites, as part of their own heritage and as points of interest for attracting Jewish tourism. A num-ber of Czech municipalities have initiated programs of synagogue restoration for cultural purposes, with excellent artistic results and a high level of historical authenticity. Their enterprise and commitment provide an exemplary standard for towns in other countries.

The existence of remarkably well-preserved ghettos in Třebíč, Boskovice, Kolín, Velké Meziříčí, Polná, Březnice, Heřmanův Městec, and Mikulov has stimulated those towns to declare the ghettos National Heritage Zones, with boundaries extended to include the Jewish cemeteries. The Czech Tourist Authority has published several attractive booklets on interesting Jewish sites and monuments in the country, and travelers are responding to this promotion. The restored Jewish Town in Prague, centered around the Altneuschul and the other old synagogues, is already one of the most popular tourist sites in Europe.

HALF ON FOOT, HALF ON HORSEBACK

Europe of the fifteenth century saw the flowering of the Renaissance. For Jews, it brought a maelstrom of pogroms, arbitrary expulsions, and search for refuge. Expelled from Austria in 1438 and from Moravian royal cities in 1454, Jews rallied in Mikulov (German: Nikolsburg), a strategic castle promontory in the Pavlov hills on the main trade route between Vienna and Brno. The area is famous for its excellent white wine, a legacy of the resident Liechtenstein aristocrats who started cultivating grapes in the Middle Ages. The Jews converged on Za hradem ulice, behind the castle, under the protection of the castle walls and the local sovereign.

Mikulov was the primary seat of the Moravian chief rabbinate during the sixteenth to the nineteenth centuries. Jews were then a majority of the town population. Escaping much of the contemporary turbulence of other Jewish towns, the tightly organized Mikulov community developed its vital role in the local wine industry. In 1550 the *kehillah* built its majestic Altschul, the only major synagogue still standing in Mikulov. Recently restored, the Altschul is an outstanding example of early Moravian synagogue architecture.

Although they could buy and own property, Jews were subject to the whims of their aristocratic protectors. Count Christopher von Liechtenstein und Nikolsburg decreed in 1560 that Jews must give 40 days of annual service to the lords of the manor "half on foot, and half on horseback," meaning with and without harness and plow. Each year Jewish homeowners paid a gold ducat and a *putschandel,* the smallest coin, as well as a live chicken at carnival time. For the privilege of electing a Jewish judge they had to supply a ton of oil to the castle on St. Mary Candlemas Day. At harvest time they were responsible for giving bread and drink as well as horses and carts to the harvesters, who nonetheless scorned them.

A new squire, Maximilian Dietrichstein, issued a *privilegium* in 1591, granting Jews a self-elected communal administration and allowing them to substitute payment in place of compulsory labor. The revised charter of 1612 removed the community from the town jurisdiction to that of the lord. As the ghetto

The Jewish quarter in Mikulov. Successively called Langegasse (Long Street), Židovská ulice, (Jews' Street), Hlavni, and Husova ulice, the main street slopes gently down to the fertile fields and vineyards that surround the town.

population increased, Jews occupied houses on the main road, Langegasse ("Long Street"), the side alleys, and down the northwest slopes to an area known euphemistically as Jews' Garden, an unpleasant, swampy area of artisans' shacks.

Although Jewish Mikulov had its share of afflictions—fires, war, and pestilence—the *kehillah* was always ready to help other Jews in distress. Ragged survivors fleeing the Chmielnicki massacres in 1648–1649 Poland found a comforting welcome. They, in turn, introduced hasidic influences to the religious life of the community.

Under quarantine without a doctor during an epidemic in 1715, only the emergency import of a physician from Vienna—at a monthly fee of 150 florins, and a fat gratuity to the town's gentile Dr. Damm—averted a calamity in the ghetto. Thereafter, as there were no Jewish doctors in Mikulov, the community prudently applied for permission to retain Dr. Josef Stella from Vienna. Attentive to opposition from the town's doctor and wary of the competition, the magistrate rejected the petition; however, he ruled that Jews who needed a physician could consult the

town doctor at his regular fee, without paying a surcharge to the town.

The fame of the Mikulov yeshivot drew rabbis and scholars. The first *Landesrabbiner* (chief rabbi) of Moravia was Rabbi Yehudah Loew ben Bezalel (1525–1609) of legendary fame. He officiated in Mikulov from 1553 to 1573 and then in Prague, where he was known as the MaHaRal. Chief Rabbi Menachem Mendel Krochmal (r. 1650–1661) edited a statute book of 311 provisions on self-government that regulated the conduct of Moravian Jewish communities.

David ben Abraham Oppenheim (1664–1736), nephew of the famed court Jew Samuel Oppenheimer, was ordained rabbi at age 20. Called to the rabbinate in Mikulov five years later, he served as *Landesrabbiner* of Moravia for 12 years before accepting the leadership in Prague. He was known and respected for his knowledge of rabbinical and halakhic literature, but he was also proficient in mathematics. Applying part of the fortune he inherited from his uncle, he organized a foundation that used income from real estate investment to support education for indigent children. Oppenheim had an unrestrained zest for books, a passion he indulged not only in extensive travel and collecting, but in sharing his finds with publishers and

Plan of the Mikulov ghetto. Hatched houses still stand. Tiny circles mark the confines of the ghetto. Stars of David mark synagogue locations. (From: J. Klenovský, *Židovské Památky Mikulova*, Mikulov, 1994.)

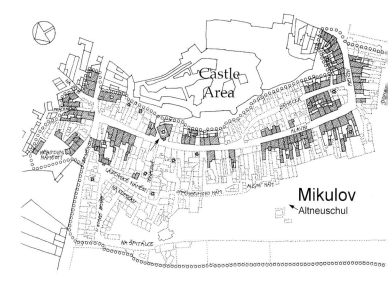

in helping young authors to publish their works. His own largely unpublished writings are preserved together with his valuable collection of books and manuscripts at the Bodleian Library in Oxford.

Hasidism was reinforced by mystic and kabbalist Rabbi Shmuel ben Hirsch Horowitz (r. 1773–1778) and again by noted talmudist Rabbi Mordecai ben Abraham Benet (r. 1789–1829), who gained fame as a "miracle worker." The last chief rabbi who lived in Mikulov was Rabbi Samson Rafael Hirsch (r. 1847–1851), who took part in the struggle for emancipation of Moravian Jewry. He advocated an intermediate position in the ideological Orthodox-Reform conflict, claiming that a combination of traditional Judaism and secular education was possible. His next post was in Frankfurt, where his successful educational system was the neo-Orthodox model applied in Germany and elsewhere.

Rabbis who passed away in Mikulov since the mid-sixteenth century were honored by burial in the Rabbis' Mount area in the cemetery, a site of pilgrimage even today for their followers. Founded over 500 years ago on the western slopes of Kozívrch (Goat's Hill), the cemetery is the most important and one of the best kept in Moravia. In 1898 Viennese architect Max Fleischer designed the ceremonial hall, restored in 1984. The 4,000 gravestones, with legible ones dating from 1605 to the early twentieth century, are archetypes of Moravian Jewish funerary art, prototypes for Jewish tombstones throughout the province. The shapes range from the seventeenth-century square or rectangular forms with pilasters on the sides, to eighteenth-century stones that culminated in a pointed triangular shield with deeply incised decorations. Moravian plant and folk motifs, such as hearts, roses, tulips, shells, and drapes are represented, as well as Jewish symbols: crowns, Levitic pitchers, hands uplifted in blessing, heraldic lions, weeping willows, wreaths, inverted scrolls, and a hand holding an alms box.

A disastrous fire destroyed the Jewish quarter and most of its records in 1719, also damaging the castle and 30 Christian houses on neighboring streets. Rioting townspeople blamed the

View from the castle terrace over the synagogue roof. The cemetery and its ceremonial hall are visible across town at the foot of Kozívrch, Goats' Hill.

Jews for the conflagration and only armed militia stopped them from perpetrating a pogrom. After the fire the duke, Walter Dietrichstein, refused to allow construction of wooden houses close to the castle hill. He erected a protective wall and committed the Jews to rebuilding their homes in brick, without chimneys on the castle side. Communities throughout Europe contributed to the cost of rebuilding, but space was severely limited because the municipality had bought up building sites to prevent expansion of the Jewish quarter.

Along with retail trade, mostly with Austrian and Hungarian villages, the community prospered through intensive viticulture, the wine trade, and transport between Vienna and Brno. Vocations shifted in the seventeenth and eighteenth centuries toward crafts and professions. Jews were furriers, tailors, trimmers, candlemakers, glaziers, button makers, braiders, goldsmiths, and soap makers, as well as physicians and musicians. Larger groups formed guilds and prayed together at their separate *shtiblekh,* small, intimate synagogues, named by craft: the *Schuster* (shoemakers), the *Fleischhaker* (butchers), and the *Schneider* (tailors), for example. Other synagogues were named by location: Upper or Lower, or by age: Old or New—and by the founders' names or origins: the Guttmann (1682), the

The Jewish cemetery in Mikulov, with legible stones from the beginning of the seventeenth century. The Mikulov peak shapes and iconographic symbols, including Moravian folk and plant motifs, and Jewish symbols—such as Levite pitchers and broken candles—were the archetypes for funereal art throughout Moravia.

Aschkeness (Ashkenazic, 1675), and the Michelstaedter (1697, extant: now a dwelling). In the early nineteenth century the Jews comprised 42 percent of the town's population, and supported 12 synagogues. There were also ritual baths, a Jewish hospital, a yeshivah, and a school for girls. Some of the synagogues closed as the population decreased toward the end of the nineteenth century. Only the Upper Altschul and the Lower Neuschul in Jews' Garden functioned after 1919.

The Imperial Vienna-Brno highway, completed in 1752, improved trade for almost a century. Many Jewish wagons rumbled along that road, carrying kegs of Mikulov wine north to Brno, west to Prague, and south to Vienna. Then in 1841 came the Vienna-Brno railroad, bypassing Mikulov and preempting most of the transport. No longer a major junction, Mikulov fell into decline. Many Jewish families left the over-crowded ghetto for Brno and Vienna, opened to them by the Emancipation.

An 1813 Brno court document yields a partial insight into the workings of the infamous Familiantengesetze (Familiants Laws), introduced by Charles VI as Rescripts 1726 and 1727, to curtail increase in the Jewish population by limiting Jewish marriage. No Jew could marry without a family number, transferable to only one son (usually the eldest) in each family after the death of the *familiant* (licensed head of a family) who held the coveted number. Other sons who wished to marry were obliged to leave the province. This law limited the number of Jewish families to 8,451 in Bohemia, to 5,106 in Moravia, and to 119 in Silesia.

A district official assigned the allotted quota of available "positions" (constituting eligibility for legal marriage) by a progressive fee according to income. Competition among the candidates was fierce. Thus, in 1813, position number 233 was granted to Gabriel Beer Skamperles for 11 florins, number 491 to Salomon Gregor Abeles for 10 florins, number 510 to Josef Sprinzeles for 13 florins, number 576 to Ahron Schlesinger for 8 florins, and number 608 to David Hirsch Misslitz for 10 florins. Possession of a "position" was necessary, but not always sufficient. A Vienna newspaper reported in January 1815 that Schlesinger was still a bachelor.

Economic development of the town progressed with active Jewish participation. During the nineteenth century Lazar Auspitz, a successful wool dealer, established a clothing mill. Rochleder set up a leather factory, Kronstein manufactured paint, Teltscher was a successful wine merchant, and Deutsch set up a grain distribution center. Jews managed 10 wholesale specialty mail-order houses for fattening geese destined for the lucrative Vienna market. The Jews in Mikulov prospered and in 1857 reached a maximum number of 3,680.

Thousands of destitute Jewish refugees from Galicia found safety in Mikulov during World War I. A year after the Czechoslovak Republic was founded, the Jewish communal autonomy in Mikulov was abolished. As a result of the postwar economic decline, the number of Jews leaving for the cities increased. The Munich Pact of September 1938 ceding Sudetenland to Germany imminently jeopardized the Jews. Since the town was within the area of the Sudetenland, whoever could fled Mikulov for the countryside. Years of fear and terror followed. In 1941 deportation squads found 39 Mikulov Jews in hiding and promptly dispatched them to the concentration town, Terezín (Theresienstadt). The few postwar survivors who returned to Mikulov met open hostility from the gentiles who were occupying their houses, and the Jews soon left. Today there are no Jews in Mikulov.

Neglected in the communist era, the Neuschul and Altschul synagogues were in danger of demolition. Without much notice the Neuschul was torn down in the 1970s by the Communist regime. Alarmed, historians and researchers of the Regional Museum of Mikulov mobilized in the late 1970s to rescue the Altschul

and to initiate restoration. Expert craftsmen worked on the synagogue painstakingly but intermittently for 12 years, as a lengthy struggle for funds took place. One extended delay resulted from a protracted search for some rose-colored marble that would closely match the original columns. Now renovated, the Altschul synagogue serves the town as a cultural center.

The restoration plan includes glass-enclosed display cases for the space where the Ark once stood, which will display Mikulov's Judaica, due for return, perhaps, from the Jewish museum in Prague. Some of these articles may have been part of the antique Judaica of great artistic and monetary value that was formerly on display in the Altschul "treasure room." The exhibit included embroidered *parokhot,* ritual utensils

Plan of the synagogue in Mikulov. A. Street level, showing Ark on eastern wall and central *bimah.* 1. entrance, 2 and 3. treasury, 4. *bimah,* 5. Ark, 6. gallery. B. Upper level with vaulted L-shaped women's gallery and nine bays in central chamber. (From J. Klenovský, *Židovské Památky Mikulova,* Mikulov, 1994.)

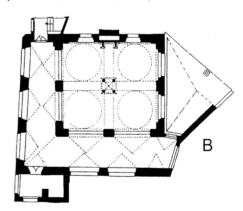

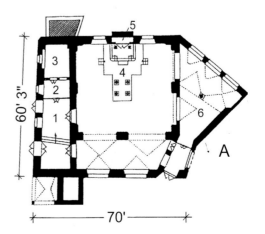

THE ALTSCHUL (UPPER) SYNAGOGUE IN MIKULOV

Masonry synagogues developed in the sixteenth and seventeenth centuries in eastern and central Europe, a quality of construction that was copied extensively in Moravia and Hungary. In contrast to the fortresslike structures of the Polish masonry synagogues, with their crenelated rooftops and narrow windows, the Mikulov Altschul, under a hip roof, has fine elegant proportions and large, round-headed windows. Unadorned exteriors were mandatory, but itinerant artists produced lavish frescoes and inscriptions on interior walls, as seen in the few remaining Polish synagogues, and in Holesov, Moravia. Within an orderly row of buildings, the Mikulov synagogue stands at an odd angle to the street so that the Ark could be located on a wall to the east.

Italian architectural influence spread northward in the sixteenth century as monarchs and aristocrats of France, Austria, and Poland invited Italian architects to design their palaces and churches. The graceful wide arches of the Altschul galleries, framing a two-level loggia, reflect this Italian Renaissance tendency. The harmonious use of domes, pendentives, and arches, and the elaborate stucco decorations on the vaults and ceiling are consistent with this notion, as is the whole concept of the interior.

The building underwent several modifications over the years. In 1688, when the galleries on north and west sides became inadequate, a triangular section was added for women on the south side, with a separate entrance. A wide set of steps leads from the two portals of the synagogue up to the castle terraces. After the ruinous 1718 fire, Johann

The Altschul on Husava ulice in Mikulov, 1550; major restorations: 1719–1723 and 1977–1989. In 1561 the corner nearest the street was accented by the construction of a one-column loggia. Such a miniature open area on the ground floor was a fashionable architectural element of the period. The Altschul is one of the two surviving synagogues in Mikulov and the only one that has been restored.

Christian Oedtl, the architect in charge of repairs to the castle, also supervised reconstruction of the synagogue from 1719 to 1723. Some features of the castle ornamentation appear in the synagogue, notably in the decorative stucco work. The main hall was rebuilt in a Baroque layout, installing and emphasizing the central *bimah*. The Ark, built in 1740, was the work of master builder Ignac Lengelacher.

The central *bimah,* constructed in 1723, with its slender marble pillars and Corinthian capitals, is in the style of the more massive four-pillared structures of contemporary Polish synagogues. The narrow space between the pillars in the Mikulov *bimah* suggest that it never served as more than a decorative architectural element. The pillars carry a multicolored marble canopy. Four arches from the central bay define the four large cupolas, and reach the peripheral masonry that supports the weight of the roof. Each of the four large corner bays contains a hemispheric dome on pendentives, in a construction similar to the system used as early as 1420 by the Renaissance architect Brunelleschi in the Pazzi chapel in Florence.

A prewar photo of the Altschul interior shows the Ark, the central *bimah,* and the stucco ceiling with Hebrew inscriptions in the cartouches below the cupolas. This and other inscriptions that graced the synagogue were omitted from the otherwise authentic restoration. The Ark was unnecessarily demolished during restoration.

Columns of the central *bimah,* with Corinthian capitals, and the stucco-decorated nine-bay ceiling, dating from the synagogue renovation of 1723.

Synagogue reopening, September 23, 1992. Galleries and sanctuary were filled with guests at the festive concert by visiting Israeli performers. (Photo provided by Wendy Eisler-Kashy.)

Prewar photo of the synagogue interior. The Ark is draped in an elaborate stucco baldachin topped by a crown. Baroque iron grille work embellishes the Ark and enhances the tall windows. The narrow *bimah* is positioned under a four-columned canopy in the center of the prayer hall. Rich stucco ornamentation covers arches and vaults. Inscription in the cartouche reads: *"Lishmoa l'Shadai melekh elyon"* ("To hearken unto the Lord, supreme King"). (Courtesy of Regionální Muzeum, Mikulov.)

Repoussé silver Passover plate from Moravia, depicting the Exodus from Egypt. The multitudes are passing through a gate on the right, which recalls the structure of the old city gate of Mikulov. Dating from the mid-nineteenth century, it measures 13½ by 10 inches. (Courtesy of Jewish Museum of Prague; inv. no. 3940.)

sculpted and cast in silver and gold, the founding books of the *ḥevrah kadishah* (1635), other illuminated books, and parchment manuscripts.

The festive reopening of the synagogue took place on September 23, 1992, with a gala concert. Town residents and dignitaries joined guests from near and far, including Vienna, Brno, and Prague, to hear Jerusalem musicians—flutist Wendy Eisler-Kashy and pianist Alan Sternfeld—who charmed the overflow audience with classical and Israeli selections. Hebrew music was heard within those walls again after 50 years of silence.

MATRIMONIAL MISCHIEF

A 500-year-old trail leads from a church in the small Moravian town of Kojetín to today's Jewish community in Maidenhead, Berkshire, England. The link is a Torah from Kojetín's former *kehillah,* one of the hundreds of sacred scrolls from destroyed Jewish communities in the Czech Republic that have found new homes abroad. The Maidenhead congregation cherishes its Torah as an inspiration, while the Protestant congregation in Kojetín appreciates the former synagogue, which is now its church. Maidenhead's Rabbi Jonathan Romain and Kojetín's Pastor Dobromil Malý have led their respective communities in the effort to keep alive the memory of the Kojetín *kehillah.*

Expelled from neighboring Olomouc in 1454, Jews sought refuge in Kojetín; however, the earliest chronicle referring to Jews in Kojetín dates only from 1566. It lists 56 Jewish families living on Judengasse ("Jews' Street"), mentions their occupations, and specifies their fixed payments to Lord Vratislav of Pernštejn. He received 20 *schock,* 7½ groschen for rent on the feast of St. George, and an arbitrary 13 *schock* on the feast of St. Wenzel. Jewish judges and elders were to ensure that no one was exempt from these oppressive assessments—the price of home and protection.

The Jews of Kojetín built their synagogue of brick and stone at the entrance to Judengasse, leaving no record of construction date; there is, however, mention of a renovation and expansion in 1614. The 1566 chronicle listing the Jews' occupations, moreover, mentions a *schul* caretaker, implying the existence of a synagogue. Unlike ghetto streets in other towns, this Judengasse was a clean and cheerful place with abundant meadows and gardens behind the houses. Most of the Jews were peddlers until they gained permission to engage in business, but some cultivated the grasslands and raised cattle.

Their bucolic peace was broken at mid-seventeenth century by events affecting Polish Jewry. Unwilling to see to the routine operation of their holdings in Poland and the Ukraine, the Polish nobility leased their estates, mills, inns, or other assets to Jews for them to administer under a system of concessions called *arenda.*

Southeast façade of the synagogue in Kojetín, sixteenth century. The Brethren who bought the building in 1953 moved the entrance, to lower right, from the north to the east. The floor is several steps below ground level, in keeping with the late medieval Jewish custom based on the verse, *"Mima'amakim karatikha Adonai"* ("Out of the depths I call You, O Lord"; Ps. 130:1).

As the proximate agents of the landowners, the Jews were perceived by the peasants as the oppressors, although Jewish control was typically more humane than the Polish. When Ukranian peasant masses and Cossacks revolted against Polish rule in the Ukraine under the ruthless leadership of Bogdan Chmielnicki (1595–1657), they vented their fury mostly against the Jews. Bloodthirsty hordes massacred tens of thousands of Ukrainian and Polish Jews during the infamous pogroms of 1648 to 1649, and more than 300 *kehillot* were destroyed. Wretched refugees of the disaster reached many Moravian towns; the Kojetín community welcomed many of them. Absorbed, at length, into the community, the new arrivals introduced Polish prayer rituals and rich talmudic lore.

In the mid-seventeenth century the synagogue lost its roof in a fire that ripped through the quarter. The *kehillah* could not afford to rebuild, so it assembled elsewhere in dingy circumstances for five decades while the synagogue remained roofless. Samson Wertheimer of Eisenstadt volunteered to pay for restoring the synagogue, but the town authorities refused his generous offer in order to prevent further Jewish use of the building on its attractive open square. On this and several other matters, the community petitioned the Chancellery of Prague. The 1718 ruling by Count Ferdinand von Khuenburg, Prince Archbishop of Prague, was favorable, granting permission to repair the synagogue and restore it to use. The Prince Archbishop granted other rights: Jewish burials were permitted, subject to an individual fee of 250 *reichsthaler;* meadow land associated with Jewish homes could continue in such use as a "temporary" measure; distribution of kosher wine on Judengasse and the appointments of Moyses Bernard as rabbi and Jacob Kantor as *ḥazzan* were all approved. But exemption of Jews from service during hunts and relief from a head tax per cow were both refused because these were "old customs worth perpetuation."

Diminished and still impoverished after the fire, the community reorganized. When the ghetto was established—on renamed Židovská ulice in 1727—500 Jews inhabited 40 houses. Small as it was, the *kehillah* became a center of important rabbis. One of the youngest was Rabbi Eleasar Flekeles, born in Prague in 1755, a student of famed Rabbi Yeḥezkel Landau, with whom he carried on a learned correspondence. At the age of 25 Rabbi Flekeles became rabbi of Kojetín, but he officiated there for only four years before he was recalled to Prague to serve as chief jurist. People fondly remembered him and his query to Rabbi Landau about a local problem over the Sabbath boundary, the *eruv.*

In his *responsum* of 1780 Rabbi Landau reviewed the issue: "Greetings to my beloved student and friend, the honorable Rabbi Eleasar Flekeles: You wrote me about the *eruv* in the Jewish quarter of Kojetín. The *goyim* often tear down the rope, making it impossible to transfer the *tsholnt* on the Sabbath from one house to another. . . . The joy of the holy day is disturbed. . . . You explored the outskirts of the town just behind the Jewish quarter and discovered a natural moat in a deep valley. Can the moat serve as an *eruv?* The answer is 'Yes.'"

And the community rejoiced. An illuminated map from 1700 in Kojetín's archive vividly depicts two rows of Jewish dwellings on a curving street that runs parallel to the moat that encircles their part of town.

Other documents from that archive illustrate the changes taking place in the Austro-Hungarian Empire toward the liberal spirit of the nineteenth century leading up to the Emancipation. The 1727 Rescript had prohibited Jews from renting houses that were Christian property. In 1827, the Imperial and Royal District Office addressed a query to the municipality regarding the observance of the draconic rescript, still ostensibly in force. The Provisions Office of Kojetín replied, in part:

In view of the progress made by the nations in the past hundred years . . . it is not surprising that a political law dating from the age of intolerance is no longer in accord with the present age. At that time Jews were regarded as depraved people with few civil rights. It led to the unfortunate state where Jews were treated in a hostile manner, almost like slaves, instead of participating in the general progress of culture and humanity. . . . The Supreme Rescript can be viewed as no longer meritorious of existence . . . the same should expressly be rescinded . . . and tolerated Jews should be permitted to rent Christian houses.

The relatively large number of Jews living in Kojetín—443 by 1830—and their high birth rate clashed with the legally established limit of 76 families. Ordered in 1830 to investigate reports of possible secret marriages among Jews, the Provisions Office displayed a pragmatic tolerance of infractions.

Here . . . single women have given birth to children . . . and since there have been no complaints as to costs of maintenance, they seem to have a secret bond with the father. There are no definite criteria for proving the existence of a secret and unlawful marriage. When, because of their businesses, unmarried Jews must maintain an individual household, they are permitted to have

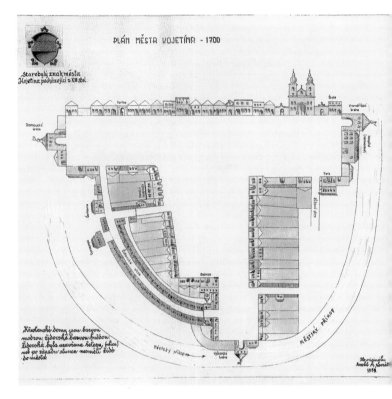

Map of Kojetín in 1700, found by Jerusalem residents Avraham and Shlomo Steiner in the Kojetín archives during a search for family roots. Young Steiner's great-great-great grandfather was one of the Jews who had to leave Kojetín under Familiants' Law restrictions and moved to Bratislava. The map depicts accurately the curving street, Židovská ulice, with its two rows of Jews' dwellings running parallel to the moat that encircles the town. Blue marks the Christian houses, and red, the Jewish ones. (Courtesy of A. Steiner. Original in Town Archive, Kojetín.)

female help. In the course of time the maid becomes a housekeeper and mother, and is scarcely distinguishable from a lawfully wedded wife in the house of her employer. This mischief cannot be countered by legislative measures. Perhaps the time has come to ease restrictions on Jewish marriages, since grounds therefore no longer exist.

The outstanding Rabbi Jacob Michael Brüll (1812–1889) served in Kojetín from 1843 for nearly 50 years. His knowledge of the entire Talmud was unequaled in his lifetime. Best known for his remarkable blending of rabbinical knowledge with a broad understanding of human nature, he was a warm hasidic rabbi, with an

The Jewish school and rabbi's house, built in 1867. A stately Classical building with five short columns accenting its facade, it stands opposite the synagogue, across a narrow street. It functioned as a Jewish school until 1910. Between 1920 and World War II, the building housed the local police. Now it serves as the residence of Pastor Malý and church offices. During the church renovation, the three Gothic windows in the rabbi's dwelling on the upper floor were changed to rectangular shape. (Illustration after H. Gold, *Die Juden und Judengemeinde in Mährens*.)

innate sense of humor. He developed a loving relationship with his congregation and kept an open mind toward modern culture and education. It was just as natural to hear strains of live classical music in his house as the tones of talmudic polemics. The Christian community respected him greatly, to the benefit of all Kojetín's Jews.

Social and cultural conditions improved in the post-Emancipation second half of the nineteenth century, a veritable golden age for the Jews in Kojetín. They pursued education and openly contracted legal marriages. They could operate businesses without discriminatory restriction. With success in trade and commerce, some moved out of the Jewish quarter, but Židovská ulice remained the busy center of social and cultural life. A lively spirit and a great

variety of activities characterized the quarter, especially on holidays, when it teemed with guests. Dwindling gradually, the *kehillah* retained a Jewish mayor until 1924.

Among the great scholars born in Kojetín was David Kaufman (1852–1899), son of one of the educated and worldly families in the town. After studying with Rabbi Jacob Brüll, he completed doctoral studies in Jewish philosophy at Leipzig. In 1877 he became one of the leading professors at the newly opened Rabbinical Seminary in Budapest. The 30 books and 500 scholarly essays he wrote testify to his creativity and exceptionally wide interests. Dealing with nearly every area of Jewish scholarship, he excelled in history, medieval Jewish philosophy, history of religion, and in the history of Jewish art—a field he pioneered.

By 1930 only 32 Jewish families remained. During the roundups of 1942 the Nazis captured 83 of the 90 registered Jews and deported them to Terezín. Few returned. The Nazis had planned to destroy the abandoned synagogue, but local residents demanded permission to use it as a warehouse. The Protestant congregation bought the building in 1953 for use as a church.

Founded by charismatic leader Jan Hus as a Christian reform movement in the fourteenth century, the Protestant Hussite church, known after the sixteenth century as the Czech Brethren, has a history that is interwoven with the surge and ebb of fifteenth-century national and social conflicts in Bohemia. Catholics accused the Hussites of being a Judaizing sect because they interpreted the Old Testament literally and rejected adoration of saints and relics. The Church burned Hus at the stake in 1415. In a striking monument in Staroměstské náměstí (Old Town Square) in the heart of ancient Prague, he still stands like a prophet in flowing bronze robes, arm outstretched and pointing. Although the Hussites generally considered the Hebrews worthy of protection because they had once been the object of Divine revelation, some Hussite leaders criticized or even tormented the Jews for their stubborn rejection of Jesus. In this ambivalence, Jews were often the victims of both sides, as the Church viciously persecuted the "heretic" Hussites.

Forced by the Catholics to convert or go into exile, some Hussites opted instead for conversion to Judaism. Certain Jewish families in Bohemia and Moravia trace their descent from these converted Brethren. After World War II local Czech Brethren acquired a total of 39 synagogues for conversion to churches. The members repaired and restored the buildings, usually covering or removing the Holy Ark and painting the walls white. Minimizing the display of Christian symbols in Kojetín, the members placed their emblem—a small cross within a chalice—high on the facade in place of Tablets of the Law, and mounted a large wooden cross inside on the western wall.

We learned of the remarkable Torah rescue project from Pastor Dobromil Malý, leader of the Kojetín Brethren. A London philanthropist had bought more than 1,500 Torah scrolls from the Czech government in 1963. These were part of

Ceramic *lavabo* on display in the synagogue anteroom, now a church columbarium.

THE SYNAGOGUE IN KOJETÍN

The old Kojetín synagogue stands surrounded by a well-kept lawn. Made of stone and brick, with space for 300 persons, it gleams under a fresh coat of white paint and a new red-tiled roof. In preparing the synagogue for their use, the Brethren made several structural changes: They moved the entryway from the north side to the east, sealed off the gallery on the north, and reversed the seating orientation, placing their altar on the west. The church organ stands on a platform near the white east wall, the former location of the Ark.

The large anteroom contains the original niche and well-preserved ceramic *lavabo* of the *kehillah*. Adapting the anteroom for Christian use as a columbarium, the Brethren installed small cubicles for funerary urns on the wall opposite the *lavabo*. This large entrance chamber with its thick walls and opposite ceiling vaults may have been the original fifteenth-century synagogue. It is the oldest extant structure in Kojetín.

Interior view of the functioning synagogue—probably from the 1930s—showing *Aron Kodesh*, seating arrangements, and decorative lamps. Window grilles to the women's gallery were sealed off in the church renovation. The small circular window above the Ark, blocked off on the outside, is covered by the taller Ark introduced with the 1718 restorations. (Illustration after H. Gold, *Die Juden und Judengemeinde in Mährens.*)

Along with the synagogue in Maidenhead, England, U.S. congregations in Fort Lauderdale, Wheeling, Chicago, and Philadelphia each received a scroll from Kojetín. Maidenhead leaders appreciated the pedagogic potential of a Torah from a lost European *kehillah.* "Adopting" the liquidated community, Maidenhead congregants researched the history of the Kojetín *kehillah,* including the biography of individual members up to the onset of the war. For an assembly in memory of the lost community—with the cooperation of Pastor Malý and Kojetín mayor Vladimír Sevela—Maidenhead congregants visited the former synagogue and cemetery in Kojetín. Other participants included Israeli representatives of the former Kojetín Jewish community and delegates from the four other congregations that had also received scrolls from Kojetín. The ceremony took place in the Kojetín synagogue in the fall of 1992, on the fiftieth anniversary of the deportation of Kojetín's Jews.

In 1574 Jan Suchanek sold a one-third part of a field for 28 *schock* "free and unencumbered . . . to the Jews of Kojetín, as heritable property, for their burials and cemetery. . . . At his expense, Jan Suchanek shall erect a fence between his field and the sold property." A fence was hardly necessary, then, to protect the dead and their monuments from vandalism. The place had little attraction for superstitious folk since the execution ramp and burial field for the town's criminals was an immediate neighbor. In the last half century, however, less inhibited townspeople have felt free to drag gravestones away from the unprotected cemetery for secondary use.

Not far from the synagogue, the cemetery on Olomoucká ulice now has the status of an historical site to be preserved. The Jewish community of Olomouc undertook to clear the weeds and to restore the existing markers, the oldest legible stone of which is from 1795. A quaint map of the cemetery, drawn in 1882 by Michael Weisskopf, locates family plots by name and surrounds them with everlasting shrubbery.

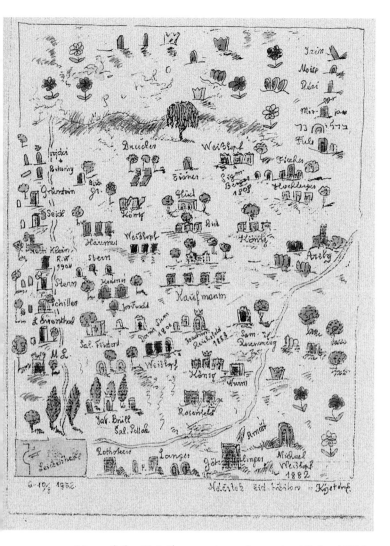

Map of the Kojetín cemetery, drawn by Michael Weisskopf in 1882 to show family plot locations. (Courtesy of Dobromil Malý. Original in Kojetín City Archive.)

the haul of Judaica that the Germans had confiscated to Prague from Jewish homes and synagogues in Bohemia and Moravia and had catalogued during the war for a projected "museum of decadent Jewish culture." After transfer to London, the 1,500 scrolls were consigned to the Memorial Scrolls Trust of the Westminster Synagogue for examination, repair, and distribution to active congregations in England, the United States, and elsewhere. A Torah scroll from the Moravian *kehillah* of Uherské Hradiště was presented to U.S. President Jimmy Carter when he visited London.

ANGELS TO GUARD YOU IN ALL YOUR WAYS

Třebíč is a pleasant highland town near Brno, famed for its outstanding collection of "Bethlehems"—miniature hand-carved tableaux dramatizing the birth of Jesus. The town also has a well-preserved ghetto, the former home of one of the largest and most influential *kehillot* in Moravia. Třebíč is a town without Jews, where a gentile octogenarian devotes his time and energy to the maintenance of the Jewish cemetery. Born in the small cottage outside the cemetery wall where he still lives, former teacher and school inspector Bohumír Pavlík carries the memory of his massacred Jewish neighbors etched on his soul. In the years since his retirement, he has steadfastly worked in the cemetery. A volunteer at first and something of a legend, he bore the expenses as well until the *kehillah* of Brno, where everyone loves and respects him, awarded him a monthly stipend.

Enterprising Benedictine monks founded a monastery in 1101 on a hill overlooking the Jihlava Valley, near the river ford at Třebíč. The monastery prospered from the traffic of pilgrims attracted to its legendary painting of the Madonna. In time a bustling market town grew up around it, with enterprising merchants and Jews among the town's residents. The date of earliest Jewish settlement is unclear. Jewish merchants had plied the trade routes in Moravia as early as the Roman occupation and during the Great Moravian era in the ninth century. The first local mention of Jews is found in a Třebíč chronicle of 1410, which records an attack and robbery perpetrated on several Jews by certain named persons who went unpunished.

Jews settled first on the south bank in Podklášteří (under the church) in mixed housing. When a local statute required the separation of Jews from Christians in 1286, they were concentrated in a Jewish quarter, Zámostí (behind the bridge), on the opposite bank beneath the castle—an arrangement that conformed to the siting of many medieval ghettos throughout Europe. We can assume that the Jewish presence was begun in the thirteenth century. The quarter developed on the north bank and ran eastward in two parallel streets, connected to each other and to the river by several narrow

Bohumír Pavlík, an octogenarian who voluntarily cares for the Jewish cemetery in Třebíč. A former teacher and school supervisor, he has restored the ceremonial hall and maintains the cemetery. "I work here every day until darkness comes, and students come often to help me. The Jews of Brno say I am sculpting a monument to myself." There is a monument at the entrance to the cemetery to the Jewish soldiers who died in battle in World War I, and another to the 290 Jews of Třebíč who perished in World War II.

alleys. Expansion of the ghetto in later years was impossible because houses had filled the area between the river and the rocky slope of Hrádek Hill. As the population increased, people exploited the limited space to the maximum, creating a tangle of houses and annexes that replaced former gardens and backyards in the inner courts. The ghetto's confined geography caused the hygienic and social problems typical of overpopulation.

By the sixteenth century, Třebíč Jews operated most of the local branches of commerce and reached distant towns and markets. Complaints by Catholic competitors in 1528 motivated Count Jan Jetřich Černohorský of Boskovice to plan an expulsion of the Jews from Třebíč and environs and to forbid participation in the fairs. The Turks, however, were at the gates of Vienna, and as the defense of Moravia depended in part on the heavy contributions from Třebíč Jewry, Černohorský deferred the expulsion. The Jews' loyalty did not, however, protect them from Hungarian troops who pillaged Jewish homes as they marched through town on their way to battle the Turks. They had done the same in similar circumstances in 1468.

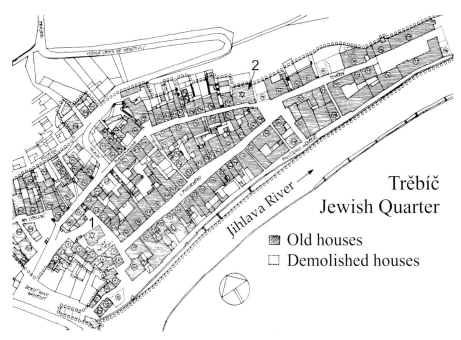

Map of the ghetto in Třebíč. Note the two main streets running parallel to the river and the synagogues identified by Stars of David. Some of the buildings on Pokorného ulice provide covered access from the street to the river bank. 1. Altschul, 2. Neuschul. (From: J. Klenovský, Židovské Památky Třebíč.)

View of the ghetto area from across the Jihlava River. Proximity to the river was considered to be an important element of security. The building marked "Zelenina" was a warehouse for agricultural produce.

Třebíč Jews had few rights and remained objects of malice and exploitation. A protection tax imposed in 1556 required them to pay half the expenses of the manorial guards and to supply forage and harnesses for the castle riding horses. They paid 120 gold coins annually for the privilege of *not* lending horses to the manor. Another payment eked out the privilege to buy agricultural products from the feudal estates, at prices determined by the aristocrats. A new owner of the estate, Count Burjan Osovský, permitted them in 1562 to erect stalls in the marketplace. They also engaged in money lending, lumber processing, soap manufacturing, distilling, and tanning. Jews were active in the production and export of a fine cloth—called *třebitscher Tuche*—famed for its beauty and delicacy. Records of 1750 list many Jewish craftsmen, including 101 master tradesmen, 23 tailors, and one bandmaster. The numerous tailors and a bandmaster suggest a fair standard of living and an interest in music.

Until the *kehillah* buildings underwent improvement around the start of the seventeenth century, children attended *ḥeder* at the homes of their *rebbes*. They studied Bible, Talmud, Mishnah, and the three "Rs" with junior teachers, while the rabbi taught the commentaries of Rashi and other scholars. History, geography, and drawing were added to the curriculum in 1740.

Ravaging armies swept across central Europe repeatedly in the seventeenth century. Lacking protective walls, Zámostí was easy prey to the marauding troops. For a hefty payment in 1621, Moravian Captain Karel von Žerotín granted a "general pardon"—protection from plunder at the hands of the military. Between 1643 and 1645 the Swedish armies of General Torstenson roamed the countryside, wreaking damage to fields and houses. With the Treaty of Westphalia ending the Thirty Years' War in 1648, a semblance of fragile peace descended.

Opposite the rabbi's house in Tiché nám (tranquil square) at the western end of the ghetto, the *kehillah* completed a substantial synagogue in 1642 to replace the wooden synagogue of the previous century at that location. Called the Front Synagogue because of its proximity to the

The Altschul on Tiché nám (tranquil square), 1639 to 1642, remodeled several times, and to the present neo-Gothic style, in 1856 to 1857. The interior was drastically altered for use as a Protestant church. External steps lead to the former women's gallery. A bronze plaque in the lobby recalls the building's Jewish origin.

ghetto entrance, it was later referred to as the Altschul when a newer one, the Neuschul, was built. The Altschul was higher than the neighboring houses, and its windows blazed with candlelight on holidays and Sabbath eve. The lights offended the religious sensibilities of Countess Marie Anna von Liechtenstein, who could see them from the castle. To remedy so grievous a fault, in 1757 she ordered the congregation to lower the height of the synagogue. Frequent fires in the town mandated numerous repairs to the structure, and major changes were made during the alterations of 1856–1857 when neo-Gothic windows were installed. The second synagogue—the Neuschul, on Blahoslavova ulice near the little square beyond the ghetto center—was built in the eighteenth century.

The community was strong enough at the turn of the eighteenth century to initiate exceptional court proceedings against the new owner of the town, Count Valdstein. Upon taking authority, he had promulgated stringent anti-Jewish measures, disregarding valid *privilegia* and documented rights. The litigation went all

the way to the court of Kaiser Joseph I, who in 1708 issued rescripts with renewed assurances of Jewish rights and equalized taxes on Jewish-owned real estate to those of non-Jews. By the end of the eighteenth century there were 1,770 Třebíč Jews—59 percent of the population.

The *kehillah* in Třebíč was served by distinguished rabbis. Rabbi David ben Isserl of Vienna, a talmudic genius and already a rabbi in Uherský Brod at age 14, served in Eisenstadt before arriving in Třebíč, where he officiated from 1677 until 1717. His learned correspondence with his father-in law, Mikulov's Rabbi Menachem Mendel Krochmal, was preserved in Mikulov until the documents were lost in the fire of 1719. Born in Třebíč, Rabbi Joachim Josef Pollak (1798–1879) studied in Třešt and later with the famed Ḥatam Sofer in Pressburg (Bratislava), and was ordained at age 18. His outstanding scholarship achieved much notice and appointment as rabbi by the Třebíč *kehillah*, which he served from 1828 to 1879. He wrote diligently for various academic journals and students from near and distant towns flocked eagerly to his side. Loyal to the city of his birth, Rabbi Pollak rejected numerous offers of appointment to other communities.

During the first Silesian War in 1742, Friedrich II, King of Prussia, marched through Třebíč with 25,000 soldiers. He spared the Jewish town in exchange for 10,000 gulden in *Brandschatzung* (fire insurance). The premium covered the military threat but not actual fire. In 1759 walnuts stored in Abraham Bauer's stuffy attic exploded from the May heat and started a conflagration. Strong winds carried blazing nuts to neighboring rooftops, setting them aflame. The fire reduced 184 houses to ashes. Successive poor crops in the early 1770s brought near famine to the town, and a few years later heavy rains swelled the Jihlava River, flooding ghetto houses. On their way to *ḥeder* in the cold winter of 1785, children trudged through high-banked snow until three weeks after Passover.

Although prices came down somewhat, army commanders clung to the ancient custom of making local populations pay for military campaigns. Before the battle of Austerlitz, when French armies marched through Třebíč in 1805, they extorted from the *kehillah* 5,000 gulden "against torching"; in 1809 with softer hearts, they demanded only 4,000 gulden.

Purim and Holy Friday fell on the same day in 1821. Palace authorities ordered the community to cancel the scheduled dance and celebration. When the musketeers arrived at the Jewish quarter to enforce the ruling, frustrated young Jews chased them away, pelting them with eggs and hot water. Unhappy results followed. Many Jews, including those from respected families, were beaten with sticks "like rebellious peasants."

From 1638 the *kehillah* was autonomous, with an elected mayor and two councilmen—though it ceded control of land registry in 1849. Three years later Dr. Simon Schuschný organized a Jewish 24-bed hospital in a single-story house in the northern corner of the ghetto and furnished it with the best medicines and equipment available. After the full Emancipation of 1861 and the subsequent population movement to Vienna and other large cities, the *kehillah* entered a period of decline.

The river was a perennial problem. It flooded severely in 1830; water inundated the entire Jewish quarter up to the second story of the buildings as well as a large part of the Christian town on the south side. Jews huddled on the rooftops, waiting for the waters to subside. In February 1862 the biggest flood since 1830 deluged Zámostí and swept away all the bridges except the one that connected the town with the entry to the Jewish quarter. As a wagoner named Grünberger drove home across the bridge in his two-horse wagon and reached the middle piers, the water suddenly swept away all other parts of the bridge. Horses, wagon, and driver stopped— stranded on the piers for three days before rescue was possible.

Emmanuel Subak, founder of a tanning factory, endowed a fund of 6,000 gulden in 1899 to provide dowries for indigent brides. He also contributed toward building the Jewish town hall at number 14, the corner of Pokorného ulice. At the turn of the twentieth century, 987 Jews resided in Třebíč. Reorganizing, the *kehillah* separated jurisdictions in 1891. The religious authority, the *Kultusgemeinde,* controlled the two synagogues and the cemetery, while civic properties, town hall,

The Jewish inn, extreme right, next to the Neuschul, in the 1920s, demolished in the 1980s. (Courtesy of the Municipality of Třebíč.)

schools, and hospital became the responsibility of the civic authority, the Israelitische Gemeinde.

In World War I the *kehillah* of 364 lost 20 soldiers. The Jews of Třebíč floated a loan of 73,000 crowns to set up an orphanage in the expanded school at number 58 Pokorného ulice. After the war the diminished community assembled only in the Altschul. Unused, the Neuschul served alternate functions, first as a leather warehouse by the I. H. Subak company and later as a vegetable storeroom by the Zelenina produce company. Decades of misuse caused the deterioration of the many colorful fresco decorations and the inscriptions that once covered the walls and ceiling.

In 1923 the community realized a long-held dream: protection against flood damage. The Moravian land administration built levees along the banks of the Jihlava River, with funds provided by the *kehillah* and the Subak family. The end of political autonomy and the dissolution of the *Israelitische Gemeinde* came in 1931. The municipality invited three Jews to participate in

The Neuschul, eighteenth century, view from the east in 1990. Note the massive buttress, the Ark protrusion, and the small round window above the Ark location.

Ghetto square, 1997, with restored synagogue (left), reconstructed inn (center), and "Synagogue Guest House" containing an art gallery.

the town government, including Dr. Julian Subak as vice mayor.

The Germans took control of the Jewish quarter in 1939. Jews from other communities of southwest Moravia were herded into the ghetto and—in May 1942—1,370 Jews (including 290 from Třebíč) were deported to concentration camps. A few women returned, only one of whom was alive in Třebíč in 1991. After the Second World War the ghetto area benefited from fortuitous neglect. There was not much interest in urban renewal until 1975, when a proposal to demolish the entire area and replace the old structures with modern dwellings died for lack of funds. With growing awareness and appreciation of the architectural and cultural value of the old quarter, the municipality has opted for preservation and has allocated funds for the purpose.

Both synagogues still stand. The Nazis used the older Altschul at Tiché nám as a storeroom. In 1952 the Czech Brethren bought it and adapted it for use as a church. They painted over the Hebrew inscriptions and the ornamental decorations, walled up the eastern windows, and closed the area of the women's gallery. Above the portal they affixed the symbol of their church, a cross on a chalice.

In medieval times Jews buried their dead below the castle walls. Early in the seventeenth century the newly arrived Valdsteins demanded that the cemetery be moved because it blocked their view as they approached the castle by coach. They appropriated land for a new cemetery "on the hill behind the town," away from the attention of aristocrats and burghers. Enclosed by a stone wall and with a gate on Hrádek ulice, it lies on the steep slope of Hrádek Hill above Týnský Brook. After the addition of a new section in 1888, it became one of the largest Jewish cemeteries in Moravia.

Plan of the Neuschul in Třebíč. A. Ground floor, B. Upper level. 1. Ark niche, 2. Entrance lobby, 3. Western gallery, 4. Northern gallery. (From: J. Klenovský, *Židovské Památky Třebíče*.)

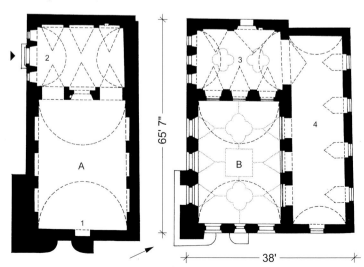

THE NEUSCHUL SYNAGOGUE IN TŘEBÍČ

The Neuschul (new synagogue) was also called "the Back Synagogue" because it was away from the ghetto entrance. It is a rugged building with deeply vaulted ceiling, and external buttress, on foundations from the late Renaissance. Carved decorations on the stone portal—and the wall thickness—suggest construction from about 1600. The current structure, including the west gallery with its entrance from the adjoining building, dates from the early Baroque, about 1700. The lavish frescoes, floral decorations, and large inscriptions were initially painted in 1707 and were renewed at later times. As the *kehillah* expanded, a northern gallery was added in 1837. Three broad arches open each of the galleries into the prayer hall. Two high, vaulted, and round-headed windows flank the Ark niche and three of them line the southern wall.

On our visits we saw a gaping rectangular niche on the east wall, the location of the missing Ark, and layers of frescoes peeling in haphazard array. Municipal plans in the 1990s to preserve the ghetto and to revitalize the synagogue as a culture hall and a museum have finally borne fruit. The old ghetto is now a protected historical zone where gentrification has begun on many of the houses. Work on the synagogue building began in 1994, and the Neuschul, in sparkling new paint with restored frescoes and inscriptions, opened its doors with great festivity to the public in September, 1977. A major exhibition on the history and monuments of the Jewish community of Třebíč was installed on January 17, 2000.

Synagogue interior after restoration, in 1997, view to the east. The synagogue has been restored by the municipality at a cost of Kč.1.5 million to serve as concert-exhibition hall and Jewish museum. (Photo: Pavelka, Třebíč.)

Women's galleries of the Neuschul on the west and north before the restoration.

נכי מלאכיו יצוה לך לשמרך בכל דרכך

Bohumír Pavlík and author display the burial cloth in front of the Ceremonial Hall. The inscription reads: "For he will order his angels to guard you wherever you go" (Ps. 91:11).

We found Bohumír Pavlík in the cemetery, busily repairing a retaining wall on a path shaded by birch, maple, and spruce trees—the ambiance of a quiet park. Pavlík left his work to show us the cemetery. Step by step, he has painstakingly rebuilt retaining walls and reset fallen stones. Among the 2,000 standing stones and the 1,600 lying on the ground, there are some Baroque markers with ornamental folk motifs. Later decorative elements include heraldic lions or deer, crowns, priests' hands in blessing, and Levites' jugs pouring water.

Pavlík showed us his achievements at the ceremonial hall near the cemetery entrance where the dead are eulogized before burial. He had recently restored to the hall two treasures that he had kept hidden in his house during the long years of Communist rule. One is an exqui-site, decorated porcelain *lavabo* that glistens in its original niche near the entrance. The other is a pair of embroidered black velvet funereal cloths, used to cover the bier during the burial service.

Pavlík told us about his nonagenarian friend Marta. He used to visit her occasionally in the old folks' home, where the same conversation repeated itself each time:

Have you finished digging my grave, Pan Pavlík? Can I die yet?

Not yet, Marta, not yet. I will tell you when.

In late 1996 Pavlík dug a new grave in the old Jewish cemetery and buried Marta Friedová, the last Jew of Třebíč.

TO DEFEND THE CHRISTIANS AGAINST SUPERSTITION

The sixteenth-century process of confining Jews to ghettos was an expression of a Christian Europe that was wracked by religious wars over the Reformation and Counter-Reformation. Although the Church had religious and economic motivations for the segregation, Jews gained a modicum of autonomy among their kinsmen. They practiced their trades and followed their culture and religion in a tight Jewish community milieu.

Though many old ghettos disappeared as they succumbed to modern urban development, some are fairly well preserved. In Polná, a way-station town between Prague and Brno, there is a ghetto complex that has been relatively undisturbed since its inception in 1681. Formerly separated from the town by upper and lower gates, the 32 houses of the complex define two courts joined by a narrow passage. The upper court is a large, unpaved open triangle sloping gently downhill—past a well, the hand pump of which still produces water, and a solitary clump of trees—to the seventeenth-century synagogue. The lower court is a small rectangle.

A *kehillah* lived in this complex for nearly three hundred years, leaving behind not much more than the synagogue, a community building, and a wooded cemetery outside the town. Without Jews since World War II, the ghetto is now a working class neighborhood that still projects something of the ethnic atmosphere of its former inhabitants. It has been proclaimed a National Heritage Zone, and local authorities have made considerable progress on restoration of the synagogue.

Polná was established in the thirteenth century to guard the commercial highway to Moravia. Some three hundred years later, it had developed into a thriving market town in which the major industry was textiles. The town attracted Jews in their familiar role as merchants and moneylenders. They settled among their Christian neighbors but were often subject to discriminatory legislation. Like so many other towns of that age, Polná has a

Polná, the larger ghetto court, northwest toward the narrow entrance near the town square.

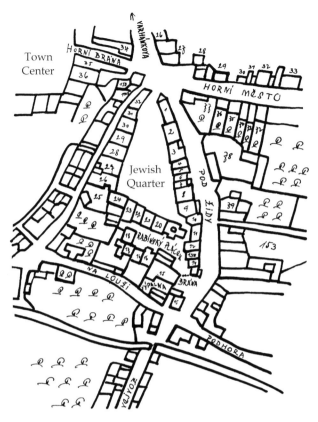

Map of the ghetto in Polná, 1711. A circle next to house number 20 identifies the synagogue complex. The ghetto encompassed houses numbers 1–32 within the larger court, (Židovské Město, and the smaller court, Rabínský Plácek. (Courtesy of Souhlasíme s publikováním, Polná.)

motley history in its relations with the Jews. Its legal Patent Book, *Právní manuál měska Polné,* contains the first documentary mention of Jews—already there in appreciable numbers in 1532.

Jews were restricted in trade; in events of friction with Christians, they had to turn to the nobility for intervention. Though scorned for their separatist religion, Jews were exempt from many civic duties. They did not stand night guard. They were not recruited into the army, nor were they required to billet soldiers. They had only to provide gold, when needed, for king and nobility.

A few sample entries from the seventeenth-century Patent Book follow:

- 1608: In response to the butchers' guild's complaint against Jewish competition, the mayor forbade Jews to sell meat to Christians. Transgressors' meat would be confiscated and used to feed hospital sick or the poor.
- 1651: Too many sick Polish Jews were traveling through Bohemian towns, laying the inhabitants open to infection. The magistrate decreed a fine of 100 thalers for anyone giving them accommodations.
- 1654: New feudal lord Cardinal František Dietrichstein of Mikulov excepted Jews from

the general exclusion of non-Catholics from his diocese. In his eyes Jews were witnesses of God's miracles and Old Testament prophesies and were worthy of protection. Presumably, the comforting convenience of their massive financial support in time of crisis bolstered his favorable discrimination.

Until Dietrichstein's time, Jews lived at will among the Christians in Polná, but the gentile merchants were uneasy. Besieging the cardinal on his state visit to Polná in 1676, the burghers presented him with a series of complaints against the Jews: "They hang their wares out in front in a way that makes Christian houses unclean. They do not weigh their wares on city scales. They sell stolen goods." The cardinal promptly pronounced social and economic restrictions, "in order to stop all religious and hygienic problems caused by Jewish and Christian coexistence." The most drastic provision was to establish a ghetto at Dolní ulice (Lower Street), outside the walls, near the small Jewish cemetery on the northwest edge of town. With poor drainage, that location was unhealthy for the inhabitants and unsuitable for shops. Local gentry for their part resented the ghetto's proximity to their lands and insisted that it be moved. The town chose a different site in 1681, just beyond the upper city gate to the southeast. The Jews moved again into the first 16 attached houses along one side of the triangular court.

Settling into its new environment, the *kehillah* received permission to form a separate municipal unit with a Jewish judge, to build a tannery, and to dig a well with an adjacent fish trough in the ghetto court. Magistrates Izak Michl, Izak Herschl, Abraham Ahron, Jakob Giml, and Elias Wolf were the leaders among the early families in the town register. The *kehillah* used a wooden hut in the yard of a member, Samuel, for assembly and prayer during the first few years in the ghetto. The modest room with benches and an Ark of unfinished lumber reminded them of the Tabernacle in the Exodus from Egypt.

Relations between the community and town authorities were amicable. On August 14, 1682, the *parnassim* and the town magistrate signed an important agreement. The town consented to build a new synagogue "from stones, bricks . . . and a nice vault up to the ceiling, and to provide all the furniture. It will also build a vaulted well and a *mikveh,* for which the Jews will pay 10 zlatý, annually, eternal interest. . . ." Of the construction costs, 474 gulden, 41 1/2 kreuzer, the *kehillah* paid 224 gulden, 41 1/2 kreuzer and promised the remainder in installments. The synagogue was completed two years later.

The legendary Prague-born Rabbi Ben Polak (1584?–1684) led the Polná community for 25 years. A *tzaddik* (righteous man) and a miracle maker, he opened a *beit midrash* (house of study), where he spent much of his time wrapped in his *tallit,* chanting prayers or studying Kabbalah. Christians as well as Jews believed in his holiness and spiritual power. People whispered

Drawing of Rabínský *Plácek* (the lower Rabbi's court). 1. the synagogue, 2. community building, 3. school and hospital, just around the bend. Below the community building is the arched passageway to the upper court, Židovské Město (Jewish court). (Courtesy of Souhlasíme s publikováním, Polná.)

that the soul of Rabbi Bezalel Loew of Prague had transmigrated to their rabbi. Rabbi Polak died shortly before the completion of the new synagogue, and Polná honored him with a funeral unlike any other. No quiet, discreet procession through the side alleys would do for the revered rabbi. The funeral cortege streamed through the main square and out the northwestern gate to the old cemetery, where he was buried with solemn ceremony. Around his grave the elders cleared an exclusive circle, saying that no one was holy enough to rest so near to the rabbi. Townspeople claim that the circle has been clear of weeds for over 300 years since his death.

With their 50 families of more than 300 persons by 1714, the *kehillah* needed a community building. An annual fee of 2 gulden and 20 kreuzer secured a permit to build a Jewish town hall. By the century's end, as the *kehillah* counted 87 families, 16 new houses completed the larger upper triangle and formed a smaller court on the south below the synagogue. The Jews were loyal patriots. When Emperor Ferdinand V arrived in 1836 for a state visit to the district town of Jihlava, a large deputation of Polná Jews went in grand procession to welcome him.

They carried aloft magnificently embroidered flags and held Torah scrolls decked in holiday mantles.

The *kehillah* reached its peak in the mid-nineteenth century, with 128 recognized families: a total of 770 persons. Large families of Jewish poor crowded the ghetto houses, while some of the more affluent moved out to the town. A descendent of Count Dietrichstein contributed 80 gulden toward the expansion and repair of the synagogue in 1861. The original vaulted ceiling had cracked despite the 40-year-old iron reinforcements, therefore its replacement was a flat ceiling on steel I-beams under a slightly peaked, tiled roof that held aloft a gilded Star of David. The interior was beautifully refurbished.

Sadly, the *kehillah* enjoyed its renovated synagogue for only a very short time. The worst fire in Polná history spread through the town only two years later, destroying most of the houses; 3,000 people, including all the Jews, lost their homes. Gifts for the victims poured in from many parts of Austria. Four Jews participated on the distribution committee. Although the community succeeded in rescuing the Torah scrolls, the *parokhot,* and much of the ceremonial silver, the synagogue was a charred shell that had to be completely rebuilt.

When the Prussian army retreated through Polná in 1866, plundering whatever valuables had survived the fire, a soldier sick with cholera infected the town. An epidemic followed that claimed 450 dead within a few weeks, most of them in the crowded ghetto. Among the victims was the physician Dr. Hoffman. In 1867, the Prague to Brno railroad began operations, bypassing Polná. The town went into a progressively severe depression that accelerated the Jews' tendency to emigrate.

The next tragedy to strike the community, the "Hilsneriada," brought Polná forcibly to the attention of all Europe. The body of a young seamstress, Anežka Hrůzová, was found in the woods near Polná in April 1899. Suspicion fell expediently on a vagrant Jewish simpleton, Leopold Hilsner. Two courts tried him for murder. The second found him guilty and sentenced

Synagogue interior, view to the west—archival photo, ca. 1930. Four round granite pillars supported the balcony. (Courtesy of Souhlasíme s publikováním, Polná.)

him to die. The affair kindled anti-Semitic passions. Enraged mobs surged through the ghetto, breaking windows, pillaging, and leaving terrorized Jews hiding behind barred doors for a year. People boycotted Jewish shops for a long time. Children marched through the streets, chanting ditties of contempt and slander:

> *Sugar, flour or coffee*
> *Don't dare to buy from a Jew,*
> *They killed our fair Anežka*
> *With eyes so pure and blue.*

Revered as the symbol of national independence and justice, Thomas Masaryk—the Czech Émile Zola—published two pamphlets demanding a

The elegant interior of the 1863 reconstruction—archival photo, ca. 1930, view to the east. In front of the Ark, the *bimah,* with reader's desk and *mizraḥ* panel, is on a platform three steps up, bordered by a light metal balustrade. The *Aron Kodesh,* two steps higher, is embellished by pilasters and a pair of gilded pillars. Gothic pilasters trim the windows and corners of the room. The semicircular inscription above the Ark is, *"Ki mitzion tetzei Torah, udvar Adonai miyerushalayim"* ("For instruction shall come forth from Zion, the word of the Lord from Jerusalem"; Is. 2:3). (Courtesy of Souhlasíme s publikováním, Polná.)

revision of Hilsner's trial, "not to defend Hilsner, but to defend the Christians against superstition." (In 1919 Masaryk became the first president of the newly established Czechoslovak Republic.) Although neither guilt nor innocence was definitely proven, Hilsner's sentence was commuted to life imprisonment, and in 1916 he went free in

Cartoon from the time of the Hilsner trial. (Adapted from: *Humoristické listy,* Prague, 1900.)

the broad amnesty that followed the death of Emperor Franz Joseph I. In 1961, as Anežka Hrůzová's brother lay dying in Havlíčkův Brod at the age of 93, he confessed to killing his sister in order to save himself the cost of her dowry.

The last rabbi of Polná, Rabbi David Alt, emigrated in 1920 after most of the ghetto houses had been sold to Christians and only 85 Jews remained. One of the last resident Jews of that period, Esther Gutman, who came to Israel in 1938, told us of her childhood:

By 1930 we were only a few Jewish families in town, and it was hard for my grandfather, the ḥazzan, to gather a minyan *for the prayers. There was no one to be a* shulklapper *to summon Jews to prayers, so he used to send my sister and me out to knock on doors and urge people to come to the Sabbath evening services. For holidays it was his custom to invite the town poor and passing Jewish travelers from Slovakia and Carpatho-Ruthenia to a festive dinner at our house so that there would be a minyan for prayers.*

The Nazis confiscated all Jewish property during World War II. They shipped documents, books, and ritual Judaica to Prague, for the projected "museum of decadent Jewish culture." Of the forty Jews deported from Polná, only two children and two adults returned. There was no one to renew community life. The abandoned synagogue served briefly as a church of the Czech Brethren, then as a storeroom as it slowly fell into neglect and ruin. The roofless synagogue and rabbi's house in Polná were among the early parcels of former Jewish property restituted in the early 1990s to the Jewish community in Prague, custodian of Czech Jewish communities.

After half a century of neglect and misuse, the Polná synagogue is undergoing a restoration funded by the municipality and the Prague *kehillah*. The work, including research, continues in earnest with support from the Ministry of Culture. The roof was restored in 1992 and scaffolding filled the interior for a long time. A small *Aron Kodesh* that turned up in the town museum storeroom in 1930 is now undergoing restoration; it served in the small prayer room but will eventually replace the large missing Ark in the synagogue. When completed, the restored synagogue will serve as a concert and exhibition hall, and it will house a museum of the history of the Jews in the Vysočiny region. One section will display selected items from Polná's Judaica, now stored in Prague's Jewish Museum.

THE SYNAGOGUE IN POLNÁ

Facing a narrow alley just off the large court, the north facade of the seventeenth-century synagogue contains two stone portals, each with an indecipherable keystone inscription. The left portal once led to a gallery that collapsed in 1969, leaving only a mound of bricks and broken plaster. The portal on the right leads to a long anteroom and, by a left turn, to the main hall. Two of the original four granite pillars still guard the entrance to the sanctuary, where weeds flourish in the cracks of the broken stone floor. A bare niche in the east wall marks the location of the Ark. A charity box had been torn from the partition wall near one of the pillars, and a plaque that blessed its donor, Yidl Filitz, has since been stolen. Built originally in Baroque style, the synagogue underwent restorations in 1863 that introduced neo-Gothic elements, the most prominent of which are the tall, lancet arched windows. Restoration work, begun in 1992 with a new roof and interior repairs, is scheduled for completion within a decade.

Interior of the synagogue toward the entrance and former gallery. Only part of the stone flooring and scattered pillars remains. The gallery wall fresco testifies to the rich decorations from 1863, when the synagogue was refurbished after a fire. Inscription to the right of the door honors the charity box donor, Yidl Filitz.

Niche for the *tzedakah* box, looted long ago. The dedicatory plaque also vanished during the early stages of the restoration.

Jan Musil, a gentile octogenarian and life-long ghetto resident, was employed by the Communists in the 1950s to strip the synagogue of valuables. When we visited he reminisced and said, with a wry smile on his ruddy cheeks, ". . . I heard about the Jewish treasure hidden in the synagogue when I was taking down the brass candelabra there. They said it was in the shape of a golden calf, buried somewhere inside. We started a hectic search. We dug all over and knocked on all the walls, but couldn't find it." Then he leaned out from the ground floor window to huddle with Josef Fencl, our translator. Both of them laughed and looked around the courtyard. Fencl explained, "People watched all morning as you crisscrossed the ghetto and the synagogue with your fancy camera equipment. They're convinced that you Jews know exactly where to find the golden calf and that you have come here to take it away."

Long-term resident in old Jewish ghetto Jan Musil (right) describes former Jewish residence in Polná to Josef Fencl for translation to authors.

LOKŠANY IS DYING

June 8 and 9, 1990 were historic days for Czechoslovakia. It was the weekend of the first free elections in that country after 40 years of Communist rule. No citizen under 60 years had ever experienced the voting booths of a democracy, and the population was drunk with the heady excitement of liberation. Election placards clamored from every surface, exhorting the vote for a bewildering multitude of ad hoc political parties. People crowded the streets, talking and greeting each other volubly among the flag-bedecked buildings. It was a time to be out in the spring sunshine and to enjoy the thrill of freedom.

Even the sleepy central Bohemian town of Březnice was celebrating in its modest way. A huge new concrete planter fairly burst with burgeoning petunias and salvia. National and local flags flew on the Baroque town hall balcony that faced the long central square, nearly empty despite the bright early morning sun. Inside, resplendent in their Sunday best, eight dignified poll watchers sat at long tables around the polling room waiting for voters to present themselves. We paid our respects,

enjoyed their hospitable coffee and cake and went off to see the synagogue.

The Jewish quarter is approached through a narrow alley at the northwest corner of the square, not far from the town hall. The well-kept ghetto is named "Lokšany" after Lord Ferdinand von Lokšan who established it on his lands in 1570 as a separate *Judenstadt* (Jewish town). The sign "Lokšany" still appears on the corner house, visible as one enters the ghetto. The quarter was initially independent of the town council and belonged directly to the state authority and the local lord.

The quarter is valuable historically and architecturally because it represents a distinctive style of urban planning. The ground plan dates from the eighteenth century: a large court around the synagogue, with a narrow alley leading to a smaller court on the way to the town square. By 1747, 22 houses boxed in the main court, many of them fine structures built in Empire style by Viennese master builder Ignaz Dientzenhofer and occupied by prosperous Jewish merchants. Since Lokšany sits in the lowest, least desirable section of the town,

Town Hall bedecked with election day flags, left, and the church, on the Březnice central square. Entrance to the Jewish quarter is by an alley, out of sight on the left.

owned six shops, it was obliged to provide the current lord each Christmas with seven pounds of pepper and eight pounds of gunpowder. For Easter they had to deliver a falcon or its equivalent in groschen. Still later, they had to keep a pair of horses for his hunting and for "reliable delivery of news." There was also the compulsory purchase of skins and pelts of slaughtered animals, or of animals that died of disease.

In 1727 Březnice Jews who had lived peacefully among their Christian neighbors in town had to crowd into Lokšany. Charles VI (1685–1740), Holy Roman Emperor from 1711 to 1740, was fanatically hostile to the Jews. Preparing to segregate Jews from Christians throughout Bohemia and Moravia, he required every town to measure and report the proximity of Jewish houses and synagogues to the local church. Jews who lived closer than a certain inviolable minimum distance decreed in the Translocation Rescript of 1727—issued in the same period as the Familiants Law—had to move further away. More than 100 of the submitted maps are still on file in Prague or in Brno. On houses and maps, it was customary to identify Jewish houses with Roman numerals and Christian houses with Arabic numerals. In Březnice the original Roman numerals are visible on many former Jewish houses around the cobblestone

it suffered from frequent flooding. Many of the buildings, including the synagogue, show the marks of water damage.

The Březnice Jews of 1586 had an obligation to deliver annually to the estate of the *Herrenschaft* (landlord) a pound of pepper—a precious condiment in sixteenth-century Bohemia. When the *kehillah* grew to 17 families in 1649 and

A map of Teinnitz, now Panenský Týnec, a small town in Bohemia. This is one of the maps prepared for Emperor Charles VI in connection with the Translocation Rescript he issued in 1727. Records confirm the existence of a prayer room in eighteenth-century Teinnitz. The location of the double-gabled Jewish house, *Das Juden Haus*, I, is shown in relation to the churches, A and B. (Courtesy of Central State Archives, Prague, 1077 FIX #24 Teinnitz über Scherodin.)

ghetto square. The numbers correspond to family and property records in the town archives.

House number III was the district rabbi's seat, the *Kreisrabbinat*. The *mikveh* was there, and a *sukkah* in the court, as well as a bench where the *shoḥet,* who also served as synagogue *shammash,* slaughtered poultry. He slaughtered larger animals in a hut behind the synagogue. House number XIV was an inn and kosher kitchen for Jewish travelers, for those who came to the market and for celebrations. There were facade frescoes on house number XV and an exact sundial high above them. The *Gemeinde* (community council) met at number LX, later the regional workers' sick fund center. A tradition holds that number XXII at the quarter's entrance was occupied by Archduke Ferdinand's mistress, the beautiful Philipine Welser, and her aunt, Katherina von Lokšan. The building has large, arched rooms, once decorated with color-

ful heraldic emblems, barely discernible now under many coats of paint.

The most famous family in the Březnice *kehillah,* the Poppers, lived in house number I. It was a large house, behind and above a store, with spiral stone steps leading to the many bedrooms upstairs. Despite the unfavorable climate, the family cultivated vineyards nearby for a limited production of kosher wine. Their expertise, however, did not lie in agriculture. For generations their sons were tradesmen and community leaders. The family founder, Wolf Popper, born in Lokšany, was land magistrate for Březnice from 1749 until his death in 1767. The "Leipzig Messgäste" record of prominent merchants reported that he and other Poppers attended the annual fairs in Leipzig. In keeping with Jewish funereal symbolism in Bohemia, his tombstone in the old Březnice cemetery carries a wolf's head carved in bold relief.

Moritz Popper, descendant of Wolf Popper, with family and employees in front of his general store at house number I in the Březnice ghetto, during the 1930s. Most of the Popper sons and daughters moved to Vienna or Prague and became prominent in business and the professions. The barely visible sign above the family symbol, the anchor, reads, "M. Popper." The heavy wooden doors have since been replaced. (Courtesy of Otto Burg.)

Popper's son, Joachim Chaim Popper (1720–1795), moved to Prague. His career was typical of his generation of eighteenth-century Jewish merchants, bankers, and enlightened benefactors of central European communities. Joachim managed a tobacco monopoly for the crown and prospered also in woolens, potash, and whalebone. Admired in business, he was a patron of literature and celebrated for his generosity as a philanthropist. An historical note by Johann Zak states: "Flour, rice, and beans supplied for the Březnice poor in the terrible famine years, 1770–1772, were, at first, unjustly distributed. The local Jew, Joachim Popper, provided the Christian poor with 20 measures of corn, and the same amount to the Jewish poor." In recognition of his many-faceted contributions to the welfare of the state, Joachim was one of the first Bohemian Jews to attain nobility, being named Edler von Popper in 1790. He bequeathed large sums for charity and money to create a synagogue in his home, where he subsidized "prayer and study in perpetuity," according to a classical custom.

As we walked through the synagogue square in Březnice, we were fortunate to meet a scion of the Popper family, Otto Burg, on a nostalgic visit from his home in Scotland. He was a grandson of Moritz Popper, the last one of the line to operate the family business in Březnice. Burg had left for Vienna with his parents at age five, but he recalled for us his excitement on the historic day in 1919 when Thomas Masaryk came to Březnice as President of the Czechoslovak Republic. Moritz Popper, representing the Jewish community, stood with the mayor and the new president on the tiny flag-draped balcony of Town Hall as the town cheered.

Rabbi Isaac Spitz, the son-in-law of Rabbi Eleasar Flekeles of Kojetín and Prague, was the first Březnice rabbi to hold the office after the Kaiser ordained the post of district rabbi in 1820. The appointment followed Spitz's five years of service in the community of Königswart, near Marienbad. When he arrived in town, *kehillah* dignitaries overwhelmed him with greetings. The members expressed their "delight that the new spiritual leader is not only a learned scholar, but also a friendly, loving father."

The late Otto Burg, born in Březnice and raised in Vienna. Burg and his cousins summered regularly during their childhood with their grandparents, the Moritz Poppers, in Březnice. Otto escaped to Scotland with his parents before World War II. In the several years before his death in 1993, he returned to Březnice on three occasions, one visit coinciding with that of the authors. When asked if he had visited Prague, he replied, "No. I have no interest in Prague. I just come here, visit the cemetery, and walk a bit through the ghetto square. Here, I remember every inch, every stone. Then I sit down to rest on my grandmother's bench and recall bygone days."

The rabbi did not disappoint his new congregants. Since the *kehillah* was too small to engage a Talmud teacher, he insisted on teaching the boys Bible and Talmud himself. Concerned for the health and well-being of the women, he built a hot-water *mikveh* for them—no more chopping ice, bathing in the river, and catching cold! More than 30 of his *responsa* appear in *T'shuvah Me'ahavah* (Responses through Love) by Rabbi Flekelis.

Rabbi Spitz's successor, observant and much-honored Rabbi Menachem Mendl Polák, was district rabbi from 1815 until his death in 1866. He and his wife Mindl adopted an orphan girl and educated her in their careful Orthodox ways. Decked out in his hallmark *schubitze* (large fur hat), Rabbi Polák traveled frequently to outlying district communities, where every visit created a holiday. He is remembered for the remarkable collection of his letters and documents, fortuitously discovered by Rabbi Alexander Kristianpoller in the Jewish Teachers' Seminary of Vienna. Most of the letters, 695 pieces written and collected during his tenure, are in Hebrew. The later ones are in German with Hebrew annotations. Family, personal, and community vignettes show up among the papers, which include permits from the lord, proposals for regulations, requests, threats, dispensations, and biographies of important personalities. The collection is an invaluable historical source of information on the development of Jewish rural communities in southern Bohemia—offering a glimpse of vanished ghetto *persona*: the *shulklapper,* who knocked on doors to call worshippers to prayer; the *maggid,* itinerant preacher; the *orei'ah,* out-of-town guest; the *melamed,* elementary grades teacher; the traveling *meshorerim* who sang their ballads at family festivities; and the itinerant peddlers of books, with sacks of family treasures.

Lokšany enjoyed a golden age between 1727 and 1872, when the head of the Kolowrat–Krakovský family controlled the town. Relations with the non-Jews were relatively free of friction. The nobles provided employment and granted contracts for the profitable potash works and the brandy distillery.

The German language school of the dwindling Lokšany *kehillah* closed in 1901; there were few children to attend, and Czech had already replaced German in daily ghetto use. Adolf Neu, the last rabbi of Březnice, was appointed in 1915 by a congregation smaller than 80 persons. The newly created Czechoslo-

vakia recognized the Jews as a national minority and granted cultural and national autonomy. By that time the Jews were actively participating in the public activities of the Christian town. In 1921 only 15 Jewish families remained in the Březnice vicinity: 41 persons, including only one child of school age.

In 1942 the Nazis confiscated Jewish property and collected it in the synagogue. They selected 273 articles of ritual Judaica, 64 documents, and 34 holy books and shipped them to Prague. The Jews were deported to Terezín and none returned. Local people exploited the synagogue building for many years as storage space for plumbing supplies, but now it stands empty. Occasional suggestions to restoring it for cultural use die for lack of interest and scarcity of funds.

Synagogue entrance on the west, with stone portal inscribed, *"Pithu li sha'arei tzedek"* ("Open the gates of righteousness for me;" Ps. 118:19). Internal steps on the right lead to the women's gallery.

THE SYNAGOGUE IN BŘEZNICE

The synagogue is a modest brick building under a red-tiled hip roof, situated in the middle of the main ghetto square. Access is by two weather-beaten doors clinging to the plain carved-stone portal of a small west-side extension. The doors open into a narrow vestibule and another door, facing the Ark, opens into the prayer room. On the north side a large room served as a dwelling for the *shammash* (sexton). The upper floor contained a window-lined *ḥeder* and a sun-filled L-shaped gallery for the women.

Close to the empty Ark niche on the east wall, nothing remains of the *bimah* but its elevated platform. The high, round-headed windows in deeply vaulted arches flood the interior with light. Stout brick pillars support the spacious gallery on the south and west sides. A Baroque design in high-relief stucco on the ceiling emphasizes the former central location of the *bimah*. Two yellow scallop shells flank a deep sunflower on a blue sky background that twinkles with gold stars.

The synagogue in Březnice, Baroque style, 1725, renovated 1821. The building, in the larger of the two ghetto squares, contained synagogue and *ḥeder*. A small east-wall protrusion marks the position of the Ark on the inside. The narrow alley, opposite, was formerly the only access to the ghetto area.

Baroque interior of the synagogue. In the vault above the *Aron Kodesh* a tired banner in a field of stylized flowers bears the message, *"V'ahavta l'rei'akha kamokha"* ("Love your fellow as yourself"; Lv. 19:18). Under deep vaults, a pair of round headed, stained glass windows with dedications flank the Ark niche.

Jaroslav Polák–Rokycana, author of the chapter on Březnice in Hugo Gold's 1934 compendium, *Jews and Jewish Communities in Bohemia*, described contemporary synagogue furnishings that survive only along with his text and perhaps in an old photograph:

In the reconstruction after the fire of 1821, the bimah *was moved from the center to the eastern end. Tastefully designed grillwork separates this part of the synagogue from the rest. On both sides of the* Aron Kodesh *there are artistic Gothic windows of painted glass. On the right side, a large brass menorah stands on a high plinth. Judging from the human figures and their costumes in its center, the menorah is apparently of Dutch–Spanish origin. Two carved wooden candelabra stand in front of the Ark. Smaller lamps of the same style hang in the galleries. The Ark doors are decorated with gilded crowns and*

View toward the ghetto entrance from the synagogue gallery.

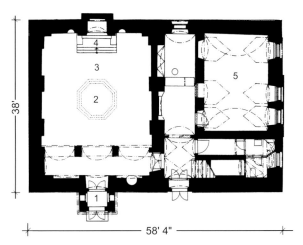

The women's gallery and ceiling. Fragments on walls, arches, and gallery pillars exemplify the foremost interior decorative element of the synagogue interior, a stylized floral fresco that reached its pinnacle in the delicate design above the Ark. Note stucco ceiling decorations.

Floor plan of the synagogue in Březnice. During restoration procedures in the mid-1990s, workers discovered the stone foundation of the earlier central *bimah*. 1. entrance, 2. former *bimah* platform, 3. principal synagogue space. 4. Ark and *bimah*. 5. *ḥeder*. (Courtesy of J. Fiedler.)

arrows, the coat of arms of the Jews' patron, the former Count Joseph Kolowrat-Krakowsky, who helped restore the synagogue after the fire of 1821. Ladislav Kuba, a Czech Academy painter, painted the wall decorations. The synagogue owns an unusually large and valuable collection of Torah decorations and embroideries. One of them is a precious parokhet *of 1793, donated by*

Joachim von Popper, who made contributions to the Březnice community and synagogue even after he moved to Prague.

Polák-Rokycana, writing in the decade before World War II, mentions the migration of the young Jews to Prague and concludes his article on the Jews of Březnice with the prophetic words, "Lokšany is dying. Another few years and the Bohemian rural ghetto will belong to history."

OF TEA LEAVES
AND ORANGE PEELS

Among the treasures of the Czech urban landscape are the Baroque town squares, preserved with their gabled row houses and arched porticos that enclose the marketplace. Such a large square matured slowly into its present shape in Jičín, Bohemia, as blocks of houses were built and variously modified over the centuries. The town lies on a hillock above the Cidlina River, near the dense forests and bizarre sandstone formations of the Český ráj (Bohemian Paradise), in the foothills of the Krkonoše mountains. Because of the strange vicissitudes of history, Protestants and Jews, in turn, fled through these passes at various times to escape persecution.

Shortly after Jičín's establishment in the fourteenth century, local aristocrats encouraged Jews to settle in the hope that they would bring wealth and help to develop trade. They designated a street, Židovská ulice, one block north of the square, for Jewish residence in 1362, and witnessed how the Jews engrossed themselves in the town's economy. Local tax registers note a plethora of early property transactions between Jews and non-Jews. In 1364 a Jičín furrier named Ješek mortgaged his house to Elias and Abraham. In 1370 a Jew, Pesach, transferred a house to a man named Jan. A widow named Zdena wrote over property to a Jew, Otlik, his wife Anna, and nephew Isaac Otlik. The latter conveyed the house to Dluhošov and Mark Rackov. In time mortgage loans by the moneylenders gave them a mortgage interest in many houses in the town. Occasionally Jews were allowed to live in these houses in lieu of receiving interest on the mortgage. One such house is listed in tax records from 1458 to 1462 as *Domus Judeorum* ("Jews' house"). By 1389 the tiny *kehillah* was managing its affairs under the jurisdiction of a *Magister Judeorum* (Jewish mayor).

In the aftermath of the 1541 pogroms in Prague, Žatec, and Litomerice, when the Jews were accused of committing arson to aid the Turkish enemy, Emperor Ferdinand I (king of Bohemia, 1526–1564) reluctantly acceded to parliament's decision to expel the Jews from the country. As an exception, the few Jews needed to supervise the sale of the confiscated property for the crown remained under temporary permits. Mindful that he would soon wish them to return, Ferdinand sanctimoniously decreed protection for the exiled Jews from brigand attack along the escape route to Poland. His "protection" proved to be ineffective. Hordes of bandits from the countryside attacked the caravan of fleeing Jews, plundering and killing. On invitation 25 years later, the Jews did indeed return to Jičín and other towns, but were obliged to wear yellow patches on their outer garments.

Emperor Ferdinand II (king of Bohemia, 1617–1637), a fanatic protagonist of the Counter-Reformation, was nevertheless dependent on Jewish financiers. In return for heavy tax payments in 1632, he protected his *Schutzjuden,* granting them privileges such as the right to engage freely in trade and a promise that they would not again be exiled from Bohemia. The situation of the Jews in Jičín improved during his reign with the arrival of new local ruler, Duke Albrecht of Wallenstein. Undertaking large-scale reconstruction of Jičín, he transformed the hitherto insignificant town into a modern urban

The large town square of Jičín, rebuilt under Duke Albrecht of Wallenstein in the period up to 1634. The view is to the west from the Renaissance tower of the Valdice Gate, the only tower that was preserved in the old stone ramparts. The square dates back to the town's beginning, early in the fourteenth century, but the prominent arched loggia reflect the influence of Albrecht's Italian architect, Nicolo Sebregondi.

complex, a superb example of early Baroque design. While artisans and tradesmen moved their shops to the side streets and eastward to the new town, the town square became the grand entrance to the ducal palace courtyard, and many of the outstanding buildings around it date from this period.

The Duke found a capable fiscal administrator for his Jičín properties in the person of a colorful court Jew from Prague, Jacob Bassevi (1570–1634), the first Jew outside Italy to gain a title. A leader of the Prague Jewish community, Bassevi had spent most of his years in large-scale trading and in providing financial expertise for Europe's nobility. A Dutch financier, Vitt, was his partner in several speculative transactions that were profitable to the duke. The success encouraged Bassevi to write to Albrecht, requesting him to lower the excessive taxes on the Jews, but the intervention was not effective. Arriving in 1632 at the ducal estate in Jičín, Bassevi financed many of the houses on Židovská ulice and became a great benefactor to the community. Unfortunately, he died only two years later, and all his privileges of nobility were invalidated. For the Jews of Bohemia, however, he remained forever a "princely Jew."

The political murder of Albrecht in 1634 brought an abrupt end to the building activity and Jičín deteriorated to the level of a provincial town. Nineteenth-century urban development of the town fortunately concentrated on the suburbs, leaving the historic buildings in the core of the old town untouched.

The nine Jewish families in Jičín in the mid-seventeenth century were happy to welcome two new families (by permission of Count Rudolf Tiefenbach): the daughters of the Mojses family and their husbands. The count also decreed that:

- Only Jews on the count's list might marry.
- Jews could purchase a field for a cemetery and pay for it annually thereafter.
- Jews could trade in a variety of merchandise: in leather, in suits, in spices, and especially in fabrics such as wool and silk. They could conduct business in shops, by peddling, and

at fairs, except on holidays. They could not deal in grains nor in products from regions infected by the plague. They were not permitted to gather early at the gates of the city to acquire merchandise being brought in, so that they could not raise the prices nor diminish the quantity of produce entering the city for sale to all the residents.

- During the three days of the Easter holiday, Jews were not permitted in the streets or in the shops but had to remain in their houses.

- Jews granted privileges by the king were to enjoy them until abrogated by the king. The *Hejtman* (local magistrate) was to protect the Jews and their privileges. In quarrels between Jews and Christians, the *Hejtman* was to adjudicate in the name of the king, and he could not discriminate against Jews.

Neo-Classical building at the corner of Židovská ulice, on the right.

The number of officially permitted Jewish families was closely scrutinized. In 1705 they included Benjamin Sobota, Abraham Goldschmied, the widow Davidová—later known as Isaková—Solomon Josel, Benjamin Mojses, Shmuel Friedlander, David Sladkes, and Joachim Josel. Others stole in and tried to establish residence in Jičín. In a decree of November 16, 1719, the count declared, "I will not tolerate the expansion of the Jewish community, especially not by foreign Jews settling in Jičín. They are living on land that is not theirs and they must leave." The new families gathered their goods and left. Nonetheless, in 1738 the number of legal Jewish families had risen to 14.

The Familiants system prevented many Jews from settling anywhere in Moravia—or Bohemia—permanently. A Jewish beggar class arose as a result. Jews wandered about the country in small groups, living outside the law, without any regular means of livelihood or economic status. This system caused tensions within the communities—with lawsuits before secular authorities, denunciations, briberies, and the occasional sale of familiant numbers to higher bidders from outside the communities. Frustrated young Jewish couples from Moravia found solutions either in conversion or migration to towns in Upper Hungary (later called Slovakia).

The 1782 Toleranzpatent of Joseph II eased the constraints on Jews in Jičín; full, legal civil rights were granted in 1848. Eager for the benefits of integration, Jews began to move to the royal cities that offered wider economic and educational opportunities. Integration in Jičín did not at first diminish the high standards of the Jewish school, enough to attract upper class gentile families. Christian children accounted for a large proportion of the pupils, and priests conducted weekly lessons in religion for them.

Language became a serious issue. The Jews had generally adopted the dominant German language of the empire in publication, daily use, and education, especially after the Toleranzpatent excluded the public use of Hebrew and Yiddish. This did not sit well with the Czech nationalists. One of their ministers denounced the Jews in a fiery Prague speech of 1866, calling them traitors for preferring a foreign language over native Czech. His followers rioted in the streets of Prague, shouting anti-Semitic slogans and branding the Jews as unpatriotic. Rioting spread to the hinterland until soldiers marched in to intervene for public safety. In Jičín townspeople poured into Židovská ulice, tearing signs in German from the shops, smashing windows, and damaging the Jewish school building. After the riots subsided, the *kehillah* erased all symbols of

Exposing the Ark to view. Storeroom workers and municipal employees pulled aside sacks of tea and orange peels stored in the synagogue to enable photography of *bimah* and *Aron Kodesh.*

German culture. Jewish officials "decided" the obvious—that Czech would thenceforth be the official language of the community and of instruction in the school.

However tiny, the *kehillah* produced doctors, lawyers, and other professionals after the Emancipation. Two famous Jewish personalities have their origins in Jičín: conservative Karl Kraus and revolutionary Rosa Luxemburg. Born in Jičín, Austrian satirist, literary historian, and poet Karl Kraus (1874–1936) was a fierce critic of the liberal culture and the permissive intellectual atmosphere of pre-Nazi Austria. After converting to Catholicism, he blamed the Jews and the Jewish press for anti-Semitism. Among his literary works were six volumes of essays, four volumes of epigrams, a gigantic drama, *"Die letzten Tage der Menschheit"* (The Last Days of Mankind), and nine volumes of lyric poetry.

Rosa Luxemburg (1871–1919) was born in Zamosc, Poland, but her family stems from Jičín, where the cemetery contains gravestones bearing the name of the family Luxemburg. Unlike her conservative contemporary, Kraus, Rosa Luxemburg was a leader of the left wing of the German Socialist Movement and paid for her ideology by

several prison terms for "revolutionary activity." Fervent in her convictions, she authored several books on radical economic theories. National self-determination, in her view, was in serious conflict with socialism, and she had no interest in a specifically Jewish labor movement. With Karl Liebknecht, she edited the Communist daily, *Die Rote Fahne* (*The Red Flag*). Both she and Liebknecht were murdered by army officers while being hauled to prison in 1919.

Like many Jews in Jičín and elsewhere in Europe at that time, Kraus and Luxemburg abandoned Jewish identification. Opposites in political and philosophical outlooks, they exemplify the ideological turmoil that faced many Jewish intellectuals in Europe after the Emancipation and the extremes to which their psyches led them.

During the First World War the sympathy of Jičín's Jews lay with Austria, but allegiance changed with the establishment of the independent Czechoslovak Republic. At the same time, the national minority status and the cultural autonomy accorded to the Jews aroused Jewish identification and sentiment. Most adult Jews in Jičín joined the World Zionist Organization, but—as had happened in so many small central European towns by the 1930s—many Jews had

The Ark exposed colorfully decorated rural Baroque *Aron Kodesh* and *bimah.* Such furnishings are rarely left intact in synagogues used as storerooms.

THE SYNAGOGUE IN JIČÍN

The synagogue is a stately two-story building, rising above the low houses around it at the east end of Židovská ulice. Rebuilt after a fire destroyed the previous synagogue of venerable but uncertain date, its present form, with gracefully arched windows and classical pilasters, dates from 1840. The community renovated the synagogue in 1932, but areas of peeled plaster on the facade testify to the neglect since then and reveal the old-fashioned construction of mixed brick and stone. It is one of the few rural Bohemian synagogues that still contains its *bimah* and *Aron Kodesh,* undisturbed when the building began to serve as a storeroom for tea and orange peels—the sacks were simply piled in. It is certainly the most fragrant synagogue we have visited! The painted Baroque Ark doors are flanked by an inner pair of helical pillars and an outer unadorned pair—all stucco—under ornate, gilded capitals. Four steps up from the synagogue floor, the *bimah* is bounded by an iron grille anchored at its ends to fluted pillars. These pillars have decorative plaster capitals topped by iron lamp stands joined by an arched iron band bearing ten small candle cups.

The upper part of the Ark is a rural Baroque structure with gilded highlights on the painted stucco, featuring two stylized urns that flank the classical round window. The relatively small prayer room was adequate for the size of the congregation. Pale blue painted decorations cover earlier decor on walls and barrel vaulted ceiling. Garlanded pilasters with scrolled capitals flank the now boarded-up windows on the north and south walls.

The men's entrance to the main hall led through a small lobby inside the arched portal at street level. Women ascended to the gallery by a narrow, covered stairway built as an addition to the front and aesthetically realized as an extension of the building's main roof. Entrance to the women's gallery before

the 1840 renovation may have been through the second story of the adjoining building, as was often the custom in eighteenth-century rural synagogues. The small front yard, fenced off in the days when the synagogue functioned, was a cheerful place for greeting friends on Sabbath and holidays.

A striking rose-colored building, with its entrance also in Židovská ulice, stands on the alley that runs diagonally across from the synagogue, leading to the central square. Its marked classical elements—broad pilasters and half-round arches in a repeated rhythm around the two facades—make it one of the finer structures of the former Jewish quarter. Adjoining this building along the street

North and east facades of the synagogue in Jičín, Baroque style with Classicist renovations, rebuilt in 1840 after a fire. The east wall protrusion encloses the internal niche of the *Aron Kodesh.*

stands the three-story community school, where the rabbi occupied the top floor. This Empire-style building was noted for its curving stone stairway and bold Doric column in the lobby. The former classrooms have become apartments.

The two portals of the synagogue. On the left, the women's entrance led to the gallery. The arched door at street level led to the main hall via a small lobby.

opted for life in the larger cities and the *kehillah* itself was headed for decline.

In the fall of 1939, when the Germans stormed through the Valdice gate into the main square of Jičín, there were only 90 Jews in town. Within a few months, in rapid sequence, the new regime deprived the Jews of rights and property, then confiscated home and synagogue treasures for loot and transfer to Prague. In 1942 Jičín Jews were transported to Terezín; most of them perished there or in the death camps. None of the survivors returned to renew the community after the war. In 1982 the municipality bought the synagogue building for restoration as a cultural hall—a mission indefinitely postponed.

Jičín's *kehillah* was always a small group, never more numerous than the 119 souls in 1930. They engaged in the typically Jewish occupations: moneylending, craftsmanship, peddling, and petty commerce. They endured the cycles of settling, exile, and return—and kept to their Judaism—just as Jews of hundreds of similar small towns did throughout Europe, through the Enlightenment and the Emancipation. And, in the end, the few Jews who were left went to their anonymous deaths in the camps, unsung in history.

Colorful flower beds now enliven the entrance and new benches in cheerful yellow replace the old wooden ones. There are no resident Jews in Jičín.

BAREFOOT ON RAW PIGSKIN

Everyone knows Pilsen beer, but who has visited Pilsen? Not many tourists take an interest in this large industrial city, famous for its beer and for its great Škoda engineering works. It has some fine parks and residential sections, but otherwise it is a gray, unattractive, smoggy city. Jews arrived here in the early Middle Ages and were part of the city for 150 years, until the township applied its royal prerogative to expel them. This exclusion remained in force for three-and-a-half centuries until the Emancipation of 1848. A period of rapid growth and prosperity followed. The *kehillah* was nearly 3,000 strong at the turn of the twentieth century and helped make the city into a great industrial metropolis of western Bohemia.

Pilsen was founded in the thirteenth century and enjoyed numerous royal privileges. At first it was called Nový Plzeň (New Pilsen), because it was situated away from the town's original 976 C.E. location; however, it soon outpaced its predecessor and became a vital commercial center. Pilsen was deeply involved in the Hussite Wars of the late fourteenth and fifteenth centuries; the Catholics strongly opposed the rebel Protestants and resolutely persecuted them. Despite the hostile climate, Jewish merchants made a niche for themselves in the city, and Pilsen was home to one of the earliest Jewish communities in Bohemia. In 1338 Count Karl of Moravia ordered the mayor and town councilors not to allow persecution of Jews in Nový Plzeň, and—if needed—to punish offenders severely.

Documents from the fifteenth- and sixteenth-century *liber Judicii* (court book) and Jewish records tell dryly of life of the small *kehillah* in Nový Plzeň. Allowed to live in the town, Jews were often subject to restrictions and deliberate humiliations, such as the Jews' Oath—prevalent in Europe until the eighteenth century. To plead in his defense, an accused Jew had to stand shirtless and barefoot on the skin of a newly slaughtered pig, while another Jew stood by him as a witness. To plead innocence, the accused recited the long-winded Oath text invoking nightmarish punishments from heaven for any falsehood. The witness was then to call out and warn him, "If your

Sketch adapted from a woodcut depicting one of the two fifteenth-century synagogues in Pilsen. Neither building survives. The woodcut is a romantic rendition, probably from the nineteenth or early twentieth century. (Drawing by Sheila Brull.)

oath is false, let you become dry like the mountains of Gilboa. . . . Let God send you fire and brimstone for nine days and nights as in Sodom. May the Earth, unable to bear your false oath, swallow you alive, like Dathan and Abiram. . . . Let the eternal God, whose name is holy, help you. *Adonai!*" (much abridged).

Other documentary evidence of the fifteenth and sixteenth centuries include:

- 1407: Lists and values of tools and clothing pledged to Jews as pawns for loaned money.
- 1501: Rules for Jewish business and private behavior established by *Ratherren* (council members) and Jewish elders. Threads and bed linen were not permissible pawns. Jews were not to sell certain items of unredeemed clothing, stolen goods, nor to buy church articles. They were not to bathe in Christian

bath houses, even if they did not yet have their own ritual bath, nor could they accept foreign Jews in town without the permission of the mayor.

- 1503: New regulations that mandated a compulsory cloak for men and veils with wide yellow borders for the women.
- 1504: One record alleged that the Holy Monstrance and the Host were stolen by a "band of Jewish criminals" in the town of Hostouň. Under torture the accused prisoners implicated Jews from Pilsen in the theft. Pilsen burghers raged. They demanded punishment for the heretical offenders and banishment of all other Jews. An edict by King Vladislav, *de non tolerandis Judaeis,* withdrawing toleration of Jews immediately followed. He granted Pilsen the right to expel Jews whenever they pleased, a right that the citizens soon exercised. Four years later they expelled the Jews under a ban that remained in force with minor exceptions until 1848.

An odd entry in the chronicle of April 1509 suggests that some Jews remained even after the expulsion: "The Pilsen court is hereby notified that young Jew Ocksenfelder, who owes 30 gulden to the Jew Turek cannot be found. His mother refuses to pay for him because the money was lent to him for gambling—and he is a minor." When the culprit turned up, he refused to pay the debt.

Excluded from the metropolis, Jews were nevertheless permitted to settle in the neighboring villages and trade in the city by day because their marketing expertise was at a premium. This was the process that scattered Jewish settlements into villages and small towns near major centers over much of Europe. On market days, streams of people poured into the city to sell or buy. Since Pilsen was a *trefe k'hile* (a nonkosher city), the *parnassim* needed temporary provision for the various physical and spiritual services Jews would use when they worked at the fairs. The *parnassim* improvised prayer rooms, set up food stands for kosher edibles, and impaneled three judges. The judges endured a heavy schedule to resolve the many business disputes and to examine teachers and butchers for license to practice. Licensing of rabbis carried special gravity and involved in-depth questioning of the candidates by the judges and by the *parnassim* of *kehillot* that were intending to appoint a rabbi.

In the later Middle Ages the city suffered the ravages of the recurrent Hussite wars and decimation from frequent plagues. It revived toward the end of the seventeenth century with the establishment of the iron, steel, and textile industries, and Jews began to reestablish a presence in the city—some without a permit. In 1790 a Jew received permission to buy a house in Pilsen. The first entries in the Pilsen civic lists, *Matricula Israelitarum . . . ab anno 1802 usque 1840,* record two November 6, 1799 births: Rosalia, to Filip Schack; and Anna, to Isak Lederer of Bušovice, just outside the city. The first funeral was on June 14, 1804—the deceased a local Jew, buried by necessity in nearby Stenovice—and the first Jewish wedding in the city took place in 1811. The Jews had returned.

An action brought by grain dealers in 1821 challenged the right of 32 Jewish merchants already residing in Pilsen to continue living there. The court ruled that six of them might remain: to manufacture brandy, but only in leased premises and under strict supervision. Another decision permitted Jews to deal in tobacco and to handle tax collections. Peddlers might ply their wares in town, but not at the regular market sites reserved for Christians; permanent Jewish stands were not permitted.

Industrialization intensified in the nineteenth century with the creation of the Burgher Brewery, the Škoda engineering works, and the first tannery. As in other communities, the unpleasant occupation of tanning was an occupational niche open—almost reserved—to Jews, and the family name of Lederer for tanners was common. The city concerned itself also with the health of its citizens: Because of complaints that tanning polluted the waters, the city obliged Joachim Kohn to build a street drinking fountain in 1837, as a condition for granting him a permit to buy land near the river for a tannery.

The first Austrian constitution, in 1848, granted the empire's Jews legal equality with others. They could live in all areas of Bohemia

Apartment house complex built by the *kehillah* in the nineteenth century. Located around the court of house number 5 on Smetana Park, it still houses a few indigent old Jews. In the same court stand the abandoned synagogues, built in 1859 and 1875.

The Great Synagogue of Pilsen. Neo-Romanesque style, M. Fleischer and E. Klotz, architects, 1892, before the restoration of 1998. Built on Nejedlého sady in the flamboyant mood expressive of the post-Emancipation expansionism and still in Jewish ownership, it is the second largest synagogue in size in central Europe. It escaped demolition by the Nazis because dynamiting it would have damaged the valuable adjacent commercial properties.

and Moravia, even in the royal towns. There were no longer restrictions on the number of families in each town. From 1852 on, the Jews could own houses—and from 1859 on, they could own land. No formal barrier now remained to self-chosen economic activity. Changes in the demographic picture followed rapidly; by mid-century the number of Jews in Pilsen had grown to 249. They organized a *kehillah* in 1859 and in the same year built a prayer house, designed by

architect M. Stelzer in neo-Romanesque style, that was used until 1892. It still stands, unused and decaying. On March 10, 1860, the rabbi conducted thanksgiving prayers to celebrate the granting of residence rights to the Jews and urged his congregation to pledge loyalty and devotion to the Kaiser and the throne.

During the long cold winter of 1861, the *kehillah* gave generously to the poor of the city. There were frequent contributions to charitable and patriotic campaigns, and prayers for the general welfare of the state. Although the *kehillah* built an additional temporary synagogue—designed by architect J. Melzer in 1875, with minor neo-Romanesque features—both buildings proved inadequate for the growing population. From 1890 to 1892, the *kehillah* followed the construction of a new, magnificent synagogue at the edge of the historical center: on Pětatřicátníků sady (Parkway)—today, Nejedlého sady.

Jews involved themselves in many facets of the growing industrialization of Pilsen, including the financing and establishment of the Pilsen Brewery that brought much fame to their city. Many second-generation Jews achieved a higher education, with the result that in the early 1900s most of the doctors, lawyers, and bankers in the city were Jews. These worldly Jews participated in the civic activities of the city, with representation on the town council from 1861. By 1864 the city counted 20,000 residents, but its 234 Jews paid most of the taxes. Only six years later, out of a general population that had grown slightly to 22,000, Jews had more than quadrupled their numbers to 1,207.

By the turn of the century, the *kehillah* was one of the five largest and most affluent in Bohemia and had a major hand in the commercial and industrial growth of the city. Within the community, however, differences in outlook between liberal German assimilationists, Czech loyalists, and Zionists made for conflict and tension. During World War I, many Jews drafted into the Austro-Hungarian army served as officers and doctors. For a few years after 1918, the community employed two rabbis: one preaching in German and the other in Czech. Rabbi Max Hoch continued alone after 1925—in Czech.

THE GREAT SYNAGOGUE IN PILSEN

Built in neo-Romanesque style by Viennese architects Max Fleischer and E. Klotz, the Great Synagogue in Pilsen rises high above Nejedlého sady, one of the city's main thoroughfares. The majesty and size of the building reflect the prewar economic strength and prestige of the *kehillah*. In the past police had to divert traffic from the main street, as throngs of worshippers filled it on the High Holy Days. The twin octagonal towers and their Oriental cupolas are a city landmark, while the vaulted brick roof protected the building against the elements during its half century of neglect. Elaborate dentilations run below the roofline. A series of half-round arches below them crown the row of narrow paired windows. Three heavy wooden doors afford entrance to a large lobby, floored in marble.

The high vaulted sanctuary has all its furniture preserved intact, a rare sight in postwar central Europe. The soaring marble Ark fills much of the eastern wall. Two sets of gray marble pillars beside the doors support a massive arched pediment with a gilded inscription, *"Kodesh l'Adonai"* ("Sanctified to the Lord"). A gilded metal screen in a delicate flower motif separates the Ark from the *bimah* platform. The Ark is set within a massive wall and flanked on each side by a high series of ten marble niches. Framed by classical arches and pillars, the panel in each niche is inscribed in gilded letters with passages from the Bible and the daily prayers.

The magnificent carved mahogany *bimah* and balustrade repeat the pattern of arches, pillars, and wall inscriptions from above the *Aron Kodesh*. Traditional gold stars on a blue sky cover the ceiling and gallery vaults, while broad bands of geometric design add color to the many arches. Stylized motifs glisten in the glorious unbroken stained glass windows and send rays of multicolored light to the dark pews.

From the choir loft, looking over the *Aron Kodesh* to the main hall. The women's galleries are behind the pillars on three sides. Decorated ceiling vaults stretch across the great expanse to the opposite wall on the west.

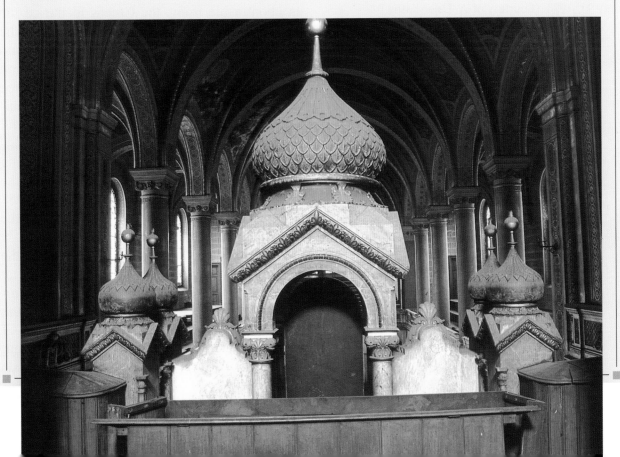

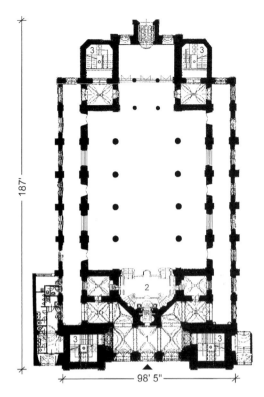

Plan of the Great Synagogue in Pilsen. 1. Entrance lobby; 2. Ark and *bimah*; 3. Stairways to the gallery. (Courtesy of J. Fiedler.)

The Jerusalem Trio—Alan Sternfeld, piano; Amalia Ishak, soprano; and Wendy Eisler-Kashy, flute—at the rededication of the Great Synagogue in Pilsen on February 11, 1998. (Courtesy of W. Eisler-Kashy.)

Community organizations played an important part in the life of the *kehillah* as its number peaked in 1921 to 3,117 and declined to 2,773 in 1930. Among the most active groups were the first B'nai B'rith Lodge in Bohemia, established in 1892; the Société, from 1911, that helped families of soldiers mobilized in the First World War; Zion, a women's organization for cultural activities to help Jews in *Eretz Yisrael;* and the Blau-Weiss (Blue-White) scout group, a forerunner of later Zionist groups. The Maccabi organization sponsored a regional athletics competition in 1934.

When Germany annexed the Sudetenland after the Munich conference of September 29, 1938, Jews of the region sought refuge in "safe" Pilsen, but it was to be an insecure haven. By September 1941 their numbers swelled to 3,106, as the Germans brought in Jews from other Bohemian communities. Mass deportation from Pilsen to Terezín began in January 1942, with the eventual transport of 2,604 Jews. By December 1944, only 242 Jews of mixed marriages remained in the city. The Nazis transferred to Prague 1,438 items of Judaica confiscated in Pilsen.

The few hundred Jews who returned to Pilsen after General Patton's forces liberated it on May 7, 1945 arrived to a hostile reception. By an abominable irony, the Czechs identified the paltry few emaciated Jewish survivors of the *Shoah* with the despised German culture and stoutly resisted their reintegration into the fabric of society. This opposition was strongly tainted with self-interest. Having usurped Jewish property, they were loath to return it to the rightful owners. Jobs, too, were scarce. Despite these difficulties, the *kehillah* resumed its functioning that year. The Jewish community cleaned up the synagogue, restored the cemetery, and in 1951 set up a monument to the 3,200 Jews of the Pilsen region who had perished in the *Shoah.*

Other tragedies unfolded in Pilsen in the Communist post-war era. The son of the former *ḥazzan,* young Bedřich Reicin, who fought heroically in the Czech army on the eastern front, achieved a Communist appointment as head of the military police. Then came the Slansky affair, the first of a series of anti-Semitic show trials held in Czechoslovakia in the 1950s. Reicin was

The synagogue is only a small distance from the central downtown square of Pilsen. Many of the visible smokestacks rise over factories established by the city's Jews during the nineteenth century.

accused of the "crime" of Zionism. Although "admitting Zionist intrigue," to please his prosecutors, he vigorously renounced his Jewish origins, as did many of the accused, and proclaimed his loyalty to Communism. He was executed with the others.

In the 1990s the *kehillah* numbered about 100 Jews, only 30 of them of unmixed parentage. They maintained a semblance of Jewish religious and cultural life, keeping a small prayer room in the community building. They also administered 60 Jewish cemeteries in the region, each of which represents a community that no longer exists. The Grand Synagogue was still in their possession, complete with all its furniture, with Ark and *bimah* intact. For many years the *kehillah* tried in vain to raise funds for restoration. Finally recognizing the cultural importance and value of this building, the Czech Ministry of Culture provided approximately 50 million Czech crowns (about 1.5 million U.S. dollars), for renovation. On Tu B'Shvat (New Year of the Trees) of Israel's 50th anniversary year—February 11, 1998—the city celebrated the rededication with great pomp and cere-

mony. Gardeners planted trees in honor of the event, and curious citizens lined the sides of Nejedlého sady, as the congregation solemnly walked by, carrying their Torah scrolls to the synagogue. Cantor Joseph Malovany of New York led the moving service in the presence of many Czech and Jewish notables. The building serves for infrequent *kehillah* functions but is used mainly as a splendid concert hall and exhibition site.

Early in the morning, just before we left the city, we walked through the undistinguished historical town square. Few people were about, even few of the usually plentiful pigeons. We climbed the tower of the neo-Romanesque St. Barthlomew's Church, built in the thirteenth to sixteenth centuries, and wondered whether its slender spire, the highest in the Czech Republic at 331 feet, was erected when the first Jews entered the city in the fourteenth century. From the tower gallery 190 feet above the ground, we caught sight of the synagogue again, stoically raising its grimy cupolas toward the skyline and nearly lost among the drab roofs and the gray mist around the distant chimneys.

Gallery area and decorative ceiling of the synagogue in Vrbové, Slovakia.

SLOVAKIA

Slovakia was a province of Hungary for nearly 1,000 years before achieving independence in newly born Czechoslovakia at the close of World War I. The Jewish history of the region was subsumed in the Jewish annals of Greater Hungary. Contemporary documents and rabbinical literature record a number of flourishing communities from the time of the Middle Ages, notably in the politically autonomous *kehillah* of Bratislava (Hungarian: Pozsony; German: Pressburg), in Trnava (Hungarian: Nagyszombat), and in Trenčín. Organized in many small, rural *kehillot,* the majority of the Jews were farmers and a minority engaged in commerce, trade, and moneylending. The fifteenth century brought in its wake blood libels and burnings at the stake, followed in 1526 by expulsion from the towns after the Hungarian defeat by the Turks at the battle of Mohács. Jews settled in the villages and brought their goods daily to the markets. The merchant guilds saw them as competitors and succeeded in keeping the towns closed to Jewish residence until 1840. Most of the *kehillot*

remained small and agricultural in nature, well after the region came under Hapsburg dominion (1699–1918). The revolution by Hungary against the Austrian crown in 1848 failed, but the founding of the Austro-Hungarian Empire in 1867 finally brought political autonomy for Hungary.

Peasant riots in Moravia in 1683, as well as the Familiants Law and residence restrictions of 1726–1727, impelled many Moravian Jews to move to Slovakia, where they settled mostly near the western border. Merchants and artisans, these industrious immigrants were welcomed by Hungarian landlords who housed them on their estates and granted them protection and privileges. The newcomers maintained their religious customs and kept up commercial and spiritual ties with the communities from which they came, but they also inclined toward worldly learning and were generally open to the gentile surroundings. In this they differed from the Galician Jews who settled the eastern regions and clung to the precepts of Hasidism, with its distinctive customs and seclusive lifestyle. Jewish communities flourished and established new centers of Jewish learning, including hasidic enclaves in Pressburg and Vrbové, among others. The most prestigious yeshivah in Pressburg owed its status to the leadership and renown of the *Ḥatam Sofer:* Rabbi Moses Sofer (1762–1839), scholar, zealous adversary of the Enlightenment, and the progenitor of a dynasty of Orthodox rabbis.

Two main social processes crystallized in the Jewish community in the first half of the nineteenth century: the battle for political rights and the *Kulturkampf* (culture conflict) that pitted Orthodox religious conservatism against a rising trend of modernization and ritual reform. The Orthodox adherents, mainly from Slovakia and Burgenland, had their center in Bratislava, while the chiefly Hungarian supporters of reform drew guidance from Budapest. The religious schism that became overt in 1868 raised havoc in all the Jewish communities of Hungary. Communities split into three factions: Orthodox, Neolog (Reform), and the small minority Status Quo Ante faction that asserted a detachment from the schism.

The new Hungarian autonomy and the Emancipation Law in 1867 brought to the fore an official policy favoring the assimilation of national minorities. Prosperous middle-class Slovak Jews welcomed the new freedom and gravitated politically and culturally toward assimilation. Jews became prominent in industry, commerce, finance, and the free professions. In the late nineteenth century, anti-Jewish riots were stirred up by supposed Jewish affluence and opposition to the influx of refugees from Galicia. Following the passing of the 1896 Reception Law that granted Jewish religion official equality with Christian faith, Slovak nationalism gained further momentum among the devoutly Catholic peasant population.

The establishment of the Czechoslovak Republic in 1918 marked a new era in the life of Slovak Jewry. The stability of post–World-War-I Slovakia brought Jews prosperity and a flourishing political and cultural life. *Kehillot* joined the National Federation of Czechoslovak Jews, an organization that was vital in strengthening the scattered Jewish communities across the republic. The first Czechoslovakian population census of 1921 counted 135,918 Slovak Jews, organized in 227 congregations, of which a majority, 167, were Orthodox. The 29 Neolog *kehillot* decided in 1926 to join the Status Quo Ante communities to form Yeshurun, the union of 60 Slovak liberal congregations. In a community atmosphere that centered around many youth movements, university-educated and politically active Jewish youth enthusiastically embraced the ideals of socialism or of Zionism.

In the 1930s the rightist national Slovak Peoples' Party incited feeling against the Jews. Conditions deteriorated rapidly after the Munich Pact in 1938 and the German occupation of the Sudetenland, dismembering Czechoslovakia. On March 14, 1939, an independent Slovak state was declared; a satellite of Nazi Germany, its regime was quasi-Fascist and anti-Semitic. On the next day, Germany proclaimed a "protectorate" over Bohemia and Moravia and occupied their territory.

Jews in Slovakia numbered over 130,000 in 1939—nearly twice as many as in Bohemia and Moravia. In March 1942, the Nazis began mass deportations of Slovak Jews to the death camps in Poland. Jews were active in the ill-fated Slovak national uprising (October 1944–March 1945). In reprisal, more than 13,000 Jews were deported to the death camps after the uprising was suppressed. Some 25,000 war-weary Jewish survivors returned at first to their towns. Their revival attempts in a few major Jewish communities faced hostile environments and most of them chose emigration, mainly to *Eretz Yisrael.*

After the 1989 withdrawal of the Soviets, Jewish learning and an interest in Jewish tradition enjoyed a revival. The Joint Distribution Committee and the Ronald S. Lauder Foundation sponsored cultural activities to attract Jewish youth. Only 6,000 Jews inhabit Slovakia today, at major centers in Bratislava, Košice, and a few other towns. Their communal organization is still the Federation of Jewish Communities, whose current difficult task is combating dangerous aspects of re-emerging anti-Semitism. Defamation has come from rightist newspapers, from elements within the Slovak Catholic Church, and from nationalist political parties. Some Jewish claims for property restitution have been slandered as international Jewish, capitalist extortion.

During World War II and the long post-war Communist rule, most of the Slovak synagogues were vandalized or used for storage, and many others were destroyed. More than 100 synagogue buildings still stand. The synagogue in Malacky was adapted in the 1980s to an art center for children, and the synagogue in Vrbové, with several interruptions, is in the midst of a slow process of restoration to a municipal concert hall. A few more projects have been initiated in recent years. Suffering economic hardships since its separation from the Czech Republic in 1993, the Slovak government has had minimal or no funds available for synagogue or museum restoration; attitudes toward funding, however, are gradually changing.

Eugen Bárkány (1885–1967) was an architect and engineer with wide interests and a concern for the Jewish community and the preservation of Jewish folk art. He wrote a history of the Jewish communities in Slovakia. An avid collector of antiques and Judaica, he initiated a modest Jewish museum in Prešov that opened on July 29, 1928. The museum's collection was confiscated during the war and brought to the State Jewish Museum in Prague. Although many of the original articles have been lost, much of the collection was returned to Slovakia in 1993. Some of the pieces are on display in the Orthodox synagogue in Prešov, but the bulk of the collection formed the nucleus for the newly founded Museum of Jewish Culture in Bratislava, dedicated on May 20, 1993.

The opening of the museum in Bratislava marks a new approach by Slovakia to Jewish cultural tradition. Scholars and municipal officials increasingly recognize the urgent need to gather, research, and preserve the material and spiritual remains of the Jewish presence in Slovakia. There is a growing awareness in the population that the destinies of the Jews, inhabitants of the country for nearly a millennium, are a permanent part of the political, economic, and cultural history of Slovakia.

Entrance to the synagogue in Svätý Jur, Slovakia. The chronogram over the stone portal proclaims, *"V'yevarkhu shem K'vodkha"* ("May your glorious name be blessed"; Neh. 9:5), denoting the year 5636/1876, the date of synagogue expansion.

THE TIME
OF THE "BARCHES"

I don't ask questions, I don't judge, I don't threaten with Divine wrath," Klára Kováčová, the *kehillah* midwife in 1920s Svätý Jur used to say as she comforted nervous patients in her spacious kitchen. Expert at births and at "more delicate interventions," Kováčová kept a blackboard on the door of her *kehillah*-owned apartment to inform clients of her whereabouts. "I know there are enough children, desired and undesired babies . . . that they pour into this world like an unending flow of lava, healthy and sick, bright and retarded . . . some who will live to adulthood and some who will live only a few days . . . some who will be happy, and some who will succumb to alcohol, poverty, or tuberculosis. All this happens with God's will; why should abortions not be God's will?" Always ready to help, Kováčová accepted with the utmost tact anything the patient could afford to pay for her services.

When their house caught fire early one morning, veterinarian Dr. Sárkanyi and his family rescued a few belongings and stood shivering on the street, watching part of the house burn down before the volunteer fire-fighters arrived. "What happened?" The maid, Kačka, weeping all the while, conjectured, "I lit the boiler to heat water for the laundry an hour ago. Some coals may have dropped on the floor. . . ." Dr. Sárkanyi comforted her, "At least the family is safe." During the war the family was less fortunate. All the Sárkanyis were taken away on a transport. Only Imrich Sárkanyi was not in town that day and no one knew what happened to him.

We did not personally meet the protagonists in these stories. They come alive in the narrative of *Čas Barchesu* (The Time of the Ḥallah). *"Barches,"* a slight corruption of the Hebrew *"brakhot"* (blessings), is the name the Slovaks adopted for ḥallah, the sweet white Sabbath bread. In this small volume, Viola Kováčová, a young Slav writer of Svätý Jur, recorded anecdotes remembered by her mother, Genovéva Kováčová, of her Jewish neighbors from the decades before the Second World War. The Jewish families of Svätý Jur—Antmans, Endlers, Gutmans, Hybsis, Königs, and others—are vibrantly portrayed in these pages.

Svätý Jur, a small, 800-year-old town on Bratislava's northern edge, named itself for the hero of legendary fame, Saint George, who galloped into the town square to save a distressed maiden and her village from a ferocious dragon. Svätý Jur's lush vineyards produced famous wines, preferred among its consumers above the well-advertised wines of Modra and Pezinok. Jews lived here for 300 years, mostly as tradespeople. They lived in the little houses along the streets with courtyards behind them, leading their daily lives in these narrow confines. Their shops were scattered on the three major streets: Bratislavská, Pezinská, and the wide main street between them, Prostredná.

A document from 1722 mentions the leasing of a shop for sale of salt and candles to Loebl Shai, for 60 gold pieces annually. In 1729 Shai received a three-year extension on his lease to sell spirits. After that he had trouble with the authorities. Despite the express prohibition on wine import without tax payment, he tried to smuggle a barrel of wine, which was promptly confiscated. In 1730 he paid a fine of 100 gold pieces for insulting the mayor during a town council meeting, but he retained his franchise until 1731, when the shop was temporarily transferred to the Bojnitzer family. Loebl Shai leased the brandy distillery until 1747, then Herschel Salomon held the lease for ten years, and after him Moshe Lippel. The franchise was important for its exclusivity. No one other than the lessee was allowed to distill brandy or sell tobacco.

The magistrate righted social wrongs between Jews. Ruth, the daughter of Yaakov Bettelheim, claimed in 1731 that Shimshe, the son of Loebel Shai, "did her a bad thing" eight days before the traditional day of mourning for the destruction of the Temple, Tisha B'Av—the ninth day of Av—and again 18 days later. The young man was apprehended while the magistrate investigated the claim that Ruth had affairs with other men. However, when the child was born and the mother insisted that Shimshe was the "only" father, the magistrate fined Shimshe 12 gold pieces and ordered the lad to marry Ruth formally under a ḥuppah.

A 1785 complaint by the Jewish judge of the community, Bojnitzer, to the town council also shows up in the chronicle. Bojnitzer claimed that they had to keep the synagogue windows open because of the summer heat. It seems that noise from the synagogue disturbed neighbor Jan Scha-

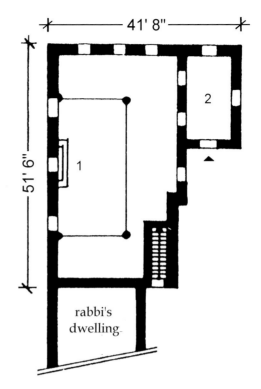

Plan of the synagogue in Svätý Jur. 1. Ark, 2. ḥeder. (Adapted from E. Bárkány and L.'Dojč, *Židovské náboženské obce na Slovensku.*)

Sketch of the synagogue as seen from the northwest. The foreground enclosed stairway to the gallery and the stone portal to the two-story annex on the right were part of the nineteenth-century expansion. A bright room with three exposures on the second floor of the annex served as a ḥeder. The large building, housing the rabbi, *shammash*, and *shoḥet*, joined the synagogue on its north wall, with internal passage between the buildings. (Adapted from E. Bárkány and L.'Dojč, *Židovské náboženské obce na Slovensku.*)

Baroque town hall of Svätý Jur (1865), standing on Prostredná—the wide, central street that slopes down-hill toward the road to Bratislava. The building serves as municipal offices and an historical museum. A distinctive attic structure flanked by a pair of Gothic-like turrets features the town emblem: St. George and the dragon.

Stone charity box, still hanging on the synagogue wall.

effer, who poured a bucket of water on the praying Jews through the open window. The council asked the sides to settle the matter between themselves, but this solved nothing, since similar complaints reappeared in the following summer.

The council ordered a census, in 1838, to check illegal residence. Then it complained about the alleged lack of Jewish participation in paying for the cost of gas for lighting the main streets at night. When the town walls were torn down and the settlement ceased to be a closed city, the council nevertheless allowed the Jews to put up an *eruv* (Shabbat boundary) despite burghers' objections. Ten florins was the annual tax per family until 1840, when a graduated income tax was introduced. Relations with the non-Jews were friendly enough, although the Jews were looked down upon because of their "backward" religion. It was common for bullying Christian children to accost Jewish children in the street and coerce them to do *pukrle,* a very deep bow. The chronicle of 1850 relates that the bullies beat a child who did not comply.

Many rabbis came to Svätý Jur to enjoy the curative powers of the phosphorus- and sulfur-rich waters of the spa. Rabbi Moses Schreiber, known as the Ḥatam Sofer of Pressburg (Bratislava), came annually and wrote many of his *responsa* in the spa's shady gardens. Generosity to synagogue and charitable institutions was so popular as to excite competition among the congregants. One of the great contributors was the wealthy Perez Neumann, who set up a foundation for the *kehillah.* Improved access to higher education after the Emancipation widened the economic horizons of the young people and they drifted away from the confines of Svätý Jur. The *kehillah* shrank from 228 in 1900 (6.6 percent of the population), to 125 in 1930, and only 86 in 1939. The 1920s and 1930s were the years remembered by the elder Kováčová in *Čas Barchesu.*

Mrs. Endler ran a general store, very popular among the many poor people of insecure income, because she accepted bundles of wood as payment for goods. Unemployed fathers collected wood in the forest. At home, the children divided and bound them into manageable parcels. How Mrs. Endler disposed of so much kindling no one bothered to ask. In the court

201

behind her store, Mrs. Endler owned one-room flats, each with a single window to the yard and an unpaved floor. She let them at low rent to poor families. On late Friday afternoons, the little gentile girl Pauline Rajkromer would come from her room in the courtyard to kindle the Sabbath fire for Mrs. Endler. Pauline and her friends enjoyed doing small Sabbath chores for Jewish families. They loved the tasty reward, a piece of the fresh *barches.*

Three Jewish doctors served the town. Dr. Halle, a tall lean man, came to a sick child even at midnight and always treated poor families for free. For the many children who suffered each winter from colds and running noses, he had one remedy: "Inhale!" This was a curative process available at no cost to all classes. The mother heated a pot of water to boiling and seated the children with her around the steaming pot. All put their heads under a blanket, inhaled together, and were cured—sooner or later. The other frequent remedy for most ailments was castor oil.

Dr. Kautz was an old bachelor with a kind heart and a clever intuition. When Duša, the son of Šiarsky, the prosperous bookkeeper, had no

Vine-covered hills that surround the town of Svätý Jur. For centuries the wine produced in the town was hailed as the best in the area of the Lower Carpathian mountains and provided the main source of livelihood for its inhabitants.

appetite, the doctor did not provide an elixir. Instead, he armed the lad with an ax and sent him into the forest with a woodsman to chop wood. Duša came home proudly dragging a large sack of kindling wood, and exulting in an enormous hunger for food.

A popular shop was the *konfitéria* (sweets shop) run by Mrs. Horecký—a small woman, fat as a barrel, with frizzy hair that suggested the preferred name of her shop, "Frizzy Horecký." It was a cramped, dark place, lit by a petroleum lamp all day, and so cold that she always sat huddled in a blanket amidst a small assortment of cheap sweets. This was a "depressed place, a depressed lamp, depressed merchandise, and a depressed saleslady"—but for Svätý Jur, it was the symbol of free spending. When children got a bit of small change for a treat they would fly down to Frizzy Horecký.

Jewish and non-Jewish children played together on the dusty streets and down at the lake among the giant thorn bushes. The girls hid from the boys in the bushes and came out with scratched legs and bruised toes. The lake would often overflow during rainy summers, flooding the surrounding area. The low-lying house of Abe Švarc, the skinner, was the first to be flooded. Beds floated around the room as thin pale children crouched on them with large frightened eyes, while the parents, armed with brooms, chased away the swimming rats. Neighbors stood by and watched the drama. All were waiting for the expert Thereza Klinková to arrive. Surefooted and confident in her high rubber boots, Auntie Thereza waded all the way out to the barrier and lifted the heavy sluicegate. The waters rushed into the river with a great noise, leaving behind puddles of mud everywhere.

Mr. Nathan sold clothing. He placed his jackets and a hand mirror on a table in a corner of the square on Sunday mornings as the Christians poured out of the three churches on the other corners. He had his own methods for fitting jackets to customers. A gentle tug from behind to gather the folds as the customer looked at the front, and a slight pull at the front as the customer looked at the mirror behind him, and the deal was set. Nathan explained to his son, Žigo, who held the

THE SYNAGOGUE IN SVÄTÝ JUR

Within a large yard surrounded by a high stone wall, the south facade of the synagogue faces an unpaved alley parallel to the main street. The brick walls are barely covered by blotches of the original plaster. High round-headed windows are crowned by stone moldings that add a touch of elegance. Two paneled wooden doors, set in a cracked stone portal on the north, open into an anteroom that leads to the wide prayer room, used now as a storeroom. Fading frescoes form a background for the farm tools hanging on the east wall. In the wide U-shaped gallery, sections of floor planking have been ripped up, and the balustrade has been replaced by a few posts, joined by rough boards. A pair of carved lions had livened up the now-missing *Aron Kodesh*. The *ḥevra kadishah* had once kept silver bowls for burial preparations, an antique *parokhet,* and the community's historical documents in a side room.

View of the synagogue interior, to the southeast from the gallery. An empty Ark niche to the left, broken windows, peeled frescoes, and scattered debris tell of abuse and neglect.

mirror for the clients, "The guy is not going to lose weight, and a large jacket will last him a long time."

Svätý Jur is in a valley surrounded by hills that are covered with rows of grapevines. Mrs. Nathan's brother, a wine merchant named Spitzer, came to buy grapes for kosher wine every year. The local grapes were good for this purpose as well as for the sacramental wine of the region's Catholic priests. Up to the weighing of the grapes, non-Jews could handle them, but if the wine was to be kosher, only Orthodox Jews could handle the grapes after the wagon came off the scales. As an interim crop, the farmers planted string beans, and the town was first to the market with its beans. Women would go out at three in the morning to pick the beans and at six the vendors would arrive to buy them for their markets. An early-morning kilogram brought 12 crowns. By the afternoon it could bring no more than one.

Southwest facade of the synagogue in Svätý Jur. The structure is rural Baroque, from the seventeenth century, and was converted to a synagogue in 1790. Entrance to the building was through a portal on the north wall. The western wing was added to expand the gallery and provide a schoolroom in the course of major repairs that were completed in 1880.

Jews in Svätý Jur, as Jews everywhere, had a problem of national identity each time there was a change of rulers. At the time of the Austro-Hungarian Empire, they saw themselves as Hungarian, and during the Czechoslovak Republic, as German. In the Slovak Republic, in 1940, when they wanted to be listed as Slovak, they were brutally reminded that they were Jews. Stripped of economic and social position, they were selectively inducted into forced labor. The remaining Jews were deported in June 1942 and Jewish property was sold at auction. Since then, Svätý Jur has had no Jewish residents and hardly any Jewish visitors.

At the north end of the Jewish quarter at 165 Edelhof Court, on Pezinská ulice, the synagogue is situated downhill from the cluster of churches in the main square. The thick walls, the shape of the windows, and the ground plan show that the structure dates from the Baroque period, early in the seventeenth century. Operated by Samuel Herschl as a pub and inn from 1785, the building was converted to a synagogue in 1790. Numbers in this small *kehillah* waxed and waned with local conditions, and there were brief periods without Jewish residence. The synagogue was reconstructed and expanded in 1880 in response to nineteenth-century growth. Other buildings in the synagogue complex included the rabbi's house, with flats for the *shohet* (ritual slaughterer) and the *shammash* (beadle) adjacent to the synagogue, as well as a *mikveh* and a *beit midrash*. A private family bought the complex in the 1980s and renovated the rabbi's dwelling to a fine apartment. For the present, the family keeps agricultural implements in the cavernous synagogue chamber and hangs laundry there, but their wish is to restore the old building some day. Other Jewish buildings and shops of the complex have been leveled.

From among their many deported Jewish neighbors, townspeople remembered the Sárkányi family with special fondness and often wondered what had happened to young Imrich. The mystery cleared up eventually. His parents had sent him to England for safety in 1939, after

The author of *Čas Barchesu* (The Time of the *Barches*), Viola Kováčová, seated, visiting Dr. Imrich Sarkany and his wife, Helen, in London, May 1995. Vignettes of Jewish life in Svätý Jur were recorded from her mother's recollections. The book was published in 1993 by the Slovak Department of Jewish Culture and was translated in London for private circulation by Dr. Sarkany, formerly of Svätý Jur. (Courtesy of I. Sarkany)

which he never saw his family again. He became a dermatologist in London and, in his retirement, pursues the fascinations of astronomy. A frustrating return visit to Svätý Jur in 1992, in search of his boyhood home and his father's grave, led to a poignant meeting two years later with *Barches* author Viola Kováčová. Charmed by her depiction of the Jews of Svätý Jur and his family, Dr. Sarkany translated her booklet from Slovak to English and published it privately for his family, "to share with him . . . the fleeting images of lost childhood and family and home."

Today there is no one left in Svätý Jur to bake the *barches*.

BARDEJOV

Banská Bystrica
Banská Štiavnica
Halič
Bratislava

THE PROPHET ELIJAH

Netanya, 1973

Dear Avram Lezer,

I read your letter and burst into tears like a child. . . . You asked me for material about our town of Bardejov for your book. What I have to tell you can hardly be expressed on paper. When we talk, the memories come rushing back. Before my eyes is the first event, on that black Shabbos *in 1938, when I saw all those respected Jews, rabbis and scholars, humiliated and dragged through the mud and dirt. . . . And that was only the beginning. Our Jewish town is no more. It has been erased. Gone are the children, gone are their mothers. The streets are empty and ravaged. The once glorious community has been liquidated. Write, Avram, describe everything, so that coming generations will know the enormity of the destruction. . . .*

Your Landsman, Naphtali Zelinger

This letter appears in *Bardejov Remembered,* privately published in 1988 by Avram Eliezer Grüssgott, who now lives in Brooklyn, New York. Grüssgott's account is one of a long series of memorial books lovingly and painfully produced by the handful of survivors of communities destroyed in the *Shoah.* These books are their way of commemorating families and friends, and the fabric of a civilization that was brutally extinguished. The library of Yad Vashem in Jerusalem contains many such volumes.

A copy of *Bardejov Remembered* went to Max Spira, one of the last two Jews living in Bardejov in the early 1990s. It was Max who showed it to us at his home and added his own experiences. Max is a familiar and respected figure in Bardejov. A widower of less than a year when we first met him, he was suspicious of strangers. He was weary of inquisitive visiting Jews and discouraged by the futility of his labors to get funds for restoring the two remaining synagogues in town. We gained his trust only with a great deal of effort, but in the end we won a friend and the benefit of his guidance in exploring his town and the synagogues.

Bardejov huddles in the shadow of the Beskyds mountain range in northeastern

Slovakia. Chief city of the Šariš area close to the Polish border, it lies south of the winding Topla River, a stop on an old lucrative trade route between the Baltic and the Black Seas. Bardejov's fourteenth-century royal charter describes an already fortified town, with walls and towers to protect a settlement clustered around a huge rectangular market place. The city has preserved some of the old fortifications.

The municipality has faithfully restored the cobblestone central square and environs, a virtual museum of Gothic, Renaissance, and Baroque buildings. In the middle of the square, the late-Gothic town hall is an architectural jewel, featuring high gables, a saddle roof edged with miniature sculptures, and an ornate staircase. Low, pastel-colored houses under steep double-pitched roofs ring three sides of the square. Bardejov, exceptional among the historic towns of central Europe, earned the prestigious Europa Nostra award for the imaginative restoration of this town square to a harmonious urban setting.

Unless they had special permission, Jews were excluded from Slovak towns for long periods of history. It is said that when a Jewish peddler entered Banská Bystrica or Banská Štiavnica, a policeman accompanied him all day and then escorted him back out of town. Jewish presence in Bardejov, sporadically documented from early in the Middle Ages, did not begin again until the mid-eighteenth century. Accord-

The award-winning town square of Bardejov, with its striking sixteenth-century town hall.

ing to documents of 1747, Jews moved to Bardejov gradually from Galicia, settling northeast of the marketplace and working as farmers in many nearby villages.

The first family to gain official entry was that of Nathan Guttmann. When he died at a young age, his capable and energetic wife, Rachel, vigorously took on his responsibilities and became known as the "mother of Bardejov Jewry." She was an efficient administrator, managing the family's mills and agricultural lands. When she died in 1828, her offspring included the Rosenwasser, Fairlicht, and Löwy families. Other community founders in 1806 included Isaac Landau, and the Sobl and Friedman families.

One of the first rabbis, Rabbi Dov Beer Spira, became a leader of village communities in the Špiš region. In keeping with the hasidic origins of Bardejov's community members, three of its rabbis, Moshe Leib Halberstam, Zalman Leib Halberstam, and Chaim Natan Halberstam, were descendants of the Galician hasidic dynasty whose founder was Rabbi Chaim Halberstam.

The Bardejov *kehillah* officially established itself and the *hevra kadishah* in 1806 and completed its first synagogue in 1830. When the numbers had grown to 181 at mid-century, two additional prayer rooms were needed. It was a largely hasidic community maintaining its traditional way of life in customs and dress, at home

Sketch of the old Bardejov synagogue. A pair of covered stairways led to the large Empire portal through which the women entered the gallery. Such prominence and grandeur for the women's entrance was rare. Men entered the sanctuary from steps down to a now-missing portal underneath. (Adapted from E. Bárkány and Ľ. Dojč, *Židovské náboženské obce na Slovensku.*)

and on the streets of the town. In Hungary's religious schism of 1868, the *kehillah* came down solidly on the Orthodox side. The *kehillah* treasured religious books and organized Ḥevrah Kinyan Sefarim, a society mandated to purchase books and set up libraries.

A booklet published by the municipality in 1935, *Old and New Bardejov*, describes the Jewish community with a modicum of sociological analysis:

There are 2,264 Jews in 450 families. Most of the Jews are storekeepers with shops on the main square. A few are wealthy, but you would not recognize them. The majority have a modest standard of living, but some are beggars who must ask for alms. Jewish poverty is caused by natural and social circumstances and by the density of the Jewish population in this poor district. In most villages, there are two to five Jewish families in a population of 150 to 400 people. No large Jewish manors exist in this region. Jews own only some of the smaller farms.

The whole town is Orthodox. They walk around in their long black kapotes *and wear traditional* shtraymlekh, *fur-trimmed hats. They value religious education. Even the youngest children go to* ḥeder, *where they receive exclusively religious training. The pupils' families pay the teachers, each according to its means. Older children attend the state school also, from 7:30 to 2:30, but they go to* ḥeder *before and after secular classes, often until 7 P.M.*

Zelinger's letter to Grüssgott corroborates this description: "I remember how as a five-year-old, I was awakened at 4:30 every morning and sent off to *ḥeder* in the cold and windy darkness. Usually, the rebbetzin was still sleeping on the long bench where we had to sit to study when I arrived at the rebbe's house. So I would wait in the corner, huddled on the floor until she woke up."

Here are some comments on health from the municipal writer in 1935:

Physical development of some boys is retarded because for 11-hour days they are sealed in the classroom without movement or fresh air. Maybe *this is the reason for the frequent occurrence of diabetes among Jewish boys. The girls are healthier because they rest more.*

Among the youngsters, girls attend libraries frequently in high proportion and enjoy reading. Older Orthodox people who come from the countryside or from Poland are not so well educated. The Jewish intelligentsia lives in town, and they include a few doctors, lawyers, officials, two veterinarians, an engineer, and a notary. Jewish business, other than the shops, includes trade in lumber that they transport to the south. They import grain and wine, which is often exported to Poland and Russia.

We met Avram Grüssgott in Israel when he came to visit his daughter. He told us:

My father, Shmuel Grüssgott, was secretary of the kehillah *from 1921 until the deportation. Jews were 40 percent of the population. On Shabbat all the stores were closed, because the owners were Jewish. The stores were closed on Sundays, too, of course, but Jews ran many of the bars and these were open after two o'clock in the afternoon. In the* kúpele, *the mineral-water spa near town, Jews owned some of the large hotels: Imperial, Astoria, Slávia, Bromberg, and Atlas. There were two synagogues there. Great rabbis from Hungary and Poland and their entourages used to come for the cure.*

In its heyday the Bardejov spa, located a few miles outside the city, was one of the most renowned in Europe. The spa is spaciously landscaped along a narrow park, bordered by gentle pine-covered slopes and dotted with decorous turn-of-the-century hotels. Jews and Armenians were among the first developers to exploit the curative springs for a health resort that European royalty soon adopted. A bronze statue, erected in a small park near the spa entrance in 1895, honors Empress Elizabeth of Austria-Hungary, who was a regular visitor.

Of the four pre-war synagogues in the city, two of them have been so completely altered for commercial use that no Jewish remnant whatever remains. The older of the two others, the Great

THE ALTSCHUL SYNAGOGUE IN BARDEJOV

Little remains of the elegant, elevated Empire-style portal of the Great Synagogue in the Suburbium. The coarse opening below the platform marks the sunken entrance to the synagogue anteroom. In the vaulted prayer room, a stone tablet mounted above the entrance tells an almost allegoric story about the construction of this large synagogue on the site of an earlier prayer room. Jozef, son of Nachum Guttmann, started the construction, but he died suddenly before the project's completion. His son-in-law, Isaac Harpuder, completed the task 22 years later in 1830.

The building, 75 by 49 feet, is one of the two nine-bay style synagogues extant in Slovakia—the other is in Stupava, near Bratislava. Colorfully painted geometric designs cover arches and high vaults, including the central bay between the four pillars over the missing *bimah*. On the eastern wall, the niche of the *Aron Kodesh* is bare. Fragments of inscriptions are visible on the east wall. There is a series of niches above the space of the prestigious benches near the Ark that may have held prayer books and shawls.

The Great Synagogue (the Altschul) in Bardejov. Empire style, 1830. The synagogue is used as a storeroom for plumbing supplies, and the facade shows the damage that comes from such use. A wall of white interior plaster below a diagonal gash of raw exposed brick locates one of the two missing covered stairways of the Empire portal to the gallery. Not much is left of the proper synagogue sunken entrance, below, except for a gaping hole.

Synagogue (the Altschul), was part of "the Jewish Suburbium," a civic complex located on Mlýnska ulica near the city's historic core. The Suburbium was the busy center of social and religious activity. Initiated at the end of the eighteenth century, the complex was planned according to talmudic regulation and became the pride of the community. The two central buildings were the large synagogue and the *beit midrash*. A spacious *mikveh* on the main street was patronized by Jews and non-Jews alike. Except for the slaughterhouse, all the structures still stand—and serve a major plumbing supply company for storage and workshops. Careless commercial use has caused considerable damage to the synagogue facade. Plumbing appliances in large cartons fill the available floor space.

When Václav Havel, president of then-Czechoslovakia, paid a state visit to Bardejov in August 1991, it was Max Spira who escorted him to the synagogue. As is typical in much of Europe, participants come from considerable distances for significant community events. There are no Jewish children in Bardejov. From Košice, an hour's distance to the south, a delegation of Jewish children came to march in the procession with lighted candles. President Havel declared the synagogue and the Suburbium to be a historical monument. A dedication tablet affixed to the south facade announces the synagogue's historic importance and its status as a protected monument.

The fourth and youngest synagogue in Bardejov still serves its congregation of one,

Plaque above entrance. Carved stone tablet over the entrance in the main hall:

Twenty-two years of the years had passed
And the hands of Jozef [Guttmann] who had started to
  build this house [faltered]
But he was plucked before his time
And thorns and thistles nearly filled the halls
Until the challenge fell on the shoulders of his son-in-law.
And Isaac came and stretched his arms upward to God
  and to the mission.
He allowed his eyes no sleep, nor did he rest nor cease
Until his God answered him and the work was
  completed, on
Rosh Hodesh Elul, in the year, "May this be a small
  temple" 5590 (1830).

Area of the *Aron Kodesh,* as seen through the four central pillars of the *bimah.* The nineteenth-century ceiling frescoes are still bright.

Max Spira. Built in neo-Gothic style in 1929 on Kláštorná ulice, a quiet street in the former Jewish quarter, the synagogue building is taller than the adjacent one-story houses. The neighborhood is blue-collar and has a few stores, a print shop and a small clothing shop. The name of the synagogue is barely visible in faded paint above the neo-Gothic windows: Klaus Ḥevrah Bikkur Ḥolim. A *klaus* is a synagogue built by and for merchants and workers. This one's name extols the virtue of visiting the sick. The rabbi lived in a few small rooms upstairs behind the women's gallery, and the *klaus* was open for prayer and

THE KLAUS BIKKUR ḤOLIM SYNAGOGUE IN BARDEJOV

In the *klaus,* tables and bookcases—crammed with sacred texts from this and the two defunct synagogues and with remnants of the acclaimed community library—crowd the *beit midrash.* A side door leads to the prayer hall, not particularly large, filled with benches facing the Ark on the street side. A wood-burning chimney/stove stands in the corner. According to Max, the *shul* was so crowded on Shabbat in the cold of winter before the war that they did not need to light the stove. The wooden Ark has simple Baroque lines and the marks of missing stucco decorations on the rounded pediment: a pair of rampant lions holding Tablets of the Law below a crown. The police recovered the stolen gilded ornaments, but instead of returning them to the *klaus,* sent them to Prague "for appraisal." A decorative black iron railing surrounds the central wooden *bimah.* The gallery face has a lower section of wooden panels in bright green, under rectangular swing windows. Panels in trompe l'oeil style on the upper part of the south wall cogently simulate an extension of the gallery. A stylized floral and geometric pattern decorates the ceiling.

The *Aron Kodesh* in the small *klaus* synagogue. The synagogue is used only by Max Spira and infrequent visitors.

study from early morning until late at night. The street entrance opens onto a narrow vestibule and gallery stairway. A small garden in the closed-in court behind the synagogue serves Max as a place to raise vegetables and keep a few chickens.

A Christian woman lived in the synagogue building during the Nazi occupation. She had the front windows bricked up to hide the appearance of a synagogue. One day, when soldiers tried to break in, she shouted invectives at them, held her ground, and refused to give them entry. This was the only synagogue in town that was not violated.

The *kehillah* of 2,700 persons functioned until May 1942 and the mass deportations. More than 2,400 Jews of Bardejov and vicinity were loaded onto boxcars to Auschwitz. After the liberation by the Soviet army in January 1945, seven Jews crept out from their hiding place, an old narrow wine cellar under a store at the square. A few returned from the camps, and Max Spira came back from the Polish forests. Bardejov became a center for refugee rehabilitation and a focal point for staging "illegal" immigration to Palestine.

We sat with Max in the *klaus* for much of a morning, while he told us how he had survived the *Shoah.* A young adult then, he started with a cousin's money, which he spent freely for places to hide. He escaped to Poland after the roundup

Max Spira and Czechoslovak President Václav Havel in the old synagogue in Bardejov, summer 1991. The occasion was the ceremonial declaration of the Bardejov Jewish Suburbium as a national monument and memorial for Bardejov victims of the Shoah. (Photo: Olga Nováková, Bardejov.)

Max Spira in front of his synagogue, Klaus Ḥevrah Bikkur Ḥolim, on Kláštorsná ulice, a few steps from the central square. The only Jew in Bardejov, Max serves in Prešov as *shoḥet,* and in Košice also as *ḥazzan* on the high holidays.

of Jews there was completed and hid on an isolated farm, surviving on turnips from the field until liberation. Now alone, he goes to his synagogue on Friday evenings and Saturday morn-

ings to chant the Shabbat service melodiously in his loud cantorial voice. Acquaintances stop him in the street to ask, "Who was with you in the synagogue yesterday?"

"That was Elijah the Prophet, who always keeps me company."

Facade of the Klaus Ḥevrah Bikkur Ḥolim synagogue, neo-Gothic, 1929.

STIRRINGS OF RELIGIOUS REFORM

The restrictive Familiants Laws of 1726 and 1727, promulgated by Charles VI to limit the number of Jewish families in Bohemia and Moravia, had a dispersive effect. It coerced many young men and women, prohibited from setting up families in their birth towns, to search for alternative places to settle. Many of them courageously crossed the Carpathian Mountains and settled in neighboring Upper Hungary, now part of the Slovak Republic. The first of them to locate in the sprawling city of Liptovský Svätý Mikuláš (St. Nicholas, Hungarian: Liptószentmiklós) in 1720 were peddlers and merchants from the Moravian town of Holešov. Convinced that Jews would enhance business activity in Mikuláš, Count Samuel Pongrácz took them under his protection without payment. Consequently, Holešov *Landsleute* (compatriots) who were banished from Moravia seven years later followed the forerunners to their new home in the Lower Tatra mountains of Slovakia. The emigrants kept loyal ties with the mother community. At Rosh Hashanah, Pesaḥ, and Shavuot, the small Mikuláš contingent undertook the long wagon journey back to Holešov, a practice that continued until they built a temporary prayer house in Mikuláš in 1728.

The *kehillah* was instituted in 1730, on Shabbat *Bereshit*--the Sabbath after Simḥat Torah when synagogue reading of the Torah starts again, from Genesis. The following year they built their first synagogue, a wooden structure near the main square, and they welcomed their first rabbi, Moshe Hacohen Ungar (d. 1772), whose patriotic surname, Ungar (Hungarian), was suggested to him by the Hungarian king. To accommodate its growing numbers and responsibility as the regional center, the community enlarged the synagogue in 1770.

Rabbi Ungar's successor, Rabbi Kunitz, established a yeshivah in Mikuláš as early as 1776. Religious and cultural life reached its zenith in the days of Rabbi Eleazar Halevi Loew, (1758–1837), one of the greatest scholars of his time. He attained the post of *dayyan* (judge) in his native city of Wodzislav, Poland, at the age of 17. Acclaimed for his many studies in all areas of halakhah, he was ceremonially inaugurated in Mikuláš in 1821, with a

Archival photo of the interior in 1977, before the synagogue was used for a warehouse. (Courtesy of Zdenko Blažek, Municipality of Liptovský Svätý Mikuláš.)

triumphal city-wide procession. Under his leadership the yeshivah flourished, selecting only the most talented applicants as students. It was not surprising that 64 of the graduates became outstanding Talmudists. During the ten years of his service, Rabbi Halevi put his considerable prestige into the losing struggle against religious reform. As the trend toward change in the community nevertheless intensified, he resigned his position as rabbi, in 1831. Yeshivah enrollment declined and the institution closed in 1861.

The tolerant attitude of the city's Protestant majority provided a favorable atmosphere for Jews and other minorities. Liptovský Svätý Mikuláš and its Jews prospered. The dense mountain forests supported a thriving lumber industry that floated endless rafts of timber down to Budapest. Jews imported products from distant parts of the kingdom, exported skins and wool, managed distilleries, and founded a successful cheese-processing plant. Eager to maintain good relations with their Christian neighbors, the *parnassim* formulated their own "ten commandments" that obligated Jews to honesty and decency in business. They lived wherever they chose, including on the main square. Most of the shops there were Jewish owned and remained closed on the Sabbath and festivals.

In the liberal spirit that swept Europe after the French Revolution, the Mikuláš *kehillah* tolerated a broad range of beliefs among its members. They supported their popular and successful yeshivah and welcomed indigent students *"zu essen teg"* (to eat "days"), a custom of free meals for the student in a different Jewish household for each day of the week. The community also encouraged secular culture and the operation of secular schools. From 1820 on, liberal community leader Yaakov Diener and other teachers established private schools in the *Haskalah* spirit where the language of instruction was German. Along with Judaic subjects, Jewish pupils studied natural sciences, geography, general history, and the works of Lessing, Goethe, and Schiller.

Prosperous members of the 300-family *kehillah* supported a secular school, opened in 1845, where the curriculum included gymnastics, singing, swimming, and skating. Christian aristocrats sent their children to this school. Illustrious alumni of the Jewish secondary school, begun in 1860, included Simon Goldstein, the first Jewish lawyer in Hungary, and publisher Samuel Fischer, who established the world-renowned publishing house in Berlin that still carries his name. Because of the high standards of its many secular and cultural institutions, the Liptovsky Svätý Mikuláš community earned the epithet "the Jewish Athens."

Many Mikuláš Jews took part in battles of the ill-fated 1848 Hungarian revolt led by Lajos Kossúth against Austria. The revolt suppressed, the Jewish community was fined 10,000 forints, an outrageous amount in those days. They were unable to raise the money on time, but their Christian neighbors tided them over with the required sum at no interest. After the political reconciliation between Austria and Hungary, Jews could vote or be candidates for elections in municipal elections. Two Jewish delegates gained city council seats in 1863. Two years later

The synagogue in Liptovský Svätý Mikuláš. Neo-Classical style, 1845; restored in 1906 by architect Lipót Baumhorn after a fire. One of the most elegant buildings in the city, its use as a storeroom ended in 1990 with the decision to restore the building to cultural purposes.

Isaac Diener won election as the first of several Jewish mayors. Others were Jozef Stern, Moric Ring, and Dr. Mano Steiner.

The spirit of the *Haskalah* and the desire to reform elements of religious practice and bring them into harmony with the conditions of modern life was widespread and growing in Hungary in the early nineteenth century. At issue were such elements of change as the use of the vernacular language in sermons, arrangement of the seating—to face a *bimah* placed close to the Ark (as in churches), rather than around the classic central *bimah*—and the installation and use of an organ in the services. Although a separate synagogue section for women was a relatively recent import to Jewish use, considering the span of Jewish history, the moderate reforms proposed by the nascent Neolog (Hungarian reform) leadership did not then challenge this practice. The controversy between the Orthodox and the Neolog intensified and became the central issue at the General Jewish Congress called by the government at Budapest in 1868. The purpose of the gathering was to define the basis for autonomous organization of the Jewish community.

At the congress 126 Neolog proponents faced 94 Orthodox representatives. Disputes broke out over religious objectives. Neologists defined the *kehillah* as "a society providing for religious needs," while the Orthodox insisted that Jews are "followers of the Mosaic faith . . . as codified in the Shulḥan Arukh." The debate was acrimonious, agreement was impossible, and more than half of the Orthodox delegates walked out of the congress.

Although the Neolog program was adopted by dint of the initial majority it commanded, the Neolog leadership reined in religious reforms sharply, taking a conservative stance in the hope of reunification with the Orthodox. At the national level, the reconciliation never took place. By 1870 the emperor allowed the Orthodox to organize themselves in separate congregations. Within the next few decades, throughout the Austro-Hungarian Empire, communities agonized, split, and reorganized themselves, mostly into the two major factions. There were some *kehillot* that preferred to avoid a decision. Calling themselves Status-Quo-Ante, or Status-Quo for short, they became a distinct though miniscule faction. This three-way split was to affect the life of Hungarian Jewry for more than 70

years, until the polemics became insignificant in the *Shoah*.

There was much discussion of religious reform in the liberal *kehillah* of Liptovský Svätý Mikuláš, one of the first Hungarian communities to split along religious lines. Here, the schism precipitated in 1843 over disagreement on where to locate the *bimah* in the grand synagogue under construction. The Orthodox wanted the traditional central arrangement, but the stronger Neolog faction insisted on placing the *bimah* before the Ark, in accordance with the changing practice. When the community voted to affiliate with the Neolog stream, the Orthodox minority seceded and set up an autonomous community, including a separate prayer room and school. The community in Mikuláš, however, was different than most. Despite the official split in 1864, they were ready by 1875 to overlook their disagreements. Making mutual concessions, they reunited to worship as one congregation in their new synagogue.

The synagogue was completed in 1845 at a cost of 42,000 forints. Congregants carried the

The synagogue interior—in blue, white, and gold—against the warm pink of the marble columns. The *Aron Kodesh* structure accentuates a complex pediment over three pairs of columns and pilasters. The verse under the splayed arch reads: *Torah tzivah lanu Moshe, morashah kehillat Ya'akov* ("Moses charged us with the Teaching as the heritage of the congregation of Jacob"; Deut. 33:4). The high proscenium arch has space in which to split a verse from Exodus 15:2: *Zeh Eli v'anvehu/ /Elohei avi v'arom'menhu* ("This is my God and I will enshrine Him/ /the God of my father, and I will exalt Him") around the central *Shema Yisrael, Adonai Eloheinu, Adonai Eḥad* ("Hear, O Israel, the Lord our God, the Lord is one"; Deut. 6:4).

THE SYNAGOGUE IN LIPTOVSKÝ SVÄTÝ MIKULÁŠ.

On their tall hexagonal pedestals, the four massive Ionic columns and pediment of the portico dominate the synagogue's pronounced neo-Classical facade. There is no trace today of the architrave inscription. The portal encloses a handsome wooden door, dwarfed between the giant, peeling pilasters. With its Art Nouveau glass knocked out, the openings are boarded up against further vandalism. Doorways at left and right provide access to the galleries. On three sides of the building, stately pilasters frame round-headed, elaborately corniced windows.

A series of broad arches spans the large interior of the prayer room. On the wide proscenium arch, an inscription proudly proclaims the well-known *Shema Yisrael* . . . . ("Hear, O Israel! . . . ."; Deut. 6:4). Four structural arches, over square Romanesque pillars from floor to galleries, border the decorated central dome. Additional arches frame the galleries, elegantly repeating the structural theme. Geometric designs in blue and gold successfully blend the classical and Art Nouveau elements that cover the many arches and vaults.

True to his custom, architect Baumhorn incorporated Jewish motifs in the design. He molded symbolic blue Tablets of the Law into the gilded column capitals. High above the Ark he draped a wide, symbolically protective *tallit* with blue stripes and fringe, frescoed across the eastern wall. This is a rare motif in synagogue art, but it appears in a much older synagogue on the other side of the mountain, in Tverdošín, only 30 miles away. Two-thirds of the windows—of stained glass in Art Nouveau designs—have been vandalized, but the municipality hopes eventually to restore them despite the high cost. As a first step toward restoration, damaged windows were removed from their settings and neatly stacked on the floor.

Capitals of the grouped pilasters at the proscenium corner. Tablets of the Law inserts were a favorite Baumhorn element. Across the east wall the long fresco of *tallitot* is a rare and effective symbol.

Zdenko Blažek, at right, with municipal and museum officials active in restoring the synagogue for cultural purposes.

A damaged stained-glass window. Stylized flowers in deep colors spread out below an expanse of alternating opalescent blue and white panes representing the sky.

Torah scrolls through the streets from the old building to the new one. District nobility and town officials participated in the ceremonies.

The synagogue suffered two destructive fires, one in 1878, and another in 1904 that nearly demolished it. The *parnassim* called on Jewish architect Lipót Baumhorn, shortly after he completed his 1903 masterpiece synagogue in Szeged, to plan the rehabilitation. He lavishly rebuilt and embellished the synagogue into the most stately structure in the city—artistically, one of the most remarkable synagogues in the Hungarian kingdom. A proud and grateful congregation dedicated it in 1906.

After World War I there was a spurt of Zionist consciousness. The large community building buzzed with youth activities: branches of Zionist organizations, Gordonia, and Maccabi Hatzair, and the sports group Maccabi. The *kehillah* maintained two tennis courts and a soccer field nearby, and an amateur young people's theater company presented plays to family and guests. By 1930 the flourishing community numbered more than 1,000.

Fifteen-hundred Jews were crowded into the city during the early years of World War II. More than 80 percent of those who were dragged away on the transports perished. The majority of the few who returned soon moved away. Today there are not enough Jews for a minyan in Liptovský Svätý Mikuláš.

The tiny post-World War II community still owned the synagogue as late as 1980, when it sold the building to the municipality. Jewish community structures—an office building, a spacious community center with meeting hall and library, houses for the rabbi and the sexton, two kosher butcher shops, and a poultry slaughterhouse—that once occupied the synagogue courtyard and the immediate neighborhood no longer existed by this time. Although the rich library in the community building had been plundered, the synagogue itself had not been desecrated. All the furniture was in place, and the broad *bimah,* bounded by an exquisite cast-concrete balustrade, was intact. The city leased the building to the Otex textile factory. The spacious interior was convenient for storing large bolts of cloth and the factory managers were apparently unconcerned that misuse and vandalism might cause structural deterioration. In contrast, the textile factory management in not-too-distant Ružomberok, similarly allotted a synagogue for storage, raised a wood partition to protect the Ark from harm.

Section drawing of Liptovský Svätý Mikuláš synagogue, in preparation for restoration, 1991. (Courtesy Zdenko Blažek, Municipality of Liptovský Svätý Mikuláš.)

Background drape for a benefit concert, featuring names of *Shoah* victims from Liptovský Svätý Mikuláš.

The Communist demise brought new forces into play. In the early 1990s public-spirited citizens formed a committee whose purpose was to save the building. The driving force of this lobby was the energetic cultural administrator, Zdenko Blažek, of the city council. Architects and museum researchers drew up detailed plans for restoration to cultural use by the city. The building received the status of an historical monument and the committee initiated a national and international campaign to raise funds for restoration work. Relieved of storage, the *bimah* stood exposed, with its balustrade shattered and piled up in the empty *Aron Kodesh* niche and the side door. Though neglected and abused in the past, the building still projects a sense of lofty purpose.

On July 28, 1991, a special benefit concert was held in the synagogue to support the restoration of historical monuments in Liptovský Svätý Mikuláš, including the synagogue. Mikuláš Jews, local dignitaries, and representatives from the central Jewish community in Bratislava attended. In preparation, gentile and Jewish volunteers came for a three-day effort to clean up the synagogue building and remove debris. For a stage backdrop over the *bimah,* they painted the names and birth years of some of the 900 Mikuláš Jewish victims of the *Shoah* on a long

drape and hung it high on the Ark. Among the names of the 18 members of the Altmann family were Emil Altmann, 1911; Edita Altmannová, 1921; Zigmund Altmann, 1893; and Paula Altmannová, 1879.

The well-attended concert was called *Mosty* (bridges), a theme that Deputy Federal Chairman Jiří Dienstbier developed in his opening address:

I do not believe that the bridges between peoples in our country and inside us were destroyed. The bridges are only damaged. Jewish culture is part of European culture. This concert and the restoration of this synagogue are the beginning of something new, something that begins with the building of bridges.

RESTORATION BLUES

No one entering Vrbové in the last hundred years could fail to notice the grand neo-Moresque synagogue on the main street near the central square. A tall building, with minarets to accentuate its height and prominent horizontal lines, the structure is still a dominant feature of the town center. In the dark wartime days immediately after the deportation of the Jews in 1942, the building stood silent and forsaken, a conspicuous reminder of its former Jewish citizens.

Faced with the question of how to dispose of a large, empty building without claimants after the war, the township, like so many others in central Europe, saw the issue in practical terms of what to do with walls and roof. They assigned the synagogue to a woodworking factory for use as storage space. A couple of generations would pass, and a change of regime, before the perspective of time would elicit a more thoughtful evaluation—taking historical, social, and cultural factors into account. The town decided in the 1980s to restore the synagogue for cultural use. The work creeps forward, but the few local Jews are divided and, at best, ambivalent over such a development.

Vrbové was a prosperous town, an important grain market for the agricultural hinterland, with a well-developed textile industry. Not by chance, the synagogue is a remarkably successful representative of synagogue architecture and art of its period in Slovakia. Its prestigious location, elaborate style, and rich decorations properly reflected the social standing and wealth of the community.

Little is known of an earlier, sparsely recorded *kehillah* of 1522. Lying in a wooded valley at the foot of the lower Carpathian mountains, Vrbové was a shelter for Jews expelled by Leopold I from Vienna in 1670. In 1683 two catastrophes befell the *kehillah*. A deadly plague felled 438 Jews in the ghetto of Ungarisch Brod, Moravia (Uherský Brod in Czech), and Kuruc horsemen galloping through the streets with brandished swords killed another hundred. The pogrom shattered the Ungarisch Brod Jewish quarter, leaving many Jews homeless. A small band of young families undertook the dangerous journey eastward through the mountains, down the River Váh to Piešt'any, and five miles west again across the valley, to Vrbové. Among the

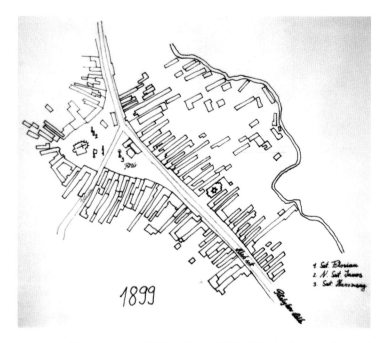

Town map of Vrbové in 1899. Marked by a Star of David, the synagogue occupies a prime location on a main street near the central square. (Courtesy of Štátny okresný archív, Trnava.)

1899

1. Sv. Florian
2. N. Sv. Jánov
3. Sv. Harmasy

founding families were Mordecai Hacohen, Abraham Samuel Hacohen, Izak Magia, and Rabbi David ben Shlomo, a *melamed* (teacher). They maintained close ties with Ungarisch Brod, even returning to the cemetery to bury the dead until 1736, when the 35 Jewish families secured a burial ground in Vrbové.

Nine smaller villages in the periphery belonged to the *kehillah.* On market days, enterprising merchants from the Vrbové area plied their wares in the large industrial and commercial center, Trnava, where new, post-Emancipation Jewish residence followed a hiatus of 250 years. By mid-nineteenth century, Vrbové counted about 100 Jewish families. They engaged in familiar occupations: tanning leather; distilling spirits; trading in grain, wool, and leather; crafts; and petty commerce. Jewish shops lined the main square, as did the craft shops. Reasonably good relations existed between Jews and Christians; during an 1848 attack on the community by brigands, Jews found refuge with their neighbors, and local Count Rudolf Ocskai gave them some protection.

Like the mother community, the *kehillah* in Vrbové was devoutly Orthodox. It attracted and

produced a number of famous rabbis. An important personality, presiding from 1829 to 1839, was Rabbi Yaakov Altkundstadt, a pupil of the famed Rabbi Yeḥezkel Landau of Prague. He was called *Reich* (German empire) in reference to his name—after his native German town Altkundstadt—but he earned the nickname, *Koppel Ḥarif* (sharp head) for his mental acumen. He established a yeshivah and was the first of a rabbinic dynasty. His grandson, Rabbi Jacob Koppel Reich, served in Vrbové from 1872 until 1890, when he became chief rabbi of Budapest. Greatly esteemed as a veteran leader of Orthodox Jewry, he was appointed in 1927 at the age of 89 to the upper house of the Hungarian Parliament, where he was the oldest and a much distinguished member.

Ḥazzan (cantor) Hefter trained a remarkable choir, among whose soloists was a child prodigy from Russia with a golden voice, Joseph Rosenblueth (1882–1933). Rosenblueth became a cantor, serving in Bratislava and Hamburg. In 1912 he emigrated to New York and inaugurated a meteoric career as Cantor Yossele Rosenblatt, *hazzan* and prolific composer of tuneful liturgical music. One of the most popular of all cantors in the United States, there was hardly a Jewish home where one could not hear recordings of his voice on a hand-cranked gramophone. He earned huge fees, but he gave generously to charity and supported his extended family and was often deeply in debt. He died suddenly in Jerusalem in 1933 while working on a Yiddish movie *The Dream of My People.*

Vrbové's last rabbi was the son of Rabbi Jacob Koppel Reich, Rabbi Samuel Reich, who officiated from 1902 until the community's end in 1942. During his long, fruitful ministry, Rabbi Samuel Reich established a Jewish secondary school: a boarding school where Jewish children from various parts of Czechoslovakia and Hungary could absorb Jewish tradition. In 1936 he set up a school for vocational training. The rabbi was one of the backers of the railroad line between Vrbové and Piešt'any.

The 987 Vrbové Jews in 1922 comprised a fifth of the population. In 1929 there were 670 persons in the *kehillah*—164 families—most of

The synagogue in Vrbové, neo-Moresque idiom, Kittel and Grätzel, architects, 1883. With its facade newly restored, the building is a striking example of architectural features favored after the Emancipation, particularly in the eastern regions of the Austro-Hungarian Empire.

whom were shopkeepers. The 24 families on public charity were the responsibility of 16 *kehillah* organizations caring for the city's poor. On the eve of the Second World War, 600 Jews still lived in Vrbové.

Riots began with the Munich Pact of September 1938, followed by worse conditions under Tiso's fascist Slovak Republic. Appointed president of Nazi-protected "independent" Slovakia in 1940, Josef Tiso had been a Catholic priest in Bánovce and a leader of the fascist People's Party of Hlinka. The primary responsibility for the deportation of Slovak Jews to the death camps was his. In March 1942 he turned a deaf ear to the pleas of a delegation of Slovak rabbis, imploring him to spare the Jews from mass deportations. Later that year he justified the deportations as an act "for the good of the Slovak nation, to free it of its pests." Slovakia paid the

Germans 500 marks per deported Jew to guarantee that they would never return.

Seeking refuge from deportation, some Jews—including about 30 families from Bratislava—fled from the cities to the Vrbové hinterland. The *kehillah* opened a kitchen to feed refugees and residents, victims of employment discrimination. Transports from Vrbové started in March 1942, first of young women, and then of entire families to camps in Poland. Only 20 Jewish families remained by the fall of 1942: those in mixed marriages or engaged in "critical" work. After his daughter and sister-in-law had been deported, Rabbi Reich and his wife hid until they were discovered in August. An order was given to take them to the collection point in Žilina for deportation on the last transport. The gendarme charged with the trip was an old friend of the rabbi's. He let the driver cruise around the countryside, arriving in Žilina late enough to miss the transport. The rabbi and his wife escaped to Budapest, where they remained until the liberation and, later, their departure for Israel in 1949.

In the summer of 1944 many Jews fought among the partisans in the Slovak uprising against the Germans. The Germans brutally suppressed the revolt, deporting or executing any Jews they found. Synagogue treasures in Vrbové, as elsewhere, were looted and the benches were burned for firewood.

About 20 Jewish families returned to Vrbové after the war and tried to rebuild their lives, but they found no peace. Hooligans stoned their windows, wrote anti-Semitic graffiti on their walls, and overturned gravestones. Most of the survivors sailed for Israel as soon as the state was established. Others left for America, Canada, and western Europe.

The small Jewish cemetery, west of the town, has gravestones, several dating from 1750 to 1762. Its brick fence still stands. Most of the sandstone markers, still in reasonable condition, are engraved in Hebrew, although a few are bilingual. Other markers are made of limestone or marble. Levite

pitchers held by a pair of lions in relief are a favored motif. Other motifs depict a Star of David or an open book and a pen. The most beautiful stones are the classical ones, dating from the early twentieth century. The tiny Jewish community takes pride in its careful upkeep of the cemetery.

The Vrbové *kehillah* built its synagogue in 1882–1883, during the leadership of Rabbi Jacob Koppel Reich, when it was at a maximum strength of 1,000 persons, about a quarter of the town population. Located near the central square on the main road to Piešt'any, the 80-by-48-foot synagogue stands to the rear of its spacious plot, leaving space for the large crowds that congregated inside and outside the fence after services.

The popular post-Emancipation trend in central European synagogue architecture influenced the Jews of Vrbové in selecting a style for their synagogue. Architects regarded the Moorish idiom as expressive of the spirit of Judaism because of its eastern sources. Not commonly used in European architecture, the style found favor by being distinctively different from the neo-Gothic of the churches. A series of new synagogues rose in central Europe, highlighting

View to the empty Ark niche. To expand storage capacity, the woodworking factory that used the building connected the three wings of the gallery with a wooden floor. The quadrefoil shape of the window above the Ark is not often seen.

THE SYNAGOGUE IN VRBOVÉ

The building was completed in 1883, when the *kehillah* was at its height. It is a stately brick structure, resplendent in light and dark horizontal stripes. The high attic has typical neo-Moresque elements: crenelations, narrow towers topped by polygonal turrets, with crowns and elements shaped like pinecones above the cornice. Additional turrets and crenelations decorate the roofline, creating the ambience of a Moorish palace. Three eight-pointed stucco Islamic stars stretch across the attic below the prominent Tablets of the Law, and a high arch defines the main portal. Two smaller doors afford entrance to the gallery stairways. North and south facades display a row of wide, round-arched windows on the ground floor and a row of triple-arched windows and two large rose windows at the gallery level.

A vaulted vestibule leads from the main portal to the large sanctuary. Broad cusped arches traverse the chamber, connecting the rows of columns and supporting the most spectacular painted synagogue ceiling in Slovakia or—perhaps—in all of central Europe. Surrounding the three central cupolas, the vaults and arches take several different shapes in unusual combination, producing a fantasy of form, geometric design, and color that spreads out to tantalize the beholder. Despite the many years of misuse and neglect of the building, most of the decorations are still gloriously brilliant.

A three-sided gallery, supported by slender cast-iron columns typical of the period, borders the prayer hall and leads the eye to the wide apse that once contained an *Aron Kodesh*. Removal of the gallery balustrades and the construction of a floor connecting the three parts of the galleries expanded the usable storage space.

Interior of the synagogue, about 1930. Carved wooden benches lined the prayer room around the central *bimah*, with its wrought-iron grille. (Courtesy of Štátny okresný archív, Trnava.)

Islamic motifs: horseshoe arches, onion-shaped cupolas on minaret-like turrets, horizontal banding, and crenelated parapets. Some prominent examples of this flamboyant style include the synagogues in Vienna, Tempelgasse, 1858; Budapest, the Dohány utca, 1859; Berlin, Oranienburgerstrasse, 1866; Florence, the Great Synagogue, 1882; and in Bratislava, the Neolog, 1895.

In the 1980s the municipality declared the building an historical monument, in recognition of its architectural and historical importance. No doubt, the potential of a renovated synagogue to attract tourists was also a factor. The plan was to restore the synagogue building and to rehabilitate the area near the town center for an enlarged and protected cultural zone. Work on the building exterior is finished, but a proper restoration of the interior is a painstaking job that proceeds slowly because of the nature of the work and because of the usual budget limitations.

The renovation of her synagogue to a culture hall troubled Eva Justová, whom we met in Vrbové's town hall. Of the three Jewish families in Vrbové in the early 1990s, only in her family are both parents Jewish. Eva and her husband Robert have two teenaged children; the daughter has visited Israel twice. Intensively Jewish in identification, they stay almost demonstratively in Vrbové in denial of the Jewish community's extinction. Eva expressed her view of the synagogue restoration in the context of a long discussion:

Now the synagogue is repaired on the outside. A town official by the name of Szabó, whose mother was said to be Jewish, got money for the restoration from the Jewish community in Bratislava and from some rich Jews. They say they will arrange concerts in the synagogue. But this is not a big town. Perhaps they'll have one or two concerts a year. I'm afraid they will turn the synagogue into a discotheque where they will dance and drink. It hurts me so much. For that, I would rather they stop all the work and burn the building down . . . It's a desecration.

Plan for the renewal of the synagogue plaza. (Courtesy of Municipality of Vrbové.)

Eva Justová, teacher of English and music in Vrbové. She and her husband, Robert, strive to impart a Jewish identity to their son and daughter by keeping a kosher home, celebrating the Jewish holidays, and sending the teenagers to visit Israel. In the wooded hills near Szarvas in southeastern Hungary, a wealthy Jew runs a camp for Jewish children and accompanying adults each summer. For several summers, Eva and her husband participated in the camp as counselors. Campers come for two-week periods for a program oriented to inculcate Jewish values that persons of each generation can reinforce in the other. "I was there last year," she told us at our meeting in Vrbové's town hall. "There were more than 200 Jewish children. I never saw so many Jewish children at one time in my life! On the first Friday evening of the camp, they blessed the candles, and I cried for joy."

THE THIRD DAY IN
THE MONTH OF ELUL

The two neo-Moorish towers of the 1892 synagogue in Trnava (German: Tyrnau, Hungarian: Nagyszombat) still stand, in echo of the austere twin spires of the seventeenth-century University Church of St. John the Baptist on the horizon behind them. The contrast between the structures—one in partial ruin, the other well maintained and in use—reflects the turbulent 700-year history of conflict between Jews and Catholics in a city known for its long history of anti-Semitism and persecution. Trnava, dotted with many Gothic and Renaissance churches, qualifies superbly for its epithet, "the Rome of Slovakia," avowed religious center of Upper Hungary for the last 200 years.

Jews lived in Trnava during the twelfth-century Great Moravian Empire period. The town's early ascendance was interrupted by the thirteenth-century Tartar invasions that devastated east Moravia and Slovakia, depopulating whole regions. Trnava overcame those hardships with the help of its markets, revenue from subject cities, and the development of vineyards and the wine trade. With the participation of Jewish merchants, the city became

the busy economic center of the region—and by the fifteenth century it was one of the largest and richest Hungarian towns.

Under tolerant Hungarian kings, the *kehillah* built a synagogue in 1335. The community of that time is remembered for Rabbi Isaac Tyrnau, who officiated in the late fourteenth century. Although his surname suggests origins in Trnava, he was born in Austria and held a post in Pressburg (Bratislava) before coming to Trnava. "Scholars became so few," he wrote after the Black Death of 1348–1350 in Germany had decimated so many communities, "I saw localities where there were no more than three or four Jews, persons with a real knowledge of Jewish customs." To fill the religious and cultural information gap, he created a guidebook of Jewish ritual, prayer, and customs of Jewish life for the annual cycle. Because of his clear language and concise style, *Minhagim l'Khol ha-Shanah* (Customs for the Entire Year; first edition, Venice, 1566) was immensely popular in eastern and central Europe and it often appeared as an appendix in prayer books.

There is a legend about a Crown Prince of Hungary who fell in love with Rabbi Tyrnau's beautiful daughter. The prince renounced the throne, converted secretly to Judaism and went to study Torah with Sephardic rabbis. When he returned to Hungary, he married the daughter in secret and continued to study with his father-in-law. Catholic clergy discovered the hidden identity, demanded that the prince return to Catholicism and, when he refused, burned him at the stake. He was not the first or last victim of brute intolerance.

The chronicler Bonfinius detailed a historical event in Trnava of 1494. A Christian child seen in the Jewish street was missing the next day. Without further investigation, Jews were accused of ritual murder. Soldiers found "traces of fresh blood" in a Jewish house and immediately arrested the owner and his family. Afraid of torture, the apprehensive Jewish women pleaded guilty to the terrible accusation. After the confessions, 16 Jews were "burned at a big stake." Later that year, 14 other Jews were convicted as accomplices. They were dragged to the fire on the third day of the month of Elul, August 22 of that year. Joshua ben Chaim composed an elegy that the Trnava *kehillah* chanted each year on the anniversary of the execution. The city council erected a statue on the Sered Gate to hallow the "murdered" child. Bonfinius enumerated the minutiae of the examinations and repeated the slander. Jews used Christian blood, he alleged:

* to remedy the wound of circumcision
* as a love-potion in food
* as a drink, to relieve the pain of menstruation, which affects Jewish men as well as women
* to shed, on principle, in some spot or other, in honor of God; in 1494 it was the turn of the Trnava Jews to perform.

Illustrated portion of a document in red ink—dated 1494—from the municipal archive in Trnava, accusing Jews of ritual murder. The historical event occurred, but the archivist who provided the document, Dr. Jozef Šimončič, claimed in correspondence and publication that the parchment might be a later forgery. (Courtesy of Štátny okresný archív, Trnava)

Incidents of Blood Libel Against Jews
(12th–20th Centuries)

Austria	5
Belgium	1
Czechoslovakia	9
Egypt	1
England	9
France	6
Germany	39
Greece	3
Hungary	4
Italy	8
Poland	18
Romania	3
Russian Empire	18
Spain	4
Switzerland	6
Syria	1
FYR (Yugoslavia)	1

The assertion that Jews used blood in matzot for Pesaḥ became fashionable later.

The medieval concept known by Jews as *alilat dam* (blood libel)—false accusations that Jews required Christian blood for ritual purposes and killed for it—began in Norwich, England in 1144. It was a diabolical inversion. Christian clerics shed Jewish blood on the stake in the name of their religion, while they justified that sadistic murder by falsely accusing the *victims* of

Interior of the prayer hall and the galleries of the Status Quo synagogue. The well-wrought classic cast-iron pillars carry no more now than the bare beams.

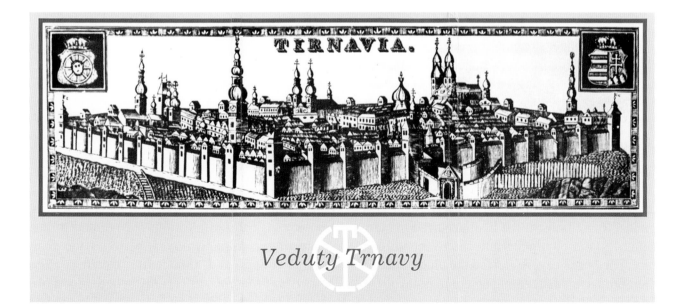

Old map of Trnava; woodcut, before 1800. This *veduta,* or panoramic picture, is typical of an art form popular in central Europe from the sixteenth to the eighteenth centuries. It renders an idealized bird's-eye view of the city in woodcut, copper, or lithograph. Fifty *vedutas* of Trnava have survived. (Courtesy of Štátny okresný archív, Trnava.)

THE STATUS QUO SYNAGOGUE IN TRNAVA

An impressive two-story structure with Moorish features, its two hexagonal towers carry eight-sided cupolas that blend harmoniously with the cluster of church towers in Trnava's skyline. A decorative wrought-iron fence once surrounded the complex, which included the rabbi's house toward the front, a *beit midrash,* and a kosher kitchen toward the rear. Rusting iron scraps and building debris now lie around the courtyard. There was a padlock on the west facade wooden doors, but access into the Status Quo synagogue was wide open through a huge hole at the eastern end of the south wall.

Eight thin iron columns with elaborate capitals support what is left of the spacious women's gallery on three sides of the hall, accessible by two stairways at the western entrance. Vandals had stripped every scrap of timber from the galleries, down to the bare beams. Building materials, abandoned when the city gave up the planned restoration, lay among the broken cement blocks, plaster, and bricks that covered the floor. The Ark and *bimah* had been ripped out, leaving the high proscenium arch agape. Details of the arch provide a clue to the original design of the synagogue interior. Paired Doric pilasters and modeled stucco rims edge an opening faced with a fresco in a geometric pattern. The Ark niche has white Stars of David in a regular array on a neutral blue ground. The synagogue shell is all that remains.

Status Quo synagogue in Trnava. Romantic style, 1892. The building was used for storage for over a decade after World War II. Soon after the community regained ownership, it transferred the building to the city to be remade into a cultural center. The city abandoned the project after a brief flurry of activity, and the building lay open to vandalism. In the late 1990s the municipality adapted the building interior for use as a gallery.

practicing the perverted fantasies of their own minds. Repetitions of the libel occurred in many countries and continued into the twentieth century. The Nazis eagerly seized the blood libel for their propaganda, devoting an entire issue of *Der Stürmer* in 1934 to spreading the lie.

Popular acceptance of the concept is still rife. A young municipal employee accompanied us with key in hand to open for us the door to the empty synagogue in Stupava, Slovakia. It was his first visit to the location. He pointed to the space of the missing *bimah* between the four central pillars and innocently asked, *"Hier macht man Blutdienst?"* (Is *this* where blood rituals are performed?)

The blood libel recurred twice in Trnava, in 1536 and again in 1537. In 1539 Emperor Ferdinand I succumbed to pressure from his subjects

Remains of the Status Quo synagogue's east wall and its colossal *Aron Kodesh* niche.

The Emperor traveled in his lands in disguise, as "Count Falkenstein." On a pilgrimage to the small town of Šaštín, not far from Trnava, he searched for accommodation but could find none. At last, he found a room in an inn owned by a Jew, Jozef Loeb Wolf. Before he left the inn, the Emperor hid two gold coins under his plate. Loeb Wolf ran after him to return the money. As he caught up with the guest, he recognized the brilliant star on the Count's coat and correctly guessed the traveler's identity. Bending, Loeb Wolf kissed the sovereign's knee in homage. The Emperor lifted the innkeeper up and offered to make a wish come true. Loeb Wolf desired no more than permission to live with his family in Trnava and Joseph II promised to fulfill the request. With the issuance of the patent, Jozef Loeb Wolf, his sons David, Mordecai, and Izaias,

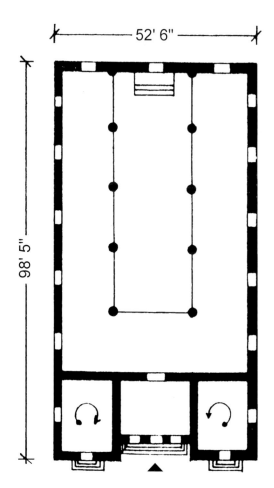

Plan of the Status Quo synagogue in Trnava. (Adapted from: E. Bárkány and Ľ Dojč, *Židovské náboženské obce na Slovensku.*)

and expelled the Jews from the city. The Jews were shamefully herded out of Trnava through the Sered Gate, thereafter called the "Jews' Gate." The expulsion remained in effect for 250 years, although after 1717 Jews were allowed to pass through the city on their way elsewhere. Curiously, the edict did not affect Jewish students at the Catholic university of Trnava, since the university had the privilege of extra-territoriality.

A legend holds that the Toleranzpatent of Emperor Joseph II had its inception at Trnava.

THE ORTHODOX SYNAGOGUE IN TRNAVA

A stark neo-Classical building, without towers or external markings, the Orthodox synagogue stands across the street from the Status Quo synagogue behind a high brick wall. Bounded by a gently sloping red-tiled roof, east and west facades have miniature, round-capped turrets along the roofline, one pair at the highest point, flanking the Tablets of the Law, another pair at the lowest corners of the roof. The spacious interior, 79 by 52.5 feet, has a large three-sided gallery with two entrances for women. Austerely designed and without wall decorations, all its color is poured into a stylized floral pattern painted on the basket-handle ceiling. The intensity of the design recalls the synagogue at Vrbové, where the painted ceiling is even more extravagant.

Western facade of the Orthodox synagogue in Trnava, built in 1914.

and his son-in-law Mandl became the first Jews to settle in Trnava. Notwithstanding their pioneer success, free access to residence in Trnava did not fully materialize until the Emancipation of 1848.

Beginnings were difficult for the young community, without rabbi, synagogue, or cemetery. Weddings and burials took place in a neighboring town. Jews gradually came into the city—78 by 1780—mostly as peddlers, and often meeting with such provocation that they needed military protection. In 1814 the fledgling *kehillah* hired a rabbi, bought a small plot of land, and built a modest prayer house, toward which some Christian burghers contributed substantial sums. During the 1848 Revolution there were anti-Jewish riots. A tailor named Schwartz organized a surprisingly effective defense action, but he was quickly expelled from the town.

Rabbi Simeon Sidon moved to Trnava, starting his 40-year career of leading the community in 1855, and opened the first Jewish school to supplant home-based education. The teachers covered general subjects in the mornings. In the afternoons, boys studied religion while girls learned to do handiwork. Teachers received annual salaries of 600 gold coins, plus lodging, from the tuition that parents paid according to means: one to five gold coins a month.

In 1862, during an expansion of the city's limits, the statue to the child martyr of 1494 was taken down and the Jews' Gate was demolished. In the foundations of the bastion, workers found ancient gravestones, stolen from the Jewish cemetery. The earliest stone, the oldest Jewish monument in Slovakia, read: "Chaim Ben Izrael, prudent and righteous man, killed on Tuesday, 22 Tammuz, July 1340, is buried here." Other stones, with legible dates of 1370, 1390, 1391, 1394, bore similar tragic inscriptions. The *kehillah* redeemed the stones from the municipal council for 10 gold coins and installed them in the walls of the old Jewish cemetery, but in recent years they have disappeared again.

The Trnava *kehillah* joined neither the Orthodox nor the reform Neolog faction in the 1868 religious split. It proposed no changes in ritual and therefore listed itself as "Status Quo." In 1892 the community built a large synagogue in Romantic style.

Despite the claims of the majority that they were making no change in the ritual, the Orthodox members did not feel at home within the Status Quo community. They withdrew from the congregation and built their own smaller synagogue in 1914. They also established a yeshivah in 1925 that became widely known in Hungary, under the leadership of the energetic Rabbi Josef Ungar.

The Zionist organization Bet Yaakov opened a Trnava branch in 1898, the first in northwest Hungary. Hamizrachi, Maccabi, and the Jewish scouts were also active. During World War I, women

Árpád Stern, former Jewish community head, and his wife. "You know, I'm missing only three years until I am one hundred," Stern told us. "When our synagogue was built, 100 years ago, it was Status Quo for all the Jews. The Orthodox wanted only strictly observant members, so they built their own synagogue 22 years later. Now, with no more than 20 Jews left out of the 150 *Shoah* survivors, we are thankful for any Jew who comes to the *minyan*." He died a year later.

teachers replaced the male teachers who went to war. They established a day shelter for soldiers' children and fed them bread and milk, sometimes a whole lunch when food was available. The municipality supported Jewish educational institutions and a theater group, Habimah. In the summer of 1919, the National Union of Slovak Jews organized a holiday course in Trnava for Jewish teachers in which 42 educators from Slovakia participated.

From 1,715 persons in 1904, the Trnava *kehillah* and its periphery increased to 2,728 in 1930—11 percent of the population.

An anti-Semitic booklet published in Trnava in 1937 swelled the growing tide of Fascism in Slovakia. After the 1938 Munich Pact which dismembered Czechoslovakia, anti-Semitic acts multiplied. Inspired by Kristallnacht in the West, an incited crowd set fire to the large Trnava synagogue that December.

After March 14, 1939, Slovakia—nominally an independent republic—became a German satellite. Jews were deprived of their basic rights in the following weeks. In 1942 the Jewish quarter became overcrowded with deportees brought in from Transylvania and neighboring villages. Some fled to Hungary and some escaped by false baptism. The transports of April 12, 1942 delivered 1,040 Jews from Trnava to death camps in Poland. In the summer of 1944 the partisan revolt against the Fascist Slovak government erupted in full force. Many Jews who had been in hiding joined the rebels in their unsuccessful revolt.

After the war, about 15 percent of Trnava's Jews returned to the city. They searched for their stolen property, mostly without success. With difficulty, they restored the Orthodox synagogue, setting up a kosher kitchen in it and appropriating the *beit midrash* as a joint prayer room for the now-unified community. They cleaned up the Status Quo synagogue from storeroom disorder to serve for memorial services and affixed memorial tablets. In 1986 the municipality started to restore the grand old Status Quo building and to maintain the Jewish cemetery, but the restoration work was stopped for lack of funds. Wanton vandalism soon destroyed much of the synagogue interior. Only a few years later, Roma squatters invaded the Orthodox synagogue and made it their living quarters. Trnava Jews discouraged us from attempting to enter. Hoping to attract visitors, the municipality refurbished the monument in front of the Status Quo synagogue in the 1990s and adapted the interior as a gallery.

THE PRESSURE OF INEXORABLE TIME

Jewish life in the smaller cities of central Europe was not quite extinguished by the *Shoah*. Here and there the remnant of a reorganized *kehillah* barely maintained its identity through the dark days of Communist misrule. With the introduction of democracy, the communities emerged as aging populations clinging to a remembered order and balancing anxiety with hope for the future of a scanty younger generation.

Where the synagogue had survived, it was the center of assembly that focused and reinforced the sense of community. Most often it was in poor condition and needed renovation. That could be done only if money were raised, possibly from overseas *landslayt* (compatriots) or other donors. In this respect, the group in Prešov was particularly fortunate and achieved a fine synagogue renovation. But it is not only the physical building and meeting in it that binds the survivors together; it is a poignant commitment to the memory of the *kedoshim,* the martyred ones killed in the Holocaust. The Prešov *kehillah* regularly holds memorial services for its *Shoah* victims, and it had deter-

mined decades ago to publish a memorial book. With the imminent approach of the synagogue's 100th anniversary, the leaders issued a call for a commemorative reunion and completed the book at last. Their concern was time and its effects.

Prešov (Hungarian: Eperjes) is an industrial city in northeastern Slovakia, dating from the early thirteenth century as a center of trade and commerce. The principal town of the Šariš district, it is the cultural focus of the Ruthenians and Ukranians of east Slovakia. Orthodox and Greek Catholic faiths are strong in the area, reminders of the Byzantine missionaries who frequented the forested hills over a thousand years ago. They left a legacy of a devout rural population and quaint wooden churches. Town planners appreciated their architectural heritage and preserved the ornate houses and stone arcades of Renaissance and Baroque times that bound the spindle-shaped central square, the site of the old town market.

To protect local tradesmen from Jewish competition in the fifteenth century, King Mattias Corvinus of Hungary granted Prešov and

Left end of the lower inscription on the inner face of the proscenium arch. It replies to the question posed at the right (opposite). *"N'ki kapayim u'var leivav asher lo nasa lashav nofsho, v'lo [nishba l'mirmah]"*; ("He who has clean hands and a pure heart, who has not taken false oath by his life, nor [sworn deceitfully]"; Ps 24:4).

other royal cities the privilege of excluding Jews from residence. The ban held until 1789, and even then it needed a Jew with influential connections to beat down the barrier. Ukrainian-born Marcus Holländer (1760–1849), a prosperous merchant well known at the Kaiser's court in Vienna, wangled a Prešov citizenship at age 30 and raised the first Jewish family within the city walls. The town council's animated protest was ineffectual against Holländer's skill and connections, and a small community gradually gained a foothold under his vigorous leadership. Marcus Holländer and his son Leo navigated the affairs of the *kehillah* for more than 60 years.

Holländer's first act was to found a synagogue outside the gates to serve the scattered but growing community in the outlying districts. Jewish immigrants to the region, driven there by the Moravian Familiants Law marriage quotas and blood libel pogroms, settled near the city to attend its market fairs, hoping eventually to take up residence within the city gates. In 1813 Holländer was elected head of the few *kehillot* in the Šariš district. Seven years later, a few of the more affluent families received permission to settle in the city. At the start, they assembled at the Holländer home for prayers. Marcus Holländer continued his international affairs, often intervening with government officials on matters of Jewish interest. He helped Jews regain their right to distribute Tokaj wine to all cities of the empire, and he personally relieved more than one *kehillah* of excessive national taxes by paying in their stead. In 1808 he roused the ire of the city trade association because of his success in merchandising wine, wool, and grain, but all efforts to expel him were futile. To show his gratitude when the city conferred some minor rights on the few resident Jewish families in 1820, Holländer paid for the construction of the lovely

Right end of the inner face of the proscenium arch. The lower border inscription reads, *"Mi ya'aleh b'har Adonai, U'mi yakmum bim'ko[m] kodsho"* **("Who may ascend the mountain of the Lord? Who may stand in His holy place?";** Ps. 24:3). **The restorer missed a final** *"mem"* **in the word** *"bim'kom."*

Poseidon fountain in Prešov's main square. Ten years later, 12 Jewish families were legally living in the city.

The first Jew born in Prešov, Leo Holländer (1806–1887), was an only child and received a private Jewish education with his father. He also attended the local high school and started to study law. After a brief stint in the family business, he transferred those concerns to his elder son, Julius, while he himself followed his father's example and concentrated on affairs of the community. In 1843 he formally founded the Prešov *kehillah*. At the outbreak of the 1848 uprising, Leo and both his sons joined the Hungarian forces. As political and economic adviser to revolutionary leader Lajos Kossúth, Leo had close ties with Kossúth and his staff; he also held the position of quartermaster at the rank of major and saw action in the defense of Komárno Fortress. After the war he continued to work for Jewish emancipation,

invoking aid from the Pope and Hungarian church officials.

At Leo Holländer's initiative and his contribution of a third of the cost, work began in 1847 on the first proper synagogue in Prešov, completed in 1849. Designed by the architect-builder, Pribrula, the building included a choir loft. When it burned down in 1887, Holländer gave 40,000 forints toward the construction of a new building. He also helped establish the Neolog (Hungarian reform) Rabbinical Seminary in Budapest. The comprehensive numismatics collection he amassed as a hobby ultimately found a place in the British Museum.

Rabbi Solomon Mayer Schiller Szinessy (1820–1890) was Prešov's most colorful Neolog rabbi. After a traditional rabbinical education he arrived in Prešov to deepen his background in the classics at the local Lutheran college. He became professor of Hebrew at the college and

THE NEOLOG SYNAGOGUE IN PREŠOV

After the community synagogue of 1849 was destroyed by fire, its 1887 replacement was designed for the use of the Neolog community. It is a bricked massive Moorish building with Romanesque cross-vaults, two curving stairways leading up to the balconies under a 37-foot high inner dome. Three broad columns on each side separate the broad interior from the side bays. The *bimah* adjoins the Ark on the east wall.

The Neolog synagogue in Prešov, ca. 1930. (Courtesy of the Jewish community of Prešov.)

Facade of the Neolog synagogue, altered after World War II.

Its pre-World War II facade was marked by horizontal stripes of light and dark brick, and featured a single onion-shaped cupola, surrounded by a ring of minarets high above the portal. In adapting the synagogue for storeroom use, the users shaved off the cupola and turrets, substituted a simple hip roof, disguised the striped facade with drab ochre paint, and squared off the distinctive circular windows to the street.

served the *kehillah* briefly as rabbi, fostering Hungarian patriotism from the pulpit. He carried his ideology to the hilt, enlisting with the rebels during the Hungarian revolution of 1848 and added the name of a Magyar hero, "Szinessy," as his surname. Wounded in battle, he escaped via Trieste to England, where he became rabbi of the *kehillah* in Manchester and was subsequently the first practicing Jew appointed to teach rabbinical and talmudic literature at Cambridge University.

In the years leading up to the 1867 emancipation of Hungarian Jewry, the question of religious

Marble monument to the 6,000 Jews of the Prešov vicinity who perished at the hands of the Nazis. Dedicated in June, 1991, the monument stands in the courtyard of the Orthodox synagogue. Expatriate Prešov Jews contributed money for the memorial, the courtyard landscaping, and painting of the facade's lower level.

gress's oldest member, he headed the conference. Active in the fields of both culture and religion, he gained distinction as one of the most effective spokesmen for Jewish emancipation.

In 1864 a group of Orthodox members petitioned the Prešov *kehillah* to allow them to conduct separate services. The *parnassim* allotted them a prayer room on condition that they remain paying members. The break became final, however, in 1870, when the majority announced a Neolog affiliation. By the following year, the Orthodox Jews in Prešov were sufficiently numerous to found a separate congregation and launch their own institutions. After some delay, they appointed Rabbi M. A. Roth to officiate. They built an impressive synagogue in 1898 and another in 1930 for the small Sephardic community; in fact, the growth of the Orthodox community was so rapid that by 1930 it had twice as many members as the Neolog group.

The two communities, Orthodox and Neolog, led separate, parallel, and unconnected lives until the outbreak of the Second World War. The last rabbi of the Orthodox group was Rabbi Moshe Chaim Lau from Rumania, who officiated from 1928 until 1935, when he accepted a prestigious post in Piotrkow, Poland. He and his wife perished in the camps, but three of their four sons survived: Yehoshua Lau, now retired, was an educator in Israel; Naphtali Lavie serves as vice-chair of the World Jewish Restitution Organization, whose mission is the restitution of Jewish property confiscated in Europe; Rabbi Yisrael Lau was appointed Ashkenazic chief rabbi of Israel in 1993.

With the establishment of Czechoslovakia in 1918, Prešov Jews were less harassed than those within diminished Hungary and were freer to express their aspirations for a Jewish homeland. They had founded a Zionist organization in 1905 and branches of others followed: Hovevei Zion, Mizraḥi, Betar, Hashomer Hatzair, and Maccabi, with a membership approaching 400 in 1930. In 1929, 29 percent of the city's population was Jewish; in 1940 its 4,000 Jews were 40 percent of the total population.

An important achievement of the community was the creation in 1928 of a modest Jewish museum, initiated by the Jewish Museum Club

reform was hotly disputed in the community. Prešov adherents of Orthodoxy vehemently opposed changes. Mobilizing to combat the dangers—as they saw them—of assimilation, they invited the participation of Rabbi Hillel Lichtenstein, a well-known opponent of reform. Using a frontal assault, Lichtenstein declared a rabbinical ḥerem (excommunication) on the Neolog community, an action that spread more fury than fear among the numerous proponents of reform. Holländer turned to the municipal authorities, who coerced the rabbi to rescind his curse and leave town. Holländer was also one of the initiators of the 1868 General Jewish Congress, intended to resolve the religious controversy, and as the Con-

THE ORTHODOX SYNAGOGUE IN PREŠOV

The facade of the Orthodox synagogue presents a restrained Moorish idiom, with horseshoe-arched windows and a portal framed by a large Moorish arch, supported on two pairs of narrow pillars. A chronogram above the entrance dates the synagogue to the year 5658/1898, *U'verakhtikha* ("And I shall bless you"; Gen. 26:24). The interior is a masterpiece of the synagogue decorator's art. It displays a wealth of geometric design and color on every possible surface, but keeps it all in balanced harmony. The gallery on three sides rests on slender cast-iron pillars. All the ceilings, above the galleries and below them, and the area directly above the Ark, display geometric patterns. Brass chandeliers hang on long chains from the flat central ceiling, which resembles an oversized Oriental rug. Much attention went into the details of the fine ceramic floor and to the carved reader's stand, produced by Bosko, a Košice sculptor.

The two-story proscenium arch is the most striking feature of the synagogue, in architecture and decoration. A high Moorish trefoil arch, decorated in a lavish floral design, delineates the proscenium area. Inside it stands the three-part marble *Aron Kodesh,* under a crenelated pediment, and topped by a flat gilded crown in its central section. Long quotations from Psalms, in traditional Ashkenazi Hebrew script, run across the interior rim of the three high arches that separate the proscenium area from the main chamber. Verses on the walls become artistic elements that color the spiritual environment. The extensive use of inscription here, even when obscured from general view, proclaims a love of learning for its own sake.

View to the Ark from the west gallery in the Orthodox synagogue. The verse on the arch proclaims: *"Mimizrah shemesh ad m'vo'o m'hulal shem Adonai"* ("From east to west the name of the Lord is praised"; Ps. 113:3). The high Moorish trefoil arch, in lavish floral design, defines the proscenium area. The *bimah* is centrally located, in conformity with Orthodox tradition.

The Orthodox synagogue in Prešov. Neo-Moresque idiom, Kollaczek and Wirth, architects, 1898; before the external reconditioning of 1991. The *kehillah* keeps an office in a building in the courtyard.

under the inspiration of Rabbi Dr. Theodore Austerlitz and Eugen Bárkány, architect and engineer. They invested 150,000 crowns to adapt the old bastion, called the *Kumst.* Reconstruction workers uncovered Hebrew inscriptions under the old plaster on the inner walls of the building. This discovery led to the speculation that the room had once served as a prayer room, presumably when the Jewish presence in the city was still clandestine.

When the museum outgrew the *Kumst,* the city allotted space in one of the town towers and added two rooms for further expansion. The museum contained documents on the history of Slovak Jews and many items of Judaica; however, the puppet Slovak government confiscated the collection at the outbreak of World War II. At war's end officials in the newly liberated Czechoslovakia transferred the collection to the Jewish Museum in Prague. Restored to Slovakia in recent years, the material is now exhibited in the Jewish Museum in Bratislava.

Refugees poured into Prešov, the district metropolis, as soon as the fascist regime took power in Slovakia in 1938. Transports of Jews from other protectorate cities and Vienna swelled the Jewish population to 6,000, prompting heroic *kehillah* measures to alleviate its hardships. Deportations started with the young people in March 1942 and ended with mass transport of the remaining Jews in May and June. After the

liberation, a few hundred survivors straggled back. Most of them had fought as soldiers or with the partisans in the hills. A minority had lived through the concentration camps. All found their homes pillaged, and the synagogues and other public Jewish buildings ransacked. Mobilizing to reestablish their lives, the Jews first set up a kosher kitchen to provide meals for the needy. They went on to revive community life, using the *beit midrash* for prayers until the synagogue was restored in 1957. However, their numbers decreased rapidly as many emigrated to Israel or to America.

In keeping with its size, the *kehillah* of Prešov successively maintained several synagogues. The first one that Marcus Holländer erected outside the town walls in the eighteenth century, at 26 Jarková, went through several renovations. It was a one-story, stone building with a gabled roof, vaulted windows, and decoratively painted wooden ceilings. Conforming to the old custom, the floor was nearly three feet below the outer pavement level. The building no longer stands.

The second synagogue, built in 1849 at 12 Konstantinová ulica, had 180 seats distributed equally between men and women. In the religous

An unsigned note, in Yiddish, in the crack of a gallery desk: "Here is where my mother, of blessed memory, used to sit."

schism of 1868, the majority at that time opted for the Neolog tradition, but the Orthodox *kehillah* broke away, and purchased a modest, one-story building in 1884 to be used as their *mikveh* synagogue. They constructed a *mikveh* underneath, and set up a women's gallery inside, on four wooden columns. The congregation increased in numbers. In 1898 they built an impressive neo-Moresque synagogue structure based on a design by Kollaczek and Wirth of Košice. It stands in a courtyard, surrounded on three sides by low buildings that once served the varied needs of the Orthodox *kehillah.* There was a row of five kosher butcher shops and a flat for Fuchs, the *shoḥet.* Also in the large courtyard stood the Jewish school, Eitz Ḥayim, a yeshivah, and a large yellow house for Rabbi Lau and his family. These buildings still belong to the *kehillah, Židovská náboženská obec* (Jewish Religous Council) of fewer than 60 persons, which rents out most of them.

At the annual memorial meeting for the 6,000 *Shoah* victims from Prešov and the Šariš district, which took place on the 20th of Sivan, mid-June 1991, the *kehillah* raised a black marble monument to the victims' memory in the Orthodox synagogue courtyard. On that occasion they laid the plans for another gathering—the purpose: to invite Jews who were born or lived in Prešov and have scattered around the world to come for one last reunion, on August 17, 1997. The 99th anniversary of the dedication of the Orthodox synagogue fell on that date. Why not wait until the 100th anniversary? The letter sent to all the invitees explained, "The inexorable time presses us to make an earlier date. We are afraid that a further delay could make it impossible for some of us to attend." The anniversary gathering took place as scheduled. Baruch Robinson, one of the participants, wrote:

About 500 of us were there, from the U.S., Canada, Switzerland, Austria, Germany, Israel, and from parts of Slovakia—all of us gathered again in Prešov. We greeted each other amidst the tearful reunions of friends who hadn't seen each other for more than half a century. On Shabbat morning we gathered in the synagogue for

The late Yakov Chajimovič, past president of the Prešov *kehillah,* in the community office. He spoke to the authors about post-war Jewish life in Prešov. "In their day, the Communists threatened to take the synagogue away from us if it was not in active ritual use. Our membership was too small to muster a minyan, and we could not hold services in the synagogue without one. The Jews of Košice came to our rescue. They made the one-hour trip every Shabbat morning to make a minyan together with us. That's how we kept the Communist wolf from the door. Now the synagogue is safely ours, but without a minyan it gets little use. We had visitors here not long ago who offered to buy the synagogue from us and move it to California. We turned them down flat; the synagogue stays here." Chajimovič came to Israel in 1993 and lived in Netanya with his son's family until his death in June, 1997, two months before the Prešov reunion.

prayers, a large crowd, just like 50 years ago . . . On Sunday afternoon the main ceremony took place. The overflow crowd in the synagogue included the mayor and many local officials, the rabbis from Prague and Košice, leaders from Bratislava, Naphtali Lavie from Israel, and local clergy. Songs in Yiddish and Hebrew opened the program, followed by a brief history of the kehillah *by Mr. Landa, the president and driving force behind the reunion. The Greek Orthodox priest spoke from the heart, with warm words that touched us all. The mayor described the important contribution of the Jews, over 20 percent of the population in the 1930s, to the economy and culture of the city. He did not mention regret, however, nor did he deplore the indifferent or hostile behavior of the Christian population during the deportations. My feeling is that somehow we did not do enough to memorialize our martyrs.*

SYNAGOGUES BORN
IN HIS HEART

In contrast to western Slovak cities such as Trnava and Bratislava, where the Jewish communities date from the Middle Ages, Lučenec and the southeastern areas of Slovakia had few settled Jews before the end of the eighteenth century. As in Bardejov, immigrants to this area often left Moravia because of the Familiants Law, or fled persecution and expulsion from Germany or Poland. By the time their communities had settled and had begun to function in this region, legal emancipation was only a couple of decades away. *Haskalah* and reformist tendencies were already part of the Jewish scene, although forces of religious conservatism opposed them. The Orthodox-Neolog schism that unfolded in Lučenec was only a local sample of the rift at the national level. Two communities existed side by side, more or less independently of each other. In an expansive mood after the First World War, the Neolog congregation had the benefit of the experienced architect Lipót Baumhorn, near the end of his long career, to design a handsome synagogue.

Lučenec (Hungarian: Losonc) sits in the southeastern agricultural heartland of Slova-kia, near a large railroad junction important for trade in fruit and wool. It is also an industrial town with factories for wood products, textiles, enamelware, and kitchen utensils. The first Jews to arrive were the Izrael Wohl family in 1808, under the aegis of Count Jozef Szillasy, an aristocrat who was ready without religious prejudice to bestow a plot of land and civil rights on his settlers. Several years later he granted land for a cemetery to the founding families—Sacher, Walles, Weiss, Grossberger, Schmiedl, Schneller, Deutsch, Herz, and Led-erer—a gift they acknowledged with a plaque in the ceremonial hall. The community's name was Tugar at first, from the Szillasy-owned vil-lage next to Lučenec, where they lived.

They organized a *ḥevra kadishah* and rented a house for a prayer room in 1825. Twenty years later they numbered 45 persons and were slowly replacing the earlier poverty with middling achievement. Until they could afford to hire a rabbi, they had the unofficial leadership of Rabbi Hogyesz. A loyal Hungar-ian as well as a devout Jew, he was arrested during the 1848 Revolution and tortured because he had supported the Hungarian cause.

Lučenec, postcard from a painting, about 1930. The town view juxtaposes the church on the left to the synagogue on the right, equally dominant on the urban skyline. Tourist publicity for Lučenec still features the synagogue as a noted landmark.

The new *kehillah* appointed Rabbi M. H. Goldzieher in 1851. A dynamic person with progressive ideas, his eagerness to promote *Haskalah* became the subject of controversy in the community. Over the heated opposition of the reform-oriented members, he was forced to resign after only seven years of service. The Orthodox candidate chosen in his stead, Rabbi Yakov Singer, was an ultra-conservative, previously rejected for the post because of his inflexibility. Friction within the community deepened until the town council had to intervene and appoint new officials for the community.

About a third of the Jews engaged in business. Some of them were affluent, owning factories for enamelware, agricultural machinery, and distilleries. A few managed large farms. Many were professionals: doctors, lawyers, teachers, and civil servants. By 1860 the expanding community numbered 120 members, mostly Neolog, and they needed a proper synagogue. They collected the necessary 23,000 forints in 1862 and built a beautiful neo-Moresque structure in the heart of town.

The old friction had not disappeared, however. The reformists could not forgive the Orthodox members for the removal of their beloved Rabbi Goldzieher. They arranged for Rabbi Solomon Braun of Putnok, an outstanding humanist and a dauntless advocate of *Haskalah,* to deliver the dedication speech for the new synagogue. Inviting Rabbi Braun was a declaration of overt intentions for reform. Moreover, contrary to custom, he gave the sermon in Hungarian. Sharply provoked, the Orthodox members reacted vigorously. Hurling accusations of divisiveness against their opponents, they withdrew from the congregation and never again set foot in the synagogue. The rupture caused great hardship to both groups. Town authorities neither recognized the Orthodox assemblage as a separate congregation, nor allowed its members to build a synagogue. Obliged to keep up the fictitious assumption of a single congregation, the Orthodox paid no dues and thereby thrust the burden of upkeep on the Neolog congregants.

The extension of full civil rights generated a feeling of strength and the Neologists were prepared for the coming decisions of the national Congress of 1868 that sealed the division. The Neolog majority kept the synagogue, while the Orthodox created and maintained institutions and organizations of their own. They found alternate quarters in 1868, but their separate identity was not recognized until 1920, after the establishment of the Republic of Czechoslovakia. Rabbi Hillel Unsdorfer, whom they chose as their leader, set up a yeshivah. An ardent Zionist, he saw his children leave to settle in Palestine. Construction of an Orthodox synagogue languished until 1927.

The Neolog group founded a secondary school in 1878, built a *mikveh* in 1885, and in 1890 bought a house for the rabbi. Community organization was strong and benefited from the enthusiastic participation of the women. Jointly with a local philanthropic group called the Patronage Union, the Jewish women's organization adopted ten orphans from neighboring Rimavská Sobota, brought them up and saw to their education. After World War I Neolog numbers grew to 470, and the congregation felt the need for a larger synagogue. They were affluent enough by then to engage the services of the foremost synagogue architect of the time in Hungary, Lipót Baumhorn.

The second half of the nineteenth century was a period of rapid expansion and creativity—in the arts, in science, and in technology. Construction was booming, and new ideas in architecture were burgeoning. Standards of living rose alongside national economies as the industrial revolution took hold throughout Europe. The recently emancipated Jews of Europe were in a good position to benefit from the prosperity. They streamed from the small towns and villages to the cities and brought their skills in search of new opportunities. The rapidly augmented metropolitan *kehillot* needed to expand their facilities, and in view of their successes many of them could manage the expense. Discriminatory restrictions on the public face of Jewish facilities no longer controlled aesthetic choices, and the Jews felt the need to assert themselves. A flurry of synagogue construction ensued, expressing the sense of identification that Hungarian Jewry felt for Hungarian culture—and the irresistible urge of the leadership for trendy ostentation.

On this horizon arrived a talented young Jewish architect, Lipót Baumhorn (1860–1932). In the varied 49-year professional career that followed, Baumhorn designed 25 synagogues in the Austro-Hungarian empire, more than any other European architect. Working in the office of mentor Ödön Lechner, of the Lechner-Partos firm in Budapest for 12 formative years left an impact on his creations. A founder of the Secessionist movement, Lechner was a trailblazer who abandoned convention and incorporated folk art elements into a dramatically new national style. Baumhorn's visits to Italy in 1893 and 1899 exposed him further to Renaissance and Oriental influences, which he willingly accepted.

Baumhorn applied Lechner's innovations in form and structure, but he preferred to combine them with historical and classical elements rather than exclusively use Lechner's avant garde ideas. Although his earliest synagogues—in Esztergom, Hungary (1888) and Rijeka, Croatia (1895)—can be regarded as refined interpretations of the popular Moorish style, the synagogue in Szolnok, Hungary (1898) demonstrated a new sophistication in his architectural language. An eclectic synagogue, it is ornate yet

Lipót Baumhorn (1860–1932), prolific Hungarian-Jewish synagogue architect. (Courtesy of János Gerle.)

harmonious—with neo-Romanesque and neo-Gothic elements, a high central dome, and large, eight-lobed rose windows. It was a striking preview of his most famous building, the synagogue in Szeged, built in 1903.

Nearly a quarter of a century and more than 20 synagogues later, Baumhorn and György Somogyi (his partner and son-in-law) designed the synagogue in Lučenec. Less grandiose and spectacular than the one in Szeged and heavier, more massive in feeling than its predecessor in Szolnok, the Lučenec synagogue carries Baumhorn's distinctive hallmarks. The great Neolog synagogue was dedicated on September 8, 1925, in an impressive ceremony described in the official handwritten town chronicle with enthusiastic detail:

Oppressive temperatures of over 102° F (39° C) did not deter the multitudes in the streets from celebrating the dedication of the new Neolog temple. The parnassim *began the well-attended procession from City Hall after a speech by Dr. Frano Oppenheimer, congregation president.*

Under four canopies, the congregants carried the Torah scrolls through the streets, from the old synagogue to the new temple.

The temple is one of the largest in the Lučenec-Spiš region, reminding one of the Hagia Sophia in Istanbul. The central bimah is of Carrara marble, carved by the master sculptor of Banská Bystrica, A. Horn. Biblical passages decorate the walls. "L'veitkha naveh kodesh" ("Holiness befits your house"; Ps. 93:5) is inscribed over the portal. The proscenium arch carries the message, "V'ahavta l'rei'akha kamokha" ("Love your fellow as yourself"; Lev. 19:18).

The synagogue became a city landmark, and its picture postcards brought greetings from residents and tourists to friends and family.

Zionist sentiment was strong in the period between the two wars, when Lučenec was part of the Czechoslovak Republic, and there were recognized national rights for the Jewish minority. Business people made generous contributions to the Jewish National Fund and to the Keren Hayesod, Israel Foundation Fund. Women were active in the WIZO organization. Young people joined the leftist Hashomer Hatzair or the general Zionist Maccabi Hatzair.

These were the years when the community's economic and social successes were visible. Many fine carriages stopped at the synagogue entrance on the Sabbath and holidays, and well-dressed worshippers alighted and made their way to seats in the magnificent temple. By 1938 the Neolog community counted more than 2,200

THE NEOLOG SYNAGOGUE IN LUČENEC

Built in a restrained Romantic style, the Lučenec synagogue faithfully represented Baumhorn's mature achievement and incorporated those characteristics of his style that generate elation. From the soaring arch of the proscenium, the feeling of uplift runs past the rounded ceiling vaults along the broad and spacious galleries to what was a grand hall below. Cusped arches and neo-Moresque dentilation throughout the building in Lučenec—as in Baumhorn's synagogues in Szeged and Nový Sad—serve as unifying elements of harmonious connection and aesthetic balance. The two-story headings of the portal blocks on north, west, and south facades set the dominant tone, repeated inside on the high Ark structure.

The interior has a large, central, domed ceiling of suspended *rabitz* construction, supported on rectangular pillars and broad arches. Three of the pendentives that join dome to pillars—always an eye-catching spot for succinct philosophical mottoes—carry an expansion of the virtues on which the world must stand from Avot 1:2, "Torah, Worship and Benevolence." The fourth

virtue added here is "Truth." Neo-Moresque dentilations along the arches, spanning the hall and the galleries, echo those that hug the external dome and the four small cupolas. Two main cupolas on octagonal turrets stand above the west entrance. A series of smaller turrets and cupolas punctuate the roofline.

Lučenec, southeast facade of the Neolog synagogue, Romantic style. Lipót Baumhorn, architect, 1925. Built of plastered brick, with cusped-arch window groups and portal pediments, it has a high central dome. The massive triple apse at the east contains choir rooms and offices for rabbi and cantor.

Three-part main entrance to the synagogue, on the southwest. Over the central door, the stately pediment rests on two squat columns, each with hexagonal plinth and square capital. Cusped lunettes over the three doors echo the theme of the cusped arch that appears many times in the building.

The capital on one of the four columns under the dome. The characteristic Tablets of the Law symbol is imaginatively molded on the capitals. Inscriptions in three of the pendentives get their inspiration from the foundations of the world, Avot (1:2): this one is Torah, the other two are *avodah* (worship), and *ḥesed* (benevolence). The fourth pendentive is inscribed *Emet* (truth).

members in 550 families. For many years Ignác Herzog, well known in all of Slovakia for his business and administrative talents, was chairman of the community. Born in 1864, he lived in Lučenec for over 50 years, owned a large, successful factory, and presided over many charitable institutions.

The splendor came to a sudden end after the Munich Pact of 1938. Hungary annexed parts of Slovakia, including Lučenec. Severe racial laws restricting Jewish employment and completely disrupting all Jewish life were applied and were soon followed by massive induction of Jewish men to forced labor. A month after the Nazis entered Hungary in March 1944, they concentrated the Jews into a ghetto that included the great synagogue on Varga ulica. Hungarian police beat and tortured wealthy Jews, hoping to discover where they had hidden their valuables. In June 1944 most of the 2,000 Jews of Lučenec were deported to Auschwitz.

Only 80 Jews returned to the city after the war. With the aid of the Joint Distribution Committee, they rebuilt the formal outlines of Jewish community life. They made repairs to the Ortho-

External octagonal dome and cupola surrounded by a ring of crenelations. Shrubs volunteer along the roofline. Note Tablets of the Law in the gable apex.

dox synagogue, set up a kosher kitchen in the courtyard, and even found funds to contribute for the defense of Israel during the 1948 War of Independence. Eighty percent of the survivors

245

departed for Israel in 1949, and nearly all the others went to the West. The Communist regime demolished the Orthodox synagogue in 1969, ostensibly to make room for apartment blocks. A handful of Jews remains in the city today.

Time and fate have been cruel to the large Neolog synagogue, and it has deteriorated into a gutted hulk. Russian artillery fire had partially damaged the building shortly before the liberation. After the war the small community sold it to the state to be repaired and used for cultural purposes. "Because of the severe lack of storage space in Lučenec," government authorities leased it for many years to an agricultural firm as a storeroom for corn and other farm products. The tenant moved out in the late 1970s and left the building open to vandals. Noting that a panel of Slovak experts unequivocally determined that "the synagogue has no historic value," journalist Katarina Kaplanová wrote a passionate plea in the national newspaper *Zmena* in September 1991 to save the landmark building. The reality is bleak. The disastrous current condition of the synagogue and the high cost of repairs unfortunately make the probability of preservation unlikely.

The interior of the Neolog synagogue today presents a picture of utter, wanton devastation. Shattered glass, broken timbers, fallen chunks of stucco, and general debris lie scattered on the floor. Galleries have been stripped bare to the beams. Sections of broken ceiling are open to the elements. General deterioration has obliterated painted decorations and most of the biblical passages from the flaking walls and ceiling. The Ark and the carved marble *bimah* have disappeared. Only style and the few Hebrew words remain to identify the ruin as a Jewish building.

Lipót Baumhorn died seven years after the dedication of the Lučenec synagogue. Under the initiative of Rabbi Immanuel Loew of Szeged, the communities for whom Baumhorn had designed synagogues were canvassed collectively to sponsor a monument in his memory. György Somogyi designed the tombstone, raised in the cemetery on Kozma utca in Budapest. A

View northeast toward the *Aron Kodesh*. Despite the synagogue's significance as one of the most distinguished buildings in Lučenec, the city allowed it to fall into neglect as a storeroom. In recent years it was empty, doors unlocked, allowing easy access to vandals. Lučenec municipal representatives asked if we might help raise money for restoration.

Inscribed stone marks the grave of Lipót Baumhorn in the cemetery on Kozma utca in Budapest. (Photo: Ilovsky Béla.)

poetic four-line epitaph by Rabbi Loew does homage to Baumhorn, under a relief of the Szeged synagogue dome among the clouds, followed by a list of 23 of his synagogues. Ruth Gruber, in her diligently researched chapter on Lipót Baumhorn in *Upon the Doorposts of Thy House,* agrees that the enigmatic eulogy in Hungarian is very difficult to translate. We propose the following version, as translated for us by László Bánszegi of Budapest:

Our inspired artist: Sky-seeking lines
Of pious synagogues were born in his heart!
His peaceful home was that of the devout:
His sky-seeking solace was born in his fatherly
and manly spirit.

HUNGARY

The earliest Jews who came to Hungary trailed after the legions that were expanding the Roman Empire northward in the third century C.E. Later waves of migration from Germany, Bohemia, and Moravia founded Jewish settlements along the Danube valley. Between the twelfth and fourteenth centuries, restrictive decrees and persecutions embittered the Jews' lives, but they persisted through medieval times and developed local and international commerce. They founded 38 communities in this period, the most important being Buda and Sopron. During the 160 years of the Turkish conquest (1526–1686) conditions were more favorable for the Jews, at least in the Turkish enclave. Jews from the Balkan countries were attracted to settle in the area, thereby adding a Sephardic element to the predominantly Ashkenazic population. Buda became a cosmopolitan city, a point of contact between Jewish East and West.

When the Hapsburgs replaced the Turks, eventually controlling almost all of Hungarian territory in 1699, the Jewish condition worsened. The burghers resented the Jewish tradesmen as competitors, and sought to banish them from the royal cities. This urban commercial conflict, exacerbated by religious bigotry, developed into an ingrained hatred, later to resurface as political anti-Semitism at the end of the nineteenth century. Impelled to move, the Jews were welcomed on the estates of Hungarian nobles such as Counts Esterházy and Pálffy, who protected them and benefited from their economic expertise.

The regime of prejudice, intolerance, and excessive taxation imposed on the Jews during the reign of Maria Theresa (r. 1740–1780) was partly modified during the more tolerant reign of Joseph II (r. 1780–1790). By 1840 Jews numbered more than 300,000. Earlier restrictions on real estate ownership were abolished in the late 1850s, after the ill-fated Hungarian revolution of 1848 to 1849 against Austria. Hungary continued to agitate against the monarchy until the Austro-Hungarian

Compromise of 1867, when it became a quasi-independent state within the renamed Austro-Hungarian Empire. The Hungarian Parliament soon enacted Jewish emancipation, removing remaining judicial and economic restrictions, allowing Jews to engage in all professions and to settle in all localities. No longer limited to the towns and villages, Jews—now counting more than 500,000 persons across the country—began to stream into the main cities.

This Emancipation period (1867–1914) brought Hungarian Jewry to a crest in political, economic, and cultural spheres. Their political position was strengthened in 1895 with the official recognition of Judaism as an equally accepted religion. Jewish enterprise and capital helped to transform the predominantly agrarian economy, to develop industries based on agriculture, and to expand banking and commerce. Jews freely entered the liberal professions and many made their mark in literature, especially journalism. By 1910 Jews were five percent of the population (numbering over 900,000), but comprised about half of the journalists, lawyers, and doctors, and nearly 60 percent of the country's merchants. Economic and political anti-Semitism increased but did not prevent the expansion of Jewish communities, primarily in the major cities: Budapest, Szeged, Miskolc, and Debrecen.

Political emancipation opened the door to higher secular education and adaptation to the outside world. Such radical options engaged Hungarian Jewry in a bitter culture conflict. The Neolog movement favored modifications of the religious ritual as well as cultural and political integration. The adaptations were opposed by the Orthodox, who resisted any change in the traditional way of life or any reduction in community autonomy. Orthodox rabbis battled the reformers from a position of power much stronger than that of the Jewish Orthodoxy in France or Germany. The conflict came to a head at the government-summoned General Jewish Congress of 1868 and precipitated the major ideological split that plagued the life of Hungarian Jewry until the Holocaust overtook all the sides.

Integration and assimilation made deep inroads into the Jewish community during the 50 years before the First World War. Hungarian Jewry became one of the most assimilated Jewish communities in Europe, with a growing tendency toward apostasy—especially among the upper classes. In contrast, Hasidism swelled in the northeast, in the Szatmar, Bereg (including Munkács), and Mármaros districts. A minority favored political Zionism.

Loyalty and patriotic participation by the Jews in the battles of World War I did not prevent overt anti-Semitic riots, known as the "White Terror," in the post-war years. Hungary was stripped of territories in 1920, including the crowded, Orthodox Jewish centers in the east that were ceded to neighboring states. The Jewish population in the country fell by almost half, to fewer than 500,000 persons. Smaller towns were abandoned as Jews concentrated in the larger cities, especially Budapest. In 1939, when Hungary regained some of her lost territories, the Jewish population expanded to 850,000.

Nazi troops marched into Hungary in "Operation Margaret" on March 19, 1944. Ghettoization and deportation followed with demonic efficiency. Toiling relentlessly before the advancing Soviet troops, the Nazis managed to murder more than half a million Hungarian Jews by war's end.

Hungarian Jewry now comprises a renewed and active community, with some 80,000 Jews living in Budapest. Nearly 20,000 more live in the rest of the country, particularly in a few of the larger cities, such as Miskolc, Debrecen, Szeged, and Pécs. Jewish cultural life has recovered to some extent, with Budapest as the center. The rabbinical seminary trains rabbis for central and east European communities. Aside from the grand Dohány synagogue (Neolog) and the Orthodox Kazinczy synagogue, 20 smaller synagogues function in Budapest.

Not destroyed by the Germans because of lack of time, nearly 100 synagogue buildings still stand in the country. Hungary, the first of the central European countries to free itself from post-war Communist rule, was a leader in restoring synagogue buildings for cultural purposes. Several synagogues were restored by municipalities and converted into concert halls in the early 1980s. With supplementary municipal funds, former Hungarian Jews living abroad financed the more recent restoration of the magnificent synagogues still in Jewish use: Szeged, Pécs, and the Dohány in Budapest,. These buildings are open to the public as museums, and the large halls serve for prayer only on the Jewish high holidays.

The synagogue in Zalaegerszeg, Hungary, József Stern, architect, 1904. Restoration to a concert hall was completed in September 1983. The original organ is still used for well-attended organ concerts.

Synagogue interior, facing the restored *Aron Kodesh*. To the right of the Ark, partly hidden behind the *bimah,* Jewish objects and documents from Apostag are displayed in several glass museum cases. The hall is popular for weddings and concerts.

MATZAH FOR THE NEIGHBORS

The remarkable synagogue restoration in the village of Apostag highlights the achievement potential of a mainly volunteer work force in substituting collective effort for scarce money. Hungary was beginning its slow crawl away from Communist domination in the mid-1980s, when a gentile schoolteacher initiated a campaign to rescue the derelict synagogue in Apostag for cultural use. He succeeded admirably.

With a current population of 2,660, Apostag still consists of one-story houses laid out among small farms and gardens on narrow streets. The village is so inconsequential that it appears only on comprehensive maps. Situated on the east side of the Danube some 50 miles south of Budapest, it claims a minor distinction as the birthplace of Hungarian writer Lajos Nagy. The *kehillah* of Apostag, too, was just another of the hundreds of village communities scattered throughout the central European heartland. This *kehillah* kept some of its Jewish population after the Emancipation opened the big cities to Jewish settlement, but Jewish life and identity in Apostag waned thereafter.

The shaded cemetery that borders the synagogue courtyard contains gravestones from the beginning of the seventeenth century, and this suggests that Jews may have lived here as early as the middle of the Turkish occupation—around 1630. In fear of Christian reprisals, Jews fled with the retreating Turks who suffered defeat at Buda in 1686. The war took a heavy toll in casualties and relocation, leaving the land fallow and under-populated. In the eighteenth century nobles and landowners attracted immigrants to resettle abandoned villages and to handle trade. Slovak farmers responded, and Jews arrived from Austria, Bohemia, and Moravia. Many of them took up farming—primarily viticulture and animal husbandry—while others were traders or crafts people.

The *kehillah* built a synagogue in 1768 that functioned until it burned down in 1820. The relatively large *kehillah*—600 persons, a fifth of the town's population—was culturally and administratively autonomous. It assumed responsibility as the religious center for Jews of still smaller villages in the region. The

The synagogue in Apostag, *Zopf* style, 1822, as seen through the trees at the edge of the cemetery. A few of the oldest gravestones among the 600 that still stand date from early seventeenth century.

parnassim maintained a genial internal discipline, enforced, if ever needed, by public punishment: fines, withdrawal of *shehitah* privileges allowing the purchase of kosher meat, or assignment of "shamed" synagogue seats to offenders.

Built in the transitional Classical, so-called *Zopf,* style in 1822, the present synagogue replaced the previous one that burned on the same site, incorporating the unchanged masonry structure from the earlier building. The new decoration, in late Baroque style, was more elaborate. The synagogue served well for the prosperous Apostag *kehillah* of 783 souls at its historical maximum in 1840. Emigration to metropolitan centers ensued in pursuit of opportunity as residence in the large cities became permissible, and within 40 years the community had dwindled to half its former size.

The first of Apostag's rabbis—from 1768 to 1818—was Rabbi Josef Moshe, who set up the *hevra kadishah* in 1772 and founded a yeshivah. His successor, Rabbi Basch, who held office until about 1860, opened a Jewish school in 1823—a year after completion of the synagogue. His congregants loved him and often visited him in his spacious house behind the synagogue.

Unhurried, the *kehillah* opted for Neolog affiliation in 1878. The school functioned until the turn of the century, when it closed its doors as parental interest in a specifically Jewish education for the children dwindled. The trend to assimilation was evident much earlier. Community organizations such as the *hevra kadishah* and a women's organization called Maskil el Dal, (education for the poor), did little to diminish the tendency to integrate into Hungarian society. Some *kehillah* members attained high government positions. Samuel Radó was inspector general of the Hungarian State Railroad, and

The rabbi's house at the northern end of the synagogue courtyard.

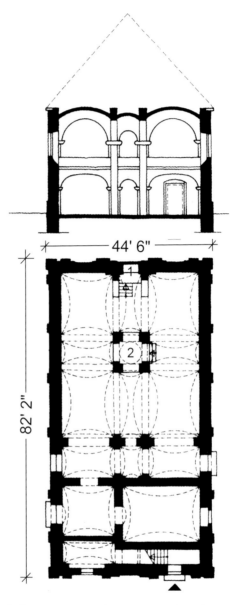

Plan of the synagogue in Apostag. 1. Ark, 2. central *bimah*. (Adapted from: A. Gazda, *et al.*, *Magyarországi zsínagógák*.)

Mór Schönfeld was the public treasurer of Apostag. There was hardly any Zionist fervor and many Jews led an assimilated life. They served patriotically in the Hungarian army in World War I, but that did not protect their shops from looting by demobilized soldiers.

With fewer than 2,000 inhabitants in 1939, the village of Apostag was nevertheless caught in the web of German conquest. The community was officially disbanded in 1947 and the synagogue was transferred to the defunct community's legal heir in Budapest, the Organization of Hungarian Jews. That organization, in turn, having no use for a village synagogue where there were no Jews, sold the building to the Apostag town council.

The building languished as a storage depot for agricultural products and fertilizer. It was in so desperate a state by the mid-1980s that demolition was on the agenda. Like other orphaned synagogues in Hungary, this one had admirable architectural and artistic features, and these stirred the idea of restoration in a perceptive village teacher. He suggested it to the council and fought tenaciously for restoration until he had council approval. As a first step, the building was listed as a national monument.

Starting with no more than village funds, the project won grants from regional, national, and Jewish sources. The benefits of this major challenge were so apparent that, in one newspaper account, it "elicited an enthusiastic profusion of local volunteer labor, including an ancient grandmother and a small child." The volunteer labor, estimated as worth 4,000,000 forints on construction and landscaping, did a major part of the heavy and unskilled work. Under planning and guidance by Budapest architect Péter Wirth, the villagers and professionals completed the restoration in less than two years and held a festive dedication in October 1987.

Renovated and well kept, the building now serves multiple purposes. The entrance lobby

THE SYNAGOGUE IN APOSTAG

Authentic except for the colors—now a dazzling white, inside and out—the restoration is a harmonious blending of the current décor with the former function and sanctity of the building. The central *bimah,* mounted between the four tall Corinthian pillars that support the original nine-bay ceiling, was aesthetically reconstructed and provided with shiny brass banisters to border the four-step approaches. Clusters of sparkling white globes illuminate with soft light.

The elaborate *Aron Kodesh* is particularly interesting for its literal and naive depiction of Mount Sinai during the Revelation, when Moses received the Tablets. The inscribed verse, *"V'hahar ba'ar ba'esh ad lev hashamayim"* ("The mountain was ablaze with flames to the very skies"; Deut. 4:11), comes to life in the lunette above the ornately carved doors. Tablets of the Law rest in a halo of puffy white clouds on a stark blue sky. A stylized mountain rises up underneath—its slopes punctuated by orderly jets of flame to illustrate the fiery and thunderous occasion. The carved wooden door decorations and—in royal blue and orange—the stucco baldachin that canopies the *Aron Kodesh* are remarkably similar to the décor of the Ark in the synagogue restored to a library in Baja in southern Hungary, also the work of architect Péter Wirth. Forty-eight cubical, upholstered armchairs in precisely aligned rows and a grand piano to the left of the Ark furnish the hall for concerts and wedding ceremonies.

Under a new, red-tiled hip roof, the Classic facade includes narrow pilasters that frame rectangular windows, possibly round headed in the original. Two lance-tipped metal urns, a favorite element in contemporary Hungarian synagogue architecture, mark the ends of the roof line. Such urns can still be seen on the roofs of the synagogues in Mád (1795) and in Albertirsa (1820).

Ark lunette of the restored synagogue in Apostag. This depiction of the Revelation on Mount Sinai—Tablets of the Law in clouds above a mountain—is rare in Ark decoration on Hungary. The theme may have been derived from Venetian Torah curtains of the seventeenth and eighteenth centuries.

Gallery library. The gallery contains a municipal library, well stocked and maintained.

contains a museum in honor of the popular Hungarian writer Lajos Nagy. The sanctuary, up a flight of steps, serves as a concert hall and as a popular wedding chapel. It also contains a small Jewish museum section. An elegant public library occupies the space of the women's gallery, where the librarians shelve the ample supply of books and periodicals behind glass in cylindrical mahogany bookcases.

Three glass museum cases at the right of the Ark contain memorabilia of the Apostag Jewish community: a *maḥzor* (festival prayer book), a *tallit, tefillin,* a shofar, and civic documents of a former resident—a Jew—some of whose papers survived. His name was Herman Farkas, serial number 429 in the *kehillah:* a male child of legal status born on August 2, 1854 to Samuel Farkas and his wife, née Sara Weisz; birth assisted by midwife Bitonia Isibram; *brit milah* performed on August 29 by *mohel* Károly Rosenthal, with

Martin Hecht as *sandek.* Another document is the birth certificate of Isidore Farkas, born February 5, 1886: male offspring of the above-mentioned Herman Farkas, tavern keeper, and his wife, née Sarolta Engel, with birth assisted by midwife Adolfina Baruch and the *brit milah* performed on February 15. The *mohel,* Ignacz Weisz, may have been a relative of the happy grandmother.

The writer Lajos Nagy was the son of an Apostag Jewish landowner and a peasant woman, Julia Nagy, from a nearby farm. In Hungarian the word, *nagy* means "big," and the property is applicable to the writer. Nagy was known as an acute observer of character. When he immortalized his native village under a fictional name in *Kiskunhalom,* a sociographic presentation of local people and their ways, the elder citizens of Apostag had no difficulty in recognizing a portrait of themselves.

Pre-war photo of Chana Wittberg and parents in front of their house in Apostag. (Courtesy of Chana Wittberg.)

Boxcars at a railroad siding in Apostag, reminiscent of those that transported the Jews of Apostag to Auschwitz.

The restored Apostag synagogue has become a showplace. Tourists and schoolchildren arrive by bus to see the building, to visit the small Lajos Nagy museum, and to hear an explanation of the Jewish past from the librarian. The Europa Nostra Federation, a volunteer organization of 22 European countries founded in 1963 to encourage preservation and restoration of historic sites, conducts an annual competition among successful restoration projects. One of the eight silver medals awarded in 1989 singled out the synagogue restoration in Apostag. Péter Wirth and town council head József Bolvári received certificates at a ceremony in Marburg, Germany, on March 19, 1989. That day was the 45th anniversary of Operation Margaret, the German invasion of Hungary.

The transports of Operation Margaret in 1944 wrenched a hundred Jews away from Apostag. Only three of them returned after the war. One was the late Chana Wittberg who came to live in Acre, Israel. "There were no Orthodox families among us. We had no rabbi in our village," Chana reminisced from her childhood in Apostag. "We had only the *ḥazzan,* Izsó Scharf, who acted as rabbi, *shoḥet,* and teacher of Hebrew and religion to the Jewish children."

"Most Jews were adults. There were very few Jewish children with whom to play. Although contacts with the goyim were limited to business, without social or cultural mixing, I did have one Christian friend, a little girl who lived next door. All of us went to the Christian school, where there were usually one or two Jewish children in each class. I had to go to school on Shabbat, but Jewish shops stayed shut on major Jewish holidays, and then our parents allowed us to stay home from school. All the Jews went to the synagogue on the holidays, even though most of them did not keep a kosher kitchen. Before Pesaḥ, when the matzot arrived from Budapest, my mother would send me around to the neighbors with some of it for them to taste. They liked the courtesy and gave me sweets. On Shavuot, I used to trim my father's seat in *shul*—and my grandfather's—with greenery.

"Everything changed for us in 1942. Jews no longer had business permits, and we were chased out of school. In 1944 my father and two other Jewish men were taken away. In June all the rest of us were packed into cattle cars and sent to Auschwitz. I came back by myself in October 1945 and found nobody. My mother, brother, father, and grandfather never returned, nor did any of my other relatives. Ḥazzan Izsó Scharf had returned a few days earlier. Together we walked the empty streets, dazed. All the Jewish houses were ransacked, empty. The synagogue was in shambles and the floor completely ripped up because the goyim had searched for valuables. The next day, I ran away from Apostag."

THE BUTCHERS
AND THE TANNERS

When young Count Ferenc Esterházy decided to build a castle at Pápa in the mid-eighteenth century, he first drained a lake northeast of the town to provide more farmland. He then had the foresight to invite Jews to his town, in the justified conviction that they would bring prosperity. For two centuries the symbiosis between the Esterházy family and the Jewish community brought benefits to both groups. Following his example, the townspeople related reasonably well with the Jews—most of the time. As in other places, however, outbreaks of anti-Semitism occurred, usually in consequence of regional or national events that raised popular emotion. At least once on such an occasion in local history, Jews stood up to riotous attack and fought back effectively.

Built on lands that once comprised the spreading estate of the aristocratic family, the city sits in the Bakony hills of western Hungary, a forest area dotted with ruined castles, mines, and industrial plants. Today, Pápa boasts one tourist attraction: the rambling eighteenth-century Esterházy castle, recently restored as a museum. It borders the highway

north to Györ and still dominates the city's entrance. Only half a mile away, the grand synagogue—once the pride of Pápa's 3,500 Jews—stands vandalized, forlorn, and locked.

Past the central square and twin-towered Baroque parish church, through the arched gate into the old town, one arrives at Petöfí Sándor utca—in the heart of what was the heavily populated Jewish quarter. It was a quiet street a little wider than the adjoining alleys in 1989, before the gentrification of the area began. The stately synagogue towers over the cramped one-story houses that crouch under low-pitched roofs and gabled fronts. The few Jews of Pápa no longer have possession of the building and it was a struggle for us to gain entry.

The 1698 town chronicle records a single Jewish family named Pintschof. A population register of 1736 lists ten taxpaying Jews, including Mattias Fischer—holder of a permit to produce spirits—and two silversmiths. The others were probably traders or provided financial services to Count Esterházy. Twelve years later the Count permitted the formal establishment of the *kehillah* near the market area. His *privilegium* (contract) allowed 15 families to live in the town, to build a synagogue, to establish a cemetery, to set up an *eruv* (Sabbath boundary), and to provide kosher meat and wine. Before building a prayer room in 1739—when there were 19 families in the community—the newly instituted ḥevra kadishhah prepared its first report. The signed document, with illuminated initials, was treasured in the synagogue archive until it disappeared in the upheavals of World War II.

Times were quiet and the community prospered. Early in the nineteenth century, Jews opened a factory for industrial and consumer ceramics. Early styles of dinnerware were copied from the English, but the artisans soon developed an authentic Hungarian style. For special orders, they painted politicians' portraits on dishes and produced embellished seder plates. The Boskovitz family established a ceramic smoking-pipe factory and the Peruz brothers founded a textile plant. There were also factories for paper, bricks, and steam production, respectively. The numerous tailors and the more than 100 families of tanners established separate Jewish guilds. Because the unpleasant odors of the tanning process clung to those who worked in the trade, tanners and their families had to live apart from the rest of the community. Although the area lacked decent sanitation, its inhabitants hardly suffered from the plague of 1830.

By 1840 the *kehillah* had grown phenomenally, reaching 2,648—20 percent of the population. The *parnassim* successfully managed a 25-acre plot of land in their possession, selling portions of it periodically to finance and maintain charity institutions. Several social associations were active: Gomlei Dalim (care for the needy), Shiur (daily Talmud study), Tiferet Baḥurim (young men's club), and a ḥevra sandek (for helping new mothers). In 1818 the *kehillah* established one of the first Jewish schools in Hungary. Eight years later it became a general school, where the children also studied subjects in Hungarian. Moses Bloch, later known as Mór Ballagi—a learned and ambitious staff teacher—was the first Jew to translate the Pentateuch into Hungarian. Ironically, he became so enamored of Hungarian culture in the process that he converted to Christianity. At mid-century the school enrolled 209 girls among its 510 pupils, a sign of how highly the *kehillah* regarded education for women.

In an attempt to mediate between the Orthodox and the nascent Neolog movement, Rabbi

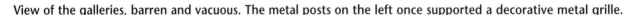

View of the galleries, barren and vacuous. The metal posts on the left once supported a decorative metal grille.

THE SYNAGOGUE IN PÁPA

Built more than a decade before the larger Dohány utca (1859) in Budapest, the synagogue in Pápa was the largest one in Hungary at the time and the first sanctuary divided into a central nave and two aisles. Parallel to Főiskola utca, its axis runs from the southwest entrance to the Ark on the northeast. The building is austere, with modest Classical facade elements such as the pseudo-stone surface division, the portal design, and the dentilation under the roofline. Florentine arches over small lunettes frame paired, round-headed windows that are separated by slender Corinthian columns.

From a large courtyard, one approaches the main entrance, now sealed with brick. Ionic columns and quarter-round pilasters under an arched pediment embellish the narrow, splayed portal. Entrance to the galleries is from more modest arched portals on the long side walls.

The proscenium arch and the Torah Ark loom high above the commodious prayer room. Paired Corinthian pilasters flank the prominent *Aron Kodesh* pillars. Above the Ark a huge rose window dominates the area. An archival photo shows a sparkling synagogue filled with benches and walls decorated with frescoes. Two elaborate chandeliers from the main ceiling and numerous smaller lamps in the galleries fill the hall with light. Elaborate metal grilles, added in a restoration of 1919, once lined the galleries between the Corinthian columns. Damaged frescoes, loose wires, and bare upright posts between the gallery columns are all that remain.

A structural rhythm works its way up from the massive square-pillared arcade at the base, to the arches between the pillars in the lower gallery, and to the overall arch of the upper gallery. The low-domed ceiling, shaped like an oval fluted shell, stretches about 70 feet above the floor. Inscriptions in cartouches on some of the square pillars are still legible: *"Pikudei Adonai y'sharim"* ("The precepts of the Lord are just") and *"Mitzvat Adonai bara"*

The *Aron kodesh* niche, rising nearly three stories. Built to provide for two gallery levels, the interior height of the synagogue is accented by the exceptionally large rose window. Two inscriptions, letter by letter, wind their way around the window, now boarded up. Above: *"Shiviti Adonai l'fanai tamid"* ("I have set the Lord always before me"; Ps. 16:8), and below, *"Da lifnei mi ata omed"* ("Know before whom you are standing"; Avot, 3:1). The large Ark structure repeats the architectural theme of the main portal: an arched pediment on pillars. At the turn of the century the frontal *bimah* was abandoned, and a central *bimah* was built. A portion of the central *bimah* base is visible in the foreground.

("The instruction of the Lord is lucid"; both from Ps. 19:9). All the pillars have heavy black marks at knee to shoulder height from the floor, suggesting that the synagogue furniture had been burned on the spot.

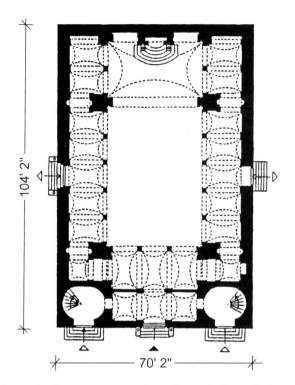

Section of the synagogue in Pápa. The inscription shown around the rose window was not used. (Adapted from: A. Gazda, *et al., Magyarországi zsínagógák.*)

Plan of the synagogue in Pápa. (Adapted from: A. Gazda, *et al., Magyarországi zsínagógák.*)

Pinchas Horowitz of Pápa organized a conference in Paks in 1844 for all the rabbis of Hungary—to no avail. Between 1844 and 1846 the eager community built the large synagogue on the then Főiskola utca (College Street), named for the Calvinist Seminary situated at the corner. The synagogue's large dimensions and its favored location on an important street indicate the strength of Jewish resources and the respected position of the *kehillah*. Count Pál Esterházy, son of the Jews' earlier patron, contributed the equivalent value of 100,000 bricks for the construction. In 1851 he supported the construction of a large school, a *beit midrash,* and community offices nearby. The *kehillah* maintained two synagogues, a hospital, a high school, and an important yeshivah that trained rabbis for many *kehillot.*

In designing their synagogue, the *kehillah* departed from tradition by keeping space open for an organ and by placing the *bimah* in front of the Ark. In an unusual change for a *kehillah* in Hungary, the congregation later affirmed its Orthodox affiliation, dropped the notion of installing an organ, and moved the *bimah* to the traditional center. Today, in the center of the

empty 34-by-71-foot prayer room, brick and concrete fragments lie on top of a bare, semi-circular *bimah* platform.

Rabbi Leopold Loew, an ardent champion of *Haskalah,* taught Hebrew at the Calvinist seminary where Jewish students also studied with him. Loew served as rabbi in Pápa for only four years—1846 to 1850—a period marked by frequent squabbles with militant Orthodox proponents. He dedicated the new synagogue in Pápa with a sermon in the Hungarian language. Called to head a congregation that was better attuned to his reformist views, Rabbi Loew moved to Szeged, where he pursued a long and distinguished career.

The 1862 *pinkas* (ledger) of the *kehillah* tells of a staunch and plucky midwife named Blau, who anticipated Zionist activism. Hearing that there was no Jewish midwife in Jerusalem, she decided to leave her busy practice in Pápa and to fill the need in Jerusalem. She packed her bags promptly and made the arduous journey to Palestine alone.

By mid-nineteenth century, the blood-libel had taken root in the Christian psyche. When a

Main synagogue portal, sealed with bricks. Paired stucco fire-pots "illuminate" the inscription: *"V'asu li mikdash v'shakhanti b'tokham"* ("And let them make Me a sanctuary that I may dwell among them"; Ex. 25:8). On the street side, another similar portal is inscribed, *"Ze hasha'ar l'Adonai, tzadikim yavo'u bo"* ("This is the gateway to the Lord, the righteous shall enter through it"; Ps.118:20).

girl from the village of Tiszaeszlár in northeast Hungary disappeared in April 1882, rumors quickly spread that Jews had murdered her in Passover rituals. Church officials coerced a 14-year-old boy to testify that he had witnessed his father and accomplices murder the girl in the synagogue and collect blood in a bowl. The press covered the trial extensively and parliament discussed it volubly. With a brilliant defense, author and politician Károly Eötvös convinced the tribunal that the evidence of guilt, as presented, was false. The defendants were acquitted, but anti-Jewish sentiment gathered momentum through-

out Hungary after the verdict, with attacks against Jews in Budapest and many other localities. In some districts, authorities proclaimed a state of emergency to protect Jews and their property.

News of the spreading riots reached Pápa, and the Jews of the town prepared quickly to protect themselves. Hearing shouts of the ruffians as they surged through the town gate on their way to the Jewish Quarter, the husky butchers and tanners rallied to the streets, brandishing their tools as weapons. They defended the community with force and effectively repulsed the attackers.

Delegates from Pápa to the 1868 General Jewish Congress in Budapest sided with the Orthodox stream. A small group that favored the Neolog trend broke with the majority in 1875, but their failure to recruit viable numbers returned them to the fold five years later. From 1870 until 1880, the 3,500 Jewish residents in Pápa comprised a quarter of the population. Organized Zionism came to Pápa early, with a branch of Hovevei Zion in 1904, that later identified itself with Mizrachi. In the 1920s Rabbi Aryeh Roth published "Zionism from the Point of View of Jewish Orthodoxy," in which he vigorously advocated Zionism in face of both active and passive opposition of many Orthodox rabbis.

From the start of the Second World War, Pápa became a center for concentrating teams of forced laborers and many conscripts were shipped out, as far as the Ukraine. Community leaders were rounded up in 1940 and dispatched to concentration camps. When the Germans took charge in the spring of 1944, they marked eight streets around the synagogue as a ghetto. Conditions were initially tolerable with a communal kitchen and doctors to care for the sick. Then the more affluent Jews were herded into the synagogue and tortured to reveal the whereabouts of their valuables. Conditions worsened. The Jews were transferred to an abandoned chemical factory, with neither food nor sanitary facilities. The municipality provided some food packets—in a rare expression for the 1940s—of humanity toward Jewish neighbors.

Deputy chairman of the Hungarian Zionist Organization and head of rescue operations, Dr. Rudolf Kastner organized transports—in

One of the few Jews whom we met in Pápa, Rózsa Vajda, an Auschwitz survivor, and her gentile husband, Pál, in the court they shared with six other families. Pál showed us the smaller synagogue and community record books. A year later, we learned that Pál had died and Rózsa had moved to an old age home in Budapest.

Orthodox synagogue in Pápa. Romantic style, 1846. The synagogue parallels a street that runs northeast-southwest, hence the orientation of the *Aron Kodesh* is more nearly north than east.

In 1935 the Jews of Pápa celebrated the dedication of a new Torah scroll in the street near the synagogue. (From: *Pinkas Hakehillot, Book of the Communities: Hungary,* courtesy of Yad Vashem.)

negotiations with Adolf Eichmann—to take Jewish leaders of Hungary to safety in Switzerland in exchange for supplies for the German war effort. Kastner's rescue list included 51 fortunate individuals from Pápa. On July 4 and 5, 1944, 2,565 Jews of Pápa and 300 more from the vicinity were forced onto cattle cars bound for Auschwitz. After the deportations, Germans stabled horses in the synagogue.

About 500 Jews returned to Pápa after the war. They buried the desecrated Torah scrolls in the cemetery, cleaned up the synagogue, set up a Jewish school, and revived Jewish life in the city. But this activity was far from long-term stability. After the revolution of 1956 many Jews of Pápa emigrated, some of them to Israel. By 1972 the community had shrunk to 50 persons, and in 1989 there remained only a handful. Unused, the synagogue again fell victim to vandals.

On our second visit to Pápa, we found that the premises were under the care of Fidesz, a new political organization of young liberals dedicated to a democratic Hungary and protection for the rights of minorities, including Jews and Roma; its office was in the former Jewish school, next door to the synagogue. Fidesz had cleaned the synagogue and used the room for meetings and exhibits, and had prepared a short videotape on the history of the Jews of Pápa. The young people gave us a cassette copy and lent us the key to the synagogue. They also told us of plans for restoring the synagogue for use as a cultural center.

Our third visit to Pápa was less productive. The Fidesz office had disappeared, the synagogue door was padlocked, and no one knew where to find the key. Who now has the key to the future of this synagogue . . . and so many others like it in Hungary?

THE PARCHMENT
OF TORAH SCROLLS

Toward the end of 1944, the tide had turned against the Wehrmacht. Its offensive on the eastern front had collapsed at Stalingrad, and the divisions were retreating in desperate disarray before a Russian counteroffensive. Instead of relaxing their extermination policy against the Jews in the face of impending disaster, the Germans intensified it. Starting in 1940, male Jews in Hungary had been drafted—to be a source of expendable, forced labor, exploitable on the eastern front. As the Germans foundered westward, they marched the Jews to deadly destinations in Austria and Germany. One of the few stopping points on the way was at the forced-labor field base in the town of Kőszeg, near the Austrian border. Kőszeg had been the home of a 500-year-old *kehillah* that cherished a jewel of a synagogue.

Situated higher than any other Hungarian town—at an altitude of 850 feet—Kőszeg has changed little since the Middle Ages, when its name was Guens. Streets in the old town are still oriented in herringbone fashion, in an old tactical arrangement designed to retard invading cavalry. It was here in 1532 that 2,500 Hungarian troops defeated an army of 55,000 under Sultan Suleiman II, causing the Turks to abandon their attempt to capture Vienna. Jews participated bravely in that legendary battle, earning awards of land and other benefits in recognition of their valor. The town's main square, named after the victorious Hungarian commander Nicolas von Jurisics, contains an elaborate neo-Gothic Heroes' Gate leading to the heart of the Belváros (inner town), where the appearance of the medieval buildings remains unchanged.

Along with nearby Sopron, Kőszeg is one of the two cities in Western Transdanubia's Vas County, where Jews lived during the Middle Ages. In 1393 King Sigismund permitted the Gara family, rulers of the fortress, to invite Jews from Bohemia and Germany to settle in Kőszeg. Jews were enticed with offers of religious freedom and the right to organize their *kehillah,* but they had to pay a tax to the crown. An extant document of 1511 annuls the requirement that Jews wear a clothing badge. Bills of lading from 1517 to 1528 of a Jew, Alexius Funck, record the extensive trading he

Dr. István Bariska, town archivist, displaying one of the many documents he found in the archive dealing with the history of the Jews in Kőszeg. This one is a decree, from 1393, by King Sigismund, extending to Jews from Germany and Bohemia the privilege of maintaining a *kehillah* and following their own religious practices, against payment of fees to the crown.

conducted with Wiener Neustadt in Austria. The list includes gold threads, reins, rugs, paper, wax, peas, oranges, saffron, clover, and assorted luxury fabrics, such as long Freiberg cloth from Munich, crimson Italian Igler cloth, short fabric from Nuremburg, and linings.

Discontented with privileges granted Jews after the 1532 battle, local burghers tried repeatedly to have them expelled but the king thwarted them each time and the threat lapsed after 1544. The Hungarian victory over the Turks was only partial, however, and Turkish rule over major portions of Hungary persisted. As Kőszeg remained an intermittently active battleground through much of the seventeenth century, some of the Jews fled to the relative safety of other Jewish communities. On one occasion, when the Jews hurriedly escaped from the town, municipal clerks found a Torah scroll amidst the confis-

cated Jewish property. Thrifty archivists cut up the parchment to bind records, such as the lists of taxes Jews had paid for the right to sell wine. Volumes of town records from 1583 to 1693 still have portions of that parchment in their bindings.

The only Jew who lived in the town in 1735, M. Schlesinger, resisted attempts to expel him by making a successful appeal to the Austrian king. Then, with the arrival of a few Jewish tax collectors and later immigrants from the "seven communities" of Burgenland, the community started to grow again. Siesel Spitzer, who owned a large house on a spacious lot with a few buildings, gave one of them to the congregation for use as a synagogue. A *parokhet* (Ark curtain) from that synagogue, dated 5529 (1769), was in the community's possession until the *Shoah*.

The Jews were active in trade, industry, and the professions. Philip Schey (1798–1891) was born to an affluent Orthodox family in Kőszeg. As an influential industrialist in 1854 he became the first Jew in Hungary to achieve noble rank. He was known for his generosity and leadership in Jewish matters, but his brothers Ferenc and Sándor, grain merchants and shippers, and Károly, a manufacturer, converted to Christianity.

Philip Schey funded construction of the synagogue in Kőszeg in 1859 and added a generous endowment for the rabbi. He also contributed a kindergarten for the town, the first in Hungary. Later, he built a hospice for the indigent chronically ill, with the interfaith stipulation that the 12 places be evenly divided among Jews, Catholics, and Protestants. Baron Schey was one of the delegates who met unsuccessfully with the district regent of Graz in 1860 to seek permission for Jewish residence in the city of Graz. In his later years, Schey moved to Austria, where he died childless, and his title passed to a nephew Friedrich, later known as Freiherr von Schey.

The *kehillah* flourished in the second half of the nineteenth century, but its number never exceeded the 266 persons of 1910. Zionism came to the fore after the First World War, and some of the young people left for Palestine.

In the spring of 1944 Kőszeg's 117 Jews were confined to a narrow, crowded space in a former grain depot and denied contact with the

The synagogue in Kőszeg, Baroque style, 1859. Tall twin crenelated towers and narrow windows give the facade a fortress-like ambiance, with the Tablets of the Law as a heraldic shield.

forced-labor battalions nearby or with Christians. On July 4 they were deported to Auschwitz. Five thousand Jews conscripted to forced labor from all parts of Hungary were then quartered in Kőszeg. Herded together in an abandoned brick factory under unspeakable conditions, they were compelled to do heavy menial work. Hani Ferenc, a gentile woman with whom we stayed briefly in Kőszeg, remembered their misery. Her mother baked bread at home and hid the loaves secretly in the bushes at night for the Jewish prisoners to find and eat.

Battalion III/4, assembled in Kőszeg, consisted of 240 young Jews conscripted from diverse Hungarian towns in late 1943, before their communities were dismembered. The battalion was shipped to the eastern front in the Ukraine, where rations for a person consisted of 17 ounces of bread a day. For the few hours of rest allowed at night, they huddled together on the floor of an abandoned synagogue. At subzero

temperatures they were forced to dig anti-tank ditches and communication trenches in the frozen ground to fortify an important railroad junction. Working in full view of the endless line of box cars rumbling westward full of deported Jews, they heard the shrieks from behind sealed doors.

In November 1944, when Russian armies were already at the gates of Budapest, the Germans still concerned themselves with the exploitation and extermination of the Jews of Hungary. They ordered the exhausted survivors of Battalion III/4 to march west through northern Hungary in the direction of Austria—320 miles, in bitterly cold weather. The unfortunates dragged themselves, under guard, for 20 days. Few attempted to escape, convinced of the futility of any such attempt. As they passed through empty villages that once thronged with Jews, the young men realized the scope of the destruction of Hungarian Jewry. Moshe Zeiri, retired now from the Weizmann Institute in Rehovot, Israel, related: "Once, in the midst of a thunderous storm on the westward march from Budapest, a wagon full of Roma rode toward us. I saw that the canopy was made of the parchment of Torah scrolls! The rain and mud had smudged most of the letters. I couldn't contain myself. . . ."

Street entrance to the synagogue complex. Memorial plaque is mounted on the building at the left, which is the former school.

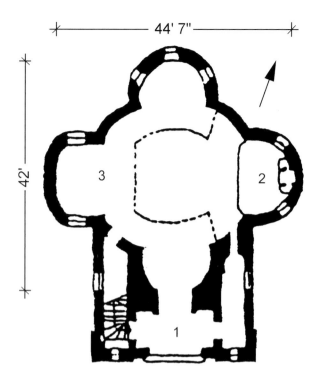

Plan of the synagogue in Kőszeg. 1. Entrance lobby, 2. Ark and *bimah,* 3. Three-sided gallery. (Courtesy of Rudolf Klein.)

Main doors with large quadrefoil panels, from the inside. Fragments of leaded glass cling to trefoil frames in the lunette. Residents of the garden cottage dry onions in the entranceway.

Not all of them reached Kőszeg again, their point of departure ten months earlier. The survivors learned that the Germans had gassed hundreds of forced laborers to death within the Kőszeg brick factory. The living buried the 2,000 dead in a mass grave in March 1945 and then were marched farther westward. The remnants of Battalion III/4 staggered toward the Austrian border. With the end of the war so imminent, there was more motivation to escape. Some tried running off into the woods, but most of them were apprehended and killed either by the Germans or by Hungarian security forces.

Ami Klein and two others tried to hide in the woods near their native town of Pápa, but a forester discovered them. He promised them a hiding place—and promptly proceeded to betray them to the Germans. Soldiers captured the hapless trio on the following day. Held for execution, their captors offered the "mercy" of a last wish. They asked to see their parents' graves in Pápa. The soldiers took them to the Jewish cemetery and shot them there. Klein was shot in the head, but, miraculously, he survived. After the soldiers left, he crawled, seriously wounded and bleeding, to precarious safety.

Forty-five years later, 60 members of the original group of Batallion III/4 were still alive. Those who had made their way to Israel after the liberation organized a survivors' reunion. Fourteen men gathered in November 1988 outside the synagogue in Kőszeg. At a ceremony attended by town notables and Mayor Freininger, as well as by older residents who remembered Jewish neighbors, the small band affixed a bronze plaque to the outer wall of the synagogue complex. Inscribed in Hebrew and Hungarian, it

The Synagogue in Kőszeg

Although it may be that the irregular lines of the plot dictated the unusual oval shape of the synagogue, the result is pleasing and possibly unique in synagogue architecture. Four apses break the oval shape: the Ark on the east and alcoves in the north and west, while the southern apse extends to form a rectangular entrance lobby. Internal steps on the left wind a way up to the gallery.

The carved and weathered wooden doors are always open now. One of them hangs disconsolately by a single hinge. Bits of colored glass adhere to leaded frames in the windows and the dome skylight. Bright sunshine does not penetrate very deeply into the dark interior. On the outside wall a marble tablet in Hebrew and Hungarian praises the patron who built the synagogue and maintained it: ". . . for an everlasting memorial to the great baron, officer, benefactor, Yom-Tov, son of our teacher Reb Moshe . . . whose wisdom inspired him to build a house for the Lord."

In the eastern apse the *Aron Kodesh* and the adjoining *bimah* stand at right angles to the entrance, an uncommon synagogue arrangement in Hungary. The empty, built-in Ark box, now without doors, contrasts sharply with the elaborate dark wood carved framework around it. Two narrow neo-Gothic pilasters ending in cathedral-like spires border the Ark with a giant metal Star of David that dominates the structure from above.

An unusual feature is the richly decorated Baroque dome. A fresco in each quarter, blotched with peeling plaster, presents a cartouche within a fanciful architectural composition. The cartouche facing the entrance contains a dedication to the sponsor, Philip Schey. The other three cartouches contain biblical inscriptions illustrated by whimsical scenes.

The synagogue, seen from the neighboring church tower. Aerial view displays the unusual plan of the synagogue: an oval structure with three rounded apses and a fourth extended to form a rectangular entrance.

The stepped gallery floor slopes somewhat, as in a theater. It has rotted away, in part, and hangs down unsupported at the far side. Broken benches lay about. Lit by round-headed windows, the gallery curves symmetrically around on three sides. In the north apse opposite the entrance, delicate Baroque arches painted on the wall frame a trio of trefoil windows.

The empty structure of the *Aron Kodesh*. The box remains, without doors, under the giant metal Star of David.

The north apse and a portion of the curved women's gallery.

commemorates the Kőszeg *kehillah* and the Jews in forced labor who perished there.

At the synagogue complex on Várkor utca, a gate opens into a spacious garden with scattered fruit trees. The path to the synagogue, centered in the far end of the garden, passes the *mikveh* shed on the right, and—on the left—the former teachers' quarters and school. The architect of the 1850s envisioned a deliberate composition in organizing these buildings toward functional and visual unity. On either side of the path, the build-

ings lead the eye to the synagogue, a striking double-bastion-type structure.

The couple who used to tend the synagogue lived in a room at the former Jewish school. They were proud of the fruit trees they had planted. Now, their daughter still occupies the modest three-room garden cottage with her husband, concert violist Zoltán Agota, and their two children. Zoltán keeps the gate locked to discourage intruders and vandals, but the synagogue building is exposed to the elements.

A fresco under the dome, inscribed to the benefactor: *"Zu Ehre Gottes erbaut von Philip Schey von Koromla"* ("Built for the glory of God by Philip Schey of Koromla"). Baron Schey, industrialist and philanthropist, was the first Hungarian Jew to achieve nobility, in 1854.

Deterioration of the structure is visible everywhere.

A local bank bought the property in the 1990s, and its officers considered plans for restoration and conversion to an antique shop. Nothing has been done, however, and the Hungarian Jewish Cultural Society still has hopes for a Jewish museum in the building. László Koday, a local metal artist, wishes to preserve the synagogue as a cultural building for the town, "Jews were prominent in the cultural life of the area. Kőszeg needs a fitting memorial to its Jewish citizens."

At the town archives, energetic archivist Dr. István Bariska found a photograph of Philip Schey and the ledger entry describing how Schey was ennobled in 1854. After much searching Bariska also found the original document, the parchment—bearing the Imperial seal—that came by special coach from Vienna and was presented by the mayor to the honoree at a festive public assembly. In the name of Emperor Franz Joseph I, Governor-General Archduke Albrecht elevated Philip Schey to "Baron, Aristocrat of Austria"—a distinction equal only to the honor conferred on him by his own community in the deteriorating fresco of the synagogue dome.

THE SANCTITY OF MAN

Győr is both an ancient city and a modern industrial center. Known in Roman times as Arrabona, it is situated at the confluence of the Rába, Rábca, and Danube rivers in northwest Hungary. The city grew up around a fortress on the present Kaptalan Hill. Restored in recent years, the fine old houses of the old city dress up one of the most pleasing Baroque townscapes in Hungary. With its sixteenth-century checkerboard layout, the large square and the narrow alleys have much the same appearance as they had when Jews first arrived 400 years ago.

According to a contemporary document, a street was set aside for Jews when Győr was rebuilt after a devastating fire in 1567. Jews paid the military governor well for his protection and for the unusual privilege of urban residence. After 1699, other than two protected families, Jews were excluded from the city and only sporadically allowed to settle on Győr's Rábca River island, Győrsziget. Entry on market days, however, continued unabated. In 1708, when the city was under siege and famine was widespread, Yitzchak Herschel managed to smuggle a large quantity of wheat into the city, but the royal patronage he hoped for never materialized.

The return to the island after 1791 came about by contract with the bishop. For an annual 400 forints, 30 families could settle, carry on trade, and build a synagogue—which they did in 1795. The city did not permit a cemetery, however, and the dead had to be ferried to another town. A stay of three days was the limit for nonresident Jews. When the mainland city was opened to unrestricted Jewish settlement in 1840, families streamed over from the island and from neighboring villages. The community flourished and expanded explosively—by fivefold to over 3,000 in only 30 years. The 5,904 Győr Jews in 1920, comprised 12 percent of the population. Since emigration was unusually low, 4,688 were still there in 1939.

After the Emancipation and remission of the Tolerance Tax in 1846, Jews enjoyed quasi-equality and a measure of prosperity, although new taxes were then assessed on all Jews in Hungary. Actively developing commercial ventures, Győr Jews played a major role in the export of grain to Serbia, Romania, and Bulgaria. They built large warehouses and worked at all levels, as merchants, agents, clerks, and providers of sacks. Factories financed and owned by Jews rose along the horizon: Adolf Schlessinger opened a distillery in 1818; Károly Neubauer founded Hungary's first match factory in Győr in 1852; Adolf Kohn became one of the greatest producers of vegetable oils in the country; and L. Schmidt operated a candy factory. In 1865 Jews established a successful maritime shipping agency, the Győr Steamship Company, which later joined the Hungarian River and Sea Shipping Company, Ltd.

The island and mainland communities functioned separately for a while, even after the mainland opened up to them, until the two merged in 1851. With their combined strength, they established a Jewish school, which gained official recognition and some renown. The internal communal organization was intense and prolific from its early days. An effective women's organization carried on varied functions, including clothing for poor school children and wedding arrangements for needy brides. As the congregation size began to exceed the capacity of the island synagogue, overflow groups conducted services in private homes, a practice forbidden by the secular authorities.

In 1861 the community announced a design competition for a new mainland building, specifying, "a large synagogue, with areas for a school building, offices . . . the whole should be monumental in size and comprise a harmonious group of buildings." Of the 33 architects from Budapest, Vienna, and Győr who submitted entries, Budapest architect Károly Benkó won the commission. The large synagogue complex stood completed in 1870, but the island synagogue continued in use—with rabbis and cantors officiating in both buildings. There were immediate repercussions, however, when the congregation majority affiliated itself with the Neolog faction and installed an organ. The Orthodox faction withdrew to set up a congregation of its own, including schools and charity organizations. Nonetheless, the Neolog synagogue and its

Inscription over the elaborate zig-zag and dentilated neo-Moresque geometrics of the main entrance: *"Habayit hazeh kadosh hu la'adonenu, Bo'u nishtaḥaveh ve'nikhra'ah lifnei oseynu"* ("This house is holy to our Lord. In it we shall bow and bend the knee before our Maker"; adapted from Ps. 95:6).

large school served as a cultural center for the community for many years.

As the Zionist movement gained strength during the early years of the twentieth century, the religious polarization within the Hungarian Jewish community was not conducive to its promotion. The Orthodox population was extremely conservative, particularly in the Szatmár and Máramaros regions of the Hungarian northeast, part of which is now in Rumania; these communities followed a dogma that mandated waiting for the arrival of the Messiah rather than to initiate change that might "hasten the redemption." Secular factions, on the other hand, sought to expand linguistic and cultural identification with the surrounding Magyar nation. At the official level, successive Hungarian governments acted to discourage Zionist activity because they were wary of *any* ethnic loyalties. They prohibited the

Corner where the school building extension meets the synagogue. All facades of the building carry eight-lobed rose windows. The four octagonal corner towers are pierced by quatrefoils and high, narrow windows.

collection of money or withheld the requisite authorizations for organizing affiliated branches. Some Neolog leaders also opposed the formal granting of such authorizations for a while, on the notion that Zionism was in conflict with Hungarian patriotism. Nevertheless, pockets of certain Zionist organizations did achieve standing as active minority voices.

The Neolog *kehillah* in Győr had no strong predilection for Zionism until it chose Rabbi Dr. Emil Roth (1907–1944) to be its rabbi in 1935. Although it was the Zionist minority who sought his appointment, the *kehillah* may have been unaware of the magnitude of his conviction or of his charismatic power to teach and convince. Unlike the dominant voice of Orthodox rabbis who declared that the gathering anti-Semitic storm of the 1930s would blow itself out with

manageable damage, Roth understood the enormity of the threat with cold prescience. He passionately promoted Zionism and *aliyah* to Palestine—especially for the youth—as the only solution for Jewish survival.

Rabbi Roth was Győr's dynamic community leader. It was he who as a young idealistic rabbi brought to this much-assimilated community a vision of the rebirth of the Jewish people in their homeland. Beginning his career, Roth first completed rabbinical studies in Budapest. Then he spent a year in Israel, first at the Hebrew University in Jerusalem and then at a kibbutz, studying modern Hebrew and observing Zionist realization firsthand. In 1932, at the age of 25, he was appointed rabbi to the 2,000-member Neolog community in Eger, in northeast Hungary. There he met and married Erzsébet Beneth.

Two-tiered galleries above the Ark, sweeping around the sides of the octagonal sanctuary. The tall neo-Moresque Ark structure of concrete and stucco on its high base stands between the curving galleries. An arched, dentilated pediment, under a squat crown behind Tablets of the Law, rests on two pairs of double columns. The small broken letters of the inscription carry the words of Joshua (3:11): *"Hinei Aron haBrit Adon kol ha'aretz"* ("The Ark of the Covenant of the Sovereign of all the earth . . .").

Their frequent outdoor arm-in-arm walks excited whispered disapproval among Orthodox elements in Eger.

Invited to take the post of rabbi of the Neolog congregation in mostly non-Zionist Győr, the tall, lean, ascetic-looking 28-year-old rabbi took charge with a determination born of inherent leadership and a firm agenda. He soon won the community's approval. His Friday night *Oneg Shabbat* sermons were so thought provoking that many an Orthodox congregant would hurry from services at his *shul* to catch the Neolog rabbi's words from standing room at the back of the synagogue.

Rabbi Roth saw his mission as that of an educator. To the few Jewish teachers at the State Women's Seminary, he taught religion and mod-ern Hebrew. To diminish the impact of the Catholic priests on Jewish youth in the late 1930s, he taught at the local high school, introducing the study of Hebrew and other foreign languages. He invested innumerable hours in extracurricular classes, clubs, scout groups, boat trips, and nature hikes, often in the face of parental opposition and growing political restrictions. He strove to inspire the youth to identify with their people and their religion. Hoping to save at least them, he promoted the not yet popular idea of returning to Zion. For those planning *aliyah,* there were classes in cooking, tractor driving, mechanics, and agriculture. Many of his students realized the aspirations he held for them. Like a biblical prophet, the rabbi warned his people by every available means of the great

THE SYNAGOGUE IN GYŐR

Viewed from a distance, across the River Rába, the synagogue complex in Győr, completed in 1870, is a prominent landmark on the city's horizon. Its segmented dome and cupolas stand out over the surrounding buildings and the luxuriant trees. Damage from half a century of neglect—bare brickwork and broken windows—is visible on every surface. Nonetheless, despite its massive feeling, the building has a pleasing architectural balance and is historically important as a precursor of Otto Wagner's Rumbach Street synagogue (1872) in Budapest. The facades show many fine details, adopted in the spirit of the early Romantic style that became popular in Hungary of the 1860s. Under the central dome and the eight-sided towers and cupolas, Moorish and Hungarian elements blend together: eight-lobed rose windows, quatrefoil windows, and dentilations along the edge of the pediment.

The interior was in poor condition from storage use before the present restoration was begun. Within the external rectangular shell, measuring 114 by 80 feet, the internal space is octagonal, under a dome 83 feet high. The upper floor of the two-level gallery—supported on eight slim columns—circles all eight sides of the hall, but the lower floor leaves an opening on the east for the massive two-story Ark. The narrow rectangular ceiling under each of the balcony sections contains a graceful eight-lobed floral motif embracing an eight-pointed star—all bordered with a narrow geometric design. Near the western entrance, a tall marble memorial stand served for lighting a *yortsayt* lamp on the anniversary of a loved-one's death. Among the inscriptions incised in the marble is the sentence: *"Ki Ata ta'ir neiri, Adonai Elohai yagi'a ḥeshki"* ("It is You who light my lamp, the Lord, my God, lights up my darkness"; Ps. 18:29). The floor was clear of debris in anticipation of restoration work.

On the eastern end of the complex, additions were built in 1926 behind the Ark, including a pair of wide entrances to the women's galleries and a large winter chapel. The chapel Ark had been ripped out completely; its plaster pillars broken to pieces, leaving only the intricately painted capitals and some twisted iron rods.

Pre-war view of the synagogue interior. (Courtesy of Marianna Spiegel.)

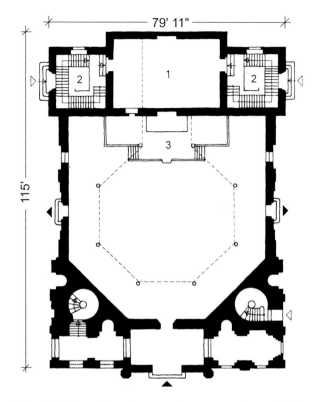

Beit midrash and eastern stairways to the galleries added in 1926. 1. *Beit midrash.* 2. Gallery stairways. 3. Ark and *bimah*. (Adapted from: A. Gazda, *et al., Magyarországi zsínagógák.*)

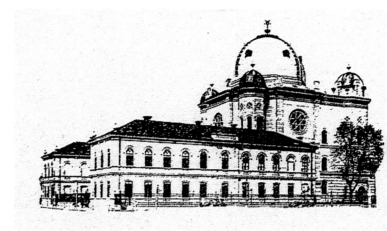

South facade of the synagogue in Győr showing west extensions for former community offices (near), and Jewish school (left). (Sketch courtesy of the Jewish Community of Győr.)

catastrophe looming on the horizon. When the racial laws were applied in 1938, the women's group still tried to find employment for Jews who lost their jobs. In mid-May 1944 the Germans moved the city's Jews to an enclosure, in extremely crowded conditions on Győrsziget island, with almost no shelter whatever. On June 7 a horde of gendarmes entered the camp, dragged people out, and tortured them in a search for valuables. The Jews were then transferred to army barracks outside the city, together with 2,500 others brought from outlying villages.

The Jewish underground had offered Rabbi Roth a chance to escape with his family in a rescue transport negotiated by Dr. Rudolf Kastner. Roth might have been on the train that left Budapest for Switzerland on June 30, but he refused to leave his congregation. On Friday night, June 10, he organized a service for which thousands gathered under the sky to pray together. The German SS brutally interrupted. They severely beat up the rabbi and members of the Jewish council. Insatiably sadistic, they shaved the leaders' heads, and, on the rabbi's bare scalp, they burned a symbolic Star of David. The transports by train to Auschwitz began on June 11, with Rabbi Roth striding to the deportation center at the head of his community. Those of his students who reached Israel after the war remember his parting words: "It is not the place that sanctifies man, but man who sanctifies the place."

Of the more than 7,000 Jews deported from Győr and its surrounding area to Auschwitz, fewer than 700 returned—but none returned who were deported as children. The survivors renewed *kehillah* life, including Zionist activity. After the anti-Russian revolt of 1956, most Jews—including all the Orthodox people—left for Israel or America. About 100 Jews still lived in Győr in the 1990s, and of those only 20 were active in community affairs.

A heavy iron fence and gate on the corner of Kossúth Lajos utca opens to the courtyard on the western side, the main entrance to the Neolog synagogue and its symmetrical wings. Stacks of planks blocked the portal, and the yard was full of scattered building debris at the time of our first visit. The community had sold the synagogue complex to the municipality in 1969 for restoration as a school and auditorium—the Franz Liszt Music Teachers College, named for the famed Hungarian composer Franz Liszt (1811–1886), who was born in the neighborhood. Financial difficulties delayed repairs on the synagogue proper, but the southern wing, formerly the community offices, was already restored and the music college had begun to function. The northern wing—the former Jewish school—was restored the following year to additional rehearsal chambers and classrooms.

At the music school in the synagogue complex, we met Marianna Spiegel—a talented teacher of the Kodály music method. She invited us to her home, where we had an informative session with her nonagenarian father, Károly Spiegel, a former leader of Győr's *kehillah*. The discussion was deferred, however, until he had carefully written preparatory notes, after which he related post-war community history with an impressive formal dignity.

Following the deportation, Hungarians and Nazis seized and looted Jewish shops and homes. The few survivors returning to Győr after the liberation found themselves exceedingly unwelcome. Many of the Christians in the city did not hide their anti-Semitism, even toward former neighbors. The Joint Distribution Committee provided food, clothing, generous funds, and professionals to help with rehabilitation. Spiegel was active in rebuilding the community. One of his first concerns was to recover the children entrusted to Christian families for the duration. Some of the little ones did not even remember that they were Jewish. The *kehillah* opened a small orphanage, housing about 15 boys and 10 girls who had been hidden or disguised during the war. An intensive educational program preparing them for *aliyah* to Israel included agricultural training and academic studies. Spiegel mourned that one of his youngsters was killed in the 1973 Yom Kippur War. He wondered what had become of the others.

The Neolog synagogue in Győr from the east, neo-Moresque. Károly Benkó, architect, 1870. The complex included a *beit midrash* on the eastern side of the main synagogue and two large extensions on the west for school and congregational offices.

The late Károly Spiegel, nonagenarian, former *rosh hakohol* (community head). As a young man after World War I, he had wanted to study medicine. A *numerus clausus* (quota) kept him out of the University of Budapest. *"Te egy zsidó vagy,"* he was told, "You are a Jew." He was rejected again in Vienna, *"Du bist Ungar!"* "You are Hungarian!" "What was I then," he asked, wistfully, "What am I today?"

Severely vandalized *beit midrash,* used before the war as a winter prayer room.

"LET THERE BE LIGHT"

The story of the *kehillah* in Szeged is inseparable from that of its two illustrious rabbis, Rabbi Leopold Loew (1811–1875) and his son, Rabbi Immanuel Loew (1854–1944). Their combined incumbency stretched from 1850 to 1944, with only a brief hiatus between 1875 and 1878. Both were great scholars in the tradition of their forefather, the prolific Rabbi Judah Loew ben Bezalel (1525–1609), popularly—though erroneously—identified with the legend of the Golem of Prague. The two rabbis officiated over a Jewish community that grew rapidly after a late start at the end of the eighteenth century and became one of the largest and most influential in Hungary.

Szeged's strategic position on the Tisza River at the southern edge of the great Hungarian plain drew merchants and traders as early as the tenth century. At a crossroads for Adriatic and Black Sea traffic, Szeged was one of the few Hungarian cities where trade and industry developed under close cooperation between the Hungarians and the various ethnic minorities: Germans, Serbs, Dalmatians, Greeks, and non-resident Jews. Szeged exercised its royal city privilege and chose to exclude both Jews and the Roma. Jews followed a familiar pattern of coming into the city for commerce and returning home to their villages at day's end.

After the first family pioneered a move inside the city's borders in 1781 and was tolerated, others plucked up the courage to join them, organizing themselves as a regulated community in 1791. The 38 Jewish families in the 1799 census included two community workers, two silversmiths, two tailors, and a brewery owner. The others were merchants and peddlers whom the municipality still tried to exclude from the annual fairs. In the course of a decade, the city council revoked the ban on property ownership by Jews and permitted them to hold real estate within a defined area. Toleration evolved in gradual steps. From 1819 on, Jews could operate hostelries. In 1833 a Jew could, for the first time, open a large retail establishment. After 1840 they had permission to establish factories wherever suitable. In mid-century the city council removed all locality restrictions on Jewish property ownership.

Prized among the treasures of the synagogue, the bronze candelabra were cast according to biblical descriptions for the construction of the utensils in the Temple. A pair of five-branched giant candelabra light up the corners of the *bimah.* The seven-branched candelabra behind them, ornamented with semi-precious stones, was modeled after the menorah on the Arch of Titus in Rome.

The Jews of Szeged prospered, which was fortunate for them since they had to pay three sets of heavy taxes: the national Tolerance Tax, the city tax, and the community tax. The city empowered the *kehillah* in 1823 to collect all of them from its members. A generation later, Hun-gary abolished the Tolerance Tax and most Jews felt relief from the burden. In reprisal for Jewish support of Hungarian independence, the Austrians initially singled out Szeged and imposed a punitive tax, requiring the *kehillah* to supply 25,000 pairs of boots to the Austrian army.

Rabbi Leopold Loew left Pápa, where he had clashed with Orthodox members of the community and accepted the offer of a pulpit in Szeged. From 1850 to 1875 in the tolerant and progressive milieu of his new *kehillah,* Rabbi Loew was a veritable prophet of the new era in a period of rapid political, religious, and intellectual changes. He brought reform to Jewish religion in Hungary, and to Szeged in particular. One of the first to deliver sermons in Hungarian, he was in speech and writing a fervent advocate of integration and full civil rights for the Jews of Hungary. Opposing the views of Hungarian liberal Lajos Kossúth, he argued that abandonment of religion must not be a condition of Jewish liberation. His scholarly research covered such varied topics as Jewish antiquities, folklore, and the history of Hungarian Jewry. He maintained a delicate balance in favor of religious reform while remaining within the framework of rabbinical tradition. During the revolution of 1848–1849, Rabbi Loew was a chaplain in the rebel Hungarian army, where his spirited sermons inspired Jewish soldiers to fight with valor for their homeland. When the revolution failed, the Austrians held him in prison for three months. As a result of Rabbi Loew's lecture before the Hungarian Academy of Science in 1868, the medieval form of the Jews' Oath was abolished in Hungary.

The city kept a close supervision over the Jewish community. The *kehillah* had to salary a city official, with powers of intervention and veto, to attend community council meetings. In return for the abolition of this practice, the Jewish council agreed to publicize its decisions in the synagogue courtyard and to appoint trustees who would verify for city tax authorities the financial status of Jews liable for taxes. Shifting the responsibility but keeping a remote control over Jewish influx, the city authorized the *kehillah* to appraise prospective candidates for new legal residence. The city

Community Secretary László Weiss at the Ark. A decorative frame of bronze rods holds the Torah scrolls upright. The doors of the Ark are made of acacia wood brought from the banks of the Nile River. Pale lavender anemones in leaded glass form a sheltering hood over the Torah scrolls.

also delegated to the council the distasteful job of expelling interlopers.

The venerable *ḥevra kadishah* institution, originally a limited mutual benefit society, became the general charitable organization and evolved into a burial society much later. Organized in Szeged in 1787, it gained considerable economic power and was a source of benefit to the poor. It seems, however, that there was a misuse of funds by some of its Szeged officials. Rabbi Loew addressed this problem in the context of his proposed radical revision of community regulations, giving the head of the community extensive control over the *ḥevra kadishah* to prevent future dishonesty.

The women of Szeged were active in community affairs. The younger women's society, Aniye Irenu (the Poor of Our City), bought food and prepared it themselves in a free kitchen for the poor. The women of Hakhnasat Kalah provided brides' necessities. Tomkhei Aniyim (Supporters of the Poor) covered hospitalization for indigents.

Szeged Jews kept a strong bond with other Jewish communities—especially in times of stress, when they mobilized to provide support. They contributed money in 1857 for destitute Jews in Palestine; in 1862 for Jews in Belgrade; in 1865 for the Jews of Graz; in 1872 for Persia;

Function and design combine in the richly ornamented Byzantine capitals on the marble pillars of the synagogue in Szeged. The familiar acanthus leaf motif is treated in a novel manner: rich classical style above and free-flowing shapes bound by a gilded band below.

in 1881 for Russia and Constantinople, and for a Vienna institute for the deaf, mute, and blind. These donations did not displace the monthly contributions to Keren Hayesod to aid settlement in Palestine. Jewish institutions extended their support to needy Christians as well, providing shelter during the First World War to refugee orphans from Germany.

The frescoes in each of the triangular ceiling vaults carry stylized floral motifs. Each panel presents a different specific plant of the Bible, such as the oleander in this one. Verses from the daily prayers fill the broad blue overall border between rows of tiny calligraphy in ancient Hebrew script.

In the decade between 1880 to 1890, the Jewish population increased by almost a third to 4,731 persons, 5½ percent of Szeged's residents. They found diverse employment and integrated into the economy. Other than numerous professionals there were 66 clerks, 51 accountants, 10 contractors, 10 insurance agents, and 8 general agents; 22 rented estates, 5 owned large estates,

5 managed clothing shops, 4 drove wagons, 3 owned restaurants, 1 contracted household help, and another produced cheese. In trade, 71 owned small shops, 30 were peddlers, and others dealt in the following items: grain 30, lumber 20, flour 11, liquor 10, textiles 10, retail 8, rags 7, wool 5, leather 4, lime and coal 4, books 3, shoes 3, horses 2, glass and porcelain 2, sewing machines 2, and iron 1. Jews also owned the local steam mill, a brewery, and factories for processing skins, and for making bricks and rope.

In 1792 the fledgling *kehillah* applied for a permit to buy a plot for a synagogue. Refused permission, they built a rabbi's house and used it for assembly and prayer. By 1803 they received a permit to build a synagogue, although limited by Church authorities to a small size. They financed it by selling the synagogue's 230 seats. In the mid-century, the city allowed construction

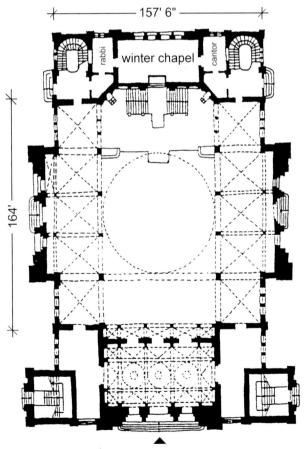

Plan of the synagogue in Szeged. Main entrance is on the west, through a triple portal into a large lobby. Ark and *bimah* are at the east wall.

283

The synagogue in Szeged, Eclectic style, Lipót Baumhorn, architect, 1903. With masterful blending of architectural styles, Baumhorn used elements such as a Baroque dome, Moorish cupolas, turrets and crenelations, splayed Romanesque portals, triple arch, and cusped windows with Gothic ribs to make a unified whole. Still owned by the *kehillah* of a few hundred Jews, the synagogue serves as a public Jewish museum since it was renovated in 1988.

of a larger synagogue on condition that it be surrounded by a fence and topped with a chimney. In the guise of a dwelling, it would not, presumably, be a source of agitation to the Christian neighbors. Architects Henrik and József Lipowsky designed the synagogue in neo-Classical style. Dedicated in 1843, it contained 400 seats for men and 260 for women in a three-sided gallery over graceful arcades.

Szeged's *kehillah* was firmly Neolog. It became a primary center of the Neolog movement around 1900, and the main office in Budapest felt its influence as an initiating and driving force. The community did not split apart because its unusual Orthodox minority chose to cooperate with the Neolog majority—out of love and respect for the Loew rabbinical family.

Although the community renovated the neo-Classical synagogue in 1879 and expanded the seating capacity, the building proved inadequate for a population that grew to nearly 6,000 as the twentieth century approached. Because they needed a synagogue, not only of much larger dimensions, but of a stature and style commensurate with their emancipation and economic status, the community announced a design competition for a new building. Among the proposals was the dramatic avant-garde Art-Nouveau design by Dezső Jakab and Marcell Komor, ultimately adopted by the *kehillah* of Subotica. The Szeged community passed over this proposal, after considerable deliberation and heated debate, in favor of the Eclectic design by Lipót Baumhorn.

THE NEOLOG SYNAGOGUE IN SZEGED

The interior is a compatible blending of Romanesque, Moorish, and Gothic elements, with lavish use of expensive materials that add to the sense of luxury and splendor. The majestic east wall of sculpted marble towers over the Ark. Semi-precious stones embellish the oversized bronze candelabra on the *bimah.* Dominant colors, from below and up to the arches and ceiling are white, blue, and gold. The profuse decorative motifs in the harmonious overall design are the product of close collaboration between Rabbi Immanuel Loew, who saw beauty in details, and exquisite execution by architect Lipót Baumhorn.

An unusual reader's desk stands below the *bimah.* Carefully chiseled, mostly of white marble, it is bounded by four rose-marble pillars with Byzantine capitals and an apron of delicately carved Moorish fretwork.

Miksa Róth, a famous and talented artist in stained glass, created the synagogue's sumptuous dome of stucco and glass that rises nearly 130 feet above the synagogue floor. Inspiration for its design came from the opening lines of Genesis (1:3), *Vayomer Elohim, "Yehi or!"* ("And God said, 'Let there be light!'").

The stained-glass windows are a fantasy of light and color depicting many universal Jewish subjects such as festivals, ritual symbols, and a profusion of biblical plants and flowers. The middle window over the entrance shows both new and old synagogue buildings. In the image of the old synagogue, a small boat symbolizes the calamitous flood of 1879 that caused havoc in Szeged and ruined or damaged many buildings. Inundating the city, the waters swirled into the old synagogue, endangering even the Ark.

The congregation commemorated the event with a concrete insert low on the facade to indicate the highwater mark:

The marble reader's stand below the *bimah.* The history of the synagogue's construction is engraved in dark marble within the Moorish portals of the upper vertical section.

In memory of the flood of many waters that rose up over all parts of our city on the night of 17 Adar, 5639 (1879). And the waters swelled to the base of the Aron Kodesh. Up to here: ———— may you come And no further.

285

Lipót Baumhorn worked closely with Szeged's Rabbi Immanuel Loew on the symbolism of the details of the synagogue dome. Twenty-four columns around the dome drum represent the hours of the day. Briar-brush flowers symbolize the earth's vegetation. The star-strewn, blue-glass dome darkens gradually to generate a sense of infinite space up to the zenith with its minute Star of David.

Flood marker. Commemorative concrete plaque inserted into the lower left corner of the facade of the old synagogue indicates the height reached by the waters during the flood of 1879.

At the age of 40, Lipót Baumhorn already had three innovative synagogues to his credit, Esztergom (1888), Rijeka (1895), and Szolnok (1898). In 1903 he completed the spectacular Szeged synagogue, the brightest jewel in the crown of 24 synagogues that he eventually built in Greater Hungary. Town authorities helped to finance construction and Christian philanthropists bought seats to distribute as charity. Rabbi Immanuel Loew, who received his father's pulpit in 1878 and remained active until 1944, was a guiding spirit in the detailed planning and design of Baumhorn's synagogue.

A versatile scholar, Rabbi Immanuel Loew edited and published his father's collected works in five volumes. Like his father, he was an eloquent speaker and published several hundred of his sermons in four volumes between 1900 and

1939. His greatest fame as a scholar derives from the monumental studies he did in the fields of talmudic and rabbinical lexicography and his extensive research in biblical flora, fauna, and minerals. During the "White Terror" of 1920 to 1921, which claimed 3,000 Jewish victims, he was imprisoned for 13 months on the accusation of having maligned President Miklós Horthy. Exploiting the time in jail, he worked assiduously, researching his opus on the botany of the Bible, *Die Flora der Juden* (Plants of the Jews). His expertise was the inspiration and the source for the extensive use of floral motifs and Jewish symbols in the synagogue decoration. Rabbi Loew served in the national parliament from 1927 as the representative of Neolog Jewry.

Jews filled positions of leadership in the civic and economic life of the city. They became financiers, managers, and trade unionists, and sent judges to the district courts. After the First World War and the short-lived counter-revolution in its wake, Szeged became the center of reactionary activity, the home base of the "White Terror" that spread throughout Hungary. Strangely enough, there was little anti-Semitic activity in Szeged itself, perhaps because many of Szeged's Jews supported the rightist government. The number of Jewish students in the university rose despite the *numerus clausus*. Cross-religious activity was at a high, with visiting clergy preaching in the synagogue and rabbis invited to sermonize in the cathedral. In 1932 there was a brief spurt of Zionist activity—in the Hashomer Hatzair, WIZO, and Hechalutz movements. Reduced in part by conversion and a low birth rate, the *kehillah* declined by about 40 percent between the wars to a low of 4,161 in 1941.

At the start of the anti-Jewish barbarity before the Second World War, a sympathetic

Interior of the synagogue. The cusped arch is repeated over the *Aron Kodesh* and side panels under a four-tiered crown-canopy. Two-story side panels frame the organ, above, and draw the eye to the inscription, *V'ahavta l'rei'akha kamokha* ("Love thy neighbor as thyself"; Lev. 19:18) on the proscenium arch. Hebrew and Hungarian words alternate to hint at Jewish integration into Hungarian society.

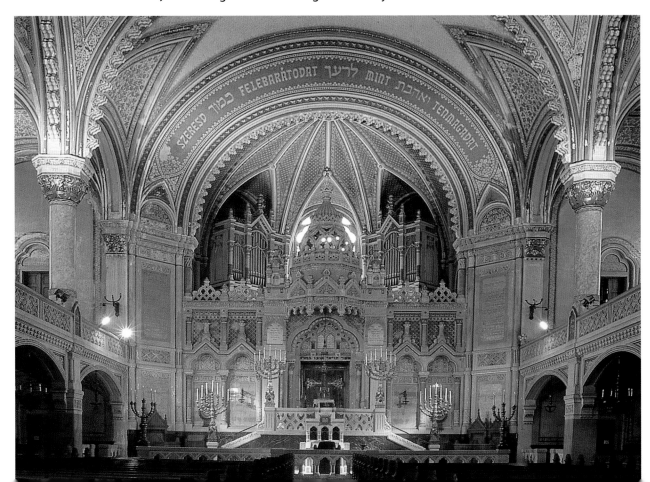

police chief quietly notified community heads in advance of impending actions and tried to help circumvent them. In May 1944 the Jews of Szeged were herded into a ghetto set up around the synagogue square. Szeged's Bishop Endre Hamvas tried to enlist Church authorities in Budapest to help rescue Jews. Cardinal Serédy, head of the Catholic Church in Hungary, tried in vain to mobilize Hungarian clergy for immediate rescue work, but he succeeded only in preventing the expulsion of 200 baptized Jews.

The Germans were insatiable. Under their orders, the police dragged Jewish women of Szeged through the streets from the ghetto to the prison, where selected midwives stripped them and systematically searched their bodies for hidden jewels. Ninety-year-old Rabbi Immanuel Loew was marched off with others in forced labor to work in the ghetto brick factory. In June 1944 the troops liquidated the ghetto and loaded the Jews onto Auschwitz-bound trains. The transport stopped briefly in Budapest, where alert Jewish workers smuggled Rabbi Loew off the train and got him to the ghetto hospital. He died there after a brief respite.

After the war, people came out of bunkers and hiding places and some returned from the death camps. The Joint Distribution Committee was able to help the 2,000 Jews of the Szeged area to re-establish the community. They reclaimed the synagogue from storeroom to community use and restored the old age home. The orphanage absorbed 400 new orphans from Budapest. By the early 1990s the diminished community numbered only a few hundred. It uses the *bet midrash* for ritual and keeps the synagogue open as a museum.

On a festive day in September 1989, the community and hundreds of guests from Budapest and elsewhere rededicated the synagogue, newly renovated with the help of a large donation from a former resident. Standing majestically on Guttenburg utca in the center of a large city lot, the synagogue is a visual symphony of eclectic architectural elements. The profusion of towers and delicate window traceries lend a festive character to the facade, the lower elevations of which are hardly visible behind the ground plantings of mature yews and pyramid oaks.

Architectural highlights of the Eclectic
synagogue in Szeged.

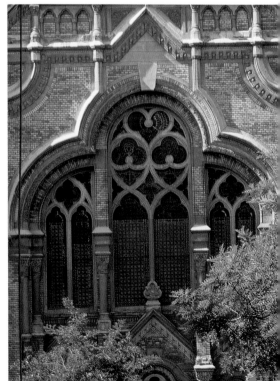

A Gallery of Women

Women, more frequently than men, are the last resident Jews in the relatively few hinterland towns in central Europe where any Jews remain at all. Widowed *Shoah* survivors for the most part, each has adjusted individually to the reality she faces. After the struggle to make a living, keeping a semblance of Jewishness in her life is usually next in importance. By default such women care for their local synagogues, sometimes in disregard of formal ownership if the building has passed to other hands. Without budgets and with few, if any, volunteers to help, they do what they can for the sake of the past and their sense of suitability. The role of women as caretakers, participants, and leaders has a venerable origin that extends back to Temple and early post-Exilic days.

The care and embellishment of the synagogue by women is an ancient tradition. Inscriptions from towns and cities of Asia Minor in post-biblical times proclaim many women by name as contributors to local synagogues. Citing the titles held by women, in a comprehensive study, *Women Leaders in the Ancient Synagogue,* Bernadette Brooten analyzes numerous inscriptions in detail. In Phocaea, Asia Minor, a woman named Tation contributed a synagogue hall and a wall around the courtyard. Her reward: a gold crown and a synagogue seat of honor among the elders. At Hamman Lif in North Africa, Juliana financed a beautiful mosaic floor, which is duly recorded in the mosaic. Different titles for a man and his wife on a Malta inscription suggest that the woman earned the title on her own merits. Brooten reviews a broad spectrum of women—as leaders and elders, as "mother" or even "father," or commonly, as *archisynagogus,* head of the congregation. She suggests that these woman leaders gave spiritual guidance, perhaps taught occasionally, read from the scriptures if no man was available, carried financial responsibilities, and represented the community to the local authorities.

Through contact with the non-Jewish world and its high rate of female participation in public and religious life, Diaspora Jews were receptively inclined to the phenomenon. Those Jewish communities that accepted many proselytes tended most frequently to elevate women to leadership positions. In *The Ancient Synagogue,* Lee I. Levine observes that the position of women as benefactors and synagogue officials was most pervasive in the Roman Diaspora. Of over a hundred donor's names on dedicatory inscriptions, up to 30 percent of them are believed to be those of women.

We salute a few of the women we met in Hungary.

Budapest

We were fortunate to meet *Eshet Ḥayil* (woman of valor) Anikó Gazda and to review with her our itinerary in Hungary. Though she lived in Budapest, she belongs to all of Jewish Hungary. Architect and historian, Anikó was the chief author of the comprehensive survey of synagogues in Hungary, *Magyarországi zsinagógák,* published in 1989, less than a year before her untimely death. She and her teenaged daughter shared a small flat in Budapest with her mother in an old apartment building overlooking the Danube. The narrow, crowded living room housed a large architect's drawing board and dozens of files filled with photos and documents about synagogues. Due to a serious illness, Anikó was under unremitting pressure and probably in physical discomfort. She had toiled on her book for more than a decade, traveling all over the country to photograph synagogues, collecting data from archives, and trying to obtain funding. Her collaboration with the other authors and with the editor, while she battled her illness privately, involved frequent conflict and frustration. She was a competent and devoted scholar. The book that she achieved is a fitting monument to her memory.

Karcag

Like widows of other times and places of whom we have written (such as eighteenth-century Rachel Guttman of Bardejov and Frumet Wolf of early nineteenth-century Eisenstadt) Mrs. Rosinger of Karcag capably manages a substantial business and holds responsibility for her erstwhile community's synagogue. Mrs. Rosinger lives up to her reputation as a tough woman. A short, stocky person of severe demeanor, she runs a large lumberyard, probably the only one in the region of

The late Anikó Gazda, architect and researcher on synagogues in Hungary.

Mrs. Rosinger and her son at the Karcag synagogue.

the central plain city of Karcag. She deals with the suppliers, taking deliveries with the help of a small staff. Contractors and do-it-yourselfers who buy lumber and building supplies respect her for fairness in business, but they know she gives nothing away as she keeps track of every transaction detail.

THE SYNAGOGUE IN KARCAG

Built in 1899, the Karcag synagogue is an imposing two-story structure with roofline crenelation and an upper row of modified horseshoe-arched windows. On entry we were impressed by the generous three-part gallery and the imposing paneled Ark, hooded by a giant, eight-lobed crown. High crenelations on the walls catch the eye, and Stars of David are plentiful. Like other Ashkenazic synagogues in Hungary, this one has a central *bimah,* three steps above the floor and bounded by an airy metal screen.

The same toughness showed up in the way she received us. With her son who helps in the business, his wife, and their son, Mrs. Rosinger's family is now one of only two Jewish families in a town where Jews numbered 1,077 in 1910—and 800 before the *Shoah.* The synagogue is at their sole disposition and Mrs. Rosinger guards it zealously. Not satisfied that Rabbi József Schweitzer, head of the Budapest Rabbinical Seminary, had telephoned her to announce our impending arrival, she demanded to see our credentials. She carefully scrutinized the letters of introduction we produced and—after some demurral—she reluctantly conceded we were the researchers we claimed to be and were entitled to cooperation. At last she allowed us to see and enter the synagogue.

Seldom used now, the synagogue had stones and broken glass scattered on floor and benches. Distraught, Mrs. Rosinger explained that she had started to prepare the synagogue for family and guests, due to arrive from Budapest for her grandson's Bar Mitzvah. Meanwhile, local hooligans had stoned the windows. "It was bad enough that the price for a rabbi from Budapest for the Bar Mitzvah was prohibitive. And now this mess. This is the second time this week the *goyim* broke the windows. The struggle never ends," she complained bitterly.

Interior of the synagogue in Karcag. Romantic style, 1899. Note the unusual crown above the Ark.

Kunszentmárton

Another woman who struggled single-handedly for her synagogue was Dr. Ágnes Nádas, a retired gynecologist and the only Jew in Kunszentmárton. From the moment of our first meeting with her, we connected as kindred spirits. As a young woman, Ágnes had joined the Zionist youth of Hashomer Hatzair, and began to train at the Hechalutz training farm near Budapest. Family opposition to Zionism diverted her from the movement to the study of medicine, and she

Dr. Ágnes Nádas at her home in Kunszentmárton.

The synagogue in Kunszentmárton. Secessionist style, 1912.

THE SYNAGOGUE IN KUNSZENTMÁRTON
This synagogue, completed in 1912, is an outstanding expression of the Secessionist style, incorporating dramatic design lines, ceramic inserts, and other Hungarian folk elements. The striking facade features two towers that rise in paired stages to culminate in conical domes and Stars of David. Secessionist decorative elements find a place in the interior, where architect Josef Doborsky used burnt brick flower ornaments from a local ceramics factory, especially over the Ark. The circular stained-glass windows on the north, south, and west facades featured stylized art nouveau Stars of David. Spiral stairways in the corner towers led to a three-sided gallery, the entire space between its branches now covered by a wooden floor for storage. Under a pyramidal skylight for daytime illumination from above, the architect designed a central *bimah*. It was removed when the synagogue was taken to be used as a storeroom.

soon lost contact with friends who left for Palestine. A stormy intermarriage ended with a son, Arpi, divorce, and Arpi's recent suicide at age 22. Ágnes' aged mother came to live with her, and Ágnes initiated an effort to promote restoration of the Kunszentmárton synagogue. "Our town of 12,000 has no cultural hall," she said. "It could use such a fine building."

The following year, we found Ágnes frustrated at the lack of interest in the synagogue restoration project and holding a file full of unanswered letters to the authorities. The municipality had bought the synagogue cheaply from the Jewish leadership in Budapest, but had little money for renovation. Roof repair already begun had been halted because of termites. As we departed, she smiled wistfully in reply to our suggestion that she visit Israel soon. "Not now," she confided, "perhaps later, when I am alone again." We saw Ágnes next a year later, after her mother had died. In the afternoon of Rosh Hashanah we walked with her along the grassy banks of the Kőrös river, where Jews used to go for the *Tashlikh* ceremony. When in parting we gave her Anikó Gazda's book on synagogues in Hungary, she welcomed the suggestion that she might translate part of it for us. After a while she sent us the chapter on Kunszentmárton in English.

Ágnes never did visit Israel. Loneliness overwhelmed her. Her last letter to us ended with a message about the records she was leaving: mementos of her days in Hashomer Hatzair, correspondence with friends, and a few political articles she had written. "These papers mirror the way for a Hungarian girl who had ideals and sentimental conceptions—from Socialism to Zionism, to Communism and internationalism and came in the end to 'nihil.'" Ten days later Ágnes was buried in the Jewish cemetery in Orosháza, southeast of Kunszentmárton.

Bonyhád

After World War II, 170 survivors—mainly from the labor camps—returned to the town of Bonyhád, about 93 miles south of Budapest. Among them was Ignác Warum, a leader of the Orthodox faction of his community. He and a few other returnees gathered the damaged Torah scrolls that were strewn on the synagogue floor and buried them—in observance of the custom—in the cemetery. Today his widow lives in their little cottage on Zsidó-köz (Jews' Alley). She recalls with bitterness that soon after the Orthodox synagogue had been sequestered for a storeroom, her husband had pleaded in vain with the Communist authorities to leave the Hebrew inscription on the facade. Nothing Jewish remains in the Orthodox synagogue building.

The Baroque Ark in the Neolog synagogue in Bonyhád and its sumptuous baldachin.

But the Neolog synagogue—also adapted for storeroom use—still shows vestiges of its Jewish origin with style and beauty.

Mrs. Warum still conducts her husband's glass shop on the main square. She perseveres in her piety and kosher diet, obtaining kosher meat from Budapest once a month. The few other widows who survived have married gentiles, so Mrs. Warum considers herself the only real Jew in town. Her son left for Chicago in 1963 and came to visit only once since then. In wistful optimism,

THE NEOLOG SYNAGOGUE IN BONYHÁD
This solidly built structure is a fine example of the Zopf style that appeared between the Baroque and Classical periods in Magyar architecture. Under a hip roof the facade has prominent pilasters and an elaborate double portal of stone on the south side. A stucco *Aron Kodesh* about 23 feet high towers over the dusty interior, flanked by Ionic pillars and pilasters. Over the Ark, a blue stucco baldachin—resplendent with gold fringe, drawstrings, and tassels—is reminiscent of draperies in opulent homes. The ornate Baroque style is typical of art by itinerant court artisans permitted by noblemen to work for *Schutzjuden,* their protected Jews. Strikingly similar baldachins appear above the Arks of the synagogues in nearby Baja and in Apostag, 50 miles up the Danube.

Renovations in 1896 included a commodious two-story annex on the west for an elegant gallery staircase. Two slender wooden posts carry the U-shaped women's gallery, bounded by a wooden balustrade and a decorative metal grille. Wide arches over the gallery support the deeply vaulted ceiling, where vestiges of Baroque floral designs bleed through the thin storeroom whitewash. The central square *bimah* is bounded by four pillars that divide the ceiling into nine bays in the manner of the stone synagogues in Poland in the sixteenth and seventeenth centuries.

Mrs. Warum at her cottage in Bonyhád.

she still hopes that one day he will send her a ticket to America, for her to join him there.

Nagykőrös

Most *Shoah* survivors fled their childhood haunts as soon as they could after they were liberated. György Feldmájer chose to start again in Nagykőrös to assert a continuing Jewish presence in his native town. He married Edit Goldstein—deported from Miskolc, but transferred from Auschwitz to forced labor in a bomb factory—and opened a law office. Before the war more than 500 Jews had lived in Nagykőrös, which was prominent in the food industry for local and export markets. Few other survivors returned, and the diminutive community was augmented at first with families from Budapest escaping post-war famine conditions in the capital. Jewish numbers dwindled rapidly, but the Feldmájers adamantly remained. They and their three children, Sándor, Livia, and Péter, constituted an exemplary Jewish family, one of the very few in town.

Four decades later we enjoyed an Erev Shabbat with the family. Daughter Livia, her husband, Meshullam Alba, and their two teenagers shared a home with the widowed Mrs. Feldmájer. As usual on Fridays, Edit baked ḥallot for the festive meal. Péter—later a president of the Federation of Jewish Communities in Hungary—and his family joined them as they regularly do. Either Péter or Meshullam chants the *kiddush* and blesses the ḥallot, and all sing familiar *zmirot* Shabbat (Sabbath hymns) in demonstrative diligence of an informed Jewish life despite the isolation. On holidays Sándor and his family come from Budapest to celebrate with the others.

Edit Feldmájer and her son Péter prepare for Erev Shabbat. Edit died on the 4th day of Shevat, 5760, January 11, 2000.

Livia Feldmájer Albané and her brother Péter Feldmájer display a ḥuppah canopy at the synagogue in Nagykőrös.

The Feldmájer and Alba children learned Jewish history and values at home from their parents and grandmother. In summer they met other Jewish children at a national camp near Szarvas. Finding a Jewish mate for her children was a serious concern to Edit years ago, when such gatherings were illegal in Communist Hungary. She sent Livia to attend a Jewish camp in

THE SYNAGOGUE IN NAGYKŐRÖS
Replacing an older building that collapsed in a 1911 earthquake, the Nagykőrös synagogue was dedicated in 1925. Almost fortress-like, the eclectic western facade has an imposing high central portion and two lower, crenelated towers; however, the tri-partite division and the stalactite-like ornamentation of the gallery portals soften the harsh, cubical shape. Inside, Livia and Péter pulled out a rare treasure from a storeroom to show us: a long unused ḥuppah (wedding canopy) embroidered with flowers and *Magen David.*

Yugoslavia, and—indeed—that is where Livia met Meshullam. The grandchildren had expanded opportunities; they toured and attended workshops in Israel.

With her children grown, Livia continues her legal practice and keeps a lively interest in politics, especially anything related to Jewish matters. She was resourcefully collecting information on the Jewish victims of the *Shoah* in Hungary: numbers, names, and records of confiscated property. The Feldmájer clan maintains the synagogue and occasionally arranges family and festival services with guests from the capital.

Jánoshalma

A short wisp of a woman and agile despite her advanced years, Mrs. Imre Samos is the widow of the last congregation head in Jánoshalma. She helps visitors locate the graves of relatives in a cemetery she herself clears of weeds. Long in advance, each year she plans the annual memorial ceremony for the town's Jewish martyrs. Some of the scattered survivors reassemble in the synagogue courtyard and later in the cemetery. They exchange reminiscences, note with restrained sorrow the recently deceased, and part again for another year. For many of them, the annual gatherings are a high point in their lonely lives.

Mrs. Samos, our hostess in the synagogue in Jánoshalma.

Mrs. Samos eagerly admitted us to the Jánoshalma synagogue, a one-story rural structure where, close to the ceiling, a three-part balcony perches courageously on four thin wooden posts. Pointing to the wide bookcase near the door that bulged with frayed prayer books, Talmud volumes, and other sacred texts, she beseeched us to take as many of them as we

wished. "There is no one here to read them now." She apologized for the dust on the furniture and convinced us to accept an old patched and faded *parokhet* (Ark curtain) and a hollow metal candlestick covered with wax. The objects later found places of honor in Kehillat Shalvah of the Conservative movement in Safed, Israel.

The tiny *ezrat nashim* (women's gallery) in Jánoshalma provoked attention to an issue that has occupied worshippers and scholars for centuries. There could never have been many full-skirted women to climb the narrow steps to that cramped gallery; space for them below was certainly ample. How traditional and how obligatory was the synagogue segregation of women? Shmuel Safrai, in an innovative article "Was There a Women's Gallery in the Synagogues of *Eretz Yisrael*," explored the question in depth. He found that, except for the Simḥat Beit haSho'eivah (the Water Drawing) festival of Ḥol hamoed Sukkot, there was a lack of references to a separate women's section in biblical and early post-biblical sources.

The first century C.E. earliest mention of *ezrat nashim* occurs in reference to the Herodian Temple and designates the women's court that

Interior of the synagogue in Jánoshalma. Classicist style, 1850; view to the gallery.

served both men and women all year long. Associating the ancient term with the women's section in synagogues since the Middle Ages has led to the erroneous perception that worshippers in the Temple were segregated by sex. However, it was only on the Simḥat Beit haSho'eivah holiday that women watched the festivities from a balcony overlooking the court. On this occasion, the revelry included paganistic aspects: libations of wine and water, tossing of lighted torches, and exhibition dancing by prominent men. The motive for that brief, temporary segregation—who knows?—may have been to free floor space for the dancing, to permit the women a better view of the proceedings, or, as is commonly supposed, to prevent the merriment from degenerating into licentiousness. In any event, segregation was the exception rather than the rule.

Archaeological remains show no evidence for the existence of a separate gallery or section for women in synagogues built before the seventh century. Susan Grossman explained in *Daughters of the King* how the prejudice of early Christian sources—that contact between the sexes led to sin—permeated Jewish thinking. The attitudes of Christianity and particularly of Islam at the time of its meteoric, forceful expansion, caused their influence on Jewish practice to be well-nigh inevitable. Pervasive Christian and Moslem models swayed Jewish intersex convention as much as they shaped synagogue architecture and art. The consequent heightened Jewish sensitivity to *yetzer hara* (evil inclination)—the untamed natural, especially sexual, passions—and the image of the annual few-nights' assignment of women to the Temple balcony overshadowed the women's previous active role in ritual.

Synagogue separation of the sexes came into practice between the seventh and the eleventh centuries. Only later synagogues, like those in Fostat, medieval Cairo, included a balcony for the women. Early European synagogues that we saw—the Altneuschul in Prague (1266), the synagogues in Sopron, Hungary (ca. 1350), and in Strážnice, Moravia (seventeenth century or earlier)—were originally built without designated sections for the women. Structural additions behind slotted partitions were added for that purpose at a later period.

Abandoning segregation of women to special galleries, modern Conservative and Reform congregations practice mixed, egalitarian arrangements that nourish family togetherness. In doing so, they renew an ancient, authentically Jewish tradition, eminently suited to contemporary life and mores.

The Italian Synagogue Through the Ages

Noemi Cassuto

Good taste, delicacy, and a sense of "nothing in excess" are intrinsic to the design and ornamentation that the Jews of Italy invested in their synagogues. The few synagogues that still feature their original décor show these qualities to an astonishing degree. The majesty of *Heikhal* and *tevah,* the ornamented and painted ceilings and the sparkling chandeliers, the fine carpentry and carving of the cherry or walnut benches, and the play of colors—all reflect the influence of the rich and artistic Italian surroundings and echo what is best from the church design traditions of their periods.

Italy merits attention as the one country in Europe that has had uninterrupted Jewish settlement from pre-exilic times. Few of the hundreds of synagogues built there have survived, however. As witnessed by documents and inscriptions from the earlier centuries of the Common Era, no fewer than 13 synagogues in Rome bore famous historical names: Augustus, Herod the Great, and King Agrippa I. Some had the names of the congregants' countries of origin, and it is likely that there were many others. No information remains about the physical appearance of these synagogues, with the exception of the first-

Carved and painted Renaissance *tevah* from Chieri, carefully refurbished and installed in the lower floor of the synagogue of Turin.

century synagogue in Ostia. Archeological findings on the site suggest that it was similar in form to the basilica-style synagogues found in the contemporary Galilee, commonly with a nave and two aisles, divided by columns. The Ostia synagogue was remodeled in the fourth century. The northern stoa, or colonnade, was closed in on the west side to create an aedicula, or niche, for storing the Torah scrolls, previously carried to the synagogue whenever they were to be read. At the west end, there was a raised *tevah* with room for a table or lectern. The *Heikhal* was placed at the east end and thereby followed the bipolar layout as in Sardis, Asia Minor, and in Gush Ḥalav of the Lower Galilee.

As depicted in the decorations on gilded chalice bases found in the Roman catacombs, the *Heikhal* seems to have been an aedicula between two pillars with classical capitals supporting a triangular pediment. The *Heikhal* is shown open, the *parokhet* pushed aside and the Torah scrolls lie on shelves, edges to the viewer. There is a Byzantine-era synagogue of the fourth to sixth centuries at the "way-station" in Bova Marina, near Reggio di Calabria. This is a basilica-style building with a mosaic floor that resembles the Byzantine synagogues of Galilee in every way. These two are the only ancient Italian synagogues that have been revealed.

There is no known structural or architectural evidence of synagogues from the end of the Classical period through the thirteenth century. Until the expulsion from Spain and southern Italy at the end of the fifteenth century, most Italian Jews lived in Rome and the south, including Sicily. Almost every small town of southern Italy and Sicily has a street named "della Sinagoga," "della Scuola," "Judecca," or something that otherwise refers to the existence of Jews, even though there have been no Jews present since the late fifteenth or early sixteenth century. In Trani, Apulia, two surviving synagogues were converted into churches. One of them, Santa Maria Scuola Nuova, is long and narrow, 49 by 21 feet, with a 36-foot-high barrel vault and what may have been a slightly raised women's gallery at the western end. This was typical of Gothic synagogues throughout Europe, such as the Pinkas synagogue in Prague. The *Scuola Nuova* had a Gothic *Heikhal* area reached by seven steps at the eastern end. The *Heikhal* had a central column that formed two separate arched openings.

The other synagogue/church, Sant Anna, evidently drew its architectural inspiration from the Mediterranean basin. The main hall—almost square, 38 by 40 feet, and Byzantine in style—was enclosed by four huge arches that supported a 26-foot-high dome. In the western arch, there was a semicircular niche covered by a half-dome that may have held the *tevah* and reader's desk. The *Heikhal* may have stood at the east end under the round window. If this interpretation of the design of Sant Anna is correct, it reveals an early bipolar synagogue—a harbinger of later developments.

At the end of the fifteenth and start of the sixteenth century, the Jews were expelled from Sicily and the Kingdom of Naples, then under Spanish control. Some of them migrated to North Africa or Ottoman lands, and others to northern Italy. It was not long before the first

Floor plan of thirteenth-century synagogue in Trani, converted in the sixteenth century to a church, *Sant Anna Scuola Nova.* (Courtesy of David Cassuto.)

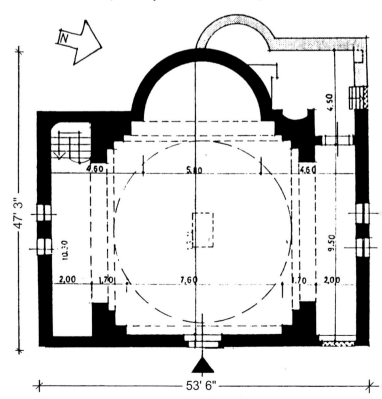

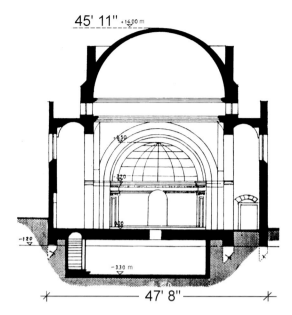

Section of thirteenth-century synagogue Sant Anna in Trani. (Courtesy of David Cassuto.)

ghettos in history appeared—in Venice in 1516, in Rome in 1555 and in Piedmont in the 1720s. Later synagogues were accordingly inside the ghettos.

Ghetto synagogues were influenced by two opposing tendencies. The first was the artistic and architectural inspiration of the nearby churches, whose designers were also responsible for the plans and details of the synagogues. The second was the desire to restrain Christian influences and to create a unique synagogue architecture that would distinguish Jewish houses of prayer. In any event, the Jews of Italy seem to have been so thoroughly involved in the artistic milieu that surrounded them that the newly arrived Jews from the Iberian peninsula and Ashkenazic lands left only a feeble imprint on synagogue design in Italy.

On the inside, Italian synagogues of this period were elegant Renaissance and Baroque salons, resembling the reception rooms of the *palazzi* of the nobility. Externally, however, the synagogues were simple severe structures because of local restrictions and the Jewish reluctance to attract attention in their alien surroundings. The layout of the interior, but not the ornamentation, may have been influenced by

Venice, Scuola Grande Tedesca, 1528. View of the *Heikhal* on the short east wall, as seen through the pillars of the *tevah* on the opposite short west wall, creating a bipolar long axis. (Photo by Graziano Arici.)

Jewish immigrants from other countries. In both Venice and Rome, Iberian Jews built bipolar synagogues, featuring an apse, or a separate elevated space in the rear, comparable to the stage of a theater, extending into the square main sanctuary. Nevertheless, it is hard to say whether this design—*tevah* at the western end, *Heikhal* on the eastern wall—resulted from Italian influence as seen in Ostia and Trani, or was brought by Jews from the Iberian peninsula. One such example is the small Isaac ben Ephraim Mehab synagogue in Cordoba, dating from 1314. The bipolar layout could, perhaps, derive from an ancient origin in *Eretz Yisrael.*

A *bimah* at the rear of the synagogue is a feature of North African synagogues also, although without the special apse. Moreover, the apse in the Cordoba synagogue is tiny. It seems plausible that had the *tevah* been located at the rear, it would not have been set into such a shallow niche. This suggests that a *bimah* recessed into its own apse could be a hallmark of Italian synagogue design. Four of the five synagogues in Venice have such a layout. The Venice synagogue that did not have a *bimah* recessed into an apse was the sixteenth-century Great Ashkenazic Synagogue, Scuola Grande Tedesca, where the *tevah* was originally in the center and was moved to the rear in the eighteenth century.

The bipolar design dominated synagogue architecture in most parts of Italy, except for Piedmont. This arrangement can be seen all across the northeastern and central portion of the peninsula in Venice, Conegliano and Vittorio Veneto, and in Pesaro, Ancona, Senigallia, and Rome, respectively. Here the *Heikhal* and *tevah* are located opposite each other on the short east and west walls. A variation on this design occurs in the Spanish and Italian synagogues in Padua, in the Scuola Talmud Torah in Venice, in the Scuola Norzi, in Mantua, and elsewhere. In these buildings, an elongated rectangular design has the *Heikhal* and *tevah* located opposite each other in the center of the two long walls, so they are relatively close together, creating a "magic" focus in the center.

Almost all the Holy Arks of the Renaissance and Baroque periods in Italy adopt the same

Padua, Spanish synagogue, 1617. Photographed in the 1950s before the transfer of the furnishings to Heikhal Shlomo, Seat of the Chief Rabbinate, Jerusalem. *Tevah* and *Heikhal* stand opposite each other in the center of long east and west walls respectively, in a bipolar, short axial arrangement. (Courtesy of U. Naḥon Museum of Italian Jewish Art.)

solution. They may be made of marble or of wood, but the style is identical, generally with upper and lower sections. In the lower, pedestal section, two small doors provide access to a closet for storing prayer books or worn holy texts. The upper section contains the two main doors of the *Heikhal,* usually ornamented inside and out. Flanking the Ark are columns that may be grooved, helical, or smooth. Occasionally, a grapevine is entwined around them, recalling the golden vine that—according to the Talmud—ornamented the columns and roof at the entrance to the Temple in Jerusalem. The columns are crowned by capitals, usually Corinthian, and support an architrave with a cornice or tympanum. This last is complete or truncated, triangular or arched, carrying a round medallion atop the cornice with additional ornamentation, usually representing the Tablets of the Law and topped by yet another small tympanum.

On the Adriatic coast, in Ancona, Pesaro, and Urbino, the *Heikhal* is adorned with a substantial dome. Surprisingly, similar domes were found on the two Holy Arks in Livorno on the western coast of Italy. One of them is now located in the Eliyahu Hanavi Synagogue in the Jewish Quarter of the Old City of Jerusalem. These Arks on west and east coasts suggest both Iberian and Levantine origins. It also may be that the Adriatic coast synagogues were influenced by the appearance of the Dome of the Rock in Jerusalem, which Jewish travelers adopted to represent the image of the Temple. Domes were, after all, a common architectural device in the Byzantine world. The Adriatic Arks have double doors, inner and outer, to create a double barrier between the Torah scrolls and the worshippers as required by halakhah. The idea may have been to obviate the need for a *parokhet.* With the trend to increasingly ornate doors, the artists considered it a sorry loss of exposure to conceal them behind curtains.

The Jewish communities commissioned famous architects to design *Heikhal* and *tevah* and even the entire synagogue. It seems that in Venice they employed Andrea Brustolon, Alessandro Ternignon, Antonio Gaspari, and the greatest Venetian architect of the seventeenth

Domed *Heikhal* in the synagogue of Urbino, built originally in 1633.

century, Baldassare Longhena. In Rome they employed Girolamo Rainaldi and later, Giuseppe Valadie. The communities in Piedmont may have employed the services of Benedetto Alfieri, architect to the royal house of Savoy.

The *bimot* of the bipolar synagogues were also objects of deliberate attention. At first, they were simply raised platforms in the rear of the synagogue, reached by two ramps—as in the Scuola Tempio in Rome and the Scuola Italiana in Senigallia. Later they were roofed over, as in the Italian Synagogue in Pesaro and the Ashkenazic Synagogue in Gorizia. In time, the posterior *tevah* gained a spatial importance of its own through the addition of an apse at the end of the synagogue. Its floor was raised about six feet above that of the main hall, almost like a stage in a theater.

The *matroneo* (women's gallery) ran around the synagogue, usually along three sides or in a complete oval, reminiscent of a theater loggia—as in Gorizia, the Sephardic and Ashkenazic synagogues in Venice, and the old synagogue in Trieste. The galleries did not always protrude into the interior space. Sometimes they were concealed behind latticed screens, doubling as wall ornaments, as in the Scuola Canton in Venice and the synagogue in Casale Monferrato. In bipolar synagogues the congregation sat in facing sections, oriented toward the central "axis" running from the *Heikhal* to the *tevah*. This central space was open and was used for processions between the two major elements.

In many synagogues the *tevah* was at the rear, but not attached to the rear wall. The smaller the space, the more feasible it was to attach the *tevah* to the western wall or recess it into an apse. Sometimes it was close to the center of the sanctuary, not as a matter of principle but merely to improve the acoustics. A large sanctuary needs a *tevah* from which the cantor can be heard. Such a central location is found in Pitigliano, Livorno, and Ferrara. This was the standard synagogue layout in most countries until the late nineteenth century.

The Sephardic synagogue in Pesaro, built in 1642, is an impressive example of the Baroque in Jewish architecture. From *Heikhal* to *tevah* and the superb stucco ceiling connecting the two poles, the unique art of this synagogue resembles an exquisitely decorated jewel box where every detail is fully justified. The *Heikhal* departs from familiar patterns and resembles a gigantic crown beneath which and in whose shadow stands the Ark itself. In this synagogue the crown can be understood as a representation of the dome typical to Holy Arks of the region.

Despite the last example, Jewish Baroque was different from its Christian counterpart, which aspired to create an illusion of the infinite, the mysterious, and the unattainable. Although Jewish Baroque was an excellent artistic imitation of the Christian model, it lacked the model's characteristic religious commitment. On the contrary, the material means of the synagogues were not intended to achieve the infinite. That goal

Resplendent *Heikhal* in the Spanish synagogue of Pesaro, late sixteenth century. Repoussé gilded doors stand under an elaborate gilded crown. (Courtesy of U. Naḥon Museum of Italian Jewish Art.)

was attainable exclusively through prayer and meditation.

The Piedmont region, close to Provence in southeastern France and to southern Germany, gives evidence of minor influences from both neighboring locales in its synagogue art. Because Piedmontese Jews were not relegated to ghettos until the 1720s and 1730s, these synagogues are particularly elaborate—the zenith of the Rococo. The *Heikhalot* resemble those already described in principle, but are more richly ornamented. The French influence is seen in the abundance of rocaille, shells, and acanthus leaves on the fluted columns.

One feature dominates all these Piedmont synagogues: their splendid central *tevot*. The

Ashkenazic influence here prevented the bipolar design from taking root. Instead, the *tevah* became a central element, as was the case in Carmagnola, Chieri, Cherasco, Mondovì, and in the oldest version of the synagogue in Casale Monferrato. The *tevah* base is octagonal, surmounted by a parapet with decorated panels on six sides, while two sides are open to allow access. Helical or straight columns affixed to the parapet rise from each vertex of the octagon and support Corinthian capitals surmounted by fantastic openwork architraves, friezes, and tympanum. All this forms an airy canopy, surmounted by a huge Torah crown. Other than the immense difference in scale, the early Piedmont *tevot* are probably influenced by Bernini's giant baldachin over the high altar in St. Peter's in Rome. In these synagogues the "magic" open center that was the hallmark of the bipolar synagogues vanishes, to be replaced by the *tevah* itself. Similar synagogues are found in the adjacent districts of Germany, especially the south, as in Ansbach.

The iconography in these Piedmontese synagogues is particularly interesting. Much space is devoted to ornaments that allude to the Holy Temple, its vessels, and other sanctified objects: the Temple itself, the vial that held the Manna, the Tablets of the Law, Aaron's staff, the golden incense altar, and the Shewbread table. They occur on a *Heikhal* from Saluzzo (now in the Old City of Jerusalem) that antedates the ghetto of 1734, where they are pictured on the inside of the Ark doors. The *Heikhalot* of Cuneo and Asti have a similar iconography.

The Asti synagogue dates from the Napoleonic era. During a major renovation in 1889, in keeping with the times, the *tevah* was moved from a central, four-pillar position to a location in front of the *Heikhal,* and the benches were all arranged frontally. The central *tevah* area, now covered by benches, is still marked by the four widely spread pillars that support a central dome. Such an architectural solution with four central pillars and a ceiling space divided into nine bays was common in Poland in the seventeenth and eighteenth centuries and was also used in Hungary—as in Bonyhád and Mád—or Slovakia, in Bardejov. In the latter synagogues the four central pillars are placed closely together. It seems that the exchange of information among Jewish

Pulpit in the neo-Moresque synagogue of Florence, 1882.

communities that was probably a by-product of Napoleon's campaigns led to mutual influence among such remote Jewish congregations.

The synagogues of the post-ghetto period, those dating from after the unification of Italy in the late nineteenth century, certainly reflected the spirit of the times. In this period the Jews got a taste of liberty and could participate in the cultural, economic, and social life of the country. Now, they built grandiose synagogues, almost cathedrals. No longer were these structures crowded with worshippers as in the ghetto. They functioned more as a symbol of Judaism, as institutional edifices.

During this period of architectural eclecticism across Europe, and especially in Italy, many old ghetto synagogues were pulled down and new ones built. It was an era in which architects drew on every style for inspiration. There were neo-Classical synagogues like the Mole Antonelliana in Turin, neo-Moresque in Florence and Vercelli, neo-Gothic in Alessandria, neo-Egyptian or neo-Babylonian in Rome, and neo-Romanesque in Trieste. These are massive structures, often frontally oriented with an elongated floor plan. The structural principle is frequently Byzantine, with four large arches supporting a central drum, topped by a dome. The facade usually sports a central rose window and two lateral spires. The largest and most famous of these, the Mole Antonelliana, never became a synagogue. Having planned a grandiose, extravagant edifice, the *kehillah* ran out of funds and sold the structure to the Turin municipality, which completed the dome and spire and turned the structure into a museum. To this day, it rises high above the skyline and has become the symbol of the city.

For the Jews of Italy, the sense of equality and emancipation was brutally eradicated during the Fascist period. Since that time the synagogues and their communities, where they have survived, have returned to their lesser, pre-Emancipation dimensions. Except for the modern synagogue in Livorno, no major synagogue building has been built in Italy since the Second World War.

The Mole Antonelliana in Turin. (From a postcard.)

Although the legacy of many generations of Italian Jewry was shattered in our time, some of its priceless furnishings have migrated to a new home. Working tirelessly during the 1950s and 1960s, Umberto Naḥon rescued as many as 40 endangered Italian synagogues or their surviving remnants and ceremonial Judaica, bringing them to new locations and uses in Israel. The Italian government has since recognized the national cultural importance of the remaining Jewish heritage on its soil and is budgeting funds for its preservation. A tourist visiting Italy may now find a growing number of synagogues restored—but empty of worshippers, a visual reminder of a glorious Jewish community that is about to disappear.

Synagogue Interior Decoration and the Halakhah

Shalom Sabar

From late antiquity the synagogue was the center of architectural and artistic creativity among Jews, both in *Eretz Yisrael* and in the Diaspora. The careful attention given to the exterior appearance of the building, the materials from which it was built, the decoration of its interior, the elaborate furnishings, and the beautification of the ceremonial objects housed inside its walls have no parallel in other areas of Jewish life and culture. Over the ages the most talented artists and craftsmen, often gentile, were called upon to transform the synagogue into the most visually pleasing space of a given Jewish environment. The form of the decoration, however, was problematic, needing to contend as it did with the halakhic proscription of figurative images.

Ancient Israel distinguished itself from contemporary cultures by its resolute rejection of idolatry. The Second Commandment was explicit: "You shall not make for yourself a sculptured image, or any likeness of what is in the heavens above, or on the earth below, or in the waters under the earth" (Exod. 20:4). This prohibition had a profound effect on the development of Jewish art, including synagogue art. Although the rabbis tended to construe the

injunction against graven images literally, their specific attitudes varied with the circumstance of time and place. In practice, synagogue decoration was often more responsive to the popular desire for figurative embellishment than to the sages' interpretation of the Commandment. The dichotomy between the subject matter depicted in synagogue interiors and the rabbis' evaluations and rulings on the underlying halakhic issue is the subject of the following discussion.

The earliest synagogues of which there are extant remains demonstrate how important their interior decoration was to the respective Jewish communities. The artistic freedom and creativity of the late Roman and Byzantine synagogues, such as at Hamam Lif in Tunisia or at Dura-Europos in what is now Syria, were unmatched by later generations. As the evidence emerged from archaeological excavations in the late nineteenth and early twentieth centuries, art historians and Jewish scholars were astonished by what was revealed. Prevailing opinion had held that "art" and "Judaism" were mutually contradictory and that Jews had little aesthetic appreciation or talent. Even Jewish art historians, especially in German-speaking lands, were unaware of—or were unwilling to admit—the existence of Jewish synagogue art. The noted connoisseur of Italian Renaissance art, Bernard Berenson, claimed that the "Judaeans" in Hellenistic times did not "possess any kind of plastic or even mechanical ability," while Jews of later periods "displayed little talent for the visual and almost none for the figurative arts."

Setting aside the prejudices of Berenson and others, how are we to explain the abundant figurative representations in the wall paintings of Dura-Europos or of the floor mosaics in *Eretz Yisrael* synagogues such as Hammath Tiberias and Beth Alfa? Even more perplexing are the ubiquitous pagan images that range from common motifs—such as Medusa, centaur, or flying Erotes—to the more intriguing sun god, Helios, figured in at least four synagogues as riding his quadriga. The images, moreover, are not limited to non-Jewish scenes: biblical episodes are abundant. A typical example is the mosaic figure of King David playing the harp in the sixth-century synagogue in Gaza. The image is modeled on the Greek Orpheus, mythological poet and musician. In another example, from the Dura synagogue, the panel depicting Ezekiel's Vision of the Dry Bones features the winged Psyche, who represented the soul in classical tradition and art.

In trying to understand these peculiar representations, scholars have offered many diverse explanations. Some dismiss the pagan motifs as simple decorative elements in the spirit of the time, while others would imbue them with deep Jewish ideas, rooted in contemporary rabbinical teachings. Such contradictory renditions demonstrate how difficult it is for twenty-first-century observers to comprehend what our forefathers really intended. Conclusive explanations are hard to achieve. One should take into account the special nature of Jewish art: the Second Commandment and other prohibitions were subject to interpretations fitting the spirit and influences of specific times. It is misleading, therefore, to employ any dogmatic principle in interpreting the evidence from the Jewish past. Each phenomenon should be examined against the socio-religious history of its particular period and place.

Helios in the center of the Zodiac cycle. Beth Alpha Synagogue, *Eretz Israel,* sixth century. (Courtesy of Shalom Sabar.)

In the case of the early synagogues, a major change in the Jewish attitude toward the image can be traced from the Late-Antique to the Byzantine eras. In the preceding Hasmonean period, Hellenistic culture threatened the basic concepts of Judaism. Figurative images and three-dimensional statues in particular were readily associated with idolatry and, as such, could not be tolerated. Even King Herod, who had a Roman education and built in the Hellenistic style throughout the Holy Land, did not dare to break this prohibition. Thus, there is no trace of figurative images in his private and public buildings.

The situation changed gradually in the second and third centuries as the synagogue institution increasingly took root in Jewish life. A period of relative tranquillity followed the stormy events of the Bar Kokhba revolt (132–135 C.E.). Relations with the Romans improved, and Jewish communal life and learning flourished in the ensuing period of economic stability. While the halakhah developed, shaping spiritual and religious life in Jewish society, idol worship among the gentiles was losing its power.

Talmudic scholars Ephraim E. Urbach and Joseph M. Baumgarten and others have shown that the Jewish literature of the time contains enough evidence to provide the halakhic background permitting the usage of images. The rule of thumb that the rabbis developed was that as long as the images do not inspire idolatry they are permissible, though not encouraged. Thus, for example, Jonathan ben Uzziel translates Leviticus 26:1, on the prohibition of idol making, as follows: "You shall not place a figured stone on the ground to worship, but a colonnade with pictures and likenesses you may have in your synagogues, but not to worship onto. . . ." Another oft-quoted passage clearly reflects the archaeological evidence on synagogue art:

In the days of Rabbi Johanan [ben Nappaha] they began to paint on the walls, and he did not prevent them; in the days of Rabbi Abun they began to make designs on mosaics and he did not prevent them" (Talmud Yerushalmi, Avodah Zarah, 3:3, 42d).

The paintings in Dura-Europos were executed during the lifetime of Rabbi Johanan ben Nappaha (born late second century, died ca. 279 C.E.), while the dates of Rabbi Abun (early fourth century) coincide with the first lavish synagogue mosaic known to us—at Hammath Tiberias.

An important factor that undoubtedly contributed to the attractive art in the ancient synagogue was competition. In that "age of spirituality," when many in both *Eretz Yisrael* and the Diaspora sought new religions, Jews felt compelled to "prove" their beliefs in a visual language intelligible to the Hellenistic-Byzantine world. Although no specific sources raise the issue, the rabbis apparently well understood the importance of images as a tool. Graffiti on the paintings in Dura-Europos reveal that they were proudly shown to visitors, possibly to affirm the might of the Jewish God and the power of Jew-

ish heroes. Images in churches and synagogues of the period were used to assert doctrinal supremacy. Indeed, the same groups of artists may have worked for all sides while employing similar visual vocabularies. Some of the Church fathers spoke vehemently against images, but the Church chose to retain and develop art as an educational tool. In *Eretz Yisrael,* where Christianity was Judaism's chief rival, competition with the Church may have influenced the popularity of synagogue floor mosaics.

While Christianity was growing more powerful, the new, militant religion of Islam came to the fore in the Holy Land. Islam preached a stricter attitude toward art in its shrines. After the Islamic conquest of *Eretz Yisrael* (636–640 C.E.), the earlier circumstances that permitted the rabbis' lenient approach to synagogue art all but disappeared. Jews in the Holy Land lost interest in producing the kind of art their forefathers had commissioned. Islamic attitudes became more influential after Khaliph Yazid II's decree, in 721 C.E., to demolish all figural representation. That influence may explain the destruction of images in some synagogues, such as the floor mosaic of the sixth-century Na'aran synagogue near Jericho. In this synagogue, built at the height of the Byzantine period and Christian dominance in the Holy Land, Jewish worshippers in the early Islamic period removed the human and animal images, but not the holy Hebrew inscriptions.

In contrast to Antiquity, the number of synagogues that survived from the Middle Ages, with or without their original interior decoration, is far smaller. While the art commissioned for the magnificent edifices of Islam and Christianity became richer, more complex, and grandiose, the physical appearance of the synagogue declined as the social reality significantly changed. Living as a religious minority whose very existence was in the hands of the host society, Jewish communities of neither East nor West could build and decorate their synagogues as they had in the past.

The meager evidence of actual synagogue buildings that has come down to us is from Christian Europe, where Jews were not permitted to build their houses of prayer on a grand scale. The most elaborate example for medieval synagogue interior decoration comes from the El Transito synagogue of Toledo. Built at about 1357, it was the private chapel of Don Samuel ha-Levy Abulafia, royal treasurer and advisor of King Pedro the Cruel of Castile. Evidently executed by master craftsmen, the single-nave hall is covered with magnificent stucco decoration in delicate *mudéjar* style, topped by a narrow frieze with calligraphic Hebrew inscriptions. Despite the richness of its decorations—and although it was the private synagogue of a court Jew—the themes of the past had all but disappeared. Biblical episodes—not to mention pagan figures or human representations—are not to be found in medieval or later European synagogues. Abulafia's synagogue was erected at the height of the Gothic period in art, when religious figurative art in sculpture, stained glass, and wall decoration flourished in nearby cathedrals. Significantly, the Jews of Toledo and other parts of Spain preferred the somewhat out-dated Islamic style. For them it not only conformed to Jewish law, but also recalled the "Golden Age" that Spanish Jews had enjoyed under Islam.

Rabbinical literature of the time supports this view. Maimonides (1135–1204), whose rulings were often quoted and relied upon by later legal authorities, adopted the relatively rigid view of talmudic rabbis. Thus, if there were pictures on the synagogue walls, he would close his eyes for fear of diverting attention from prayer. Human figures in relief were not allowed in any context, although they were permitted in "sunken form," under certain conditions, such as in painting or embroidery. Flora and fauna, on the other hand, were accepted even in relief, all in parallel with Islamic standards.

Similar opinions were expressed in medieval Ashkenaz, where the Second Commandment was more strictly observed than in Spain. The enigmatic animal-headed figures of illuminated Ashkenazic manuscripts, for example, demonstrate the iconophobic tendency to avoid the human face in Hebrew codices. A number of German rabbis attempted to discourage the use of images in religious contexts. Regarding the images in his contemporaries' prayer books, Rabbi Meir Ben Barukh of Rothenburg (known

Interior wall decoration. El Transito Synagogue, Toledo, fourteenth century. (Photo by Shalom Sabar.)

by the Hebrew initials of his name as the Maharam, ca. 1215–1293 C.E.) found them improper, "since when [the worshippers] contemplate these figures they will not incline their hearts to their Father in Heaven" (Talmud Bavli, Tosafot to Yoma, 5a).

On the other hand, the Spanish grammarian Profiat Duran (1361–1444) was of the opinion that, "The contemplation and study of pleasing forms, beautiful images, and drawings broadens and stimulates the mind and strengthens its faculties. . . . As with God, who wanted to beautify His Holy Place with gold, silver, jewels, and

Jews with birds' heads collecting the manna from the *Birds' Head Haggadah*, Germany, ca. 1300. Jerusalem, Israel Museum, Ms. 180/57. (Courtesy of the Israel Museum, Jerusalem.)

precious stones, so it should be with His Holy Books" (*Ma'ase Efod,* 19, translated by J. Gutmann in *Hebrew Manuscript Painting*). Indeed, many Hebrew manuscripts, haggadot in particular, and even a Bible codex from medieval Spain are elaborately illuminated with biblical episodes showing complete human figures. The prohibitions were more carefully observed, however, in synagogue interiors, although Profiat Duran recommends the beautification of "God's House of Prayer" in the same passage, without elaborating on the nature of the decorations.

The more restrictive attitude in Ashkenaz was apparently influenced by the contemporary ascetic tendencies of some Christian circles, such as the monastic order of St. Bernard of Clairvoux. While that approach failed to be generally adopted by other Christian orders, most rabbis in medieval Germany accepted Maimonides' attitude for the interiors of their synagogues. Rabbi Isaac, son of Moses of Vienna (ca. 1180–1250), known for his important halakhic work, *Or Zarua,* reported that painted trees and birds embellished the walls of his childhood synagogue in Meissen, Saxony. However, like Maimonides and the Maharam, he disapproved, for the figures distracted attention from prayer and lessened devotion.

Certain Ashkenazic rabbis were more lenient. With approval by the relatively liberal local rabbi, Ephraim, son of Isaac (1110–1175), walls of the twelfth-century synagogue of Regensburg were decked with figures of animals and birds. A more important halakhic authority of the time, Rabbi Eliakim, son of Joseph of Mainz, objected to this practice. He ordered the removal of the "lions and snakes" motifs that reportedly decorated the stained-glass windows commissioned for the synagogue of Cologne.

Despite these negative opinions, we learn that the reality was always at least one step ahead of the official halakhah. Synagogues in medieval Germany had wall paintings and—in the spirit of the time—stained-glass windows featuring flora and fauna, possibly of a symbolic nature. These themes were carried over, as we shall see, to later periods.

The decisions of the great medieval authorities, particularly Maimonides and Rabbi Eliakim of Mainz, shaped the opinions of the subsequent legalists. Both authorities are quoted by the great halakhist Joseph Caro (1488–1575), compiler of the Shulḥan Arukh. Caro repeats the argument of distraction and rules against paintings and relief figures in the synagogue (*Tur Yoreh De'ah, Hilkhot Avodah Zarah*). His view was also expressed in a case that stirred up many leading rabbis in Italy and the Sephardic world in the early sixteenth century, invoking intervention by local authorities. The case in question took place on the island of Crete, then under the dominion of the Republic of Venice. A wealthy patron of the local Jewish community founded a synagogue and wished to place above the Ark a three-dimensional figure of a crowned lion, carved in marble and gilt—apparently his family's heraldic device (*arme*). According to extant sources, the community "bewailed" and tried all

Floral and faunal decorations. Synagogue in Holešov, Moravia, 1560; paintings from 1737.

Italian Torah Arks of the Renaissance and Baroque eras were lavishly decorated, employing a wealth of decorative and symbolic elements that testified to the deep acculturation of Italian Jews. The two pairs of columns flanking the Torah Ark in the synagogues of Ancona and Biella, for example, have helical form. This recalls the columns used by the noted Italian artist Bernini for the massive baldachin he erected in the church of St. Peter's, Rome, between 1624 and 1633. Some of the *bimot* in Piedmont, such as in Chieri and Carmagnola, display similar twisted pillars, but not merely in imitation of the popular church architectural feature. With deep Jewish meaning, the twisted "Solomonic" columns symbolized the pillars of the Temple in Jerusalem, the precious remains of which were carried off to Rome. By placing Solomonic columns in their synagogues, Italian Jews wished to convey the message that the synagogue is indeed a "miniature Temple." Only temporarily does it replace the Jerusalem Temple, which will be rebuilt in the end of days. This meaning was enhanced by painting Temple implements on the inner side of the Ark doors, as in Casale Monferrato. During the service, when the doors are opened and all rise in honor of the Torah, the community would be reminded of the Temple's glory. Other communities, such as Asti, depicted Temple implements on the outer doors.

The Italian rabbis, who were more open to the host society than their colleagues in other lands, did not object to such "borrowings," perhaps because of the special meaning given to it. Jewish writers in Italy frequently justified the borrowing of "gentile practices" by saying that the practices were originally Jewish and were now "reclaimed by us." This is how Gedaliah ibn Yaḥya (1515–1587) explains the adoption of family insignia in his comprehensive *Shalshelet ha-Kabbalah* (Venice, 1587): The twelve tribes carried emblems before the medieval knights had them. In a like manner, Italian Jews of the Renaissance believed that church or synagogue music was first inspired by the instrumental ensembles of Levites in the Temple. Thus, the interior of the synagogue could be highly attractive and sumptuously ornate—in sharp contrast

manner of persuasion to stop him. When he persisted, they bribed the civil authorities to prevent the installation of his lion. Although all the rabbinical authorities consulted in that case ruled that such figures could not be permitted within the synagogue, there were Italian rabbis in later periods, such as Abraham Joseph Graziano (d. 1684) of Pesaro, who allowed the use of an Ark that rested on two wooden lions.

Torah Ark with helical columns. Synagogue in Biella, Italy, ca. 1750.

to the austere facade—as long as it did not contravene talmudic injunctions and those by medieval authorities. Figurative drawings and paintings were privately displayed at home, as reported by Leone da Modena (1571–1648), the famous rabbi of Baroque Venice. He notes that this was done by his co-religionists in Italy despite the Second Commandment prohibition, but reiterated that such art could not conceivably decorate the walls of the beautiful synagogues.

The spread of visual motifs first used by Italian Jews into other communities in Europe,

North Africa, and the East is unparalleled. Features such as the helical columns were imitated first by communities who were closely associated with Italian Jews—such as Dubrovnik, and later by Ashkenazic communities also, such as Jičín. However, not all "imported" motifs were welcomed by the Ashkenazic rabbis, especially in countries such as Hungary and Poland. A case in point is the pair of Tablets of the Ten Commandments placed above the Ark in so many synagogues. Despite the popular notion that the Decalogue is a venerable, inseparable element of synagogue interiors, it is, in fact, a relatively new feature. The Ten Commandments were first depicted on the inner faces of Ark doors in fifteenth- and sixteenth-century Italian synagogues. In the seventeenth century we find them above the Ark in the famous Esnoga, the Portuguese synagogue of Amsterdam, completed in 1675. The symbol was probably adopted in imitation of a practice of the Reformed Church in Holland, whose doctrine held that the Decalogue is one of the pillars of Protestant belief. Unaware of this connection, congregations throughout Europe adopted the symbol for their synagogues. The tablets were usually given a double round-top shape although that property, too, stems from Christian art. Its earliest appearance occurred in an anti-Jewish context. The tablets were held upside down by the humiliated figure of "Synagoga," representing Judaism and the Jews, besides the triumphant "Ecclesia" representing the Church. Dozens of Christian works of art on this theme were executed throughout the thirteenth and fourteenth centuries, including, for example, the sculpted figures in the south porch of the Strasbourg Cathedral, or the stained glass lancet window in the Troyes Cathedral.

The Decalogue was originally an essential part of the daily liturgy, recited together with the *Shema* (Bavli, *Berakhot,* 12a), but the practice became problematic as early as talmudic times. Because the believers of the new religion, the Christians, turned the Ten Commandments into a central pillar of their faith, the rabbis ordered the recitation to stop. For Jews, every word in the Torah counts equally, without preference of any section over others. This reason is quoted by the

Temple implements, on the carved and gilded doors of the Torah Ark, synagogue in Asti, Italy, early nineteenth century. Ark dated 1809.

influential Moravian talmudist and Mishnah commentator, Rabbi Yom Tov Lipman Heller (1579–1654).

Long after the Tablets became a permanent feature of the synagogue we hear rabbinical objections, particularly in Hungary and Galicia. Interestingly, in the nineteenth century, when many synagogues in emancipated Europe proudly featured the Decalogue on their facades as well, the criticism of the hasidic rabbis became even sharper. Rabbi Solomon Judah Leib Tabak (1832–1908), the chief rabbi of Sziget, Hungary; Rabbi Hayyim Eleazar Shapira (1872–1937), the *Admor* of Munkacs; and others, associated the Decalogue on the facade with the new trends of the emancipated Jews whose knowledge of Torah "is meager and contaminated."

Along with the criticism against the "new Jews," some hasidic rabbis also looked disparagingly on the decorations in the synagogues built by the most pious communities. Based on the cherished saying of Rabbi Judah ben Temah in *Avot* (5:20): "Be strong as a *tiger,* light as an *eagle,* fast as a *deer,* and mighty as a *lion* to fulfill the will of your Father in Heaven," many synagogues in eastern Europe featured the four "holy animals." Sometimes, as in Nyíregyháza, Hungary, the images were accompanied by the entire verse from the Mishnah. Despite the pious intentions of both patrons and artists, opposition was raised on the grounds that the act of bowing before the wall upon which such images appeared might imply idolatry. The same opposition was raised by the noted Ashkenazic chief rabbi of *Eretz Yisrael,* Rabbi Abraham Isaac Kook (1865–1935), regarding the popular images of the twelve signs of the zodiac. Such pronouncements against the zodiac and "holy animals" were not taken seriously. Artists were invited to decorate synagogues in eastern Europe

315

with such motifs even in the early twentieth century. A major exception took place in Safed in 1857, far away from the shtetls. After the renovation of the Ashkenazic Ari synagogue, a recent immigrant from Kolomea in Galicia was commissioned to carve the wooden Torah Ark. In accordance with the style of his native town, he incorporated the cherished animal figures, tirelessly carved with his pocket knife. These figures infuriated the local hasidic community, who claimed they could not use the synagogue, and called their rabbi, Samuel Heller, to resolve the conflict. In a lengthy *responsum,* issued as a separate book entitled *Sepher Toharat ha-Kodesh* (Safed, 1864), Rabbi Heller admits that synagogues in Europe display such images, "but in *Eretz Yisrael* we should be more pious." His decision was accepted without question, and by the east European rabbis with whom he consulted as well. The "forbidden animals" were removed. That beautiful Ark, without the animals, still stands in the Ashkenazic Ari synagogue in Safed.

Finally, questions were raised not only about images, but also about Hebrew inscriptions. Rabbis dealt at length with this issue in Bohemia and Moravia, where it was customary to write sections of the prayers and other sacred quotations on the synagogue walls in large, quadrangular Hebrew letters, e.g., Boskovice, Březnice, and Třebíč. The problem arose during a synagogue renovation that required new plaster on the walls, with the question: Is it permissible to cover or obliterate verses or holy names? When the synagogue of Mikulov burned down in 1719, the problem was posed to the head of the local *bet din,* Rabbi Menahem Mendel (r. 1705–1747). What should be done with the remains of the inscriptions on the walls? His impractical recommendation was, "carefully peel off the plaster carrying the holy names, so that the words would not disintegrate and bury them in the *Genizah.*"

The rigorous views presented here tell us more of the decorations of the synagogue over the ages than of the intentions of the halakhic authorities. Despite harsh rabbinical views based on strict interpretation of the early sources, communities continued to decorate their synagogues as they found fit and appropriate. Only in rare cases did the communities significantly alter

"Four Holy Animals," wall painting in the synagogue in Nyíregyháza, Hungary, 1923.

316

Wall painted with Hebrew inscriptions in the women's gallery, synagogue in Boskovice, Moravia, late seventeenth century. Inscriptions date from nineteenth century.

synagogue decorations to eliminate the "forbidden images." Furthermore, many authorities who found discrepancies between the halakhah and their daily reality relied on the honorable and beloved traditions of their respective communities, and did not recommend change. Pleasant childhood memories and the scenes one grew accustomed to view and appreciate could not easily be erased.

The sources and reading list for this essay can be found on page 341 in the general bibliography.

Spirituality and Space

Rudolf Klein

Architecture is an expression of cultural history: A society's image of the world—and of man's role in it—determines the way it organizes its sacred space. Accordingly, the space conception of sacred buildings is virtually a replica of how a civilization comprehends the universe. Although cultures differ, development of their respective sacred spaces can be remarkably similar from place to place. Historically, early sacred space was often center-oriented and rooted materially in particular hallowed locations. By a process of varied, culture-specific stages, sacred architecture came to be independent of geography, centerless and flowing freely *between* inside and outside.

Jewish sacred architecture differed from that of other religions in that it lacked direct links between the spiritual, the Torah, and the spatial—a quality that was not codified in religious teachings. For example, a minyan can hold services in any room or, indeed, out of doors. Space, however, is an unavoidable aspect of human existence; it expresses an order, in the nonvisual sense, and establishes a link between religion and the more tangible world—architecture. The spatial arrangement of synagogues usually exceeded the merely functional level, and the

codification of their space eventually related to the spiritual. As a minority living among an alien population, Jews accorded great importance to maintaining their group identity, a stance that forced them into a position of intellectual "self defense." Paradoxically, this implied the acceptance of the dictates of the gentile environment. Jews could not, therefore, avoid taking a certain interest in architecture, even if it was a negative one. This interest became increasingly significant over the centuries, despite the pre-eminently textual character of Judaism.

The history of architectural space parallels the development of metaphysics, cosmology, and whatever is considered sacred, in a range from the primitive, *touchable* divine to total secularization. In architecture the development was a gradual one, from the mostly material to the pre-eminently immaterial—the spatial. According to Siegfried Giedion, author of *Space, Time and Architecture,* the history of Western architecture may be divided into three major periods: first is the sculptural phase in which sacred architecture is observed from the outside; second is the phase in which the interior dominates; the last phase, in which these two concepts mingle, is evident in modern architecture. Although Giedion defines his classification formally, the development of physical architectural space relates to the notion of what is sacred in each period. Religious buildings of a society reveal the character of the sacred in that society, and how it relates the sacred to the profane.

The first concept of space, the *topographic,* is related to the *touchable sacred.* This type of architecture is geographically rooted, connected to a particular historical or mythical place representing a point of contact between the earthly and the divine. Space in the topographic period is usually an architectural exterior without strict separation from nature. It expresses a world view that man is an integral part of nature. An interior, if it exists, is usually of minor significance. Consequently, there is no firm boundary around the focal center, implying a gradual transition from the sacred to the profane. The architectural form may take the shape of a phallic structure, such as an obelisk, or it may be like a Greek temple, a sacred structure with no significant interior. This treatment expresses a certain distance from the deity. The exterior and the shape of the monument can be understood at first glance. Members of the congregation face each other in an arrangement that promotes a strong communal feeling, and the structure is usually a place for sacrifices. Total experience of the sacred requires proximity, pilgrimage, or physical contact. Although the topographic concept applies chiefly to idol-worship and to polytheistic cultures, it may exist in the architecture of later phases as a component in a complex situation. The Roman Catholic church, for example, has an elaborate space conception, but it still contains physical focal centers, such as altars and pulpits.

The second concept, the *transcendental* stage in the development of Western architecture, relates to the *intellectualized sacred.* It originated under the Roman Empire, but dominated mainly in the Middle Ages. The sacred is more or less geographically independent and its space strives to achieve spiritual contact with the divine. Such contact requires a strict separation from profane nature, which is why the sacred interior space was created. We must walk up the nave or the aisle in order physically to comprehend the interior.

The third space concept, termed *isotropic,* relates to the *denied* or *dispersed sacred.* It appeared in twentieth-century European culture as the final stage of modernization. Public and private buildings tended to lose firm physical boundaries as a consequence of perforated walls, sometimes totally glazed or completely omitted: the centerless space flows freely between interior and exterior. In practice, these ideal cases are frequently mixed up, but one or another component is almost always dominant.

Throughout history synagogue and church architecture differed from each other fundamentally in how they functioned to transfer ideas. Church architecture and its decoration transmitted religious teachings. Synagogues, on the other hand, had no explicit architectural guidelines; the Jewish emphasis on an ethical rather than a theological approach leaves some questions open. For example, the prescriptions that synagogue interiors should be entered by means of two doors, and the differences in floor levels—such as the few steps before the *bimah* and Ark—are far from enough to form a coherent building program. Although Jewish symbols and decorative elements were also created, they were too few to solve the problem.

The centrality of text, the neglect of the visual, and the lack of ideological content that architecture might convey paves the way for the introduction of alien elements. Those elements selected from the Christians included building materials and techniques, and some neutral decoration. These are "textual" elements—the *language* of architecture. Opposed elements are those of content—the arrangement of interior space.

Roman Catholic church interiors symbolize a sacred path that is also a life path. It is spatial and temporal, having a clearly defined beginning—at the church entrance, birth—and an end—at the altar, death, or the beginning of heavenly life. The congregation forms a homogeneous, elongated rectangle, but the spiritual focus of the interior is far from either the geometrical center or the mass of people. When there are several altars, the only important interior orientation is the main altar; the same relation holds for services performed before a secondary altar.

In sharp contrast, the prevalent pre-Emancipation Ashkenazic synagogue interior had a central arrangement. The congregation sat around the *bimah,* a focus that was usually at or close to the geometrical center of the interior. There was, however, another important direction: the *Aron Kodesh,* on the eastern wall. With each focus possessed of distinctive qualities, this double focus was the basic spatial concept of the synagogue interior.

The first focus has a specific topographic center, the *bimah,* the place where the Torah is read. In contrast to the sacred buildings of idol-worship or polytheism, where mere presence and proximity were enough to experience the sacred, here an intellectual effort is needed for participation in the service. The physical building is not of itself sacred as a stone, a limb of a god, or a saint—it is sacred because of the scriptures it contains. The emphasis is on the *ethical,* on the acceptance of certain religious laws and interpretations, rather than on the character of the divinity. The Torah is "active" at the place where it is read, at the *bimah.* In its passive state it rests in the eastern structure, the *Aron Kodesh.*

The centrality of the *bimah* contrasts also with the temporality expressed in the church interior of Western Christianity. The aim of Judaism is not outside our actual being, but within ourselves. Human life on earth is not a preparation for a future eternal life, but a duty to be realized in accordance with the Law. The structures around the *bimah*—a decorated grid in the Romanesque and Gothic periods, and a separated space within four columns in the Renaissance and Baroque nine-bay structure—reinforce its physical presence.

The central arrangement, where the congregants look into the faces of the others opposite, emphasizes a sense of belonging to a coherent community. Belonging is reinforced by the custom that the first row of worshippers, usually community elders, faces not the *bimah,* but the other members sitting around it. Unlike real topographic architecture, such as a pagan temple,

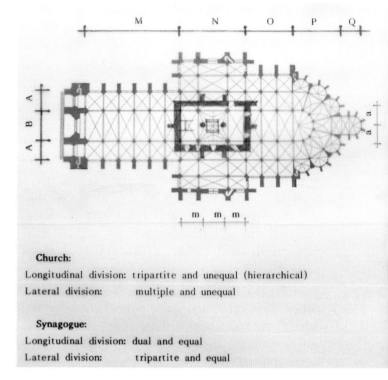

Church:

Longitudinal division: tripartite and unequal (hierarchical)
Lateral division: multiple and unequal

Synagogue:

Longitudinal division: dual and equal
Lateral division: tripartite and equal

Medieval church-synagogue distinctions. Although both may have used the Gothic architectural *language,* the church is tri-partite, with a nave and two aisles and a variable number of bays. The medieval synagogue (central rectangular insert), such as the Prague Altneuschul or the Stara Bóźnica of Crakow, was divided into two aisles and six bays. (Drawing by Rudolph Klein.)

the synagogue seldom has a special relationship with its location. The site is of minor significance and may even be an unfavorable one allotted to the tolerated minority.

The second spatial idea prevalent in the synagogue interior is partly similar in its philosophy to the transcendental concept. It relates to a spiritual focus outside the congregation, neither *here* nor *now.* Orientation of the Ark and interior space toward the east reminds the Jews that they are in exile, that their presence in all its apparent solidity is only a temporary solution—an interim phase. Housing the Torah, the Ark mediates between Jerusalem and any present place and is thus a materialization of the Eternal. The Ark is the focus of interest during a certain proportion of the service only and not at all times, as with the Christian altar. Although the Ark position compares to that of the altar, the Ark is less

The Renaissance Shakh synagogue in Holešov, Moravia (ca. 1560), with central *bimah* and its walls covered in ornamental frescoes and inscriptions.

emphasized in function than the altar and is eclipsed by its "rival," the *bimah.*

The ritual underlines the double focus of the synagogue interior; the focus changes if there is a sermon. Bifocality is more than a religious issue: It gives rise to an attitude of toleration to duality—the co-existence of two entities under one roof—and marks an aptness to change viewpoints, to observe things from various angles. Later, in the nineteenth century, when Jews began to assimilate, this double focus, being contrary to the Christian way of thinking, was abolished.

Apart from conceptual differences between the Christian church and the synagogue, sacred space for Jewish use was also distinguished by technical or instrumental means, such as certain details of vaulting, decoration, and so on. These specific elements of the synagogue originated from intellectual self-defense. As a result, the

synagogue was able to preserve its identity even when, as in Renaissance synagogue interiors, they slightly resembled contemporary churches.

The usual architectural classification of synagogues according to stylistic periods of the Christian environment—the Romanesque, Gothic, Renaissance, Baroque, neo-Classical, and so on—does not properly characterize synagogue space. As direct Christian influence was present only on the level of the architectural *language*—features such as structural solutions, building materials, details, and decoration—but not on the level of space concept, a real classification cannot be based solely on the stylistic approach.

The conception of space in the synagogue interior remained essentially unchanged for nearly a millennium: from the early Romanesque period to the nineteenth century, and to the twentieth century in some remote areas of eastern and central-eastern Europe. Although there was often a genuine attempt at differentiation during this time, synagogues borrowed language elements from gentile architecture and omitted certain forms that had Christian connotations.

The six-bay structure, exemplified in Prague's Altneuschul or Stara Bóźnica in Cracow, differs from a church interior in its proportions and in its distribution of space and vaulting. In the synagogue this is merely a technical issue, whereas church construction linked technique to ideology and its all-embracing spiritual system. Technical solutions containing explicit Christian elements were unacceptable in the synagogue. Thus, while the church had a tripartite division along the transversal axis, synagogue space was divided into two equal naves as a matter of design, not numbers. The situation was similar along the longitudinal axis, where the Gothic church uses the unequal intervals that result from the cruciform plan. The Romanesque- and Gothic-period synagogue was divided into three or four equal bays, without emphasis on the central bay of the six-bay structure, if there was one.

During the sixteenth and seventeenth centuries, the differences in proportion between church and synagogue interiors disappeared as both of them adopted a nearly central arrangement. The synagogue in central and eastern Europe, however, retained its identity during the Renaissance and Baroque periods through the widespread adoption of the four-column, nine-bay arrangement, thus resolving the clash between the *bimah* and the central row of columns. Eliminating the columns also resolved the conflict between bearing structure and content. As the view and way from the *bimah* to the Ark are no longer blocked by two central columns, the bearing structure reinforces the space concept.

This relatively small change in synagogue design was paralleled by contemporary radical changes in church design. A central space suddenly appeared, implying that the Church had relaxed its commitment to the "sacred way," the religious fulfilment associated with longitudinal church orientation. For the Christians, the world ceased to be an incomprehensible divine miracle

The slightly irregular ribbed vaulting of the Gothic-Renaissance Pinkas Synagogue in Prague (fifteenth century), recently renovated.

and became, instead, a readable, geometrically representable entity, exemplified in the clear shapes of the Renaissance church. Apparently, due to the centrality of the church, it became similar to the synagogue. However, in spite of the similarity in proportions, the nine-bay synagogue structure still featured a significant difference compared with the central space of both the Renaissance Catholic or Reformed churches. The church center was void and heavy with

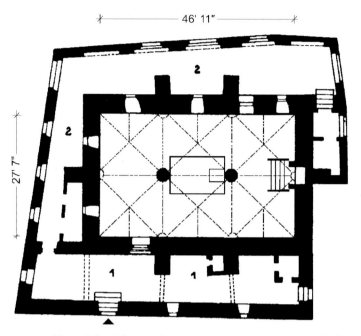

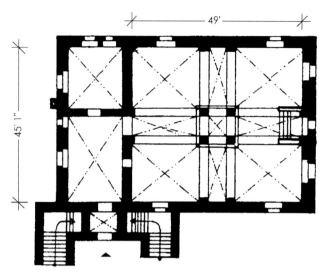

Plan of the synagogue in Bardejov, Slovakia (1830), illustrating the nine bays derived around the four central pillars of the sanctuary. (Adapted from E. Bárkány and L'. Dojč, *Židovské náboženské obce na Slovensku.*)

Plan of the Altneuschul synagogue in Prague (probably late thirteenth century): 1. Southern vestibule, added in the fourteenth century. 2. Women's annexes. The western annex was added in the sixteenth–seventeenth centuries and the northern one in 1723. (Adapted from R. Wischnitzer, *The Architecture of the European Synagogue.*)

sentinel pillars around it. The opposite applied in the synagogue: the mass was in the center, but it was perforated. Thus, the Renaissance play between the material mass and the void is less noteworthy in the synagogue interior.

The empty center of the Renaissance church interior draws us into the space under the dome like a magnet, as—for example—in Bramante's version of St. Peter's in Rome. The moment we reach this point, however, we realize that we are in the center of the space. It is our *individual being* that is the subject of admiration rather than some religious concept, or a meaning that refers to something outside our personal existence. In contrast, when we step up to the central *bimah* of the nine-bay synagogue, we are not in the center of the universe, but rather in a confined—if visually open—space; our movement is restricted, but the view is unimpaired. The feeling, however, is not so much one of confinement as of protection inside a railing that surrounds us.

The distribution of spans also highlights the difference between Christian and Jewish con-

cepts. The Renaissance church usually has a larger span in the middle—where the void is large—and narrower spans at the sides. The nine-bay synagogue structure, on the other hand, usually has a smaller span in the center—around the *bimah*—and bigger spans on the outside. A vertical section reinforces what the floor plan suggests: the church is highest at the central cupola, whereas the synagogue center is lower than its surroundings. This distinction is interpretable as a retention of hierarchical thinking by the Church, while the synagogue remains nonhierarchical. Even as a void, the church center is still important.

The Counter-Reformation attempt to re-establish the pre-Renaissance longitudinal arrangement created a synthesis in church architecture. This trend did not affect the synagogue interior, apart from changes in Baroque vaulting techniques and the application of period decoration, such as the festoon. The same situation applies for the neo-Classical period. Stylistic alterations on the exterior marked changes in the language of architecture only, primarily affecting the decoration. Changes in the synagogue since the Renaissance, the consequence of employing Christian master builders, were superficial and left the synagogue essentially unchanged.

The most significant changes in the synagogue interior occurred during the nineteenth century, mainly as a result of emancipation and assimilation. The proportions of interior space changed, as did the relation between architecture and spiritual issues—between space and language, and the synagogue service. Although Jewish symbols remained, the synagogue lost its previous architectural identity and acquired a new one based on gentile elements and ways of thinking. Even in the selection of symbols, the Jews introduced a form of self-censorship. They omitted emblems that are specifically Jewish, such as the menorah—icon of Israeli statehood—or the shofar. Instead they favored universal symbols stressing values common to Judaism and Christianity, such as Tablets of the Law or the *Magen David* star.

The *Haskalah* was influential in introducing Western order into the synagogue. It accepted the notion that architecture should explicitly convey religious concepts, rather than be autonomous of them. The intention was to express synagogue space—such as the central *bimah*—in an intrinsic architectural language rather than in borrowed details of style, such as Gothic or Baroque. In practice, the hoped-for change did not occur. The Jews dismantled tradition in the attempt to establish a real synagogue style, but success eluded them.

The central arrangement and the interior double focus were readily abandoned while a unified eastern *mizrah* was established, comprising Ark and *bimah* in one monumental composition. Sometimes there were interim solutions and compromises during these transformations: a longitudinal floor plan and a central *bimah,* or a central floor plan with an eastern *bimah.* Although the Orthodox modified their synagogues more conservatively, many of them adopted longitudinal floor plans or placed the *bimah* in front of the Ark. This positioning served two ends: By creating an emphasized nave, as in the church, the positioning allowed a longitudinal arrangement and the simplification of the previous space complexity.

The changing focus was very irritating for Christians. In the times of the great synagogue service reformers, numerous publications waged a war against "the unsystematic course of the

Massive Ark and *bimah,* unified on the eastern wall of the synagogue in Pilsen (1893), Bohemia.

synagogue service," meaning the deficiency of Christian order of ritual practices such as unison prayer, singing, and so forth. Though seemingly chaotic, the order of the Jewish service was in fact well defined but did not follow Christian patterns. Its philosophic meaning was incompatible with Western Christian values, or so believed both assimilated Jewish intellectuals and most of the non-Jewish majority. In particular, Christians interpreted the spatial duality of the synagogues as showing instability of behavior and lack of loyalty to a single system. The duality implied changing views, and a questioning of the position and some of the basic values and axioms of the host society. People who attended such a service could not become loyal subjects of a kaiser and reliable citizens of a society requiring discipline and austerity. The inevitable radical changes of the future had to abolish existing features and introduce and codify new ones.

Depriving the synagogue of its essence could only be achieved by proposing a substitute that maintained its identity. An architectural interpretation was needed that could be part of the Christian system and would combine nineteenth-century historicism with some specifics relating to the Jewish past. The solution was the neo-Moresque language. Infrequently used by the Christians, it was available, whereas other major historic styles—the Gothic, Renaissance, and Baroque—were already spoken for. It did not matter that the neo-Moresque was a somewhat inferior architectural expression. The Jews were extremely happy with it because it offered them a chance to become part of a system that had previously denied them entry. Introducing the Moorish appearance was justified by reference to the glorious past of Jewish culture in medieval Spain.

In the new form, the Jews relocated the *bimah* and embraced a longitudinal floor plan. They wanted to underline the fact that the basic content of their religion was the same as that of the Christians; it differed only in expression by an alternative, seemingly different, architectural language. Thus, the neo-Moresque was an ideal interim solution because it appeased the Jewish conscience, reassuring the Jews that their identity was not entirely forgotten, while it told the Christians that the Jews were still clearly distinguishable.

The Jubilee Synagogue in Prague, W. Stiassny, architect, 1906. Moorish style influenced by Art Nouveau.

The neo-Moresque never became a "style." It remained at the level of a language that had a set of decorative elements but no immanent spatial implications. Usually, but not always, it was employed together with a longish floor plan and was not codified in combination with any spatial arrangement—as the Gothic style was, with its longitudinal church interior. The neo-Moresque was codified only as a "clothing," a type of decoration.

A sacred *style* of architecture carries a spiritual as well as a formal dimension and uses the *language* of shape and decoration to create the *space* that gives it expression. If nineteenth-century European Jews had succeeded in creating a style, their innovation would have brought to a close the dissonance between space and language that had existed in synagogues since the Romanesque period. It also would have signalled the completion of the assimilation process. The fact that the neo-Moresque could not form an ideologically and formally coherent system underlines the fact that it was only a language composed of arbitrary architectural elements. Thus, the duality between language and space continued during most of the nineteenth century, paving the way for another change at its end that brought back the central space concept and led gradually to the abandonment of the neo-Moresque—a language that became untenable as assimilation continued and Jewish influence increased. Previously needed to boost the diver-sity of the urban context, as did the Tempelgasse Synagogue in Vienna or the "Dohány Temple" in Budapest, the neo-Moresque was an exotic style that lost interest or even became frightening for some gentiles.

By the end of the nineteenth century, community leaders and architects who tried to reform synagogue architecture were attempting to convince the public that the neo-Moresque expression was unjustified: Jews were Germans, Austrians, or Hungarians of the Jewish faith and should not have a separate language of architecture. In the most assimilated communities, the neo-Moresque was abandoned and the identity of the synagogue yielded to a spatial arrangement; however, it was not the previous central synagogue interior with the *bimah* as a focus. Now, the center was empty and the central arrangement resulted from formal considerations: the dome was idealized as the sky, or the desert tent. It gave identity and significance to a building in an urban context and was distinguishable from church spires. The central arrangement resulted in a theatre-like interior where people were able to watch one another. In the cities, gallery ladies—no longer enclosed by grids— used opera glasses to watch each other and their husbands or boyfriends on the floor below. These gentlemen were perceptibly different from the spouses of theatre-goers, by virtue of their head-coverings—no longer a kippah, but a top hat.

APPENDIX: SYNAGOGUE RESTORATION

Restoration and preservation of synagogue buildings in towns and cities with small or zero Jewish populations today is a haphazard event, dependent usually on local initiatives. A few outstanding projects are supported by organizations such as the World Monuments Fund or the Getty Foundation, but most restorations depend on national, local, and private (sometimes Jewish) support. The funding is ordinarily slow in relation to real costs, with the result that the work can take many years to complete. Current synagogue restoration, intended mostly for cultural purposes, is more often directed toward the creation of a Jewish museum than in earlier post-war years, or includes a section devoted to a Jewish memorial.

The following summary relates to restorations in progress, planned, or completed in the last two decades of the twentieth century. In countries with few remaining synagogues, the list includes some synagogues in Jewish use, or ancient sites without reference to restoration. The first date refers to the year of synagogue completion.

AUSTRIA

Eisenstadt: ca. 1700—Jewish museum
Graz: 1892—Destroyed in 1938; new synagogue under construction, dedication scheduled November 9, 2000
Innsbruck: 1993—New synagogue built on the site of synagogue destroyed in 1938
Kobersdorf: 1860—Restoration planned
Linz: 1968—Destroyed 1938; new synagogue dedicated April 4, 1968
Salzburg: 1901—Damaged in World War II; in Jewish use, restorations done in 1946, 1968, and 1988

St. Pölten: 1913—restored 1990s, Institute for the History of the Jews in Austria
Stadt Schleining: 1715—restored as Austrian Institute for Peace Research
Vienna:
    Seitenstettengasse: 1826—In Jewish use
    Tempelgasse: 1858—Former synagogue offices; remodeled post-World War II to synagogue

CROATIA

Dubrovnik: 1408—Restored, 1998
Rijeka: 1928—Sephardic Orthodox; in Jewish use, good condition
Split: 16th century—In Jewish use, restored 1997

Zagreb: 1867—Destroyed 1941; prayer room and Jewish community center bombed in 1991, reconstructed later that year

CZECH REPUBLIC

Batelov: 1797—Garden club

Boskovice: 1698—Restoration of synagogue and its murals, work on a Jewish museum, and restoration of Jewish quarter in progress since 1991

Břeclav: 1868—Restoration including restoration of murals nearing completion in 2000

Březnice: 1725—Restoration work, 1995–1999, contains Jewish exposition

Brandýs nad Laben: 1829—Restoration in progress

Čáslav: 1890—Prepared in 1999 for restoration

Český Krumlov: 1909—Prepared in 1999 for restoration

Čkyně: 1828—Synagogue owned by Society of Friends of Israel; restoration planned

Dolní Kounice: 1652—Restoration in progress

Habry: 1825—Prepared in 1999 for restoration

Heřmanův Městec: 1728—Synagogue and ghetto restoration in progress since 1997

Holešov: 1560—Restored to Regional Jewish Museum of Moravia

Hranice: 1864—Reconstruction completed in 1996 to Jewish museum

Jičín: Reconstructed in 1840 after a fire Prepared in 1999 for restoration

Kasejovice: 1762—Renovated, 1994; houses new ethnographic exhibit of Jewish and local folk art

Kolín: 1696—Partially restored; work on Jewish quarter in progress

Krnov: 1871—Flood damage repaired, 1998

Ledeč nad Sázavou: 1739—Restoration begun, 1998

Lomnice: 1785—Restoration completed June, 1997; contains Jewish exhibit

Loštice: 1805—Restoration planned

Luže: 1780—Restoration begun, 1995

Mikulov: 1550—Main synagogue restored, 1980–1992; ghetto restoration in progress

Nová Cerekev: 1855—Prepared in 1999 for restoration

Nová Kdyné: 1863—Renovations begun in 1999

Pilsen: 1892—Great Synagogue restored; opened to the public in February 1998; the two nineteenth-century synagogues in restoration

Polná: 1684—Reconstructed several times, lastly in 1863 and 1935; current restoration near completion in 2000; restoration of Jewish quarter planned

Prague:

  Altneuschul: 1270—Restoration completed, spring 1999; in Jewish use

  Ceremonial Hall: 1908—Restored January 1998; museum

  High: 1568—Restored as museum, 1996

  Jéruzalémska: 1906—Restoration completed; Jewish services resumed

  Klaus: 1694—Restored in 1996 as museum

  Meisels: 1592—Restored in 1991 as museum

  Pinkus: 1535—Names of Czech Holocaust victims restored on walls, 1996

  Smíchov: 1863—Restoration begun in 1999

  Spanish syn.: 1868—Restoration completed November 1998; Jewish exposition

Radnice: 1750—Synagogue owned by nature preservation society; restoration planned

Rakovník: 1764—Synagogue restored as concert hall, 1992; adjoining community building as Václav Rabas art gallery, 1989

Rychnov nad Kněžnou: 1787—Restored to Regional Jewish Museum, a memorial to Jewish humorist Karel Polaček

Slavkov: 1850—Restored as archive building, spring 1998; Jewish museum in entrance hall

Strážnice: 16th-century origin—Rebuilt 1869, roof repairs, 1994–1997; Jewish historical exhibition planned

Terezín: Ghetto synagogue discovered, 1995

Třebíč, Neuschul: ca. 1700—Restored as Jewish museum and concert hall, September 1997; conservation of gallery murals 1998–1999; exhibit on history of region's Jews, January 2000; ghetto under restoration

Třešt: Rebuilt in 1825 on older synagogue foundations—Restoration sponsored by Czech Brethren and municipality begun in 1997

Úsov: 1784—Restoration begun, 1998
Úštčk: 1794—Restoration begun, 1995
Velké Meziříčí:
  Old syn.: Early 16th century—Exhibition gallery and small Jewish museum, 1995

  New syn.: 1867—Rented as business premises; restoration planned
Žatec: 1872—Planned restoration

HUNGARY

Apostag: 1822—Restored, serves as concert hall and wedding chapel; Lajos Nagy; museum and town library
Baja: 1846—Restored; municipal library
Budapest:
  Dohány: 1859—Restored in 1996; open to the public
  Kazinczy: 1913—Orthodox, restoration in progress
  Rumbach: 1872—Restoration in progress
Cegléd: 1905—Restoration in progress
Debrecen: 1909—Restored
Győr: 1870—Restoration in progress; community buildings restored as Franz Liszt Music Teachers' College
Hódmezővásárhely: 1856—Restored in 1990s to concert hall
Jánoshalma: 1850—Restoration in progress
Kaposvár: 1864—Restored
Karcag: 1899—Restored
Kecskemét: 1871—Completely altered; convention center, museum of classical sculpture
Keszthely: 1894—Restored
Kiskőrös: 1873—Music school and concert hall
Kiskunhalas: 1860—Restored

Kisvárda: 1901—Ethnographic museum
Mád: 1795—Restoration in progress
Makó: 1870—Restoration in progress
Matészalka: 1857—Restoration in progress
Mezőtúr: 1835—Former art gallery, now vacant
Miskolc: 1863—Restored
Nagykanizsa: 1805—Restoration in progress
Nagykőrös: 1925—Restored
Nyíregyháza: 1923—Restored
Pápa: 1846—Restoration planned
Pécs: 1864—Restored in 1995; open to the public
Siófok: 1986—In Jewish use during the summer
Sopron: 14th century—Restored as Jewish museum
Szeged: 1903—Restored in 1989; open to the public
Szekszárd: 1896—Concert hall and gallery
Szolnok: 1898—Concert hall and gallery
Szombathely: 1880—Concert hall; interior completely altered
Tata: 1861—Museum of Greek and Roman art
Tokaj: 1890—Concert hall, nearly completed
Várpalota: 1839—Art gallery
Zalaegerszeg: 1903—Concert hall and gallery

GREECE

Aegina: 5th century C.E.—Remains of synagogue mosaic floor
Athens:
  In the *agora*: 3rd century C.E.—Remains of a probable synagogue
  Beth Shalom: 1930—In Jewish use, renovated 1975
  Ioanniton: 1904—Sparse Jewish use
  Saoul Modiano Retirement Home: 1982—In Jewish use

Corfu, Scuola Greca: 17th century—Sparse Jewish use; open to the public
Halkis: 1854—In Jewish use
Hania: 17th century—Restored, rededicated on October 8, 1999
Ioannina: 1829—In Jewish use
Kos: 1934—Converted to municipal cultural center
Larissa, Etz Hayyim: 1860—In Jewish use; collapsed roof repaired, 1991

Rhodes, Shalom Syn.: 1577—Sparse Jewish use; open to the public
Salonika:
    Monasterioton: 1927—In Jewish use
    Yad l'Zikaron: 1920—Rebuilt in 1984, in Jewish use

Trikkala:
    Kahal Yavanim: 19th century—In sparse Jewish use
Veroia: Mid 19th century—In restoration
Volos: 1960—In Jewish use

ITALY

Carmangola: 17th century—Under restoration
Casale Monferrato: 1595—General restoration work completed; museum expanded
Gorizia: 1699—Restored 1984; contains small Jewish museum
Mantua: 1751—Partial restoration, in community use
Mondoví: ca. 1700—Restored in the early 1990s
Pesaro, Spanish: 17th century—Restoration in progress

Pitigliano: End of 16th century—Restoration of synagogue and ghetto completed mid-1990s
Sabbioneta: 1824—Restored 1994
Soragna: 1855—Restored in 1980s as Jewish museum
Venice:
    Scuola Grande Tedesca: 1528—In restoration
    Scuola Italiana: 1575—In use
    Scuola Levantina: 1538—In use
    Scuola Grande Spagnola: 1635—In use

SERBIA

Belgrade: 1907—In Jewish use; well maintained
Novi Sad: 1909—Under long-term major restoration
Pancevo: 1902—Nationalized and maintained

Subotica: 1903—National cultural monument; initial restoration begun by World Monuments Fund; work suspended for lack of funds
Zemun: 1867—Completely restored by Serbian radical party to restaurant and gambling house, 1998

SLOVAK REPUBLIC

Bardejov, old syn.: 1830—Protected monument but still in use as storeroom
Brezno: 1902—Under restoration to Jewish museum, temporary interruption in 1999
Kokava: ca. 1900—Restored, vacant
Košice, Tajoskoho: 1930—Culture house, concert hall
Liptovský Svätý Mikuláš: 1845—Rebuilt 1906; restoration to concert hall suspended for lack of funds
Malacky: 1886—Completely altered to children's arts and crafts center
Prešov, Orthodox: 1898—Restoration funded by overseas Jews; in limited Jewish use
Ružomberok: 1880—Restoration planned

Spišské Podhradie: 1905—Restoration to Museum of Jewish History for the Spiš Region in progress, funded by Getty Grant Program
Stupava: 1803—Purchased by ARTEP, international media concern; restoration to offices possible
Trnava: 1892—Status Quo Synagogue initial restoration to exhibition hall–small Jewish museum
Trenčín: 1913—Art gallery
Trstená: 1732—Completely altered, youth club
Vrbové: 1883—Restoration to concert hall; exterior nearly completed, interior awaits funding

ACKNOWLEDGMENTS

A work such as ours is never the product of the authors' efforts alone. As strangers to the sites of interest and ignorant of most of the relevant languages, we were particularly dependent on others for assistance. We accepted help in preparing and planning our forays to central and southern Europe, and received more help when we were there. At home we needed translations of the interviews and historical material we had collected. Beginning with a slide lecture at Yad Vashem, we asked for volunteers. Most of the respondents were Israelis who had emigrated from the countries we were researching—retirees like us who had completed careers in other fields. They were young in spirit and captivated by the idea of keeping alive the memory of depopulated Jewish communities. They harnessed themselves to the task, happy to use their skills purposefully and grateful for exposure to the sources.

We owe a special debt of gratitude to Sheila Brull, formerly an editor with a London publishing house. She accompanied the book from its inception, transcribing, translating from tape, and reading the texts critically through innumerable revisions. Still with us until final edit, Sheila produced two lovely drawings to adorn the work.

Our first translator was Jana Mihulová Pokorná, whom we met in Bohemia. She lived with us for six months, improving her English while translating a portion of the Czech and Slovak material. Working as a team, Yochanan Magen who is still indispensable, translated orally from Hungarian, Czech, Slovak, or German into Hebrew, while Nitza Shiffman—with us twice a week during a Sabbatical year—typed the information in English. Sheila Brull, Ruth Mittelmann, and Eva Kondor came to work at our house regularly. Social staff lunches in our sunny kitchen were a highlight of the week.

In Jerusalem we thank Ernest E. Rosenbluth—who translated several historical booklets—and Chana ben Abba, Elfrid Bergmann, Tova Bilitzer, Lassar Brueckheimer, Gideon Lefen (translations and maps), Yoel Litke, Elaine S. Feffer, Esther Shiloh, and Karla Yaron for multiple achievements over extended periods. We have met only a few of the following Israeli mail correspondents, but they had faith enough in our goal to translate from the pages we sent and return packets time after time: Eliyahu Arbel, Laura Gentili, Matityahu Galambosh, Walter Kirshbaum and Rachel Halevi in teamwork; Asher Lestovsky, Baruch Robinson, Ladislav Rotter, Penina Petian, Avri Salamon, and our most distant colleague, Ladislav Stein in Bonn, Germany, who is fluent in all European languages.

Also helpful were Levi Arieli, Romi Ascarelli, Nora Aviad, Michal and Shimon Be'er, Chana Boguslavsky, the late Hans Brull, Doris Budovsky, Lina Castelnovo, Ruth Dominitz, Shlomo Ehrlich, Yehudit and Yaron Erenreich, Gila Fatran, Rachel Gallin, Esther Gutman and Tzippie Sapir (a prolific mother-and-daughter team), Esther Herskovics, Meir Livnat, Aryeh Louv, Yosef Mittelmann, Danny Reiss, Inge Sadan, Tzvi Sarid, Peggy and Eliezer Schwartz, Edit Solar, Bettina Spoerri, Gizella Sternbach, and Yehudah Weiss. Young summer research assistants were precious: Rachel Abrams, then a university student in London, and Dina Pollock, a social worker from New Haven, Connecticut.

All these volunteers gave their time willingly. We hope they approve of the result as much as we appreciate their generous assistance.

Relevant information, books, manuscripts, personal memoirs, or graphic material that came from *Israel:* Edna Amit, Paolo Colbi, Berti Eckert, the late Yaakov Keren, Eitan Lederer, Lee I. Levine, Yaakov Meiman, Faigel and Harry Rosenberg, Eliezer Shavid, Chaya and Ephraim Shen, Giora Solar, the Steiners—David, Avraham, and Shlomo—and their cousin, Natan Steiner, Yaakov Timnat, and the late Chana Wittberg; *England:* Leonard Brown, Neil Pike, Rabbi Jonathan Romain, and Imrich Sarkany; *Scotland:* the late Otto Burg, Airdrie; *United States:* Abraham Grussgott, Michael and Barbara Shulman; and *Switzerland:* Robert Tausky.

At Yad Vashem in Jerusalem, we had cooperation from Elie Dlin, Director of the Valley of the Communities, and Nina Springer of the photo archive. At Beth Hatefutsoth, The Diaspora Museum in Ramat Aviv, Ruth Porter of the photo archive division and Miriam Hajnal of the research department provided assistance. The late Geoffrey Wigoder, editor of the *Encyclopedia Judaica,* offered valuable suggestions. Shalom Sabar, department head of Jewish and comparative folklore at the Hebrew University in Jerusalem, and Rudolf Klein, professor of architecture at Tel Aviv University, have been patient consultants, enthusiastic about our research and valued contributors to this volume. Rabbinical advisers and avid project supporters are Rabbi Yosef Heckelman and Tziporah Heckelman of Kehillat Shalvah in Safed. Rabbi Aryeh Zimmer of Jerusalem clarified certain elements of halakhah and identified scriptural sources of obscure verses.

We thank David Cassuto, architect and expert on Italian synagogues, for excellent guidance to synagogues in Italy, and Noemi Cassuto for her chapter on Italian synagogue architecture. In the late 1980s, other than the Italian *Guida All'Italia Ebraica,* by Annie Sacerdoti, there were no comprehensive guide books to Jewish sites in European countries in any language. We were fortunate to meet the authors of other books that have since been published on the topic while they were still in the making. In Budapest we consulted with the late architect Anikó Gazda, the Jewish authority on synagogues in Hungary, who—together with Rabbi József Schweitzer, of the Rabbinical Seminary—helped us plan our route in Hungary. In Bratislava we met the late L'udovít Dojč who was then compiling the manuscript of the late scholar Eugen Bárkány on communities in Slovakia. At the then State Jewish Museum of Prague, Bedřich Nosek and Arno Pařík suggested locations to visit in the periphery, while Chana Mayer and Vlastimíla Hamačková helped us gather archival information and photos.

Jiří Fiedler, former book editor and now researcher for Prague's Jewish community was indispensable. During 12 years of weekend photography excursions on his bicycle to synagogues and castles, he researched the Jewish-built heritage and its history in Bohemia and Moravia. Responding to our mail inquiry, Jiří sent us annotated lists of 318 standing synagogues in Czechoslovakia, coded to maps he included. His excellent travel guide, *Jewish Sights in Bohemia and Moravia,* appeared in 1991. Engineer-architect and historian Jaroslav Klenovský, adviser on synagogue restoration to the Jewish community of Brno, was equally indispensable. He freely shares his expertise and information on Moravian communities and synagogues, sends his monographs on Jewish communities as they appear, and updates us on restoration progress. We thank Jaro and Jiří for their friendship, open communication, and phenomenal patience.

Our project generated interest wherever we turned in Europe, and we were fortunate to find help and cooperation in nearly every town and city. Among our European friends, we especially thank young Ružica Maraš who was a student at the Pentecostal Seminary in Osijek, Croatia. She sent packets of useful photos, articles, pamphlets, and archival materials garnered in her travels and church work in the former Yugoslavia, Romania, and Hungary.

We thank our cooperative informants in Italy: Rabbi Artom, Turin; Paulo Benedetti, Asti; the Cavaglion family, Cuneo; Elvira Colombo, Vercelli; Cesare Finzi, Mantua; Marco Levi, Mondovì; Esther Moscati, Urbino; Sylvio Norzo, Alessandria; Adriana Ottolenghi, Casale Monferrato; the Pugliese family, Ivrea; Rabbi Elia Riccetti, Trieste; Beppe Segre, Saluzzo;

Roberto Segre, Cherasco; Massimo del Sette, Biella, and Federico Steinhaus, Merano.

Miriam Reiner of the Hebrew University helped plan our itinerary in the former Yugoslavia. Among our contacts there were Mirjam Ferera, Dubrovnik; Demeter Gabor, Subotica; Boris Helman, Skopje; Zdenko Kohn from Osijek, now in Carmiel, Israel; Pepice Mišič, Split; Livia Stein, Novi Sad, Rifke Slosberg, and architect Ivan Ceresnjes, Sarajevo. Ivan has since moved to Israel, where he is the emminent expert of the Center for Jewish Art of the Hebrew University on synagogues in the former Yugoslavia and our adviser on the topic.

Yaakov Shibi of the Jewish Agency had good suggestions for our Greek odyssey. Contacts there were: Eliyahu Arom and Obadia Sabatta, Trikkala; Kamelia Begas, Larissa; Moise and Semos Eliusaf, Ioannina; Raphael Frezis, Volos; David Koen, Veroia; Perla Soosis, Corfu; and Lucia Sulam, Rhodes.

Austrian contacts include Manfred Fuchs, mayor of Kobersdorf; Martha Keil and Klaus Lohrmann, Institut für Geschichte der Juden in Österreich, St. Pölten; Mr. Klein, Jewish community, Graz; Juta Kronar, librarian at the Austrian Institute for Peace in the former synagogue in Stadt Schleining; Inez Muller, art historian, and Barbara Sandler, journalist, Vienna; and Kurt Schubert of the Jewish Museum in Eisenstadt.

Museum, archive, and municipal personnel in the Czech Republic who spared no efforts on our behalf: Milan Augustin of the Okresní archiv, Karlovy Vary; Otá Balek, vice-mayor, and Charles Burianek, Kasejovice; Dobromila Brichtová of the Regionální muzeum, Mikulov; Jiří Černý of the Okresní muzeum, Pelhřimov; Jaromír Hysman, historian, Budyné nad Ohří; Zdeněk Jelínek of the Regionální muzeum, Kolín; Jaroslav Kos, mayor, Rychnov nad Kněžnou; Jaroslav Liška, cultural administrator, Velké Meziříčí; Pastor Dobromil Malý, Kojetín; Zuzana Miškovská of the Okresní archiv, Kolín; Danuša Pašiaková of the Ministry of Education, Prague; Bohumír Pavlík, keeper of the Jewish cemetery, Třebíč; František Plech, historian, Jevíčko; Jan Podlešák, historian, České Budějovice; Paula Kapčarová, Okresní archiv, Boskovice town council; Jaroslav Prokop of the Městský muzeum, Nový Bydžov; Kneta Rková of the Památkoví ustav, Brno; Bohumír Roedl of the Okresní archiv, Louny; Eliška Šmídová of the Okresní muzeum, Rakovník; Jan Šmitka, historian, Svéradice; Milan Topinka, historian, Lomnice; Marta Vomelová of the Muzeum Vysočiny, Jihlava in Polná. Other loyal contacts include Karel Beck, Žatec; František Farber, Kroměříž; Max Gross, Prostejov; Walter Günsberg, Pilsen; Ruth Halová, Český Krumlov; the late Lily Holmesová, Brno; Ladislav Mareš, Heřmanův Městec, and Josef Švagr and family, Pilsen.

In the Slovak Republic we owe thanks to Zdenko Blažek, cultural administrator, Liptovský Svätý Mikuláš; the late Jakov Chajimovič and Ján Koma, folklorist, Prešov; Jozef Duchoň of the Ostslovak štátny múzeum, Košice; Jaroslav Franek and Robert Kardoš of the Jewish community in Bratislava; the Gati family and daughter Christina, Královský Chlumec; Armin Haber, Trenčin; Eugen Haber, Michalovce; Julius Levický, Humenné; Jozef Šimončič of the Štátny okresný archív, Trnava; Jozef Petrovič of the Štátny okresný archív, and Max Spira, Bardejov; Pavel Spišiak, historian, Kokava nad Rimavicou; Madlena Tomková of the municipality in Banská Bystrica; Juraj Turcsány of the Okresní archív, Modrá; Beata Vlasáková of the Vlastivedné a literárne múzeum, Svätý Jur.

Thanks to our friends in Hungary of whom the most prominent is Marianna Spiegel in Győr. Other advisers were archivist István Bariska, Kőszeg; Ilona Benoschofsky of the Jewish Museum in Budapest; József and Edit Engelmann, Pécs; historian József Farkas, Mátészalka; researcher Anna Gabor, Budapest; former Jewish Community President Péter Feldmajer, Nagykőrös; architect János Gerle, Budapest; Cantor Marton Klein, Szeged; Arthur Kővesi, Szolnok; Lajos Lőwy, Tokaj; Pana and Tamás Marosváry, Budakalász; the late Ágnes Nádas, Kunszentmárton; Edith Perkovác, journalist, Sopron, and Riczu Zoltán, researcher, Nyíregyháza.

We appreciate the helpful suggestions of the experts on the respective countries who read and commented on our chapters: *Italy,* David Cassuto, Jerusalem; *former Yugoslavia,* Miriam

Aviezer, and Ivan Ceresnjes, Jerusalem, and Rudolf Klein, Tel-Aviv and Budapest; *Greece,* Bracha Rivlin, Jerusalem; *Austria,* Martha Keil, St. Pölten, and Sylvia Noll, Beit Shemesh; *Czech Republic,* Avigdor Dagan, Jerusalem, Jiří Fiedler, Prague, and Jaroslav Klenovský, Brno; *Slovak Republic,* Yehoshua Büchler, Kibbutz Lehavot Havivah and Livia Rothkirchen, Jerusalem; *Hungary,* Michael Silver, Jerusalem. If, despite their diligence, we have retained any errors, the fault and the responsibility are ours alone.

Israeli experts who helped include: Moshe Golden, programmer in the Faculty of Engineering at Ben Gurion University of the Negev, who volunteered his professional Macintosh expertise to produce the small chapters maps; Allyn Rothman who untangled weird computer problems; Lenny Prager of Haifa University who guided us on Yiddish terms; Zvi Reiter, who produced excellent photo lab work and also prepared our photo exhibit on synagogues in Hungary for Yad Vashem, and Dov Lieblein and his staff at Tafsar L. Ltd., who digitized the photo material for publication.

At the Jewish Publication Society, we are grateful to Ellen Frankel, CEO and Editor-in-Chief for her guidance, her vigorous support where it was needed, and her long-term faith that a significant book would result from our labors.

Our thanks to managing editor Carol Hupping for superb management and valuable suggestions, and to developmental editor Sarah Swarz, copyeditor Suzanne Snyder, and proofreader Clifford Shubs. We appreciate the efforts of Becky Barnhart and her staff at Shepherd for quality production of the book.

Gifts from Louis and Mollie Dorfman, Tzipora and Zalman Siegel of Brooklyn, and Martin and Roberta Zissblatt of Katonah, New York, are gratefully acknowledged. The project award, "Prize of the Minister of Education for Innovators in Jewish Culture, 1993," carried a welcome grant.

Thanks are due our family, Rose Golden, and Adina and Joseph Lazar, for help in office work, for persistent encouragement, and for tolerant, critical listening to chapters along the way. From our children and grandchildren—Alfa and Ilan Peri, their children, Yoli, Noa, and Hadar; Rachel Victor and her children, Sara and Eitan Yehiel—we request forgiveness for the many months we spent abroad and for the hours of family togetherness we had to forgo as we immersed ourselves in the writing. We are indebted to Rose and Walter Pollock, of West Simsbury, Connecticut, our dedicated anchor in North America.

BIBLIOGRAPHY

GENERAL SOURCES

Becker, Avi, ed. *Jewish Communities of the World*. Jerusalem: Institute of the World Jewish Congress, 1996.

Breffny, Brian de. *The Synagogue*. Jerusalem: Steimatzky, 1978.

Brown, Francis, S. R. Driver, and Charles A. Briggs. *Hebrew and English Lexicon of the Old Testament*. London: Oxford University Press, 1962.

Brooten, Bernadette J. *Women Leaders in the Ancient Synagogue*. Atlanta: Scholars Press, 1982.

Encyclopædia Judaica. Jerusalem: Keter Publishing House, 1996.

Encyclopædia Britannica, London: William Benton, 1993.

Fleming, John, H. Honour, and Nikolaus Pevsner. *Dictionary of Architecture*. London: Penguin Books, 1991.

Folberg, Neil. *And I Shall Dwell Among Them*. New York: Aperture Press, 1995.

Grossman, Susan, and Rebecca Haut, eds. *Daughters of the King*. Philadelphia: The Jewish Publication Society, 1992.

Gruber, Ruth Ellen. *Jewish Heritage Travel*. New York: John Wiley and Sons, 1992.

_____. *Upon the Doorposts of Thy House*. New York: John Wiley and Sons, 1994.

Huberman, Ida. *Living Symbols*. Tel Aviv: Massada Press, 1988.

Jacoby, Ruth, and Rina Talgam. *Architectural Glossary*. Jerusalem: Center for Jewish Art, Hebrew University of Jerusalem, May 1988.

Kraemer, Shepherd. *Her Share of the Blessing*. New York: Oxford University Press, 1992.

Krinsky, Carol Herselle. *Synagogues of Europe*. New York: Architectural History Foundation, 1985.

Levine, Lee I. *The Ancient Synagogue: The First Thousand Years*. New Haven: Yale University Press, 1999.

Loukomski, George. *Jewish Art in European Synagogues*. London: Hutchinson and Son Ltd., 1947.

Meek, H. A. *The Synagogue*. London: Phaidon Press Limited, 1995.

Pevsner, Nikolaus. *Outline of European Architecture*. London: Penguin Books, 1955.

Roth, Cecil. *Jewish Art*. Tel Aviv: Massada P.E.C. Press, Ltd., 1961.

Safrai, Shmuel. "Was There a Women's Gallery in the Synagogues of Antiquity?" *Tarbiz* 33 (1963–64): 329–338.

Tanakh (Hebrew)

TANAKH, the Holy Scriptures. Philadelphia: The Jewish Publication Society, 1985.

Tigay, Alan M. ed. *The Jewish Traveler*. Northvale, New Jersey: Jason Aronson Inc., 1994.

Tuchman, Barbara. *A Distant Mirror*. New York: Ballantine Books, 1978.

Wigoder, Geoffrey. *The Story of the Synagogue*. Tel Aviv: Beth Hatefutsoth, 1986.

Wischnitzer, Rachel. *The Architecture of the European Synagogue*. Philadelphia: The Jewish Publication Society, 1964.

Yaniv, Bracha, Zohar Hanegbi, and Shalom Sabar. *Hebrew Inscriptions and Their Translations*. Jerusalem: Center for Jewish Art, Hebrew University, 1988. Reprint. New York, 1995.

AUSTRIA

Geschichte der Juden in Südost-Österreich, Gedenkschrift (hereafter: *Südost-Österreich*). Graz: Israelitischen Kultusgemeinde für Steiermark, Kärnten und die politischen Bezirke des Burgenlandes Oberwart, Güssing und Jennersdorf, 1988.

Gold, Hugo, ed. *Gedenkbuch der Untergegangenen Judengemeinden des Burgenlandes* (hereafter: H. Gold, ed. *Burgenlandes*). Tel Aviv: Olamenu, 1970.

Gold, Hugo, ed. *Geschichte der Juden in Österreich* (hereafter: H. Gold, ed. *Österreich*). Tel Aviv: 1971.

Krautheimer, Richard. *Medieval synagogues.* Jerusalem: Bialik Institute, 1994. (Hebrew.)

Kult und Kultur des österreichischen Judentums (hereafter: *Kult und Kultur*). St. Pölten: Kulturzentrum Ehemalige Synagoge, 1984.

Allerhand, Jacob, "Die Funktion der Synagoge im Judentum," *Südost-Österreich,* 178–181.

Barb, Alphons A., "Ein Ghetto in Österreich," H. Gold, ed. *Burgenlandes,* 51–57.

Böhm, Erich. "Die Eisenstädter Wolf-Familie," H. Gold, ed. *Burgenlandes,* 37–50.

Eidelberg, Shlomo. *Jewish Life in Austria in the XV Century.* Philadelphia: Dropsie College, 1962.

Genée, Pierre. "Als die Synagogen brannten," *Zentrum* 18 (September 1988): 22–24.

_____. "Die Juden des Burgenlandes und ihre Synagogen," *David* 3 (December 1989): 6–13.

_____. "Die neuzeitlichen Synagogen in den südlichen und westlichen Bundesländern Österreichs," *David* 4 (April 1990): 12–16.

_____. "Die neuzeitlichen Synagogen in Niederösterreich," *David* 1 (January 1989): 7–11.

_____. *Wiener Synagogen 1825–1938,* Wien: Löcker, 1987.

Goerlich, Dr. Ernst Joseph. "Das Burgenland. Historische Überblick," H. Gold, ed. *Burgenlandes,* 11–16.

Gold, Hugo. "Geschichte der Juden in Eisenstadt," H. Gold, ed. *Burgenlandes,* 17–24.

_____. "Zur Ältesten Geschichte der Juden Im Burgenland," H. Gold, ed. *Burgenlandes,* 7–11.

Grünzweig, Leopold. "Die Instandsetzung der ehemaligen Synagoge in St. Pölten," *Kult und Kultur,* 4–6, 1984.

Gutkas, Karl. "Geschichte der Juden in St. Pölten," H. Gold, ed. *Österreich,* 81–86.

_____. "Geschichte der Synagoge St. Pölten," *Kult und Kultur,* 7–13.

Haeusler, Wolfgang. "Geschichte, Religion und Kultur des österreichischen Judentums," *Kult und Kultur,* 22–28.

Hammer-Schenk, *Synagogen in Deutschland.* Hamburg: Deutsches Architekturmuseum, 1981.

Jewish Austria, Yesterday and Today, Institut für Geschichte der Juden in Österreich, Vol. I, 1998.

Keil, Martha, and Klaus Lohrmann. "Die Geschichte der Juden in Österreich im Überblick," Personal communication. October 1995.

Kitlitschka, Werner. "Die kunstgeschichtliche Bedeutung der St. Pöltner Synagoge," *Kult und Kultur,* 14–16.

Mayer, Eugen. *Burgenland in alten Ansichtskarten.* Eisenstadt: Burgenlandisches Landesmuseum, 1981.

Reitter, Gudrun. "Die Geschichte der Israelitischen Kultusgemeinde Graz 1914 bis zur Gegenwart," *Südost-Österreich,* 151–177.

Saltzer-Eibenstein, Gerhard. W. "Die Geschichte des Judentums in Südostösterreich von den Anfangen bis ins 20. Jahrhundert," *Südost-Österreich,* 27–149.

_____. "Geschichte der Juden in Graz," H. Gold, ed. *Österreich,* 9–19.

Scheiber, Alexander. "Die Anfange der Jüdischen Kunst in Burgenlands," H. Gold, ed. *Burgenlandes,* 121–124.

Schubert, Karl, ed. *The Austrian Jewish Museum,* Eisenstadt, 1989.

Steines, Patricia. "Symbolik auf jüdischen Grabsteinen," *David* (December 1988): 22–30.

Zimmerman, Fritz. "Die Ortsnamen der Jüdischen Gemeinden im Burgenlandes," H. Gold, ed. *Burgenlandes,* 125–133.

CROATIA AND SERBIA

Ceresnjes, Ivan. *Caught in the Winds of War: Jews in the Former Yugoslavia.* Policy Study No. 17. Jerusalem: Institute of the World Jewish Congress, 1999.

Fischer, Leopold, ed. "Nešto iz povijesti židovske bogoštovne opčine u Osijeku, u gor. gradu," *Jevrejski Almanah za godinu* 5688 (1927–1928): Vršac, 193–197.

Freidenreich, Harriet Pass. *Jews of Yugoslavia.* Philadelphia: The Jewish Publication Society, 1979.

Grgurovac, Martin. *Razglednice starog Osijeka.* Osijek: Produkcija Art, 1990.

Hostein, Lisa. "Yugoslavia, a Jewish community that refuses to die," *Jewish Exponent* (February 2, 1990).

Klein, Rudolf. "A szabadkai zsinagóga mint a Gótikus Templomok Ellentéte," Abstract in *Létünk* (Novi Sad, 1987): 471–512.

_____. "A szabadkai zsidóság felemelkedése és hanyatlása," *Múlt és Jövő, Zsidó Kulturális Folyóirat* 1–2 (1995): 143–160.

Kumic, Franc. *Zidje v Prekmurju.* Osijek, 1990.

Locker, Zvi, ed. *Pinkas hakehillot, Yugoslavia (Encyclopaedia of Jewish communities: Yugoslavia).* Jerusalem: Yad Vashem, 1988; "Dubrovnik," 89–111. "Osijek." 28–31. "Subotica," 218–231. (Hebrew.)

Malcolm, Noel. "The Jews and Gypsies of Bosnia," *Bosnia, a Short History.* London: Papermac, 1994: 107–118.

Nickels, Sylvie. *Yugoslavia.* London: Collins, 1984.

Pinterović, Danica. "Da li je u rimskoj koloniji Mursi postojala sinagoga?" *Zbornik radova centar za znanstveni rad Jugoslavenske akademije.* Osijek: Znanosti-umjetnosti, 1967.

Sabo, "Ovaj hram je bog sačuvao." *Izvori* (July–August 1981): 11–13.

Shaw, Avigdor Levy, ed. J*ews of the Ottoman Empire.* Princeton: Princeton University Press, 1994.

Singer, Mark. "Trapped in the memories of another war," *Al haMishmar* (December 12, 1991). (Hebrew.)

Sorić, Ante, ed. *Jews in Yugoslavia.* Zagreb: Muzejski Prostor, 1989.

Stulli, Bernard. *Jews in Dubrovnik.* Zagreb: Yad Vashem, 1989.

CZECH AND SLOVAK REPUBLICS

Gold, Hugo. ed. *Die Juden und Judengemeinden in Vergangenheit und Gegenwart Böhmens* (hereafter: H. Gold, ed. *Böhmens*). Tel Aviv: Olamenu, 1934.

_____. *Die Juden und Judengemeinden in Vergangenheit und Gegenwart Mährens* (hereafter: H. Gold, ed. *Mährens*). Brno: Jüdischer Buch und Kunstverlag, 1929.

Altshuler, David, ed. *The Precious Legacy.* New York: Summit Books, 1983.

Atlas, Mosche. "Die Jüdische Geschichte der Stadt Bartfeld und des Bades Bardejov in der Tschechoslovakei," *Zeitschrift für Geschichte der Juden* 3–4 (1966–1967): 17–32, 151–170.

Bardejov a jeho okolie dávno a dnes. Pamphlet. Bardejov, 1935.

Bárkány, E. and L'. Dojč. *Židovské náboženské obce na Slovensku.* Bratislava: Vesna, 1991.

Berger, Natalia, ed. *Where Cultures Meet.* Tel Aviv: Beth Hatefutsoth, Ministry of Defense Publishing, 1990.

Brown, Len. "Kojetín-Maidenhead," *Ḥadashot,* Monthly Newsletter of Maidenhead Synagogue (June 1989: 2; January 1990: 4; May 1990: 3).

Dienstbier, Jiří. "Mosty, Odkial'? Kam?" *Liptov* (August 7, 1991): 1,5.

Falková, Elena. "Prešov during the Occupation," Personal communication. Zvolen, 1991.

Fiedler, Jiří. J*ewish Sights of Bohemia and Moravia.* Prague: Sefer, 1991.

Gerö, Ignác. "Vývoj židovského školstva st. quo," *Trnava 1238–1938.* Trnava: Municipality of Trnava, 1938, 296–303.

337

Gold, Hugo. "Dějiny v Polné." H. Gold, ed. *Mährens,* 508–511.

_____. *Gedenkbuch der Untergegangenen Judengemeinden Maehrens.* Tel Aviv, 1974. N.p.

Gruber, Samuel, and Phyllis Meyers. *Survey of Historic Jewish Monuments in the Czech Republic.* New York: Jewish Heritage Council, World Monuments Fund, 1995.

Grünwald, Shmuel. "Kurze Geschichte der Gemeinde Vrbové," *Verbo: Gedenkbuch der Gemeinden Piešťany, Vrbové, Myjava und Umgebung.* Jerusalem: Grünwald, 1969, 17–20.

Grussgott, Abraham L. *Bardejov remembered: A Memorial to the Jewish Community of Bardejov, Czechoslovakia, 1734–1945, Second Edition.* Brooklyn: Grussgott, 1998. (Hebrew.)

Hamáčková, Vlastimila, and J. Sedinová. "The Jewish Cemetery in Třebíč." *Judaica Bohemia* XXVII, (1991): 82–94.

"HaNoda b'Yehudah, matayim shana l'ptirato," *Yated Ne'eman, Special Edition.* Bnei Brak, *Parashat Bahar b'Ḥukotai,* 5753–1993. (Hebrew)

Hoch, Max. "Geschichte der Juden in Plzeň." H. Gold, *Böhmens,* 479–488.

Iggers, Wilma Abeles, ed. *The Jews of Bohemia and Moravia.* Detroit: Wayne State University Press, 1986.

Kaplánová, Katarína. "O Lučeneckej Synagóge Zachráni ju niekto pred zánikom?" *Zmena,* (September 1991).

Klenovský, Jaroslav. *Židovské Památky Mikulova.* Mikulov: Regionální muzeum v Mikulově, 1994.

Klenovský, Jaroslav. *Židovské Památky Třebíče.* Brno-Třebíč: Židovská naboženská obec v Brně, 1995.

Kořatek, Jakob. "Geschichte der Juden in Trebitsch," H. Gold, *Mährens,* 523–537.

Kováčová, Viola. *Čas Barchesu.* Bratislava: Slovak Ministry of Culture, 1994. Translated by Imrich Sarakany as *The Time of the Barches.* London: Published privately, 1995.

Lalková, Jarmila, ed. *Bardejov, mestská pamiatková rezervácia.* Bratislava: Slovenský ústav pamiatkovej starostlivosti. 1991.

Landa, Dezider, *Storočnica.* Prešov: Židovská náboženská obec v Prešove, 1997.

Lányi, M., and H. Propperné Békefi. *A Szlovenszkói zsidó hitközségek története.* Bratislava, 1923.

Martinek, A. "Dějiny Židů v Jíčíne," H. Gold, *Böhmens,* 199–203.

Nosek, Bedřich. "The Old Jewish Cemetery at Mikulov," *Judaica Bohemia* XV, 42–59. Prague: Státní židovské muzeum, 1979.

Novotný, Vladimir, ed. *Pamět' Měst, Městské památkové rezervace v českých zemích.* Prague: Odeon, 1975.

Pařik, Arno. "Synagógy v českých zemích," *Umění a řemesla* 91 (1991): 19–28. Prague.

Pavelek, Juraj. *Svätý Jur.* Martin: Osveta, 1958.

_____. "Dejiny židovstva vo Svätom Jure," *Dejiny Židovstva na Slovensku.* Svätý Jur: Mestské múzeum, 1942.

Pavlík, Bohumír. "Historie Židovské obce v Třebíči do jejiho zániku v roce 1940," Essay. Třebíč, 1940.

Polák-Rokycana, Jaroslav. "Geschichte der Juden in Březnice," H. Gold, ed., *Böhmens,* 63–69.

Polišenský, J. V. *History of Czechoslovakia in Outline.* Prague: Bohemia International, 1980.

Poulis, Suri. "Journey to Kojetín." Unpublished essay, Maidenhead Synagogue, November 1992.

Rérych, Břetislav. *Prameny dějin židů v Polné.* Polná, 1935. N.p.

Rezač, František. "Budova bývalé židovské synagogy v Kojetíne," Pamphlet. N.p., n.d.

Romain, Jonathan. "Kojetin-Maidenhead, 1150–1989," *Ḥadashot,* Monthly Newsletter of Maidenhead Synagogue (July 1989:2; August 1989:3).

Rothenberg, Ruth. "Slovak historian finds lost Jew in Hampstead," *Jewish Chronicle* 9 (June 9, 1995).

Sedlák, Jan. *Polná.* Brno: Krajské středisko, Státní Památkové, 1970.

Šimončič, Jozef. "The History of Trnava," *Dejiny Trnavy,* 472–476. Bratislava: Obzor, 1988.

_____. "Židia v Trnave v stredoveku," *Acta Judaica Slovaca* 2 (1995): 83–98.

Steiner, Artur. "Geschichte der Juden in Kojetein," H. Gold, ed. *Mährens,* 279–287.

Telscher, Richard. "The Altschul Synagogue of Mikulov," *Jews of Czechoslovakia* 2: 547–559. Philadelphia: The Jewish Publication Society, 1968.

Town chronicle, Lučenec. Synagogue dedication. September 8, 1925

Trapp, Bruno Mauritz. "Geschichte der Juden in Nikolsburg," H. Gold, ed. *Mährens,* 417–450.

Vachá, Z. "Zámer obnovy pamiatky synagógy vo Vrbovom," *Zastavovacia Objemová Štúdia Synagógy Vrbové.* Architectural study for synagogue restoration. Bratislava, 1986.

Vlasáková, Beáta, and Františka Hlaváčiková. *Svätý Jur, prechádzka mestom.* Bratislava: Alfa Plus, 1994.

Yehezkel ben Yehudah. *HaNoda b'Yehudah: sh'elot ut'shuvot.* Prague, Rosh Hodesh 1, Adar 1, 5540/1780: *Siman* 112. (Hebrew)

"Židia v Trnave v Stredoveku." *Acta Judaica Slovaka* 2 (1995): 83–95.

GREECE

Benvenisti, David. *The Communities of the Jews in Greece: Impressions of a Journey.* Jerusalem: Committee of the Sephardic Community, 1979: 32–34, 66–69. (Hebrew.)

Dalven, Rae. *The Jews of Ioannina.* Philadelphia: Cadmus Press, 1990.

D'Angel, Marc. *Jews of Rhodes.* New York: Union of Sephardic Congregations, 1978.

Harris, Alan C. "The Jew of Verroia," *Reconstructionist* 17 (January 3, 1963): 11–16.

Lamdan, Ruth. "The Ancona Boycott Affair," *Yehudei Yavan l'Dorotam: Diyun Katedrah.* Volume V. *MiLisbon l'Saloniki v'Kushta.* Zvi Ankori, ed. Jerusalem: Yitzchak Ben Zvi Institute, 1986: 135–154. (Hebrew.)

Levy, Isaac Jack. *Jewish Rhodes: A Lost Culture.* Berkeley: J. L. Magnes Museum, 1989.

Levy, Rebecca Amato. *I Remember Rhodes.* New York: Sepher Herman Press, 1987.

Liberles, Adina Weiss. "The Jewish Community of Greece," *The Balkan Jewish Communities,* edited by Daniel J. Elazar, 102–126. Lanham: University Press of America, 1984.

Messinas, Elias V. *The Synagogues of Salonika and Veroia.* Athens: Gavrielidis Editions, 1997.

Molkho, Michael. "Annals of the *kehillah* in Veroia," *Minḥah l'Avraham* (Jubilee volume to Avraham Elmaleh). Jerusalem: Jubilee Committee, 1959: 192–196. (Hebrew)

Nellhouse, Arlynn. "Distinctive Spirit," *Jerusalem Post* (November 26, 1993): 14.

Rivlin, Bracha, ed. *Pinkas hakehillot, Yavan (Encyclopaedia of Jewish Communities: Greece).* Jerusalem: Yad Vashem, 1999; "Ioannina," 131–143. "Rhodes," 392–407. "Veroia," 110–116. (Hebrew)

Stavroulakis, Nicholas P. *Jews of Greece.* Athens: Talos Press, 1990.

_____, and Timothy J. DeVinney. *Jewish Sites and Synagogues of Greece.* Athens: Talos Press, 1992.

Yoffe, Ruth Agmon. *Veroia and Kastoria, light and shadow in the life of two communities in western Macedonia in the sixteenth and seventeenth centuries.* Masters thesis. Tel-Aviv University, 1988. (Hebrew.)

HUNGARY

Ben-Haim, Natan, ed. *Rabbi Dr. Yoel Tsvi (Emil) Roth.* Netanya: Former Residents Organization, Győr and Surroundings, 1994. (Hebrew.)

Benoschofsky, Ilona. "The History of the Jews in Hungary," Budapest: Committee of the Central Board of Hungarian Jews, 1988.

_____, and Alexander Scheiber. *The Jewish Museum of Budapest.* Budapest: Corvina Kiadó, 1987.

Blumenthal, Michael. "Synagogue fights threats in silence," (Kőszeg). *The Budapest Sun,* vol 4. July 13–19, 1995.

Fidesz. *Pápa és a Zsidóság.* Videocasette. Pápa: 1989,

Gazda, Anikó, András Kubinyi, Pamer Nóra, Klára Póczy, and Károly Vörös. *Magyarországi zsínagógák.* László Gerő, ed. Budapest: Műszaki Könyvkiadó, 1989.

Gerle, János, Attila Kovács, and Imre Makovecz. *A Századforduló Magyar Épitészete* (Turn of the Century Hungarian Architecture). Budapest: Szepirodalmi Konyvkiadó, 1990.

Greenwald, Y. Y. *The Jews in Hungary.* Vac: M. A. Kahan, 1917. (Hebrew.)

Gruber, Ruth E. "Hungarian synagogue comes to life again," (Szeged). *Jerusalem Post* (September 12, 1989).

Heller, Imre and Zsigmond Vajda. *The Synagogues of Hungary, an Album.* New York: World Federation of Hungarian Jews, 1968.

Orbán, Ferenc. *Magyarország Zsidó Emlékei, Nevezetességei.* Budapest: Panoráma, 1991.

Pinkas hakehillot, Hungaria (Encyclopaedia of Jewish Communities: Hungary). Jerusalem: Yad Vashem, 1976. (Hebrew.)

Sivan, Gabriel. "Monument to the Past," (Apostag). *Jerusalem Post* (March 22, 1989).

Somogyi, György, and János Gerle. "Baumhorn Lipót zsinagógái," *MIOK évkönyv,* edited by S. Schreiber, 355–365. Budapest: Magyar Izraeliták Országos Képviselete, 1979–1980.

Somorjai, Ferenc. "Die Synagoge von Szeged," Pamphlet. Szeged, 1989.

Strom, Yale. *The Last Jews of Eastern Europe.* New York: Philosophical Library, 1986.

Szabó, Joseph, and Stephen Török, eds. *Album of the Tokaj-Hegyalja.* Pest: Vinicultural Society of the Tokaj-Hegyalja, 1864, reprinted 1984.

Szegő, György, et al. *Baumhorn Lipót, építész, 1860–1932.* Budapest: Magyar Zsidó Muzeum, 1999.

Ujvári, Péter, ed. *Magyar Zsidó Lexikon.* Budapest: *Magyar Zsidó Lexikon kiadása,* 1929.

Winkler, Yehudit. "March of the returnees to Kőszeg," *Haaretz,* May 2, 1989. (Hebrew.)

ITALY

Amram, D. W. *Makers of Hebrew Books in Italy.* Philadelphia: Julius H. Greenstone, 1909.

Arnaldi, Roberto. "Immagini di un passato ebraico nel Monregalese," Extract from *La Ghisleriana.* Mondovì, November 1982.

Bolaffio, Giuseppe. "Sfogliando l'archivio della comunità di Gorizia," *Rassegna Mensile di Israele (RMI)* 23 (1957): 537–546; 24 (1958): 30–40, 62–74, 132–141.

Bulfoni, Claudio, *La Sinagoga di Gorizia.* edito dal comune di Goriza, 1987.

Cassuto, David. "The Story of a Synagogue," *Compilation in Memory of Shlomo Umberto Nahon.* Jerusalem, 1978: 176–207. (Hebrew)

_____. "Medieval Synagogue architecture in Southern Italy," *Ninth World Congress of Jewish Studies.* Division D, Volume II. Jerusalem: World Union of Jewish Studies, 1986: 1–6. (Hebrew)

Colbi, Paolo. "The Golden Age of Hebrew Literature in Trieste," *Sinai* 83 (Nisan–Iyar 5738/1978): 70–79. (Hebrew)

_____. "Una pagina di storia ebraica Triestina, di un'antica famiglia ebraica di Trieste," *RMI* 17 (1951): 122–129.

Comunità Israelitica di Torino. *Ebrei A Torino.* Turin: Umberto Allemandi & Co., 1984.

Curiel, Riccardo. "Le origini del ghetto di Trieste," *RMI* 6 (1931–1932): 446–472.

Davidovitch, David. "Design of Italian Synagogue Interiors," *Fifth World Congress of Jewish Studies,* Volume IV: 37–43. Jerusalem: World Union of Jewish Studies, 1969. (Hebrew.)

de Benedetti, Claudia, ed. *La sinagoga degli argenti.* Turin: Pluriverso, 1991.

Eckert, Tamar. *Pioneering Zionism in Italy between the two world wars.* Tel-Aviv: Hakibbutz Hadati, 1970. (Hebrew.)

Fishof, Iris. "Synagogue Architecture in Italy," *P'amim,* Volume 8: 3–19. Jerusalem: Yitzchak Ben Zvi Institute, 1981. (Hebrew.)

Foa, Salvatore. "Appunti d'archivio di storia ebraica monferrina," *RMI* 15 (1949): 113–121.

Fortis, Umberto. *Jews and Synagogues, Venice, Florence, Rome, Leghorn, A Practical Guide.* Venice: Edizioni Storti, 1973.

Gattinara, Rabbi Joseph Jehuda Halevy. "Per il Centenario del Purim dei Tedeschi nella

Comunità di Casale Monferrato, 29 Marzo 1849," *RMI* 15 (1949): 260–266.

Hartt, Fredrick. *History of Italian Renaissance Art.* London: Thames and Hudson, 1987.

Levi, Giuseppe. *Le iscrizioni del Sacro Tempio israelitico di Casale Monferrato.* Casale Monferrato: Giuseppe Lavagno, 1914.

Mann, Vivian, ed. *Gardens and Ghettos.* New York: The Jewish Museum, 1989.

Mehling, Franz N., ed. *Italy: A Phaidon Cultural Guide.* Oxford: Phaidon Press, 1985.

Ottolenghi, Leone. *Brevi cenni sugli Israeliti Casalesi e sul loro sacro oratorio.* Casale Monferrato: Amministrazione dell'Università Israelitica, 1866.

Pagella, Vivetta Valacca. "Il Tempio Israelitico di Casale Monferrato," Extract from *La Provincia di Alessandria.* October 1981.

Pinkerfeld, Jacob. *The Synagogues of Italy.* Jerusalem: Bialik Institute, 1954. (Hebrew.)

Rosenfelder, Reuven. "The Region of the Finzis and the Condotta," *Eretz* January–February, (1995): 59–63.

Roth, Cecil. *Dona Gracia of the House of Nasi.* Philadelphia: The Jewish Publication Society, 1977.

_____. *The History of the Jews of Italy.* Philadelphia: The Jewish Publication Society, 1946.

_____. *The Jews in the Renaissance.* Philadelphia: The Jewish Publication Society, 1959.

Sacerdoti, Annie. *Guida All'Italia Ebraica.* Casale Monferrato: Marietti, 1986.

Saracco, Roberto. "Quattrocento anni di vita per la sinagoga di Casale," *Vita Casalese* September 29, 1994: 5–6.

Schreiber, Bruna. *La scuola media ebraica di Trieste durante il periodo razziale.* Trieste: La Comunità Israelitica di Trieste, 1980.

Simonsohn, Shlomo. *History of the Jews in the Duchy of Mantua.* Jerusalem: Kiryat Sefer, 1977.

Sonne, Isaiah. *From Paul IV to Pius V.* Jerusalem: Bialik Institute, 1954. (Hebrew.)

Sorani, David, Laura Colombo, and Mauro Masoero. *Sei Comunità Ebraiche piemontesi: Un itinerario didattico,* Scuola Media Ebraica "Emanuele Artom." Turin: Emanuele Artom, 1982–83.

Stock, Mario. *Nel segno di Geremia.* Udine: Instituto per l'Enciclopedia del Friuli–Venezia Giulia, 1980.

Vitale, Anna Bises, Carlo Viano, Diego D. Mora, eds. *Ebrei a Torino: ricerche per il centenario della sinagoga 1884–1984.* Turin: Umberto Allemandi, 1984.

Volli, Gemma. "La nazione ebrea a Trieste," *RMI* 24 (1958): 206–214.

SYNAGOGUE INTERIOR DECORATION

PRIMARY SOURCES

Caro, Joseph. *Shulḥan Aruch (Tur Yoreh De'ah, Hilkhot Avodah Zarah),* Venice, 1564–65. (Hebrew)

Ha-Levi, Isaac b. Moses (Profiat Duran). *Sefer Ma'aseh Efod.* Vienna, 1865. (Hebrew)

Heller, Samuel. *Sefer Toharat ha-Kodesh.* Safed, 1864. (Hebrew)

Isaac b. Moses of Vienna. *Or Zaru'a.* Zhitomir, 1862. (Hebrew)

Kook, Abraham Isaac. *Responsa Da'at Kohen.* Jerusalem, 1942. (Hebrew)

Maimonides. *Mishneh Torah: The Book of Knowledge,* tr. by Moses Hyamson. Jerusalem, 1965.

Mendel, Menahem. *Responsa Zemach Zedek.* Altdorf, 1766. (Hebrew)

Modena, Leone da. *Historia de riti hebraici.* Venice, 1637.

Talmud Bavli, *Avodah Zarah, Yoma.* (Hebrew)

Talmud Yerushalmi. *Avodah Zarah.* (Hebrew)

SECONDARY SOURCES

Barasch, Moshe. "The David Mosaic of Gaza," *Assaph. Studies in Art History.* Tel-Aviv University 1 (1980): 1–41.

Baumgarten, Joseph M. "Art in the Synagogue: Some Talmudic Views," *Judaism* 19 (1970): 196–206 (reprinted in Gutmann, *The Synagogue,* 79–89).

Berenson, Bernard. *Aesthetics and History.* London, 1950.

Beth, Hatefutsoth. The Nahum Goldmann Museum of the Jewish Diaspora, archival printouts.

Blumenkranz, Bernhard. *Le juif médiéval au miroir de l'art chrétien.* Paris, 1966.

Dothan, Moshe. *Hammath Tiberias.* Jerusalem: Israel Exploration Society, 1983.

Grabar, Oleg. *The Formation of Islamic Art.* New Haven and London, 1971.

Gutmann, Joseph. *Hebrew Manuscript Painting.* New York, 1978.

_____, "How Traditional Are Our Traditions?" *Beauty in Holiness: Studies in Jewish Customs and Ceremonial Art,* ed. J. Gutmann, New York, 1970: 417–419.

_____. ed. *The Image and the Word: Confrontations in Judaism, Christianity and Islam.* Missoula, Montana, 1977.

_____. ed. *The Synagogue: Studies in Origins, Archeology and Architecture.* New York, 1975.

Kahana, Isaac Z. "Synagogue Art in Halakhic Literature," *Bet ha–Knesset,* edited by M. Ha-Cohen, Jerusalem, 1995: 255–308 (Hebrew).

Kaufmann, David. "Art in the Synagogue," *The Jewish Quarterly Review* 9 (1897): 254–269.

Kotler, David. *Art and Religion,* Jerusalem, 1971. (Hebrew).

Kraeling, Carl H. *The Synagogue: Excavations at Dura-Europos. Final Report.* VIII/1. New Haven, 1956.

Narkiss, Bezalel. "On the Zoocephalic Phenomenon in Medieval Ashkenazi Manuscripts," *Norms and Forms: Essays in Honour of Moshe Barasch.* Jerusalem, 1983: 49–62.

_____. "Pagan, Christian and Jewish Elements in the Art of Ancient Synagogues," *The Synagogue in Late Antiquity,* edited by Lee I. Levine, Philadelphia, 1987: 183–188.

Ovadiah, Asher. "The Mosaic Workshop of Gaza in Christian Antiquity," *Ancient Synagogues: Historical Analysis and Archaeological Discovery, Vol. 2,* edited by D. Urman and P.V.M. Flesher, Leiden, 1995: 367ff.

Roth, Cecil. *Jewish Art.* Tel Aviv: Massada P.E.C. Press, Ltd., 1961.

Sabar, Shalom, "On the Difference in Attitudes towards Visual Arts between Sephardim and Ashkenazim in Eretz Israel in the Late Ottoman Period," *Pe'amim: Studies in Oriental Jewry,* 56 (1993), 75–105. (Hebrew).

_____. "The Tablets of the Law at the Bibliotheca Rosenthaliana," *Bibliotheca Rosenthaliana. Treasures of Jewish Booklore,* edited by A. K. Offenberg et. al., Amsterdam, 1994: 78–79, 127.

Urbach, Ephraim E. "The Rabbinical Laws of Idolatry in the Second and Third Centuries in the Light of Archaeological and Historical Facts," *Israel Exploration Journal,* 9 (1959): 149–165, 229–245.

Weitzmann, Kurt, ed. *Age of Spirituality.* New York and Princeton, 1979.

Wischnitzer, Rachel. *The Architecture of the European Synagogue.* Philadelphia: The Jewish Publication Society, 1964.

GLOSSARY

Adar (He) Hebrew month corresponding to February–March

Admor (He) Acronym for *Adonenu, Morenu, ve-Rabenu* (our lord, teacher, and master), the hasidic title for particularly distinguished rabbis

aedicula shrine or other opening, with two columns supporting a **gable,** lintel, or plaque

alef (He) first letter of Hebrew alphabet

aliyah (He) going up, term used for immigration to Israel, or—in synagogue ritual—for going up to the Torah reading

Altschul (Ge) old school, term used for old or earlier synagogue

Anschluss (Ge) annexation of Austria by Germany in 1938

apse, apsidal vaulted semicircular recess at the end of a chapel

architrave supporting horizontal beam extending over two columns (*see* **entablature**)

Aron Kodesh (He) Holy Ark in which **Torah** scrolls are kept

Art Nouveau (Fr) nineteenth- and early twentieth-century style of fine and applied art, characterized by complex curvilinear motifs derived from natural forms

Ashkenazim (He) Jews originating from Germany and northern France

auto-da-fé (Sp) public burning at the stake of persons condemned by the Spanish Inquisition

Av (He) Hebrew month corresponding to July–August

avodah (He) work, also used to mean worship—as in prayer

Avot (He) abbreviation for *Pirkei Avot,* Ethics of the Fathers

B.C.E., before the common era, B.C.

baldachin ornamental canopy, often in drapery form and made of painted stucco

barches corruption of **brachot,** (He), in reference to the blessing over the **ḥallah,** also the **ḥallah** itself

Bar Mitzvah (Bat Mitzvah) (He) adult status, also the ceremony conducted when a boy reaches 13 years (12 for girls) to mark his (her) arrival to adult status

Baroque ornamented style of art and architecture developed mainly in seventeenth- and eighteenth-century Italy, characterized by exuberant decoration

barrel vault also called tunnel vault. Continuous vault of semicircular or pointed sections

basket-handle ceiling, shaped like a flattened basket handle, then sloping slightly

beit midrash (batei midrash) (He) house(s) of study, often a room within the synagogue

bet din (He) religious court

Betar (He) Zionist youth movement inspired by Joseph Trumpledor; founded in 1923 in Riga, Latvia, and widespread in eastern Europe; later identified with Revisionist ideology

bikkur ḥolim (He) visiting the sick

bimah (bimot) (He) cantor's platform(s) in the synagogue, location of desk for **Torah** reading; called *tevah,* box, in **Sephardic** usage

bipolar in **Sephardic** or Italian tradition, having two focal points located at opposite sides or ends of a synagogue: one is the *Heikhal—* Holy Ark—and the other, the *bimah,* also called *tevah*—reader's platform and desk

Blau–Weiss (Ge) Blue–White, first Jewish youth movement in Germany, based on the German Wanderfogel; founded 1912

B'nai B'rith (He) Sons of the Covenant, widespread social organization promoting interests of Jews and the wider community; founded 1843 in New York by German Jews

brakha (brakhot) (He) blessing(s)

brit milah (He) ritual circumcision of Jewish males at age of eight days

C.E., common era, A.D.

caftan (Tu) long garment worn in Near East, with long sleeves and tied at waist with a girdle

capital uppermost portion of a column

Cardo main street of town in Classical Antiquity; from Greek, *cardio,* heart

cartouche rounded, convex surface as a base for a painted or low-relief decoration, usually surrounded with ornamental scrollwork

chronogram inscription in which marked Hebrew letters, on being added together by their standard numerical values, designate a Jewish calendar year

Classical a style of architecture based on Greek or Roman precedents

columbarium sepulchral vault or other structure with recesses made to receive containers with the ashes of the dead; from the Latin: *columba,* dove

condotta (condotte) (It) contract(s) to open loan banks in medieval Italy

converso (Sp) Jewish or Moorish convert to Christianity; also see *Marrano*

Corinthian the most ornate of the five classical architectural orders of ancient Greece; pillars more slender than the **Ionic,** with decoration of two rows of acanthus leaves on the **capital**

cornice projecting ornamental molding along top of building, wall, or arch (*see* **entablature**)

crenelation, crenelated alternating low and high portions on top of a wall, as a parapet or battlement

cupola small **dome** crowning a roof or **turret**

cusp angle or point; form of arch rising to an angle at the center

dayyan (He) judge in Jewish religious court

dentils, dentilations small, closely spaced rectangular blocks used in **cornices** of **Classical,** and neo-Classical architecture

dhimmí (Ab) non-Moslems living in Moslem countries as "protected" people held at low status

divan council of state in Turkey and other Middle East countries

dome a vault of even curvature on a circular base

domical domelike

Doric the earliest style of **order (column, architrave, frieze)** used in Greek architecture

double-pitched roof rectangular roof slanting down in four directions

Eclectic style of architecture combining elements from two or more historical styles

Elul (He) Hebrew month corresponding to August–September

Emancipation The liberation of individuals or groups from servitude, legal restrictions or political and social disabilities; in this volume the reference is to liberation from inequities applied specifically to Jews and to the period of such liberation in the countries discussed: approximately from the middle to the late nineteenth century.

Empire restrained style of French architecture, 1800–1830, based on classical Greek or Roman designs

entablature upper molded element in a building, comprising **architrave, frieze,** and **cornice**

Eretz Yisrael (He) Land of Israel

Erev Shabbat (He) the evening preceding the Sabbath day, starting with candle-lighting just before sundown.

Eros (Erotes) ancient Greek god(s) of love, identified with Cupid by the Romans

eruv (He) a mixing—an insertion of the forbidden into the permissible; commonly applied to the nominal fence, usually a wire on poles, defining an extended boundary within which Jews may carry objects on the Sabbath, and other practices

Eishet Ḥayil (He) woman of valor

etrog (He) citron, one of the four species blessed during **Sukkot;** central ornamental motif on Israelite coins, synagogue walls, and mosaic floors during Second Temple period and later

ezrat nashim the first of the three forecourts in the ancient Temple area, the only one where men and women stood together, now applied to the women's section of synagogues

familiant (Ge) licensed holder of a heritable family number under the **Familiants Law**

Familiants Law legislation introduced by Charles VI in 1726–27, regulating the number of Jews entitled to marry and found families in Bohemia, Moravia, and Silesia

festoon a horizontal looped ornament, draped and tied at both ends

finials *see rimmonim*

firman administrative order of Ottoman (later, Middle Eastern) sovereign

Florentine arch double arch with pointed outer curve, semi-circular inner curve; developed in Florence between thirteenth and fourteenth centuries

foil architectural term for arc or rounded space between points. Number of foils indicated by prefix, e.g., **trefoil, quatrefoil**

fresco wall painting done on a moist lime plaster surface

fretwork geometric ornament of attached horizontal and vertical straight lines, repeated to form a band

frieze middle division of **entablature,** usually decorated; decorated band along upper part of internal wall, immediately below **cornice**

gable triangular upper portion of wall at the end of a **pitched roof**

Gemeinde (Ge) community council or other administrative form

Genizah (He) hidden material; applied to unusable scraps of sacred writings or torn prayer books put aside to accumulate for burial; also, the place of such storage

Golem (He) in Jewish folklore, a sculpted human figure mystically endowed with life

Gothic a style of architecture originating in twelfth-century France with pointed arches, ribbed vaults, fine wood- and stonework, and interior walls reduced to a minimum by spacious arcades

goy (goyim) (He, Yi) non-Jewish person(s)

Habima (He) The Stage, a theatrical group, using the name of the first major Hebrew theater; founded in Moscow, 1916

"Ḥad Gadya" (Ar) "Only One Kid," a traditional parable sung at the close of the **Passover seder**

haggadah (haggadot) (He) Telling; the book(s) of blessings, prayers and rabbinical comments, read and discussed during the **seder** feast on **Passover** evening

hakafot (He) ceremonial processions around the synagogue with **Torah** scrolls on **Simḥat Torah**

hakhsharah (He) agricultural training, or training farm, preparatory for immigration to Israel

halakhah (He) laws and ordinances of Jewish religious practice

ḥallah (He) braided sweet white Sabbath loaf

ḥalutz (ḥalutzim) (He) pioneer(s), Zionist workers on the land in Palestine

Haman (He) a chief minister of ancient Persia, villain in the **Purim** story in the Scroll of Esther

ḥamsa (Ab) five, amulet in form of a stylized hand, of Near Eastern origin

Hanukkah (He) dedication, eight-day festival of lights at the winter solstice, in celebration of the rededication of the Temple by the

Hasmoneans after their victory over the Greeks in 164 B.C.E.

Hashomer Hatzair (He) the Young Guard, Socialist Zionist youth organization dedicated to *aliyah;* origin in Vienna during World War I

Hasid (Hasidim) (He) member(s) of any of several sects founded in eighteenth-century Poland that focused on religious zeal and mysticism

Haskalah (He) Enlightenment, a movement to modernize Judaism, to bring secular studies into Jewish education and to prepare Jews to function in the modern world; begun in mid-eighteenth century Germany

Hasmoneans a priestly family of Jewish rulers and leaders in Judea in the second and first centuries B.C.E.

ḥazzan (He) cantor

Hechalutz (He) the Pioneer, Zionist youth organization dedicated to *aliyah*

Hechalutz Farm farm for pre-*aliyah* training in agriculture

ḥeder (He) room, traditional religious one-room primary and elementary school in the house of the **rebbe,** teacher, where boys started Bible study at age 4 or 5

Heikhal (He) Temple, term for the Holy Ark in **Sephardic** synagogues

Heshvan (He) Hebrew month corresponding to October–November

ḥevrah (Ar, He) society, friends

ḥevra kadishah (Ar, He) holy brotherhood, a local organization originally active in all aspects of social aid but more recently focused exclusively as a burial society

hiddur mitzvah (He) enhancement and embellishment of a commandment, e.g., providing beautiful mantles and silver ornaments for **Torah** scrolls, or elegant utensils for rituals practiced in the home

hip roof a pitched roof with sloped instead of vertical ends

ḥol hamo'ed (He) half holiday, intermediate days of **Passover** and **Sukkot** when secular activities are permitted

ḥuppah (He) bridal canopy; also the wedding ceremony

iconostasis richly decorated screen typical in Byzantine churches, separating the sanctuary from the nave, usually pierced by three doors

Ionic one of the five classical orders of ancient Greek architecture; the capital of the columns characterized by inverted scrolls

isotropic of equal physical properties along all axes

Israelitische Gemeinde (Ge) Jewish civic authority

Jews' Oath *Oath More Judaico* (La) a degrading form of oath that Jews were compelled to take in lawsuits with non-Jews; applied in Europe from the Middle Ages until late nineteenth century

Judengasse (Ge) "Jewish street"

judenrein (Ge) "cleansed of Jews"

Judenrichter (Ge) administrative head of the Jewish community

Judenstadt (Ge) "Jewish town"

Jugendstil (Ge) **Art Nouveau** as practiced in German-speaking countries

Kabbalah (He) esoteric teachings of Jewish mysticism

Kaddish (He) prayer recited by mourners

kadosh (kedoshim) (He) holy, holy one(s), martyred Jews

kaf (He) eleventh letter of Hebrew alphabet

kapote (Yi) long black coat worn by **Hasidim**

kashrut (He) Jewish dietary laws

kehillah (kehillot) (He) Jewish community(ies), congregation(s) or assembly(ies)

ketubbah (He) document, Jewish marriage contract in Aramaic with ornamental frame; often beautifully decorated. It is a contract recording financial obligations that a husband undertakes toward his wife, declaimed during the marriage ceremony

kiddush (He) blessing recited over a cup of wine

kippah (He) skull cap

Kristallnacht (Ge) "night of the broken glass," when Jews were attacked, and synagogues vandalized and destroyed in Germany and Austria, November 9–10, 1938

kuf (He) nineteenth letter of Hebrew alphabet

Kultusgemeinde (Ge) Jewish religious authority

Landesrabbiner (Ge) chief rabbi of a country

Landjudentum (Ge) an agrarian Jewish community

landsman (landslayt) (Yi) compatriot(s)

Landsman (Landsleute) (Ge) compatriot(s)

lavabo anteroom basin for ritual hand washing

Levite of the tribe of Levi

loggia a gallery or arcade open on one or more sides, often lined with pillars

lulav (lulavim) (He) palm leaf shoot(s), bound together with willow and myrtle branches and blessed in the ritual of the fall festival **Sukkot**

lunette an opening above another, framed by an arch or vault; usually semicircular

Maccabi (He) Maccabi World Union, international Jewish sport organization; formalized in 1921 after two decades of activity

Magen David (He) Star of David

maḥallasi (Tu) neighborhood

maḥzor (He) festival prayer book

Marrano (Sp) term of opprobrium used to designate and denigrate the New Christians of Spain and Portugal; probably from Spanish word for swine; see also *Converso*

matrikel (Ge) register of population, events

matroneo (It) women's gallery of the synagogue, in Italy

matzah (matzot) (He) unleavened bread eaten at **Passover**

Megillah (He) scroll or book, especially the Scroll of Esther, read on **Purim**

meḥitzah (He) partition screen designating women's places separate from men in the sanctuary; term used to designate the women's gallery in synagogues in Greece

me'il (me'ilim) (He) coat(s), decorative covering for **Torah** scroll

melamed (melamdim) (He) elementary level religious teacher(s)

menorah (He) candelabrum, symbol of Judaism, after the seven-branched predecessor that once stood in the Holy Temple; eight branches plus one for lighting, for **Hanukkah**

meshorer (meshorerim) (He) poet(s)

mezuzzah (mezuzzot) (He) doorpost, also—especially—the encased small parchment scroll inscribed with verses from Deuteronomy and affixed by tradition to the right hand doorpost in Jewish buildings

micrography art form using calligraphy of sacred or other texts in tiny letters to form images, often in floral or animal shapes

mikveh (He) ritual pool or bath of running water for ritual cleansing

minhag (He) custom, rite

minyan (He) quorum, the ten men required for communal prayer

Mishnah (He) section of the **Talmud** comprising the post-biblical Oral Law

Mizrachi (He) Easterner; religious Zionist organization; founded in 1902

mizraḥ (He) east, designation of the direction for prayer, often indicated by an artistic wall plaque inscribed with *"mizraḥ"* in Hebrew

mohel (He) person who performs ritual circumcision

Monti di Pietà (sing. Monte, It) Funds of Piety, loan banks founded by Franciscan friars in medieval Italy

moreh (morim), (He) teacher(s, m.)

mudéjar (Sp) Spanish Christian architecture of the eleventh–sixteenth centuries, produced under Moorish influence

mullion vertical post dividing a window or other opening into two or more openings

nave principal longitudinal area of a church, usually flanked by two aisles

Neilah (He) closing, concluding prayer on the Day of Atonement

neo- prefix denoting later adaptation and modification of an earlier, named architectural style

Neolog a religious movement of the communities in Hungary belonging to the European Reform in Judaism

ner tamid (He) eternal lamp, a light that burns perpetually before the synagogue Ark, electrified in modern times

neshamah (He) soul

Neuschul (Ge) new school, new synagogue

numerus clausus (La) closed number, specified maximum number of discriminated persons admissible to a profession, institute of higher learning, professional association, or public office; historically applied against Jews in particular

ogee arch an arch, each side of which is a double curve, convex below followed by concave above

Ohel Mo'ed (He) Tabernacle, portable sanctuary of the Israelites in the wilderness

oleh (olim) (He) person(s) going up, i.e., immigrant(s) to pre-1948 Palestine or now to Israel

Oneg Shabbat (He) celebration in enjoyment of the Sabbath on Friday evening

order in architecture, an arrangement of columns with an **entablature**, e.g., **Doric, Ionic, Corinthian**

palmette fan-shaped decorative motif

parapet low, protective wall at the edge of a roof or balcony

parnas (parnassim) (He) official(s) of the community

parokhet (parokhot) (He) curtain(s) in front of the Holy Ark in the synagogue

Passover festival commemorating the Exodus of the Jews from Egypt

pediment low-pitched **gable** above doors, windows, or a group of columns

pendentive spherical triangle, typically formed between arches supporting a **dome**

Pesaḥ (He) **Passover**

pilaster column projecting only partially from a wall and conforming to one of the classical architectural **orders**

pinkas (He) register, usually of the **kehillah**

pitched roof roof slanting down in two opposite directions

plinth pedestal, base of wall, column, or **pilaster**

portico structure consisting of a roof supported by columns, usually attached to a building as a porch

privilegium (La) contract, between the ruler and the Jewish community, delineating rights and responsibilities of each party

proscenium arch a decorative arch separating the stage from the auditorium; in synagogue architecture, the arch before or above the niche containing the **Torah** Ark

proseucha a Latin parallel to the Greek synagoga, applied to Jewish prayer rooms in the Hellenized Eastern Empire

Purim (He) Feast of Lots; joyous spring festival celebrating deliverance of the Jews in ancient Persia as described in the Scroll of Esther

quadrefoil see **foil**

quadriga in classical antiquity, a two-wheeled chariot drawn by four horses harnessed abreast, often driven by emperors or gods

rabitz type of suspended ceiling construction using reeds and plaster

Rashi (He) acronym for Rabbi Solomon ben Isaac (1040–1105), commentator on Bible and Talmud, Germany,

Rathaus (Ge) City Hall

rebbe (Yi) teacher, often a rabbi

rebbetzin (Yi) wife of a rabbi

repoussé ornamented design raised in relief by hammering on reverse side

rescript edict or decree, or a document written by an authority in reply to query or petition

responsa (responsum) (La) reply(ies) of a rabbi or scholar to **halakhic** inquiries

rimmonim (He) pomegranates, ornaments, usually silver, mounted on the two posts of a **Torah** scroll

Risorgimento (It) the movement for liberation and unification of Italy, or its period, 1750 to 1870

rocaille (Fr) rock, shell, and plant forms in fantastic, ornamental combinations, found in **Rococo** decoration

Rococo style of architecture and decoration originating in eighteenth-century France as the final stage of **Baroque** and marked by richer decoration and elegance

Romanesque style of architecture preceding the Gothic; prevailed in western and southern Europe from ninth–twelfth centuries, characterized by heavy masonry construction with narrow openings, round arches, and groin or barrel vaults

Romaniots Jewish population resident in the Byzantine empire before the sixteenth century, and their descendants

rose window circular window decorated with circularly symmetrical tracery

rosh hakohol (He: *rosh hakahal*) titular head of a Jewish community

Rosh Hashanah (He) Jewish New Year, first and second days of **Tishrei**

Rosh Ḥodesh beginning of each Jewish month, at the new moon

rusticated rough-surfaced, masonry cut in massive blocks, separated from each other by deep joints

saddle roof normal **pitched roof,** used over a tower

Sambatyon legendary river beyond which the ten lost tribes of Israel were exiled; its waters were turbulent on six days of the week and rested on the Sabbath

sandek (He) person, usually grandfather or another male relative worthy of honor, who holds the child on his lap during the circumcision ceremony

Sanhedrin (He) from Greek word for assembly, the highest Jewish legislature and court, of 71 members; functioned from the Roman period to *ca.* 425 C.E.

schul (Ge) school, synagogue

Schutzjuden (Ge) Jews protected by a specific nobleman

Scuola Italiana (It) synagogue using the Italian rite

Scuola Levantina (It) synagogue using rite of the Levantine Jews, hailing from the Ottoman Empire

Secessionist (Ge) A style of art in Germany, Austria, and Hungary concurrent with and related to **Art Nouveau**

seder (He) **Passover** feast; the participants retell the story of the Exodus from Egypt from the **haggadah;** certain foods are arranged as symbols on a special **seder** plate

Sephardim (He), Jews descended from Jews of pre-expulsion Spain or Portugal

Shabbat (He) Sabbath

Shabbos (Yi) Sabbath

shammash (He) beadle or sexton of synagogue

Shavuot (He) Pentecost, Feast of Weeks, one of the three festivals of pilgrimage to the Jerusalem Temple

sheḥitah (He) ritual slaughter for kosher meat or poultry

Sheva Hakehillot (He) the seven Jewish communities established in the seventeenth century in Burgenland, Austria

Shewbread the 12 Sabbath loaves placed by the high priests on the table in the Holy of Holies of the biblical Tabernacle and on a gold table in the Temple of Jerusalem

shin (He) penultimate letter of Hebrew alphabet

shiur (He) lesson in **Torah, Talmud**

shiviti (He) votive plaque or tablet, usually inscribed with the verse, *"Shiviti Adonai l'negdi tamid"* ("I am ever mindful of the Lord's presence"; Ps. 16:8) and decorated

Shoah (He) the Holocaust

shofar (shofarot) (He) the ram's horn, an ancient musical instrument, sounded to this day in the synagogue on **Rosh Hashanah** and **Yom Kippur;** one of the oldest Jewish symbols

shoḥet Jewish ritual slaughterer for kosher meat or poultry

shtadlan (He) advocate, a representative who pleads the Jewish cause before princes, kings, and governments *shtetl* (Yi) diminutive of *shtot,* town; village in central and eastern Europe where Jews were often a majority and had some autonomy

shtibl (shtiblekh) (Yi) small, intimate synagogue(s), often in homes

shtrayml (shtraymlekh) (Yi) fur-trimmed hat(s)

shul (Yi) school, synagogue

Shulḥan Arukh (He) Code of Jewish Law, composed by Joseph Karo and published in 1555

shulklapper (Yi) person who knocked on doors to summon congregants

siddur (He) prayer book for daily use

Simḥat Torah (He) festival of Rejoicing in the Law at the end of the **Sukkot** week

Sivan (He) Hebrew month corresponding to May–June

splay spread of an opening, such as sides of a portal, at an obtuse angle

stoa in Greek architecture, a covered colonnade; in Byzantine architecture, a covered hall, its roof supported by one or more rows of columns parallel to rear wall

sukkah (sukkot) (He) booth(s) or tabernacle in which Jews live for a week during the **Sukkot** festival

Sukkot (He) Feast of Tabernacles, one of the three pilgrimage festivals to the Jerusalem Temple

taf (He) last letter of the Hebrew alphabet

tallit (tallitot) (He) prayer shawl(s)

Talmud (He) code of laws and commentaries composed between the third and fifth centuries C.E., the most authoritative source of Judaism after the Bible

Talmud Torah (He) Hebrew elementary school

tambour circular wall carrying a **dome** or **cupola**

Tammuz (He) Hebrew month corresponding to June–July

Tashlikh (He) rite performed on the afternoon of **Rosh Hashanah,** symbolically to cast off sins by throwing crumbs into flowing water

tefillin (He) phylacteries, worn during daily morning prayer: two black cubes containing

Torah passages on parchment, attached to thin leather straps; one is placed on the forehead and the other is wound around the left arm

Terezín former garrison town in northwest Bohemia, emptied of troops and adapted by the Nazis in World War II as a concentration area, mostly of Jews, but of other deportees as well. Built for about 3,700, it held a maximum of 54,000 inmates in 1942; as new arrivals were incarcerated, older inmates were transferred to death camps in Poland.

terrazzo (It) cement floor containing stone or marble chips, ground and polished in place

tevah (He) In the Sephardic or Italian traditions, the reader's platform holding the table used for reading the **Torah,** or the reader's table

Tisha b'Av (He) ninth day of **Av,** a day of fasting and mourning for the destruction of the First and Second Temples

Tishrei (He) Hebrew month corresponding to September–October

Toleranzpatent (Ge) edict of tolerance issued by Emperor Joseph II in 1782 for Vienna and Lower Austria, guaranteeing existing rights and obligations of Jews and laying down new ones

Torah (He) the Pentateuch, the Five Books of Moses, written law; handwritten parchment scrolls

trefoil *see* **foil**

tri-stoa *see* **stoa**

trompe l'oeil (Fr) trick of the eye, a painted visual deception often creating a three-dimensional effect

truss timbers framed together to bridge a space, e.g., in a roof

tsholnt (Yi) an **Ashkenazic** dish, stew of meat and vegetables for the Sabbath, prepared beforehand and kept hot on continuous low heat

turret small, slender tower

tympanum area between lintel of door and the arch above it, also triangular space enclosed by moldings of a **pediment**

tzaddik (tzaddikah) (He, m/f) righteous person

tzedakah (He) charity

tzitzit (He) fringes, the knotted cords on the corners of a **tallit** or the small garment traditionally worn by Orthodox men under their upper garments

tzitzit cord cord used for knotting fringes on a **tallit**

ulica (Cr, Sl) street

ulice (Cz) street

Ustaša (Cr) Nazi puppet regime and its adherents in Croatia during World War II

utca (Hu) street

vault arched structure of ceiling or roof

Volksdeutsche (Ge) ethnic Germans living in countries neighboring to Germany

volute spiral scroll or ornament, usually on an **Ionic** capital

Wehrmacht (Ge) armed forces of Germany

wimple a linen **Torah** binder made from a boy's **brit milah** swaddling cloth, embroidered with

blessings and presented, on the boy's first visit with his father, to the synagogue

WIZO Women's International Zionist Organization, promotes child welfare and vocational training for women in Israel; founded in 1920

yeshivah (He) academy for the study of **Talmud** and **halakhah**

Yom Kippur (He) Day of Atonement

yortsayt (Yi) death anniversary date, for remembrance of the deceased

Zimmer (Ge) room(s), for rental to visitors

zmirot Shabbat (He) Sabbath hymns

Zopf (Ge) a transitional building style between Baroque and Neo-Classicism in central Europe characterized by restrained decoration

Židovsk-á, é, ý, (Cz, Sl) Jewish

Žudioska (Cr) Jewish

INDEX